KOREA IN THE PACIFIC CENTURY

KOREA IN THE PACIFIC CENTURY

Selected Speeches, 1990–1992

ROH TAE WOO

President of the Republic of Korea

A Companion Volume to
Korea: A Nation Transformed,
Published in 1990 by
Pergamon Press

Lanham • New York • London

Copyright © 1992 by
The Embassy of the Republic of Korea

University Press of America®, Inc.
4720 Boston Way
Lanham, Maryland 20706

3 Henrietta Street
London WC2E 8LU England

All rights reserved
Printed in the United States of America
British Cataloging in Publication Information Available

The following articles were reprinted with the permission of
Newsweek, Inc. All rights reserved.

"Riding the Trends of History."
Newsweek, June 18, 1990

"Untying the Last Knot of the Cold War."
Newsweek, September 30, 1991

"I Expect the United States to Remain Involved."
Newsweek, November 18, 1991

Library of Congress Cataloging-in-Publication Data
Roh, Tae Woo, 1932–
Korea in the Pacific century : selected speeches.
p.   cm.
1. Korea (South)—Politics and government—1988–   2. Korea
    (South)—Foreign relations.   I. Title.
DS922.4635.R64   1992   951.9504'3—dc20   92-23251 CIP

ISBN 0-8191-8851-4 (cloth : alk. paper)

The paper used in this publication meets the minimum requirements of
American National Standard for Information Sciences—Permanence
of Paper for Printed Library Materials, ANSI Z39.48–1984.

Contents

Preface xi

Introduction xiii

I. Democracy and Prosperity: Policy for the Republic

1. Opening Remarks at the New Year's News Conference, Seoul, January 10, 1990   3

2. Remarks at the Dinner for the Diplomatic Corps in Seoul, February 8, 1990   14

3. Address on the 71st Anniversary of the Samil Movement, Seoul, March 1, 1990   17

4. Over the Wall Toward Peace and Prosperity—A New Era of Soviet-Korean Friendship and Cooperation; Address at Moscow University, December 14, 1990   21

5. Overcoming Difficulties and Marching Forward; Opening Remarks at the New Year's News Conference, Seoul, January 8, 1991   33

6. President Pins His Hopes on Moscow and Peking; Interview, *Far Eastern Economic Review*, May 9, 1991   41

7. South Korea's President Wants a Polity to Match Its Economy; Interview, *Los Angeles Times*, June 23, 1991   44

8. Opening Remarks at the New Year's News Conference, Seoul, January 10, 1992   50

9. Reshaping a Nation: Korea's Quiet Revolution; article, *Britannica Book of the Year*, 1992   57

vi   *Contents*

II. Toward Reunification of the Nation

10. Riding the Trends of History; Interview, *Newsweek* Magazine, June 18, 1990 — 77

11. Special Announcement on Major Inter-Korean Exchange Visits, Seoul, July 20, 1990 — 80

12. Commemorative Address on the 45th Anniversary of the National Independence Day, Independence Hall, August 15, 1990 — 83

13. Remarks at the Dinner in Honor of President Richard von Weizsaecker of the Federal Republic of Germany, Seoul, February 25, 1991 — 87

14. Interview with CNN Television News, September 22, 1991 — 90

15. Declaration of Non-nuclear Korean Peninsula Peace Initiatives, Seoul, November 8, 1991 — 96

16. Special Announcement on a Nuclear-free Korean Peninsula, December 18, 1991 — 99

17. Special Statement on the Occasion of Coming into Effect of the Basic Agreement Between South and North Korea, Seoul, February 19, 1992 — 102

III. Korea's Place in the World

18. Remarks at the Banquet in Honor of President Daniel Toroitich arap Moi of the Republic of Kenya, Seoul, September 17, 1990 — 107

19. Congratulatory Remarks on the Awarding of the First Seoul Peace Prize, Seoul, September 25, 1990 — 110

20. Remarks at the Banquet in Honor of the President of the Socialist Federal Republic of Yugoslavia and Mrs. Borisav Jovic, Seoul, November 8, 1990 — 112

21. Remarks at the Dinner for the Diplomatic Corps in Seoul, February 12, 1991 — 115

22. Address at the Ground-breaking Ceremony for Taejon Expo '93, Taejon, April 12, 1991 — 119

23. Remarks at the White House Welcoming Ceremony, South Lawn, Washington, D.C., July 2, 1991 — 123

24. Remarks at the State Dinner Hosted by the President of the United States of America and Mrs. George Bush, The White House, Washington, D.C., July 2, 1991 — 125

25. Korea: Emerging World Power; Interview, *Leaders* Magazine
 (U.S.A.), July 1991   127

26. Remarks During the Reception at the 17th World Jamboree
 Mondial, Kosung, Korea, August 12, 1991   137

27. Toward a Peaceful World Community; Address to the Forty-Sixth
 Session of the United Nations General Assembly, United Nations,
 New York, September 24, 1991   140

28. Untying the Last Knot of the Cold War; Interview, *Newsweek*,
 September 30, 1991   149

IV. Northern Policy: Opening to Socialist and ex-Socialist Countries

29. Opening Remarks at the News Conference Following the Summit
 Meeting with President Mikhail Gorbachev of the Soviet Union,
 San Francisco, June 4, 1990   153

30. Remarks at the Banquet in Honor of the President of the Republic
 of Hungary and Mrs. Árpád Gönez, Seoul, November 15, 1990   156

31. Responses to Questions Submitted by the Soviet Press,
 Tass-Izvestia-Pravda, December 10, 1990   159

32. Remarks at the Banquet Hosted by President Mikhail Gorbachev,
 The Kremlin, Moscow, December 14, 1990   167

33. Opening Remarks at the News Conference, Moscow, December
 15, 1990   170

34. Remarks at the Luncheon with Business and Academic Leaders,
 Moscow, December 15, 1990   175

35. Remarks at the Luncheon Hosted by Mayor Anatoly Sobchak,
 Leningrad, December 16, 1990   178

36. Written Interview with *Far Eastern Affairs* (U.S.S.R.), Vol. I, 1991   181

37. Remarks at the Dinner in Honor of President Gorbachev of the
 Soviet Union, Cheju-do, Korea, April 19, 1991   189

38. Remarks at the Banquet in Honor of the President of the
 Mongolian People's Republic and Mrs. Tsevelmaa, Seoul,
 October 23, 1991   191

V. Relations with Japan: Reconciliation with a Neighbor

39. Remarks at the State Dinner Hosted by the Emperor of Japan,
 Tokyo, May 24, 1990   197

40. Korea and Japan: New Relations in a Changing World; Address Before the Japanese Diet, Tokyo, May 25, 1990 — 199

41. Remarks at the Luncheon Hosted by Japanese Business Leaders, Tokyo, May 25, 1990 — 208

42. Remarks at the State Dinner Hosted by the Prime Minister of Japan and Mrs. Toshiki Kaifu, Tokyo, May 25, 1990 — 213

43. Opening Remarks at the Luncheon for the Japanese News Media, Tokyo, May 26, 1990 — 216

44. Remarks at the Banquet in Honor of the Prime Minister of Japan and Mrs. Toshiki Kaifu, Seoul, January 9, 1991 — 218

45. Remarks at the State Dinner in Honor of the Prime Minister of Japan and Mrs. Kiichi Miyazawa, Seoul, January 16, 1992 — 221

46. Opening Remarks at the Joint News Conference Following Summit Talks with Japanese Prime Minister Kiichi Miyazawa, Seoul, January 17, 1992 — 223

VI. Korea as Leader in the Asia-Pacific Region

47. Address to the 23rd International General Meeting of the Pacific Basin Economic Council (PBEC) (via satellite transmission), May 20, 1990 — 227

48. Remarks at the Banquet in Honor of Dato Seri Dr. Mahathir bin Mohamad, Prime Minister of Malaysia, and Datin Seri Dr. Siti Hasmah, Seoul, September 12, 1990 — 230

49. Opening Address at the 47th Session of the Economic and Social Commission for Asia and the Pacific (ESCAP), Seoul, April 1, 1991 — 233

50. Congratulatory Message on the Occasion of the 40th Anniversary of the Colombo Plan, Seoul, May 1, 1991 — 237

51. Message to the 24th General Meeting of the Pacific Basin Economic Council (PBEC), May 4, 1991 — 239

52. Room for Joint Ventures with Canada, *The Globe and Mail* (Canada), June 29, 1991 — 241

53. Korea's Emerging Role in a New Pacific Order; Speech Given at the Hoover Institution, Palo Alto, California, June 29, 1991 — 243

54. Remarks at the Welcoming Ceremony on the Occasion of the State Visit of the Yang Di-Pertuan Agong IX [King] of Malaysia, Seoul, September 13, 1991 — 253

55. Remarks at the Banquet in Honor of the Yang Di-Pertuan Agong IX of Malaysia, Seoul, September 13, 1991 — 255

56. Keynote Address to the Third Asia-Pacific Economic Cooperation (APEC) Meeting, Seoul, November 12, 1991 — 258

57. I Expect the United States to Remain Involved; Interview, *Newsweek*, November 18, 1991 — 263

VII. Korea and the West: Europe and the Western Hemisphere

58. Remarks at the Banquet in Honor of the Prime Minister of the Hellenic Republic and Mrs. Constantine Mitsotakis, Seoul, November 14, 1990 — 267

59. Remarks at the Banquet in Honor of the Prime Minister of Denmark and Mrs. Poul Schlüter, Seoul, June 12, 1991 — 270

60. Remarks upon Arrival in Canada, Ottawa, July 3, 1991 — 273

61. Opening Remarks at the Joint News Conference with Prime Minister Brian Mulroney of Canada, Ottawa, July 4, 1991 — 275

62. Remarks at the Banquet Hosted by the Governor-General of Canada and Mrs. Ramon Hnatyshyn, Ottawa, July 4, 1991 — 277

63. Remarks at the Welcoming Ceremony on a State Visit to Mexico, Mexico City, September 25, 1991 — 280

64. Remarks at the Dinner Held by President Carlos Salinas de Gortari of Mexico, Mexico City, September 25, 1991 — 282

65. Opening Remarks at the Joint News Conference with President George Bush of the United States, Seoul, January 6, 1992 — 286

66. Remarks at the State Dinner in Honor of the President of the United States of America and Mrs. George Bush, Seoul, January 6, 1992 — 288

Appendices

1. Grand National Harmony and Progress Towards a Great Nation; Special Declaration on June 29, 1987 — 293

2. We Can Do It; Inaugural Address, February 25, 1988 — 298

3. A Single National Community; Special Declaration in the Interest of National Self-Respect, Unification and Prosperity, July 7, 1988 — 304

4. Feelings of Great National Pride; Remarks on the Eve of the Seoul Olympic Games, September 14, 1988 — 307

x   *Contents*

5. Dialogue for Peace; Address at the Forty-Third Session of the General Assembly of the United Nations, October 18, 1988 — 310

6. Partners for Progress: ROK-U.S. Relations in a Changing World; Address before a Joint Meeting of the United States Congress, October 18, 1989 — 318

7. Partners for a New Era of Harmony; Address to the Hungarian National Assembly, November 23, 1989 — 324

8. Declaration on General Principles of Relations Between the Republic of Korea and the Union of Soviet Socialist Republics, Moscow, December 14, 1990 — 333

9. Agreement on Reconciliation, Nonaggression and Exchanges and Cooperation Between the South and the North, Panmunjom, Korea, December 13, 1991 — 336

Preface

As the 21st century nears, hopes run high for a brighter future and for a more peaceful, equitable and prosperous world.

During the past four years, we have seen powerful currents of openness and reform sweep across the former Communist world and the subsequent collapse of the dreaded Cold War system. The Cold War post mortem continues to this day, in some places violently, but efforts to improve international relations and to increase cooperation among nations continue apace with promising prospects.

While Europeans look forward to an integrated community, transcending national boundaries, the Pacific Rim countries have begun in earnest to promote "Asia-Pacific cooperation" in anticipation of a Pacific Century.

The Republic of Korea is proud to have joined this historic process—first by hosting the highly successful 1988 Olympic Games in Seoul, then by opening formal diplomatic relations with all the former Eastern bloc countries, save China and North Korea, and then by promoting the Asia-Pacific Economic Cooperation (APEC), a unique intergovernmental consultative body now consisting of 15 members of the region.

As soon as I became president in February 1988, I put forward democracy, prosperity and unification as the primary goals of my administration. The process of Korea's democratization is fully reported over the last several years. And, our economy, despite symptoms of stagflation, continued to grow by an average of nine percent per year. Following on the success of the Seoul Olympic Games, we opened diplomatic relations with all Central and Eastern European countries, including the countries of the former Soviet Union. Even stubborn North Korea agreed to our proposal and entered the United Nations along with us. Subsequently, a "Basic Accord" and a "Joint Declaration on Denuclearization of Korea" have been signed between the two governments. Although many hurdles do remain between the two Koreas, these documents are certain to serve as the basic framework for future inter-Korean relations.

The following pages contain all the major speeches and public statements I have made over the last three years, with emphasis on foreign relations of the last two. A few major statements of previous years are also included in an appendix. The speeches reflect important landmarks in our foreign relations as well as my efforts to articulate some of the vital issues the nation has faced. Some of them, such as the democratization program, have been fully carried out, while others, such as relations with China and North Korea, have yet to see fruition. Given the current international climate and our resolve to build a more harmonious world, I am confident that we will, in good time, succeed in these efforts as well.

I sincerely hope that this book will serve the needs of general readers and researchers alike in their attempts to better understand Korea, her situation today and her dreams for tomorrow as we move toward a Pacific Century.

Roh Tae Woo
Seoul
June 1992

Introduction

A major emphasis in President Roh Tae Woo's public statements is the impact of world change. New nations are forming. Popular demands for justice, equity, and political participation are growing. Old-fashioned national aggression has been met by international force. Communism is discredited. The end of the East-West struggle of the Cold War has been marked with the disintegration of the Soviet Union, bringing to the fore the North-South debate over the allocation of resources among rich and poor nations. A new world order is emerging, in which the Asia-Pacific region is playing a leading role.

The Republic of Korea is also changing. Strategically, economically, and politically, it is clearly destined to be a major regional player in the new world order and the coming Pacific Century. This destiny reflects the Republic's dramatic economic and political development since liberation in 1945.

Economic development was slow at first, because of the legacy of Japanese colonial control and the ravages of the Korean War. Korean energies, supported by initial foreign assistance and mobilized by a disciplined government, burst into action in the 1960s and have carried the nation to the top among industrializing countries.

Political development began later. Like most other long-established nations, Korea had a history of autocratic government, and its politics were almost totally suppressed during the forty years of Japanese control. Both its people and its postwar leaders therefore lacked experience in the practice of truly free and representative government. After the nation's liberation in 1945, priority was necessarily given to defense against a renewal of the Korean War and to escape from poverty.

As the risk of war receded and living standards rose, Korean energies burst forth once again in the 1980s—this time in the political arena. The story of President Roh Tae Woo's leadership in the democratization of the Republic is told in the first volume of his speeches, *Korea: A Nation Transformed*.

That story continues in this second volume. The texts of sixty-six of the

President's most significant speeches, statements, and interviews in 1990, 1991, and 1992 are presented in the following pages, beginning where the first volume left off. Taken together, these volumes bear impressive testimony both to the growing maturity and national power of the Republic of Korea and to the quality of its president's leadership and vision.

During the period covered in the second volume, President Roh's speeches emphasized the process of political and economic development within Korea, its problems and its prospects. They spoke eloquently of the supreme aspiration for reunification of the Korean Peninsula, divided for over forty years against the people's will. They expressed the development of the President's Northern Policy—of improving relations with the former Socialist bloc— taking advantage of the dramatic developments of the past few years in that bloc to further the cause of reunification and to advance Korea's security and prosperity. President Roh's speeches also stressed Korea's desire for peaceful, friendly, and cooperative relations with other nations of the world, including the United States as principal ally for security and principal trading and investment partner, and Japan, next most important trading partner. With Japan, particularly, President Roh used the occasion of his meetings with the emperor and prime minister to call for reconciliation and understanding, putting past enmity aside.

The President summarized his vision for Korea in his article for the *Britannica Book of the Year, 1992:* "I believe that the Korean Peninsula . . . can play a unique and vital role in forging a new world order. Korea is neither a wealthy nor an advanced country. But we have demonstrated to other newly emerging countries that it is indeed possible to pursue economic and political development simultaneously. . . . Korea must be a bridge between the advanced and emerging countries, while striving to become advanced itself."

* * *

For convenience in reference, the texts in this book are somewhat arbitrarily grouped into seven categories, based on their points of primary emphasis. The reader must bear in mind, however, that their content often spreads across many or all of the categories, as one would expect of statements by the President of a major nation addressing both his own people and the leaders and citizens of other countries. The main themes expressed in each category are briefly summarized in this introduction. However, it is to the speeches themselves, and not to this unofficial summary, that the reader should look for an authoritative statement of the Republic's and the president's policies.

For background reference, the appendix includes nine of the major documents of the Republic's domestic and foreign policy during President Roh's administration.

I. Democracy and Prosperity: Policy for the Republic

In his New Year's message of January 10, 1990, President Roh spoke of Korea's future in terms of "decades of hope for the Korean people, who have suffered unspeakable tragedies in the past." This future, however, "hinges on whether or not we can successfully cope with the current global as well as domestic challenges and move the nation on to a higher level of progress." He noted that the ongoing process of democratization had unleashed long pent-up demands, resulting in "structural asymmetries and societal contradictions" that had caused economic progress to lose momentum. Nevertheless, "our only choice . . . has to be a more vigorous pursuit of economic progress in a more democratic setting."

The President stated his view that the weakening of Korea's international competitiveness was due in large measure to the decline in morale and work ethic among both industrial managers and workers. He said that "political, social, and economic leaders should lead and encourage the general public by setting paces in moderation, conservation, cooperation and sacrifice." For his part, he promised that "during my tenure as president, I plan to implement various reform measures to make our country a land of hope in which the benefits of economic progress are evenly distributed among all citizens." He listed a number of specific measures. However, the first step was to "make the [economic] pie bigger so that each individual will get a larger share later."

The President identified five urgent domestic tasks: reduction in crime and violence, educational reform, promotion of science and technology, environmental protection, and alleviation of traffic congestion. He concluded with a vision of Korea in the year 2000: an economy three times the present size; a per-capita national product of $15,000; even low-income workers able to save and buy their own homes; a satisfactory standard of living. "We will then have built a prosperous society that will guarantee well-being for all," and "before the end of this century . . . we will attain our long-cherished goal of building a democratic, unified, and prosperous nation."

A month later, taking note of the merger of the government political party with two opposition parties, the President said that "politics in Korea has now moved to a new, higher level of maturity based on mutual trust." He pointed out that there had been some counterproductive developments in the transition from authoritarianism to democracy, like the swing of a pendulum. "We have to wait patiently for the pendulum to return to a normal range of motion."

March 1, 1990, marked the anniversary of the Korean unarmed national popular uprising for independence from the Japanese occupiers in 1919. The President paid homage "to our patriotic forefathers for their noble sacrifice and courageous struggle for freedom at home as well as in such far-away places as China and the United States." He continued, "We shall never forget that we lost our national sovereignty early this century because our nation was weak and poor. During this decade, therefore, we must build a proud and respected nation that will play a leading role for peace and prosperity in the world."

Speaking to academicians and officials at Moscow University in December, the President noted that the liberation of Korea in 1945 brought jubilation which was short-lived because "foreign powers decided to impose a territorial and national division on the Korean Peninsula," and in 1950 "the Cold War imploded into the Korean War," which devastated the land and inflicted "millions of casualties. As a result, when the Republic of Korea launched plans for social-economic development in the early sixties, we had scant resources, hardly any capital and little technology. . . . Korea was one of the poorest countries in the world." Yet "finally, the Korean people stood up." At the 1988 Seoul Olympics, "what the world saw . . . was not the long lines of hungry refugees that they saw during the Korean War, but a new nation of vibrant energy, freedom and prosperity." And, in 1987, an "honorable revolution" succeeded in Korea, bringing the nation into an era of rapid democratic development. "The experience of the Korean people shows that free competition and creativity are the sources of human progress in a pluralistic society. And, respect for human dignity, liberty and individual drive for the pursuit of happiness are vital motivating forces not only for individual successes but for the progress of a nation as well."

In recounting Korea's progress, and the sacrifice that had made it possible, President Roh introduced an autobiographical note: "Originally, I planned to become a medical doctor. When the Korean War broke out I fought in defense of my country, still wearing a high school uniform. This is the reason behind my military career." Two years later, in an article for the *Britannica Book of the Year, 1992*, the President commented that in attending the Korea Military Academy, "I learned a lot more about Communism, but I also learned a great deal about American democracy. Thanks to General James A. Van Fleet, then commanding the Eighth Army in Korea, our curriculum was modelled on West Point's [the U.S. Military Academy]."

In the *Britannica* article, the President also commented that as a member of the National Assembly and chairman of the government party, "inevitably, I came to be impressed with the important place of the legislature in a democracy. I became convinced that the National Assembly alone—through debate, dialogue, and compromise—could effectively reflect the views of the people." He continued, "Our past presidents managed to develop the economy rapidly, enhance education, and strengthen national security. . . . However, there is no denying that we lagged behind on building a truly democratic society. . . . As our society grew more affluent and sophisticated, however, I realized that authoritarian methods could no longer be used to deal with the needs, demands, and conflicting interests that had surfaced as a result of our accelerated modernization."

In a May 1991 interview in *Far East Economic Review*, the President said, "I have been so busy in the last few years that there has hardly been time to think over what I would do in retirement. . . . I just hope to hand over to the next president my personal efforts and experiences from the pursuit of northern diplomacy and reunification." Regarding the qualifications of his successor, he said that person should be "someone who is capable of mastering the course of our democratization efforts, of satisfying the increasingly diverse aspirations of our people; it should be someone who can stand up to the task of our times. . . ."

President Roh's news conference in January 1991 marked the beginning of the fourth year of his administration, out of the five in his constitutionally allotted single term. The President chose to report progress "on what is being done rather than making new pledges and commitments." He took note of pledges already carried out: freedom of the press, removal of authoritarian style of government, construction of two million housing units, development of west coast areas long neglected, northern diplomacy toward the former Socialist bloc, and a push toward reunification.

The President called attention to the forthcoming local elections, in which five thousand local council members would be chosen, in order to "encourage participation by local leaders and to realize the welfare of the people through local representation." He emphasized the need for fair, just, clean elections: "You, the voters, must bring about what amounts to a revolutionary change in our election practices." He noted the task of politicians "to transform the style of our politics from confrontations that breed instability to compromises and dialogue that produce national harmony and integration," and added, "I will do my utmost to transform the ruling party [the Democratic Liberal Party, formed by the three-party merger a year previously], based on a thorough-going self-criticism. . . ."

Addressing public concern at increased rates of crime, the President noted his October 1990 "Declaration of War on Crime," and the ensuing New Life, New Order campaign. He said the government would continue strict law enforcement and eradicate crimes, violence, and unlawful and disorderly behavior. "To reform society, we will address the trend toward delinquent behavior and decadent pleasure-seeking." But the public, too, must cooperate.

Turning to economic problems, the President repeated his call for "infusing vitality into economic, industrial, and technological structures and . . . introducing fresh approaches to business management and the national work ethic." He listed external economic problems—the Persian Gulf crisis, unstable oil prices, worldwide stagflation, the Uruguay Round of trade negotiations and the related frictions—and the internal problems of wage and price rises, energy costs, and slow recovery of competitiveness. To meet these problems, the President said, a "societal consensus" was needed for stabilizing wages, prices, and labor-management relations, fiscal restraint, and holding the inflation percentage to single digits and wage increases within price increases.

The President said the government would implement a plan for recovery of industrial international competitiveness, including relief of the money supply and labor shortages and development of technology, supporting corporate research and development. The social infrastructure would be expanded. Efforts would continue at eradicating illicit real-estate investment activities and discouraging expansion of non-productive service industries. Unrealistic control measures would be removed, and farming and fishing villages modernized. But the people, as well as the government, must contribute.

Noting four priority areas for action—housing, transportation, environment, education—the President mentioned specific actions to be taken in each, and noted, "During my tenure, I am determined to implement effective long- and intermediate-range environmental protection programs to preserve our natural environment and to provide clean air and clean water. . . ." Regarding education, he called for adjustment in the popular attitude "that everybody should go to college or that everyone should graduate from college. . . . We should find a better way of educating our children, and the government is currently in the process of restructuring the college entrance exam and high school education systems. . . ."

In a June 1991 *Los Angeles Times* interview, the President took stock of the eight political reforms promised in his famous declaration of June 29, 1987. Of these, he said the most successful was the direct election of the President and the release and restoration of rights of politicians and others, including the prominent opposition leader, Kim Dae Jung. Least successful had been efforts to remove authoritarianism. "Rather than grasping and resolving popular demands and frictions, the ruling and the opposition parties have tended to escalate them. . . , engrossed in self-serving maneuvers to advance the interests of only their parties, factions, or themselves personally."

Regarding regional antipathies that had plagued Korean politics, particularly between the southwest Cholla and southeast Kyongsang provinces, the President said these feelings, which had been growing over the past generation, were partly due to the tradition of blood and community ties, and partly to the focus of economic development on the eastern side of the country. The antipathies had been enhanced by the competition for election of Kim Young Sam [a Kyongsang politician formerly in the opposition] and Kim Dae Jung [a Cholla politician and principal opposition leader], and fueled by the suppression of the 1980 Kwangju uprising. The government's remedial actions had included compensation for the victims of violence in Kwangju, and economic development of the west coast. "Within ten years, the west-coast axis will be strengthened . . . and regional antipathies softened."

Concerning the Korean security agencies, longtime targets of popular fear and resentment, the President said that their management had been improved, and the National Security Law had been modified. "Unlike the old days of authoritarian rule, political surveillance of opposition politicians is not possible. Opposition parties and politicians are not restricted in their political activities. . . . It is no longer possible even to imagine military intervention in politics."

As the President entered his final year in office, he held a press conference in January 1992. He took note once again of progress made in carrying out the political reforms promised in 1987. He noted, also, the successes of his Northern Policy, including the entry of both North and South Korea into the United Nations and the North-South agreements signed the previous month. Yet although the economy was growing, South Korea had "not yet been able to fully overcome the difficulties stemming from democratization, internationalization, and market opening." Given the changing world, in which "nations and regions are increasingly involved in fierce competition for prosperity," the Republic "must weather these changes and surge ahead."

Top administration priority, the President said, would be on restoring economic vitality, as the nation entered the first year of its seventh Five-Year Economic and Social Development Plan, "designed to fully transform our economy into an advanced economy," with per-capita income reaching $11,000 by 1997. To achieve stability, the government would lower economic growth to 7 percent in 1992, continuing its emphasis on holding wage increases within productivity increase, controlling inflation, checking speculation and the growth of service industries, improving education, and curbing consumption.

The President reemphasized the promotion of competitiveness, saying, "If our businesses do not try harder to produce a range of products that can meet international standards of excellence, they will lose out in today's international marketplace." To this end, he said, his administration would support technological development and export industries, especially small and medium industry. Additionally, the program begun in 1991 to improve social infrastructure would continue, with ground-breaking for high-speed railways and a new international airport. The Korean financial market had already been opened to foreign investors. Agriculture and fishing would be modernized. "What is important . . . is the concerted effort of workers, farmers, fishermen, and all other citizens to adapt to the changing circumstances."

Turning to political and social matters, President Roh noted, "We have ahead of us a great task of electing representatives of the people who will lead our efforts to achieve national prosperity and unification and thus lay a foundation for the establishment of a new government" through parliamentary and presidential elections in 1992. "We cannot, however, let the forthcoming elections disturb the national economy, split national unity and destroy social morale. We must build a consensus on the need to revitalize and further promote national development." The government would crack down on illegal practices, but "it is impossible to ensure fair elections without the active and spontaneous participation of the people. In fact, the political climate is in the hands of the people."

The President went on to state the political agenda for 1992. Parliamentary elections, in which co-chairman Kim Young-Sam would lead the government party, would be followed by a convention of the ruling party at which a presidential candidate would be nominated by democratic procedures. There would be no revision of the Constitution during President Roh's term of office. Elections of local government heads would be postponed because of the likely impact on the economy and social stability; their timing would be determined by the newly-elected National Assembly. Efforts toward reunification of the nation would continue.

Programs for social stability and improved living standards noted by the President included public security (continuation of the war on crime), construction of housing units (2.14 million by the end of 1991), declining housing prices and rising home ownership; local education autonomy, introduced in 1991; investment in water treatment and sewage disposal; and increase in liquid natural gas supply in major cities. The President commented, ". . . A mature civic consciousness has been the underlying force for the ongoing New Life-New Order campaign to drive out excessive consumption, depraved lifestyles and social disorder. . . . We will be assured of a better future as long as we remain conscious that we are the masters of our country, that we must develop our own community, and that it is for us to choose our own future." He concluded, "I will do my best to accomplish what I can. I will never neglect to sow seeds for the future."

II. Toward Reunification of the Nation

Hardly an utterance of the President omitted mention of the task of reunifying North and South Korea. Some statements, however, gave it particular attention. In a June 1990 *Newsweek* interview, following his historic meeting with Soviet President Mikhail Gorbachev, President Roh said, "We do not want the North Koreans to be further isolated. . . . I think the North Koreans will experience some shock [at the meeting], but in the future they will recover their reason. Eventually, they will follow the trends of history." Noting that the Korean War resulted from the vacuum following the withdrawal of U.S. forces, the President expressed his hope that the United States "will maintain its necessary presence" in the future.

Regarding the possibility of closer U.S. relations with North Korea, the President said he had no objection in principle, but noted "absolutely essential preconditions": North Korea should first abandon its hostility, aggressiveness, and huge offensive military deployment toward the South, and its international terrorist and subversive activities. "If North Korea abandons such activities and attitudes, and if there is true openness and reform in North Korea, the relationship of the United States with North Korea can improve." ". . . Kim Il Sung has ruled North Korea single-handedly for the past 42 years. Under those circumstances, there is little chance that the Gorbachevian movement for reform and openness will affect the North Korean attitude in the near future. But in this modern age no country can erect watertight walls against the outside world. . . . Eventually North Korea will start to crack and open up. We cannot be too optimistic about this, but once Kim Il Sung is out of the picture, whoever succeeds him will be quite different."

As one attempted step toward cooperation with the North, on the emotion-laden issue of reuniting separated families, President Roh in July 1990 proclaimed "the five-day span around [August 15, the 45th anniversary of Korean liberation] a period of grand inter-Korean exchange visits. For five continuous days beginning on August 13th, we will keep Panmunjom [the site of the Military Armistice Commission, between the North and South] open and will accept our brethren from the North without restrictions. . . . We will also permit our citizens to visit North Korea through Panmunjom, without restrictions. . . . If we succeed in such a free exchange, . . . we should be able to permit mutual visits on and around . . . national holidays" and thus "clear the way for free interchange throughout the year. . . ." North Korea, however, did not agree.

When the August 15 anniversary came, the President noted in his commemorative address, "Today is the first Independence Day of the 1990s, and we greet it with the determination to build within the decade the proud homeland that our patriotic forefathers dreamed of . . . We must usher in a new century of glory during which our brethren will live in freedom and prosperity in a single homeland. . . ." ". . . The time has come," he said, "for the responsible authorities of the South and North to hold talks on an entire range of issues, from the joint renunciation of the use of military force to the signing of a non-aggression pact, and from the replacement of the present armistice agreement with a peace agreement to the establishment of permanent representative offices in Seoul and P'yŏngyang. In particular, we are willing to discuss earnestly the issue of arms control in our efforts to eliminate threats of war on the Korean Peninsula, end South-North confrontation, and usher in an era of national reconciliation." Thereafter, renewed attempts at contact were positively received by the North. The prime ministers of North and South Korea met in Seoul in December 1990, the first in a series of subsequent meetings.

In February 1991, the President reaffirmed his government's determination to pursue dialogue with the North, and commented, "The peaceful and democratic unification of Germany inspires us with courage to seek that goal. I am convinced that just as unified Germany is underpinning European peace, so will the unification of the Korean Peninsula bolster peace in the Asia-Pacific region. . . ." In September, in a CNN interview, he said, "I believe the political development and evolution of the Soviet society will have a very positive impact on the Korean Peninsula." Noting the admission of both Koreas to the United Nations, he observed, ". . . Now that we are members of the United Nations which pursues peace and prosperity of all mankind, I believe the Cold War system and confrontation on the Korean Peninsula will proceed to a relationship of cooperation and mutual trust, and that, I believe, would be another step toward realization of Korean unification." He continued, "The Republic of Korea has pursued northern diplomacy, which is to seek friendship and cooperation with North Korea's friends and allies, [so that they would] persuade North Korea and promote cooperation and friendly relations with the Republic of Korea."

In the same interview, the President took note of the North Korean "attempt to develop nuclear weapons," which "is a source of grave concern for all of us" in the light of past North Korean adventurism and confrontation. "Consequently, we cannot be assured of our safety. . . ." Moreover, "The North Korean development of a nuclear device will pose threats, not only to the Republic of Korea, but to China and Japan as well. Therefore, North Korea should immediately and unconditionally sign the nuclear safeguards treaty with the International Atomic Energy Agency, and submit all its nuclear material and nuclear-related facilities for international inspection."

Looking toward future developments in North Korea, the President noted two schools of thought among experts—one, that North Korea would "undergo a rapid transformation and perhaps even rather unfortunate bloody developments" after its leader, Kim Il Sung, passed from the scene; the other, that the North Korean political system, "maintained so long under rigid control," might continue for some time. He expressed his own belief in both possibilities, and said, "What the Republic of Korea wants is . . . a smooth transition to democracy, even if it means time is required, and we do not want any violence and bloodshed on the part of North Korea." Notwithstanding the universal desire of the Korean people to achieve unification as soon as possible, "it is absolutely essential that we achieve unification without incurring any unfortunate turn of events in the process, and we should speed up the process prudently. . . ." He noted the effect of changes in the Soviet Union and Eastern Europe, and called for the continuation of the U.S. military presence as "not only essential, but . . . critical for the maintenance of peace and stability on the Korean Peninsula, and the Korean Peninsula, of course, plays a key role for the maintenance of stability of the entire Northeast Asian region." He expressed the belief that China would also "want reduction of tension on the Korean Peninsula, and the development of a cooperative and friendly relationship between the two Koreas . . . ," and hoped that the Chinese would contribute toward the promotion of such relations.

In November 1991 came the President's historic pledge that the Republic of Korea "will use nuclear energy solely for peaceful purposes, and will not manufacture, possess, store, deploy or use nuclear weapons" and that it "will continue to submit to comprehensive international inspection . . . and will not possess nuclear fuel reprocessing and enrichment facilities." In addition, the Republic "will actively participate in international efforts toward a total elimination of chemical-biological weapons and observe all international agreements thereon." The President called on North Korea to take immediate corresponding steps, and said that as soon as the North did so, his government would "initiate bilateral discussions on other military-security issues" and seek to resolve them through high-level South-North talks. In a separate statement, the President was able to say that there were no nuclear weapons in South Korea—meaning that the United States had removed any such weapons that it might have deployed there.

These statements hastened negotiations between North and South that led to the signing on December 19, 1991, of an "Agreement on Reconciliation, Nonaggression and Exchanges and Cooperation between the South and the North" and a "Joint Declaration of the Denuclearization of the Korean Peninsula." The previous day, the President said of the signing that it, together with the joint entry of both Koreas into the United Nations, was "an epic milepost on our road to the resolution of the Korean Question and the attainment of national unity." He noted that his government, in consultation with the United States, had proposed simultaneous nuclear inspections of facilities in the South and North, including U.S. military bases. "To open the military bases of a nuclear superpower to international inspection is a truly exceptional precedent, but we have reached this decision for the sole purpose of a peaceful and smooth resolution of the Korean Peninsula nuclear issue."

III. Korea's Place in the World

Many of President Roh's speeches dwelt on Korea's place in a changing world. One of the most eloquent on this subject was his address to the United Nations General Assembly in September 1991, after the Republic, together with North Korea, had been admitted to UN membership. "The world is undergoing epochal changes," he said. "Systems that oppressed freedom and human dignity are being dismantled and the tragedies stemming from dogmatic ideologies are coming to an end everywhere. Around the world nations are seeking to chart their own destinies.

"What is truly momentous about this process is that history is being advanced not by the forces of bloody revolution but by the power of reason and free spirit. . . . This epic change brings enormous opportunities and is the source of hope for all mankind. Even so, we must travel a long and tortuous road before we can successfully mold the current process into a new order of world peace. . . . We have to recognize that any attempt at reform, however minor, is bound to require an element of sacrifice and pain. . . . In the case of the Soviet Union and the Eastern European countries, . . . moving away from a system of strict control that pervaded every aspect of their lives for decades, the difficulties and costs of creating new structures must be enormous.

"We all know that throughout the Cold War period, the nations of the world spent an exorbitant amount of resources on national security and military preparedness. Now, the success of current reforms promise to bring benefits the world over in the form of peace. . . . As the benefits of peace are shared, it is only fair that the burdens and sacrifices should also be shared. Consequently, I call upon all the well-to-do nations to extend active support and assistance to the countries that used to have centrally planned economic systems, in their transition to democracy and free market economies.

"As a nation that has risen only a generation ago from the ashes of war, and as a recently democratized nation that is growing in prosperity, the Republic of Korea feels a special affinity toward the emerging democracies, and understands from experience the acute imperative that these nations are facing together: to achieve democracy and economic development in tandem. Korea is neither a wealthy nor an advanced country. But we are prepared to extend support to the reform efforts not only in Eastern Europe and the Soviet Union but in all parts of the world, and to offer them cooperation to the best of our ability."

In speaking of the Korean desire for peace, the President commented, "The recent war in the Gulf region confirmed that the United Nations is the only independent global body capable of asserting and giving force to the rule of law in today's international community. . . . Now as a member [of the UN], we will participate more actively in all UN endeavors toward the peaceful settlement of disputes as well as the enforcement of international justice. Peace can be built only when a common conviction prevails that nations do not threaten each other and that we may in fact live in peace. We shall never win faith in peace so long as we let our safety hinge on the might of formidable weapons that can reduce this world to ashes in an instant." Welcoming the recent signing of the START arms reduction treaty between the United States and the Soviet Union, the President expressed the hope that it would "accelerate arms control negotiations around the world." Further, "The Republic of Korea fully supports a complete elimination of all chemical weapons, and will readily join an international convention as soon as it emerges."

Speaking of Korea's economic role in world affairs, the President said, "Many countries around the world as well as the United Nations itself rendered assistance in the process of Korea's development, and became our partners for common prosperity. Today, the Republic of Korea lies at a midway stage between the advanced and the developing countries. As such, we hope to return the benefits we received from around the world by playing an active role in solving the global North-South problem. In addition to sharing our experience and know-how with the developing countries, we will seek to play the role of a bridge between the advanced and the developing world by promoting global exchanges and cooperation and by facilitating the flow of commodities, capital and information. . . .

"We encourage the advanced countries to move forward with the horizontal specialization of industries among nations by speeding up the process of readjusting their domestic industrial structures. In addition, they should refrain from monopolizing information and technology. . . . Global markets should be opened wider and the expansion of trade should be encouraged. Tendencies toward protectionism and mutually exclusive economic blocs should be discouraged. The international community should adopt a more positive posture toward the solution of these critical problems within the framework of the United Nations system. In addition, we should jointly meet such new and serious global challenges as drug trafficking, terrorism and environmental damage."

In September 1990, the President awarded to Juan Antonio Samaranch, President of the International Olympic Committee, the Seoul Peace Prize established after the 1988 Seoul Olympics. As he did so, the President said, "With the dawning of a new century fast approaching, waves of openness and reconciliation are sweeping the whole world. When, at this propitious time, the sacred Olympic flame was lit in Seoul, symbolizing a universal yearning for peace, we came to believe that peace was within our reach, if only we remained as united as on that uplifting occasion. The Seoul Peace Prize embodies this fervent desire."

In November 1990, at a dinner in Seoul for the visiting President Borisav Jovic, President Roh noted the "momentous change" in process, and the collapse of the Cold War system. "The ideological barriers and political blocs that used to divide humanity and the nations of the world are being removed. Human dignity, freedom, and democratic pluralism are now being accepted as universal values." Paying tribute to the Yugoslav contribution as a leader of the Nonaligned Movement, the President commented, "Korea probably is the world's worst victim of the Cold War." Later in his speech, he said that Korea's policy was to cultivate "friendly and cooperative relations with all nations of the world. We believe this is the way to promote not only universal prosperity but world peace and global cooperation as well."

Breaking ground for the 1993 Taejon International Exposition, President Roh noted that it would be the first international exhibition to be hosted by a developing country, "tantamount to the Olympic Games of the fields of economics, science, and technology." He described it as a Korean contribution to global understanding. "It is here that we shall discover in two years fresh ideals and challenges of mankind, and how modern technology proposes to fulfill our dreams and aspirations. . . . The Expo '93 is certain to provide as well a meeting ground for the peoples of the world as a festive occasion for reconciliation and harmony among nations and cultures. . . . The remarkable changes which have taken place have brought with them the realization that a world of harmony in which we can live in friendship and peace is not a mere dream, but is in fact, a realistic possibility."

On the other hand, the President noted, while "advances in science, technology, and industrial development have brought us all together as neighbors in a single global village, . . . technological development continues to exacerbate the gap between advanced and developing nations, intensifying the already wide gap between North and South.

"It is also true that the rapid process of industrialization carries within it the seeds of destruction, threatening nature and the environment of our one and only planet earth. Energy and natural resources will be depleted within a few generations if the current rate of consumption should continue.

"All of these are formidable challenges, but together through Taejon Expo '93, we shall discover ways of coping with these challenges, and enhance the happiness and prosperity of all mankind."

Welcomed by U.S. President George Bush in Washington in July 1991, President Roh once more spoke of the changing world and Korea's role in it. "We must now focus our attention to removing the legacies of the Cold War from the Korean Peninsula and Northeast Asia so that a durable peace and stability may be secured for the entire Asia-Pacific region. He continued, "As the world saw during the 1988 Seoul Olympic Games, Korea's dynamic energies and cooperative spirit encourage a new faith in freedom and hope for prosperity around the world. The Korean people have now become a dependable friend and ally of the American people, and they promise to assume appropriate international responsibilities and make a greater contribution to the international community."

Later the same day in Washington, the President noted, "The Gulf War victory has established that the international community will no longer tolerate wanton aggression and that the rule of law shall prevail in our world. We are at an historic juncture at which a new world order of freedom, justice and peace is being established."

In an interview published in the American magazine *Leaders* in July 1991, President Roh emphasized support for international free trade. "Because the Republic of Korea has achieved economic development through international trade, we shall continue to promote trade with all the countries in the world. Moreover, we must step up cooperation for the promotion of free trade and guard against protectionist tendencies and the proliferation of exclusive economic blocs. Since the world economy today must resolve not only the North-South problem but also the East-West problem stemming from the reforms of socialist countries, we must bring the Uruguay Round [international trade] negotiations to fruition in a spirit of cooperation and for the common prosperity."

In the same interview, the President noted that world change "is now moving toward this area of Asia, toward China and North Korea. As soon as . . . they pursue economic development and take advantage of such systems as free trade, market economies and economic cooperation, the trade volume between East and West will certainly see a quantum jump." However, "The prospects for the North-South problem are not very promising. . . . A majority of developing and underdeveloped countries are suffering from chronic poverty and foreign debt. So the gap between the North and the South is expected to further widen, particularly in view of the rapid pace of progress in modern technology. Thus, if we are to succeed in building a more peaceful and harmonious world, we must step up international cooperation and find effective solutions to the North-South problem."

Korea's global reach was illustrated by the visit of President Daniel arap Moi of Kenya to Korea in September 1990. In the course of his welcoming remarks, President Roh noted, "The world today offers opportunities as well as challenges. I therefore believe that cooperation among developing countries like Kenya and Korea is more essential than ever before."

IV. Northern Policy: Opening to Socialist and ex-Socialist Countries

Dramatic change in the Soviet Union and Eastern Europe during the period covered by this volume was a major theme in President Roh's statements. The effects of the change were a vindication of the President's Northern Policy, enunciated at the beginning of his term of office.

In June 1990, President Roh met with Soviet President Gorbachev in San Francisco, signalling the success of the Korean President's Northern Policy. President Roh said on that occasion, ". . . Our historic meeting represents an important turning point. After talking with President Gorbachev today, I am convinced that prospects for peace and the eventual unification of the Korean Peninsula are bright. . . . President Gorbachev and I are both encouraged by the fact that the progress toward openness and reform is forging a new world order of harmony and cooperation. We have agreed to make joint efforts to facilitate the development of the new order." As to the situation in Northeast Asia, President Roh said, "I have made it clear to President Gorbachev that we do not want North Korea to be isolated. It is my hope that the Soviet Union will continue to maintain interest in and further develop its existing links with North Korea even as the USSR and the Republic of Korea promote constructive relations. . . ." He further said, "The northern policy of the Republic of Korea will serve to convince socialist countries of the effectiveness and efficiency of democracy and free trade system and help them carry out reform."

As envisaged at the June meeting, the Republic of Korea and the Soviet Union established full diplomatic relations in September, thus ending an 86-year hiatus in Russian-Korean relations and dramatically reversing the hostility of the post-World War II period. (Following the dissolution of the Soviet Union in 1991, Russia continued the newly-established diplomatic relationship.) In December 1990, responding to questions from the Soviet publications *Tass, Izvestia,* and *Pravda,* President Roh commented, "The rapid development of Soviet-Korean relations is an encouraging sign to many nations in the area that a new era of reconciliation and cooperation is dawning in the Asia-Pacific region as well." Further, ". . . the road for mutual exchange is wide open. This year alone recorded a total of one billion dollars in our trade and there have been more than 12,000 visitors between our two countries." The President recalled that the Soviet athletic delegation to the 1988 Seoul Olympics had "received an enthusiastic welcome by the Korean people, and the performances of the Bolshoi Ballet and the Leningrad Philharmonic Orchestra have seen enormous successes in Seoul."

In answering other questions, the President noted, "Our two countries are not only close geographically, but our economic structures share complementary characteristics. . . We have developmental techniques and experience under the market economy. . . , the capabilities to build merchant marines and automobiles, to manufacture and produce electronic appliances and consumer goods . . . , the material and technology for construction, communications and other social infrastructure . . . skilled manpower and managerial abilities. . . . These are all items that can provide realistic help in the process of restructuring the Soviet economy. On your part, the Soviet Union has a large potential market, a wide expanse of territory and abundant natural resources including oil, gas and timber. And, we can benefit from your advanced scientific technologies. In view of these complementary features of our two economies, the expansion of trade and economic cooperation will benefit us both and contribute to our common prosperity." The President called attention, among other things, to the possibility that Korean businesses could "through direct investment or joint ventures, build factories in the Soviet Union and provide the products to our markets and export to the world market."

President Roh visited Moscow in December 1990. At a press conference there, he said, "the Soviet-Korean Joint Declaration that President Gorbachev and I signed yesterday will serve as a charter as our two countries open a new era of friendship and cooperation." He continued, "Our bilateral rapprochement can be described in terms of confluence between my 'northern policy' which sought to remove Cold War confrontations and build a world of harmony and cooperation, and President Gorbachev's perestroika which has brought on phenomenal changes around the world. The philosophy that we share has provided the basis for our talks. . . ." He noted, "During my visit agreements on trade, avoidance of double taxation and science and technology cooperation were signed between the two governments. Now, a solid framework is in place for further development of exchanges and cooperation between our two countries."

At a banquet for the visiting Hungarian President Gönez of Hungary in November 1990, President Roh told his guest, "We Koreans feel particularly close to the Hungarian people, for Hungary was the first among the Central and Eastern European countries to establish diplomatic relations with us, thereby contributing to a new world order of reconciliation." He noted that this second meeting within a year had "firmly established a framework and we were able to confirm the rapid increases in bilateral cooperation in economic, cultural, scientific and technological sectors."

In October 1991, during the visit of the President of Mongolia, President Roh said, "Our partnership has transcended the barriers of the Cold War and is . . . at the forefront the human progress toward a harmonious world community. Furthermore, it means that in the Asian continent also a new era has arrived." He continued that in welcoming the Mongolian President, he felt himself to be "among old friends who have been away. . . . Perhaps you are also struck by the fact that it is very difficult among us to distinguish guests from the hosts. Indeed, our two peoples are as close to each other as our features are similar. . . . Our two nations, both belonging to the Altaic cultural sphere, have been engaged in close interchanges from time immemorial. . . . I am convinced that [the reforms in Mongolia] carried out under the banner of *Shmechlel* (reform) and *Eerchlelt* (openness) will mark an historic beginning in new Mongolia of freedom and prosperity. The Republic of Korea pledges to render its support and encouragement to the reform efforts of the Mongolian government and people." President Roh recalled that formal diplomatic relations with Mongolia had been opened in March 1990, and said, "As soon as a favorable environment for foreign investment emerges, many Korean businesses will decide to participate in various Mongolian projects, including the utilization of abundant livestock resources for woolen products, the foodstuff industry, joint exploration of natural resources, expansion of social infrastructure such as highways, railroad and communications, and construction of residential housing."

V. Relations with Japan: Reconciliation with a Neighbor

In May 1990, President Roh visited Tokyo, and the Emperor of Japan hosted a banquet for him. On that notable occasion, the President philosophically viewed the course of the long relationship between the two countries, placing the traumatic forty-year Japanese occupation of Korea (1905 to 1945) in historical perspective and looking toward the future. He said:

"Since time immemorial, Korea and Japan have had close contact as neighbors. Through interactions across the narrow straits, our two nations have exercised significant mutual influence on each other's cultural development. We have shared many positive things together, but in more modern times, we have also experienced pain. But, compared to the long history of neighborly and amicable relations, the period of darkness was relatively short.

"To be sure, it is not possible to erase, nor should we forget, historical facts. But, I do not believe we should remain bound up in the past. Our two nations must now forge a new era of friendship and cooperation based on proper historical perspectives, and put the wrong-doings of the past behind. . . ." He continued, ". . . Our two countries ought to combine our efforts to take a leading role in promoting peace and prosperity throughout the Asia-Pacific region, the new center of world attention, by harmoniously combining the merits of the East and the West. Furthermore, our two nations should endeavor to make greater contributions toward the well-being and prosperity of the world at large. This, I believe, is our duty before history and mankind."

The following day, as the first Korean head of state ever to address the Japanese Diet, the President again spoke of the prospects for Korean-Japanese cooperation. "For some time now," he said, "it has been predicted that the Asia-Pacific region will emerge as the hub of world civilization in the new century. We now see that prediction coming true. With boundless potential, this region is now bursting with dynamic development. I think it is a mandate of our time to develop an Asia-Pacific community in keeping with the current trends toward regional integration in this increasingly multipolar world.

"The well-being of both Japan and Korea in the twenty-first century will also be directly linked with the peace and prosperity of Asia and the Pacific. Our two nations must thus be partners in shaping a Pacific Era. To that end, we should develop an efficient and effective framework for cooperation to benefit all nations on the strength of openness and diversity in this region. Our bilateral relationship is now the concern of our two nations and is also the basis and focal point for Asia-Pacific cooperation."

As to the present Korea-Japan relationship, the President said, ". . . [O]ur bilateral relations are characterized by mutual beneficial interdependence. This is particularly true in the economic field. Korea and Japan have now become each other's second largest trading partner, next only to the United States of America. . . . It can be clearly seen that Korea's development contributes to Japan's prosperity, too. The presence of a prosperous country as its closest neighbor will be an advantage in the future for Japan, also. Korea's development will also help to strengthen the economy of East Asia as a whole. I solicit your cooperation in ensuring the continuing expansion and strengthening of trade and economic cooperation between our two nations from such a broad perspective."

The President went on to call for attention to "the chronic trade imbalance between Korea and Japan," and to the furnishing of technology to Korea. ". . . Rises in exports from my country have always led to rises in our imports from Japan at a similar pace. It is my sincere hope that with the realization that Korea's development is in the best interests of Japan also, you will join us in urging and promoting active technological and scientific cooperation between our two countries."

Noting the travel of two million people a year between the two countries, and "private-level exchanges and cooperation in the political, economic, social, cultural and other fields," the President said, "In particular, exchanges between young Koreans and Japanese are expanding fast and efforts in both countries to study and understand each other are growing more and more enthusiastic." While calling for all citizens of both countries to be "involved in exchanges and mutual help in every possible area," the President noted, ". . . There still remains a psychological barrier that hinders the evolution of genuine friendship between our two peoples. . . . The negative vestiges of the past era continue to hamper the development of our bilateral ties" while former European enemies are joining in a single community. ". . . Depending on how we tackle it, we now have an opportunity to discard the shackles of the past and purge the negative residues of what took place in bygone days. . . ." In particular, the President called attention to the situation of the 700,000 Korean residents "who for historic reasons have come to live in Japan. . . . Only when they become able to live in this land as good neighbors of the Japanese and without artificial convenience, will both our people feel genuine friendship to each other."

During the same visit, President Roh met with Japanese business leaders. Noting that "in the process of development, Korea has learned and received much help from Japan," he expressed his "gratitude to Japan and the Japanese people for their cooperation, especially to the business leaders present here." He said, "The active involvement of Japanese businessmen, especially the senior business leaders present here, is essential to improving economic cooperation between Korea and Japan." He appealed for their cooperation in several specific fields: bilateral industrial cooperation, including transfer of technology; redressing the trade imbalance by lowering tariff and non-tariff barriers and permitting Korean businesses to participate in large projects in Japan; sharing of capital and technology with countries in East Asia and the Pacific Basin. Finally, he expressed the hope "that Japan will also assist in effectively coordinating policies of the industrialized nations to stabilize the world economy and curriencies, especially the yen. . . ."

After President Roh's state visit to Japan, two successive Japanese Prime Ministers, Kaifu and Miyazawa, visited Korea in January 1991 and January

1992. In a joint press conference with Miyazawa, President Roh again stressed the need for Korean-Japanese cooperation in the international arena, noting that the two countries "have agreed to closely cooperate with each other in the Asia-Pacific Economic Cooperation forum and the Uruguay Round of trade negotiations." At the same time, the President called on the Japanese government "to actively probe into the tragic events of the past, including the issue of the Korean 'comfort women' [mobilized for the benefit of Japanese soldiers in World War II] and to take appropriate measures if the results so warrant."

VI. Korea as Leader in the Asia-Pacific Region

The Republic of Korea played an active role in the organization of the intergovernmental forum called Asia-Pacific Economic Cooperation, erected on the foundation of a private-enterprise grouping known as Pacific Basin Economic Cooperation. In an address via satellite to the 23d meeting of PBEC in May 1990, President Roh noted the anticipated integration of the European Community in 1992 and the Community's prospective expansion, and said, ". . . We must guard against the appearance of regional blocs and protectionist tendencies that hamper the growth of the world economy." Pointing out that the Asia-Pacific region had achieved "a higher rate of economic growth than any other area in the world," the President said, "By combining Western influences with Eastern culture, the Pacific promises to serve as an even greater source of global prosperity in the 21st century. . . . But, multilateral cooperation in the Pacific region remains underdeveloped. . . . We need to develop a mutually complementary system of cooperation unique to our own region, which will function as an efficient mechanism to harmonize historical, cultural, and economic differences of Pacific nations. Since regional cooperation will have to be based on principles of the free market and free trade, it is private enterprise that should be the driving force behind growth. . . . The Asia-Pacific Economic Cooperation (APEC) conference, which met for the first time in Canberra last November, will no doubt serve as a conduit for government-to-government cooperation in our common efforts to encourage and support private-sector activities."

The President then listed the principles that he believed "essential to a productive Pacific cooperation":

1. Openness—"for all to effectively serve the cause of free trade and free enterprise throughout the world. . . ."

2. Mutual respect—". . . to foster cooperative independence within this region of diversity."

3. Market economics—"We should encourage creative, private initiatives and free economic activities with the goal of promoting mutually beneficial and balanced regional development."

4. "A more active system of cooperation"—which "should be built on the basis of mutual understanding and friendship among the peoples of this region."

Malaysian Prime Minister Mahathir visited Seoul in September 1990. At a banquet in his honor, President Roh spoke of relations both with Malaysia and with the East Asian region. ". . . Our practical bilateral cooperation has taken unprecedented big strides in all sectors following my visit to your country [in 1988]. Investments in Malaysia by Korean businesses have been rapidly on the increase in recent years, and major Korean corporations are launching their investments in the field of Malaysia's heavy chemical industries. Our bilateral trade rose from US $1.7 billion in 1988 to over $2 billion last year. As our two economies are complementary in character, I expect that bilateral trade and economic cooperation will continue in the years ahead."

"We are well aware, Mr. Prime Minister," the President continued, "of your vigorous pursuit of the 'Look East' policy and its magnificent accomplishments. I am confident that Malaysia and Korea will develop a model partnership for building a prosperous East Asia. . . . Through closer cooperation with each other, our two nations should make increasing contributions not only to the development of the Asia-Pacific region but also to the pace and prosperity of the world in general." In particular, President Roh noted the need for closer cooperation between the Republic of Korea and the Association of Southeast Asian Nations (ASEAN), of which Malaysia is a member, and Korea's interest "in developing a framework for regional cooperation through the ministerial conference on Asia-Pacific Economic Cooperation, or APEC. . . ."

In September 1991, the King of Malaysia also visited Korea. On that occasion, President Roh noted the rising levels of trade and investment, expanding "from primary goods and light industries into heavy industries such as steel and chemical products." He said, "I am especially grateful for the role Malaysia played as the Chair country of the Association of Southeast Asian Nations in inviting Korea as a full dialogue partner last July. I also appreciate the support Malaysia has given in the process of our entry into the United Nations."

The Republic of Korea was host to the 47th session of the Economic and Social Commission for Asia and the Pacific, an affiliate of the United Nations, in April 1991. In his opening address to the group, President Roh commented on the great transformation of the region, and noted, "Exchanges and cooperation between and among the nations of the region have also increased in a rapid and progressive manner. . . . this in a region that lacked any cooperative experience between the geographically distant countries. The nations of this region of diversity have long been alienated from one another, but they are now rapidly forming a strong and friendly partnership for cooperation."

Later in his address, the President said, "The primary challenge before us today is to turn this vast region into a zone of open doors and mutual cooperation by marshalling the unbounded potentials of Asia and the Pacific, the region's enormous dynamism toward progress and our aspirations for peace and prosperity." Noting the Commission's pursuit of industrial restructuring and adjustment, the President opined that it "will undoubtedly facilitate and accelerate technology transfers and horizontal division of labor on the basis of complementary features of the regional economies. . . . Because the Republic of Korea, rising from the ruins of a war, has become a newly industrializing country within one generation, we are perhaps in a unique position, and we are prepared to actively share with everyone our developmental experience and know-how." Additionally, "Korea is prepared to actively contribute to the promotion of a harmonious regional cooperation by playing the role of a bridge between the advanced and developing countries and between the market and socialist economies. . . ."

Although emphasizing the need for cooperative mechanisms, the President told the *Toronto Globe and Mail* in a June 1991 interview that "conditions for multilateral Asia-Pacific security cooperation are not yet ripe," since "major local conflicts still rage in this region and the interests of many Asia-Pacific countries still diverge sharply. The over-all situation in this region is thus still very complex and in flux."

At the time of the President's first meeting with Soviet President Gorbachev in San Francisco in June 1991, he also addressed the Hoover Institution for Disarmament and Peace at Stanford University. Taking note once again of the rapid change in the world, the President termed it "a revolution . . . not one of rivalry and conflict, but of peace and promise for all mankind." He then proposed a plan of action for the Asia-Pacific area, based on four fundamental principles:

- "First, we must build a solid foundation for international stability across the Asia-Pacific region by removing the last vestiges of the Cold War. . . . All the regional countries, including the United States and Japan, must actively support China and the Soviet Union in their pursuit of development, free market economies, and democratic choices. The efforts of those nations to join international arenas of cooperation must also be facilitated." However, ". . . all the countries in the area seem to recognize the need for the United States to continue its leading role if regional stability is to prevail. . . ."
- "Second, we must work toward a sustained Asia-Pacific prosperity through openness, free trade and economic cooperation. The free trade system, as we all know, is what has brought to this region unprecedented growth and prosperity. The share of intra-regional trade in the total trade of the Asia-Pacific nations exceeds 65 percent, indicating a greater interdependency than that which exists in the European Community."

- "Third, we must direct our efforts toward harmonizing and capitalizing on the diversity of economic structures, developmental stages, cultures and ethnic origins that characterize the various regional states. . . . By combining the complementary features of our respective economies, we can enjoy the true benefits that come with cooperation. . . ."
- "Fourth, based on a new Asia-Pacific identity, we must then proceed to develop a formal framework that can help us achieve our objectives. That framework should embrace the entire Asia-Pacific region. The appearance of sub-regional groups that compartmentalize the region would not, in my view, be desirable because sub-regionalism tends to cause friction and rivalry, and contribute to protectionist tendencies. In this context, I would look to the Asia-Pacific Economic Cooperation to develop into a respected instrument for the realization of our common prosperity."

The President noted three major challenges faced by the postwar world: "The first of these has been the disparity between the haves and have-nots, the so-called North-South problem; the rivalry between different ideologies and systems—the so-called East-West confrontation—the second; and the struggle to build a world which will guarantee human dignity and freedom, the third." He then expressed his belief that "the achievements of the Korean people despite difficulty and adversity can stand . . . as a model for others. Our experience may indicate approaches to the solution of larger global problems." Demonstrating Korea's rapid progress with statistics on national product and trade, the President said, "The Korean experience is testimony to the fact that nowhere can today's poverty justify the poverty of tomorrow, nor can poverty ever be justified by a lack of resources."

The third ministerial meeting of Asia-Pacific Economic Cooperation was held in Seoul in November 1991. It was noteworthy in that the People's Republic of China, the Republic of China on Taiwan, and Hong Kong were admitted to membership, joining the original twelve countries. In his keynote address to the conference, President Roh expressed his view that the group "should develop along the following principles and directions:

—"First, APEC should seek to shape the world economy of the 21st century into an order of economic globalism by first setting an example of open regionalism under the principles of free trade . . . within a stable multilateral trading system. . . . To this end, we should exert our utmost efforts for a successful outcome of the Uruguay Round negotiations. . . . We should also develop close cooperative relations with other regions to prevent them from drifting toward inward-looking regionalism. . . .

—"Second, APEC should play an increasingly active role as a region-wide cooperative body, which includes such sub-regional groups as ASEAN and NAFTA [North American Free Trade Area] within our region. In view of the vastness and diversities of the Asia-Pacific, the appearance of sub-regional groups may perhaps be inevitable . . . [but they] must also seek to develop in harmony with the open and cooperative order of the region. Asia-Pacific Cooperation should not, in any case, develop into a competing relationship between East Asia and North America. On the contrary, it should play a central role for the promotion of a harmonious and balanced development of trans-Pacific relations. . . .

—"Third, APEC should seek to narrow the economic gap between the advanced and the developing economies of the region, to support Socialist economies of the region in their efforts toward openness and reform, and to encourage these economies to join the Asia-Pacific economic mainstream. To this end, the advanced economies should facilitate market access to the developing economies as well as to those economies that are in the process of transforming into market economies, and should more actively share capital and technologies with them. . . .

—"Fourth, APEC should explore, in the long run, the possibilities of moving toward a free trade area encompassing the entire Asia-Pacific."

VII. Korea and the West: Europe and the Western Hemisphere

Korea's relations with the West received somewhat less attention in the President's speeches during the period 1990 to 1992 than in the previous period—not, presumably, because these relations, particularly with the United States, were less important, but because they were well-established and relatively stable, in contrast to the changes in the ex-Socialist countries and progress in the dialogue with North Korea. Nevertheless, the President often referred in passing to the importance of the relationship with the United States both for Korea and for the Asia-Pacific region.

In November 1990, the Prime Minister of Greece, Constantine Mitsotakis, visited Korea. At a banquet in his honor, President Roh took note of the influence of Greek culture in Korean art and education and as a source of "values such as democracy, equality, human dignity and the love of freedom." He cited the Greek contribution to the Korean War, and Greek support for the Seoul Olympics. Expressing the hope for expansion of exchanges in all areas between the two countries, President Roh said, "Korean businesses would also be interested in joint ventures with their Greek counterparts for third-country business opportunities within the framework of the European Community."

Poul Schlüter, Prime Minister of Denmark, paid his third visit to Korea in June 1991. At a dinner in his honor, President Roh compared the two countries: "Like Korea, Denmark is a peninsular country surrounded by powerful neighbors. Neither of us is endowed with rich natural resources. And yet, the people of Denmark, known for their unequalled independent and cooperative spirit, have successfully built the best-managed welfare state in the world, which is a model for our nation." Denmark, too, was recognized for its contribution to the Korean War, in the form of the hospital ship *Jutlandia*, and its support for a major medical center in Korea following the war.

During a visit to Canada in July 1991, President Roh spoke warmly of the bonds between Canada and Korea, beginning with early Canadian missionaries such as James Gale, Frederick McKenzie, and Frank Schofield, "pioneers who made enormous contributions to Korea's modernization in such areas as religion, medicine, and education." Over 26,000 Canadians fought in the Korean War. The two nations had become important commercial partners, and "bilateral economic cooperation and trade are certain to expand. . . . Korea is prepared to increase its investment in Canada in such areas as steel, automobile and resource development."

In September 1991, President Roh visited Mexico. In a welcoming ceremony, he noted that he was the first Korean head of state to make an official state visit to Latin America. At a banquet given by Mexican President Salinas, President Roh was given the highest medal of Mexico. After accepting it, he said, "Pacific Rim countries, including Korea and Mexico, should improve mutual understanding through active interaction, and should stimulate trade and economic cooperation by cultivating mutually complementary economies." He noted that trade between the two countries had increased by 40 percent a year in the past five years, and that "Mexico is . . . our most important economic partner in Latin America."

U.S. President George Bush visited Korea in January 1992. At a joint press conference, President Roh said he had "emphasized the roles of our two countries in promoting lasting peace and prosperity in the Asia-Pacific region. . . ." There was a joint reaffirmation of the shared ROK-U.S. position that North Korea "must sign and ratify a nuclear safeguards agreement without delay and that the recently initialled Joint Declaration for a Non-Nuclear Korean Peninsula [by North and South Korea] must be put into force at the earliest possible date. We also discussed ways in which the United States' contacts with North Korea might be gradually expanded, provided that close consultation is maintained between our two countries and progress both on the North Korean nuclear issue and in intra-Korean relations is made."

While pledging cooperation in promoting free trade, including the Uruguay Round, President Roh noted that "in the agricultural sector, I explained that because of our peculiar situation, it will be exceedingly difficult to fully open our market in the immediate future. . . ." He said that the two presidents had "agreed to institute Korean-U.S. Subcabinet Economic Consultations to develop ways to promote economic partnership between our two countries. We agreed on the need to further expand bilateral cooperation in the fields of science and technology."

At a state dinner given for President Bush, President Roh praised the American president's initiatives in the Gulf War and in Arab-Israeli peace negotiations, repeated his commitment to uphold "the principles of free trade and market economics," and paid tribute to the "support and assistance of the United States" in Korea's development. He noted the closeness of the ROK-U.S. relationship "that has become an inseparable part of our daily lives, in many realms: political, economic, cultural and scientific." He concluded, "Our two countries are partners for freedom and democracy, and we are partners for a new world order. We have today become partners for free trade and market economics that will bring common prosperity to all mankind."

Part I

DEMOCRACY AND PROSPERITY: POLICY FOR THE REPUBLIC

1.

Opening Remarks at the New Year's News Conference, Seoul, January 10, 1990

Good morning, ladies and gentlemen, I wish all of you a Happy New Year.

Decade of Hope and Challenge

The 1990s will be a decade of hope for the Korean people, who have suffered unspeakable tragedies in the past. We all look forward to a fulfillment of our national aspirations in the course of this decade. If the past years were a period of fruition of our sacrifices and hard work, I am convinced that the coming decade will be one of great harvest.

As the 21st century draws near, the world is in the midst of epochal change. The Cold War politics that divided our land and forced upon us a fratricidal war are receding. A new international order, however, has yet to emerge. Although a tide of reconciliation is sweeping across the world, the anxieties and uncertainties persist everywhere. As a result, competition between nations is intensifying, which in turn seems to encourage the appearance of exclusive regional blocs.

No one can predict with certainty when and in what manner the waves of reform, which are currently sweeping Eastern Europe, will reach East Asia and the Korean Peninsula. In our own country, long pent-up demands have erupted across the nation in the wake of democratization, and structural asymmetries and societal contradictions, which had remained latent during the period of rapid growth and industrialization, have begun to surface. Although we do not know in detail the nature and scope of these challenges, it is certain that our potential for progress will ultimately be put to a rigorous test.

Our future hinges on whether or not we can successfully cope with the current global as well as domestic challenges and move the nation on to a higher level of progress. We must therefore renew our resolve to meet the challenges facing the nation in the late 20th century.

Our generation of Koreans has undergone profound social, economic, and political changes within the span of our lifetime. But, rising from the devastation of war, we have built a nation of per capita GNP of $5,000. The Korean experience is indeed unique.

For a long time, we have fought for individual rights and genuine democracy. The checkered record of innumerable hurdles and sacrifices in the forty-year history of our constitutional government is testimony to our torturous and turbulent path to democracy.

Three years ago, the June 29th Declaration of Democratic Reforms ushered in a new era of genuine democracy. The arrival of a new era in our political development and the ensuing democratic reforms instilled in us confidence and pride. Our concerted efforts laid the groundwork for a successful hosting of the internationally acclaimed Seoul Olympic Games.

Over the past three years, however, unreserved individual demands and pressures have brought on a new national debate. As the need to restructure the social, economic, and political arrangements of the past era increased, we were faced with the formidable task of having to completely rebuild the framework itself. In the process, our economy has lost much of its momentum, vitality and dynamism.

Throughout the process of democratization, all of us have had to sustain enormous difficulties. Responsible for the affairs of the state, I too have had to carry enormous burdens and undergo periods of personal anguish. But, no matter how great our sacrifices and suffering, we must not backtrack. If our democratic development were to sustain a setback, hopes for the future of our nation would be all the more dampened. Our only choice then has to be a more vigorous pursuit of economic progress in a more democratic setting.

The next several years will be crucial for the nation as they will divine whether we will join the ranks of the advanced countries or will fall behind in spite of years of effort and sacrifice. The administration this year will carry out various programs mindful of this historical imperative.

Overcoming the Economic Crisis

As we enter the first year of the 1990s, we find ourselves confronted with many economic uncertainties. Our national economy today is undergoing a very difficult stage due to a combination of political, social and other factors stemming from our reforms. Consequently, I plan to issue the administration a set of extraordinary guidelines with which to overcome the looming economic crisis.

Last year, our economy grew by 5.6 percent, while consumer prices rose by 5.1 percent. Our exports reached $62.3 billion, with a current account surplus of $5.1 billion. On the face of it, such economic figures do not indicate any serious problems. However, what concerns us deeply is the gradual weakening of the competitiveness of our businesses. We have seen a sharp decline in growth as well as in exports, and our balance of payments surplus is rapidly shrinking.

Clearly, the cause lies in the decline in morale and work ethics among the major economic participants, including businessmen and workers. In other words, our economic difficulties have been caused not necessarily by external variables beyond our control, but by internal factors.

There are two other major reasons for our economic downturn: Our businesses neglected to keep up their international competitiveness by upgrading their technology and improving their style of management during times of brisk exports and booming economy. In addition, wages have been driven up rapidly and the productivity declined as a result of labor disputes. Should wages be raised again this year by as big a margin as last year, many businesses will have no other choice but to fold, which in turn will force a large number of workers out of their jobs. Businessmen would then lose the incentive to reinvest in capital goods, and this would further weaken our international competitiveness.

Consequently, nationwide cooperation is imperative if we are to avert the impending economic crisis and achieve continued growth. Political, social, and economic leaders should lead and encourage the general public by setting the pace in moderation, conservation, cooperation and sacrifice. Only when the entire nation exercises self-restraint will it be possible to cope with the present difficulties.

We must bring together our energy to overcome the current difficulties. We have the capabilities to do so. We have faced far greater challenges in the process of our national modernization, including two global oil shocks in the 1970s. In 1980 alone, prices soared more than 40 percent with runaway inflation. However, workers, businessmen, farmers, fishermen, public officials, indeed, the entire nation banded together to successfully survive all those crises by voluntarily participating in burden sharing. As a result, we not only met the challenges, but moved on to register one of the highest economic growth rates in the world.

We must marshal our experiences and capabilities. For it is incumbent upon us to avoid the folly of cutting off our own lifeline—the national economic development. In order to solidify the groundwork which will enable our country to enter the ranks of the advanced nations within this decade, I will do everything in my power to bring about improvements in the economy, social cohesion, and our national resolve toward progress. My administration will provide maximum support to export-oriented businesses, manufacturing, and small- and medium-sized industries in order to help them overcome present difficulties, and to buttress their competitiveness.

Actions will be taken to train a skilled and talented workforce, to promote research and development, and to foster high-tech industries so that our economic structure will become more sophisticated and advanced. Efforts will also be made toward an early removal of economic uncertainties and toward the creation of a stable business environment in which our businessmen can vigorously pursue productive activities.

During my tenure as president, I plan to implement various reform measures to make our country a land of hope in which the benefits of economic progress are evenly distributed among all citizens. Our workers, for their part, also should refrain from demanding the resolution of all income distribution issues simultaneously; we should first make the pie bigger so that each individual will get a larger share later.

As an integral component of democratization, the government has guaranteed the three basic labor rights, and wage scales and working conditions have been greatly improved. The workers are likely to lose everything if they merely insist on their demands regardless of profitability and competitiveness. They must refrain from demanding wage hikes over and above the rate of increases in productivity. At the same time, businessmen should adopt a fresh managerial approach rather than dwell on practice that prevailed during the years when businessmen were given priority treatment by the government. The business sector must make greater efforts to bring innovation to management and technology. This, together with harmonious labor-management relations, will enhance their international competitiveness.

The government will deal firmly with any illegal union activities and labor-related violence. We will seek to maintain private sector stability by enforcing general rules practiced in most of the Western democracies.

Building A Land of Hope

The government will firmly enforce economic reform measures to remove structural contradictions and asymmetries in our economy. It is essential that we remove the causes of "relative deprivation" among the people, for the nation to become advanced and for national harmony. The government is fully committed to building a land of hope in which the hardworking ordinary people will get their fair share and be assured of stable living conditions. To that end, the following steps will be taken:

First, institutional reforms aimed at securing further economic justice will be carried out. The law of limited land-ownership and the aggregate land tax will be enforced starting this year. Bogus accounts in banking and financial transactions will be phased out gradually to ensure fairness in individual tax assessments. At the same time, the administration will implement the second phase of tax reform. We will seek to remove inequities in the distribution of wealth by stamping out real estate speculations and by imposing heavier taxes on profits derived from excessive land holdings and speculative financial investments.

Second, the business conglomerates will be discouraged from undue wealth accumulations. Large corporations will be encouraged to separate the management from ownership and upgrade their management system. The inheritance and gift tax systems will be revamped and oligarchical stock ownership will be discouraged. Small- and medium-sized industries will be protected so that they will grow to form the backbone of our manufacturing industry. All these measures are intended to promote free enterprise and free-market economy at a higher level of maturity.

Third, two million housing units will be built by the end of 1992 to help ease the acute housing shortage. This will include 900,000 units supplied by the public sector for lease or sale to low-income families. Of these, 150,000 units will be available for sale, and 100,000 units for lease, in the vicinity of industrial districts to provide improved housing for workers. Greater tax incentives and special loans will be provided to those businesses that will build housing units for their employees, so that workers with about ten years of service will be able to own a house of their own.

Although few students fail to receive a secondary education for financial reasons, the government will provide additional funds for relatively poor high school students. Now that a nation-wide medical insurance system has gone into effect, efforts will be directed toward improving the quality of medical care. Social welfare programs for the underprivileged will continue to expand as the level of our economy improves.

Fourth, a total of sixteen trillion won will be invested by 1992 for a comprehensive development of rural areas. This should bring significant improvements to rural living conditions. Within a decade, those investments are forecast to increase the proportion of off-farm income to 70 percent of the total farm income. These changes will contribute to the much-needed restructuring of our agricultural and fishing industries.

Fifth, as we elect autonomous governments later this year, local communities will be able to develop their own region through independence of economy, public administration, education and culture. The ensuing vitality will greatly help overall national development and usher in an era of healthy decentralization.

Sixth, keeping abreast with the national economic growth, efforts will be made to bring about a balanced growth of all regions by expanding and improving the social infrastructure such as roads, railways, and harbors. Also, in view of the relatively small land area of the Republic, a massive project will be launched to reclaim tideland along Korea's western coastline.

Five Urgent Tasks

There are five urgent problems that not only have a significant influence on our daily lives, but must be resolved to ensure a brighter future for the nation, and I fully intend to deal with them immediately. They are crime and violence, educational reforms, promotion of science and technology, environmental protection, and traffic congestion. Each task requires considerable financial outlays, and we will find necessary revenues from the tax reform measures discussed earlier.

1. Crime Prevention

In spite of sustained government efforts, violent crimes and larceny still plague our society. All law-enforcement agencies will have to redouble their efforts to ensure public safety by strengthening preventive measures and detection devices. The government will reexamine manpower, organization, equipment, and communications of our police with a view to improving them to the level of advanced countries. Pleasure-seeking establishments and other hotbeds of crime will be closely policed in an effort to revive a crime-free climate. The educational system will be revamped so that young people who fail to continue education at higher levels can still find productive roles in society. Cultural and sports facilities will be expanded to promote a healthier social environment. These measures are part of an effort to help solve the crime problem.

2. Educational Reforms

We will have to reform our secondary education system so that high schools will produce the academically talented as well as the skilled manpower needed for an industrial society. Around this time every year, more than 500,000 young people who are unable to continue their education at colleges and universities despair in frustration. This is indeed a national problem. The government will overhaul the present schooling system which is geared exclusively to preparing students for college entrance exams. We will develop an educational system that will enable our high school graduates to pursue respectable careers even without college educations. Open colleges and adult education programs will be expanded and improved to accommodate those who seek to obtain college degrees at mid-career. In fiscal 1990, the government budget on education has increased by 500 billion won for purposes of improved educational facilities and teachers' salaries. More than 25 percent of the 1990 government budget of 3.4 trillion won has been earmarked for education. More than any time in the past, more government funds are being allocated on educational improvements.

3. Promotion of Science and Technology

We are determined to become in the next ten years one of the seven most technologically advanced nations in the world. Accordingly, the government will provide maximum support to research and development activities of the private sector, including universities and institutions. In addition, more high-tech "research parks" will be created with governmental assistance. Large amounts of investment will be directed for the training of scientists and engineers and for international joint research projects. Steps will also be taken to encourage the manufacture of state-of-the-art semiconductors, supercomputers, and communication satellites. For example, research on promising areas such as fiberoptics, electronics, super-ceramics, and biotechnology are likely to receive priorities.

4. Environmental Protection

As our industrialization proceeds, the preservation of clean water, clean air and unspoiled nature have become critical problems. The government will take necessary steps to clean up and protect the sources of drinking water. The rate of sewage treatment today stands at about 30 percent nationwide. The government will improve this to a higher level at the earliest possible date. But, cooperation of the public is essential for the protection of our own environment.

5. Urban Traffic Problems

Barring government intervention, the number of motor vehicles on the road is projected to double in eight years, and this will undoubtedly worsen our traffic congestion. Accordingly, strong emphasis and highest priority will be placed on the construction of subways, the expansion of road networks and parking spaces to alleviate traffic and transportation problems.

These are some of the more important projects that must be tackled immediately if we are to enjoy a decent and comfortable life as an advanced nation.

Toward Reconciliation and Unification

Ladies and gentlemen,

On the strength of the successful Seoul Olympics and the timely and effective Northern Policy, we have been able to stay ahead of the epochal changes around the world. In so doing, the Republic of Korea has been able to facilitate global reconciliation rather than exacerbate the Cold War confrontation. We will continue to pursue our Northern Policy on the basis of closer and stronger ties with our traditional friends in the Asia-Pacific region, especially the United States and Japan, as well as with our partners in Europe.

Our newly established diplomatic relations with Hungary, Poland, and Yugoslavia will be strengthened, and at the same time we will seek to establish formal relations with other Socialist countries in Eastern Europe. Nowadays, more than 20,000 people annually travel between our country and the People's Republic of China, and our airlines fly over Soviet airspace on their way to Europe. These are some of the developments that were unimaginable until a few years ago. All of these developments will put us in a position to cultivate more substantive relations with Socialist countries including China and the Soviet Union, with which we have recently established consular relations.

The waves of reform in Eastern Europe toward freedom and prosperity are bound to reach North Korea before long. We hope that such reform movements when they arrive in North Korea will be both peaceful and orderly. The historical trend in the world today is toward freedom and prosperity. And because we want North Korea to share prosperity with us as a single national community, we will do everything possible to persuade North Korea to open its doors and join the current trend.

North Korea should no longer be regarded as our rival. We are approaching the half-century mark of our territorial division. Now, the two parts of Korea should open an era of dialogue, exchanges, and cooperation to build mutual confidence, so that one day we may achieve national unification. In my inaugural address in February 1988 and again in my speech before the United Nations General Assembly, I have repeatedly emphasized that South and North Korea must form a single national community. I believe unity can be achieved by dismantling the barriers and allowing free inter-Korean travel as well as political, economic, and cultural exchanges.

I issued a six-point declaration on July 7, 1988, and in the summer of 1989 I proposed a Korean National Community Unification Formula. On both occasions, I called on North Korea to join us in the formation of a "national community" by promoting openness and exchanges between the two parts of Korea. For this reason, I welcome the North Korean leader's New Year's Day proposal to allow free travel between the South and the North, despite the strange preconditions attached to it. These issues, I believe, can be resolved through talks between the authorities of the South and the North, especially at the highest level. It is in this context that I call for South-North summit talks at the earliest possible date, and I sincerely hope that North Korea will respond positively to my proposition.

The reality today is that not a single letter nor telephone call, let alone separated family members, can cross the Demilitarized Zone between South and North Korea. If it is difficult to reach an agreement on free travel and full-fledged exchanges, we must at least allow correspondence, telephone calls, and visits by family members. If these appear to be unacceptable to North Korea, then we should at least arrange for family members over sixty years of age to meet their loved ones.

We urge North Korea to show sincerity in these humanitarian issues. We hope to conclude with North Korea an inter-Korean travel and communications agreement. Cooperating in projects that are mutually beneficial would be a most practical way to improve inter-Korean relations. If North Korea is agreeable, we are prepared to enter into various joint projects, including the tourism development of the scenic Mt. Kumkang. We will continue to take realistic steps to promote economic cooperation with North Korea, including inter-Korean merchandise trade.

At present, we are engaged in talks to form a single Korean team to represent both Koreas at the Beijing Asian Games in September of this year. I hope the formation of a single Korean team, if agreed upon, will lead to more inter-Korean sports exchanges and cooperation.

In an effort to demonstrate our commitment toward South-North dialogue and the easing of tension on the Korean Peninsula, the Republic of Korea has agreed with the United States to scale down the annual joint military exercise, Team Spirit 1990, this year. In view of the continuing military tension on the Peninsula, we have taken this initiative, so that North Korea too will take a corresponding action. We invite North Korea, the People's Republic of China and all four member countries of the Neutral Nations Supervisory Commission to send observers to Team Spirit 1990 to verify the defensive nature of the exercise. At the same time, we urge North Korea to invite our observers to their military maneuvers.

Despite our efforts toward peace and reconciliation, the reality is that the situation on the Korean Peninsula remains cold and grim. That North Korea persists in its rigid policy of self-imposed isolation is truly unfortunate. In fact, uncertainties on the Korean Peninsula seem to increase as the external pressures for change mount. We will have to be on guard of our national security to ensure peace under any circumstances. And the ROK-U.S. security cooperation needs to be firmly maintained.

A Vision of Korea 2000

If we successfully meet the challenges of today, we will become by the year 2000 an advanced nation with exports reaching $200 billion and a per capita

GNP of $15,000. The Korean economy would by then be flourishing with sophisticated technologies, high-value products and information industries.

If our policy of balanced growth succeeds, even workers with relatively low income will be able not only to purchase their own homes without difficulty, but to save a substantial portion of their income for a better tomorrow. They will form part of the stable middle class and be able to enjoy a satisfactory standard of living. The fruits of development will make the country affluent, but they should also be fairly distributed among all citizens, who have contributed to the development. We will then have built a prosperous society that will guarantee well-being for all.

By the year 2000, our national economy will grow to a size three times larger than it is today and the heartbeat of modernization will be felt strongly everywhere in the land. High-speed rail service and express highways should permit cross country travel in matters of hours, and a full range of modern facilities and conveniences should be available everywhere. Not only will we become materially affluent, we will also have a highly educated and sophisticated public enjoying a rich cultural environment. It is very likely that within the next ten years, opportunities for national unification will present themselves. The road to national unity will surely open up, and the exchanges, trade, and cooperation between the South and the North will increase. As inter-Korean travel becomes a reality, separated families will also be able to meet their loved ones. All of us will then be able to enjoy visits to Mt. Kumgang and Mt. Paekdu in North Korea.

The Republic of Korea is expected to emerge in the 21st century as an important actor in the Pacific. At the turn of the century, the Korean people had been unable to preserve their sovereignty. More recently, we suffered from the tragic division of our land. Before the end of this century, however, we will attain our long-cherished goal of building a democratic, unified, and prosperous nation. We can and will realize that dream. The 1990s will be the propitious opportunity to realize our national goal.

We will face many challenges on the road to peace and prosperity. The tasks before us may appear daunting at times, but we must not give up. With unity and resolve, we shall cope with any challenge on our road to greater progress.

To build a good nation, the government will draw on our great national strength. Through a compromise, the government and opposition political parties have now set aside the problems of the past. Our politics will function in a manner that will inspire our people with hope. I sincerely believe that the latest party merger marks the beginning of a new era of Korean politics for a brighter future.

As president, I will take the lead in establishing a new order in a spirit of dialogue and compromise, as we approach the 21st century. Now that the

1990s are upon us, I urge all of you, my fellow citizens, to march toward the new century, and triumph over the challenges. Together we will achieve democracy, prosperity, and national unification.

Thank you.

2.

Remarks at the Dinner for the Diplomatic Corps in Seoul, February 8, 1990

Ambassador Anibal Raul Casal, Dean of the Diplomatic Corps, Your Excellencies, distinguished guests, ladies and gentlemen,

It is a great pleasure for me to share this evening with you. As we usher in a new decade of hope and promise, I wish all of you peace and prosperity in the new year.

Our traditional new year, Sol, has just ended. Last week, we saw the heaviest snowfall in many years, and it caused considerable inconveniences and loss of property.

Some unfortunate occurrences aside, many of you, particularly those who come from countries without snow, would agree that the snow-covered Korean scenery was full of breathtaking beauty, and I hope you will enjoy the season and its many sports to your hearts' content.

As we approach the 21st century, astonishing and fast-paced changes are sweeping across the world. In the several months since last autumn, we have witnessed a series of revolutionary upheavals in the Soviet Union and other Socialist countries in Central and Eastern Europe. One-party Communist dictatorships that once appeared invincible have collapsed like falling dominoes in the face of mounting popular aspirations for freedom and prosperity. Barbed-wire fences between East and West Europe have been removed and the Berlin Wall has crumbled.

Our nation has been suffering from the painful division of our land and the tragedy of a fratricidal war caused by Cold War confrontations. Because the old international order has been a source of national torment, we now greet the 1990s with fresh hopes and expectations that a new order will emerge to replace the old.

Last week, I was delighted to receive a unique gift. It was a gold disc issued to celebrate the sale of nine million copies of the record "Hand in Hand," the

Seoul Olympic theme song. The great popularity of that song, I believe, stems from the fact that it superbly expresses universal aspirations of all mankind. As the song begins, "Hand in hand, over the walls . . . ," so the barriers separating mankind are collapsing all over the world, in the wake of new waves of harmony and progress.

Today, we are eager to see similar changes take place on the Korean Peninsula. The 155-mile-long Demilitarized Zone that separates our land into southern and northern halves still remains as frozen as ever. There are no human footprints on the fallen snow, and the North remains frozen at a point in time in the fifties, when the guns of the Korean War fell silent.

However, I do not believe that North Korea can remain a frozen land at a time when the warm winds of change are sweeping over the entire face of the globe. I believe that the warmth of spring will soon come to the North as well. We shall continue our efforts to build trust between the two Koreas by promoting dialogue, exchanges, and cooperation. It is my sincere hope that the nations that you represent will continue to support our efforts to end the Cold War confrontation on the Korean Peninsula and to replace it with peace and reconciliation.

The Republic of Korea has been making remarkable progress with the hope that one day it will be able to take an active part in building a more harmonious world, and I believe we are now ready to meet the challenges of the new era.

Over the past several years, Korea has been undergoing fundamental changes, and inevitably various transitional phenomena have appeared. In the course of transition from a prolonged authoritarian rule to democracy, some counterproductive developments have also appeared. I could perhaps compare this to the movement of a pendulum. When the pendulum is pushed to one extreme, the return swing is bound to be great. Consequently, we have to wait patiently for the pendulum to return to a normal range of motion.

Today, we are on the threshold of successfully coping with the difficulties stemming from this transition. Many of those who once raised their voices for radical reforms have begun to exercise self-restraint, and as a heightened civic consciousness prevails among our citizens and as a public consensus emerges, a sense of balance is taking hold in our society.

Recently, three of four major political parties have agreed to merge themselves into one to form a majority party, ending a 40-year-old rivalry among political parties. This was the first such event in our national political history. The announcement was truly a surprise. This change in our political map signaled the closing of an era of factional politics where the tendency was to dissect all arguments into simplistic black or white.

Politics in Korea has now moved to a new, higher level of maturity based on mutual trust. This trust should provide a firm foundation for both democratic and economic progress in the '90s. Bolstered by a more stable political system, the Republic of Korea will be in a better position to make greater contributions to the community of nations.

I recall what I said to you this time last year. I suggested that in Korea, when you must bet on the outcome of a situation, you should always choose the optimistic side. Recent history has shown, time and again, that the Korean people have a talent for turning a bane into a boon. With an optimistic frame of mind, we will strive toward a world of democracy, prosperity, peace and friendship. In the new year, we renew our resolve to do our best to carry out the Republic's responsibilities as a member of the international community.

I wish to express my gratitude to the distinguished members of the Seoul Diplomatic Corps for the energetic activities in the course of last year to promote ties of friendship and cooperation between my country and yours. In particular, I would like to take this opportunity to convey once again my deep appreciation for the warm welcome and hospitality extended to me by the government and people of the United States and the five European countries that I visited last year.

Ladies and gentlemen,

Please join me in a toast to your good health and the progress of your home countries and in wishing that the 1990s will be a decade of peace and prosperity for all mankind.

Thank you.

3.

Address on the 71st Anniversary of the Samil Movement, Seoul, March 1, 1990

My sixty million fellow Koreans, distinguished guests, ladies and gentlemen,

Today we commemorate the 71st anniversary of the Samil Independence Movement of the year 1919. On March 1st of that year, 20 million Koreans rose to demand liberation from foreign oppression. Our patriotic forefathers defied the iron-fisted rule of the Japanese imperialists and rallied across the entire Peninsula with shouts of "Man-se!" (Long live Korea!) They proclaimed to the whole world their right to determine their own destiny and declared independence from Japanese rule.

Following the Samil Declaration of Independence, a provisional government of the Republic of Korea was established in Shanghai, China to carry out a vigorous and sustained national independence movement at home and abroad with the ultimate aims of recovering national sovereignty and independence.

As the decade of the 1990s begins, let us recall once again the lofty ideals of the Samil Movement, and pay homage to our patriotic forefathers for their noble sacrifices and courageous struggle for freedom at home as well as in such far away places as China and the United States. We have been able to preserve our history and tradition through the darkest days of foreign domination owning largely to the devotion and sacrifices of those courageous national heroes. That we stand tall and proud in the world today is testimony that their sacrifices have not been in vain.

Fellow Koreans,

The Samil spirit of independence has been burning brightly from the day of the uprising to the present, even as we prepare to usher in the 21st century. Our forefathers bravely rose to demand national self-determination. Our sovereignty was lost for the first time in our long history because it was too weak to resist foreign encroachment. The echo of their heroic cries served as a constant reminder for us to stake a proud claim on the world stage as a strong nation.

By building a prosperous, unified and democratic nation, we will be fulfilling the historic aspirations held by our ancestors for which they sacrificed themselves, braving all forms of hardship. We are now on the threshold of achieving this cherished dream of our people. But this can be realized only if we successfully harness our national strength to overcome the many internal and external challenges.

Within 10 years of the collapse of our monarchy at the hands of a foreign power, our forefathers sought to build a democratic state in Korea. The Constitution of the provisional government clearly defined Korea as a "democratic republic."

Over the past three years, the nation has ushered in a new era of democracy, reflecting the ideals of the Samil Movement. The new birth of freedom and individual initiatives will serve as the driving force toward building a model democracy and a prosperous nation in Korea.

Having overcome age-old poverty and the devastation of war, the Korean people have successfully propelled the country forward into the ranks of the top 10 trading nations in the world. The 1988 Seoul Olympics was a magnificent festival of global harmony and put the Republic of Korea prominently on the world scene. On a symbolic level, the Seoul Olympics was a propitious opportunity to display the maturity of our nation before the whole world. It was truly a landmark event in our history.

Over two-thirds of the nations of the world gained their independence since the end of World War II. Few of them, however, have made as strong advances into the ranks of the industrialized countries as the Republic of Korea.

In a period of rapid transition, we also suffered internal instability as we made the transition from authoritarianism to democracy. The nation's democracy is taking deep root in an increasingly stable and favorable climate. By pooling the strength of our people, we can overcome the current economic adversities and attain prosperity.

Fellow Koreans,

It is for us to make the 1990s a decade of hope. In the course of this decade, our people, presently divided into South and North, should come together into a single community in the process of achieving national reunification. We shall never forget that we lost our national sovereignty early this century because our nation was weak and poor. During this decade, therefore, we must build a proud and respected nation that will play a leading role for peace and prosperity of the world.

Today, the world is engulfed in historic changes. The Soviet Union and other Socialist countries in Eastern Europe are undergoing fundamental transformations as evidenced by the sweeping waves of reform and openness.

The Berlin Wall has crumbled, and one Communist dictatorship after another is falling. East and West Germany are making rapid progress toward reunification.

The world has become a global village as a result of advances in science and technology, especially in the field of information. Under these circumstances, it would be impossible for any political system to suppress forcibly the aspirations of the people for freedom, democracy, and prosperity. The day will soon come when North Korea also will abandon its rigid isolationism and open its doors to the world.

We have successfully paved a road for trade and exchanges across ideological and political barriers, which had separated the Communist bloc from us for nearly half a century. Today, more than 20,000 people travel between the Republic of Korea and the People's Republic of China annually. Our airliners fly scheduled routes to Moscow, while Soviet passenger jets are also planning flights to Kimpo International Airport. Our diplomatic relations have already been normalized with Hungary, Poland, and Yugoslavia. Czechoslovakia, Bulgaria, and other Socialist countries are expected to follow suit.

During the painful Japanese occupation period, many of our people fled to Manchuria, mainland China, the Soviet Far East, and Sakhalin to escape from the oppression that befell them with the loss of national independence. They now freely visit their homeland and reunite with their parents, brothers, sisters, and other relatives. Under these circumstances, there is no reason why our people, separated by a narrow Demilitarized Zone, should not come and go freely and live together as a single community.

We will continue to make our best efforts to achieve reconciliation with North Korea, and by restoring one national community we will bring freedom and prosperity to our brethren in the North.

I once again urge top leaders of North Korea to accept my proposal for a South-North summit meeting to discuss any and all inter-Korean issues, including political and military matters. If political issues are too complicated and difficult to resolve at this time, we can still make progress in other issues such as travel and cultural exchanges. What is important is the development of an atmosphere of mutual cooperation.

I make it clear that we are ready to resume talks, immediately if necessary, between our representatives on economic cooperation in such areas as trade, tourism, land resources development, and construction.

It must be emphasized, however, that mutual trust is the key to opening an era of genuine reconciliation and cooperation between us, and North Korea should demonstrate its willingness to abandon the illusion of unifying the country by military force or through a "class struggle" in the South.

Fellow Koreans,

The Samil spirit is that of sacrificing oneself for the love of country. It is a call to join forces in the interest of the nation, regardless of political affiliation, religion, or social station. Now more than ever, we must unite and translate this spirit into action. The Samil Declaration of Independence envisioned an end to the era of force and the beginning of new civilization based on humanitarianism. Seventy-one years later, world-wide reforms are making this dream a reality.

The time has come for our nation to make the hopes of our people into reality. By nurturing freedom and prosperity, we can bring closer the day of national reunification. Only then can we return the sacrifices made by our forefathers and sustain the Samil spirit. A world of challenges and opportunities awaits our participation. This is the stage for a brighter future.

Let us join in paying tribute to our national heroes and to their families, who have made it possible to build this nation into what it is today.

Thank you.

4.

Over the Wall Toward Peace and Prosperity—A New Era of Soviet-Korean Friendship and Cooperation; Address at Moscow University, December 14, 1990

Honorable President Anatoly Logunov, distinguished guests, professors and students of Moscow University,

It is a great pleasure and honor for me to have the opportunity to discuss with you some of the vital issues of our time. Probably no one, not even your most eminent professors, would have thought it possible a short while ago that the president of the Republic of Korea would be speaking from the rostrum of this world-renowned institution, known for its long history and brilliant tradition.

The forces of great historical change sweeping across the world today have brought us together here this afternoon. Hopes run high in the world that mankind may at last be able to live in peace in one global village, free from fear of war, confrontation and rivalry.

Future historians will record this enormous change as the most brilliant achievement that mankind has accomplished in the twentieth century.

The forces of perestroika have created huge tidal waves of change around the globe and brought to an end strains and tensions of the Cold War. As I recall, this university was the standard bearer and birthplace of perestroika, and I pay my respects to you for your vision and courage. President Logunov, Vice President Tropin, professors, indeed the entire Moscow University, were at the forefront of the "new thinking," and many prominent leaders of the reform movement, including President Gorbachev, were educated on this bastion of new ideas.

In this connection, let me recall the poor descendant of a fisherman whose unequalled vision and lofty ideals led to the establishment of an institution of higher learning for the first time in this part of the world. The lifetime contribution of Mikhail Romosonov, the founder of this great university, will be long remembered by men of ideas everywhere.

Since this great man opened this university 235 years ago, a countless number of literary giants and artistic geniuses. Turgenev, Goncharov, Chekhov, and Kandinsky, like the brilliant stars in the Milky Way, walked on this beautiful campus. Influential thinkers and scholars debated their ideas and refined their theories—among them, Belinsky, Herzen, Vernadsky and Kyeldish, to name but a few.

The genius and wisdom of many great men flourish in this university. It is the cradle of intellect, leading the progress of this country and the world and enriching the history of mankind.

Professors and students of Moscow University,

A prominent graduate of this university and eminent writer, Goncharov, was the first Russian to leave us with journals of his impressions of Korea. In his description of Korean character, we can get a glimpse of his prescient wisdom whose relevance continues today.

In 1854, he accompanied Admiral Putjatin and became the first Russian to come ashore. From the depth of tracks of cow-drawn wagons on the mud-roads in old Korea, he discovered that Koreans were very diligent and energetic, and said it was quite strange to find that even poor peasants were literate enough to write poems. This is part of what he wrote in his journals:

"Koreans tell the truth when queried. They are not afraid to say what they know . . . People living elsewhere in East Asia would not have said those things . . . This is why I think the Korean people will be able to approach Europeans quickly and without any difficulty . . ."

How very true, indeed.

The driving forces behind Korea's rapid development were openness, diligence and the desire to learn, as he perceptively pointed out long ago.

However, in order for the characteristics that he observed to really work for us, we had to wait more than one century.

For a century, the Korean people had to tread a history of trials and tribulations due to great power rivalries and Cold War confrontations. The great power rivalries early this century resulted in the sacrifice of our country, which we had defended successfully for several millennia, to the forces of colonial expansionism. Nevertheless, throughout our darkest years, our people at home and abroad never ceased to fight for national liberation and independence.

At the conclusion of the Second World War, Korea was liberated from the yoke of colonial occupation and the entire nation was jubilant. But, the jubilation was shortlived . . . and a national trauma set in as foreign powers decided to impose a territorial and national division on the Korean Peninsula.

In 1950, the Cold War imploded into the Korean War.

The war lasted over three years, devastating our land and inflicting millions of casualties. As a result, when the Republic of Korea launched plans for socio-economic development in the early sixties, we had scant resources, hardly any capital and little technology. At the time, our per capita GNP was $82 and our total export volume was $40 million, and Korea was one of the poorest countries in the world.

Finally, the Korean people stood up.

With unremitting confidence in the mind of every citizen that we "can do," the entire nation stood up for "national reconstruction." Twenty-six years later, a "big festival for harmony of mankind" was opened in Seoul. The entire world gathered in Seoul under the Olympic flame. The 1988 Seoul Olympiad was a festivity for the youth of the world, and reaffirmed friendship and progress, transcending all barriers extant among men—race, religion, ideology, national boundaries. . . .

What the world saw during the Seoul Olympics was not the long lines of hungry refugees that they saw during the Korean War, but a new nation of vibrant energy, freedom and prosperity. Looking at the flame of peace over their divided land where the threat of war persisted, the Korean people reaffirmed their self-confidence and hopes for the future.

Today, Korea has become a newly industrializing country with per capita GNP of $6,000 and an annual trade volume of $130 billion. A backward, agricultural country that had little manufacturing ability thirty years ago has become the world's 12th largest trading nation. Korean products are now exported across the world. They include hair-thin fiber-optic cables and thumbnail-sized computer chips as well as ocean-going vessels.

The Republic of Korea has pursued the goals of liberal democracy since its inception. But, the road leading to democratic development has not been smooth. We had to undergo a series of trials and errors due to such socio-political traits and legacies as Confucianism, colonialism and authoritarianism.

Three years ago, an "honorable revolution" succeeded in Korea when the nation produced a national consensus on the basis of the June 29 Declaration that I proposed. The Republic of Korea has now entered an era of rapid democratic development.

Professors and students,

When Goncharov wrote 140 years ago that Koreans had a propensity for learning, he was simply referring to the educational tradition of the Korean people. Even in the aftermath of the Korean War, farmers used to sell plots of farmland and tilling cattle so their children could receive university educations. It simply illustrates part of the resolve our people had at the time to eliminate poverty within the span of our generation.

Perhaps, Korea is unique in the world in that an average of 10 percent of household income is spent on education.

You may be surprised to learn that there are 107 four-year colleges in a country of 43 million people. The month of December is the annual college entrance examination season, and you will be interested to know that, in addition to the student himself, every member of his family comes to the aid of the student during this season of college examination.

Over 700,000 high school graduates will apply for college this year, and less than 20 per cent of them will be admitted to colleges and universities. To gain admission to a prominent university such as yours is so hard that students call it "reaching for the stars in the sky."

Koreans of my generation had to sacrifice to the tragic war not only their youth but, for too many, their lives as well. Originally, I planned to become a medical doctor. When the Korean War broke out I fought in defense of my country still wearing a high school uniform. This is the reason behind my military career.

Compared to the Korean War generation, young Korean men today look happier and brighter. University campuses are full of freedom and youth. This is the result of sacrifice by those of us who underwent difficult times.

Most students enjoy academic and youthful pursuits in Korea today. But, we also have our share of students who idolize the Bolshevik Revolution.

Korean universities just like your school here try to excel in every field such as philosophy, academic research, advanced science and technology, and political science.

Soviet studies in Korea are a good example. Seven years ago, only two universities had Russian language departments, and research pertaining to the Soviet Union was limited to a small number of universities. Today, there are thirteen universities that have Soviet studies departments, and the universities are competitively setting up Soviet study research institutes.

Korean universities encourage multiplicity and diversity but they also serve as a big furnace of ideas for development and progress of the nation. The success of Korea today is owed greatly to the quality of its people and high levels of education.

Professors and students,

During the 28 years since Korea implemented its first development plan, our GNP has grown at an average rate of 8.6% per year. Such a sustained high growth rate may be attributable to the balance struck between the Korean people's untiring efforts and creativity and the government's effective development policies. From the outset, we pursued a strong export-oriented development strategy.

During the initial stages of development, we had to import everything from foreign countries including raw materials, manufacturing facilities and technologies. Given our weak capital base, we had to depend on foreign loans in a number of areas. The government therefore made deliberate efforts to concentrate scarce funds on core and export industries and the manufacturing sectors that had promising import substitution effects.

Highest priority was placed on export for reasons of foreign currency liquidity. As soon as the government decided on the basic direction of its development strategy, private industries began to demonstrate their creativity. They developed plans in compliance with the basic direction of the government, and built factories and other industrial facilities with the help of foreign capital.

In the process, employment increased and the labor force worked around the clock. In order for a firm to grow in an open market economy it needs to compete both in pricing and quality control. For this reason, the management and labor combined their efforts to produce high-quality, low-cost products. The result was that Korean businesses successfully exported their products to the world market and accumulated foreign currency reserves, which they reinvested for expansion purposes. The process continues to this day.

In the 1960s and 1970s, the majority of Korean exports consisted of such labor-intensive items as textile products, wigs, plywood and toys. By the latter half of the 1970s, however, the focus began to shift to such areas as heavy chemical industries and high-technology products.

When we first launched our development drive in the sixties, there were few industries worthy of mention. In order to nurture and husband domestic industries, the government supported private business efforts to construct factories by providing investment capital through loans from foreign sources. The government also extended payment guarantees for acquisition of modern machinery through deferred payment schedules.

Together with such incentives, the government also developed core industries that were beyond the capabilities of the private sector such as electricity, communications, steel, fertilizer, and petroleum, while expanding social infrastructures such as roads, railways and ports.

With the increasing capability of private businesses in the 1980s, we are making a concerted effort to privatize core industries in a transition to a private sector-led economic system and to achieve take-off into yet another stage of economic growth.

Currently, the Republic of Korea is concentrating on education, national medical insurance, housing and environmental protection. We are in the process of building a welfare state in which the benefits of economic development are equitably distributed to all citizens.

Professors and students,

Korean businessmen and laborers have made enormous contributions in the process of our national development. Let me relate to you an episode in connection with the construction of Hyundai Corporation's Ulsan Shipyard, which is the largest in the world. In the early 1970s, the corporation was in need of loans to build the shipyard. After studying the feasibility plan and related photographs, a British banker was not convinced because Hyundai planned to build a shipyard, which would take five to six years for the British to complete, in two and a half years. But Hyundai engineers and management insisted it "can be done."

From then on, Hyundai employees worked day and night. The night shift worked under the glare of several thousand lights and torches. And, exactly two years and three months later, two gigantic dry-dock facilities with a 500,000 ton capacity each were completed—on schedule.

Not only was the world surprised at the new record for the building of dry-dock facility, but also because a huge 260,000-ton oil tanker was constructed and launched with the completion of the dry-dock. And, next to the two docks, a third was being built, this time a one million ton capacity dock.

Openness was a critical factor in Korea's economic development, and I would like to illustrate this point by describing the experience of a particular fur company. This company has recently set up a joint venture firm in the Soviet Union. I am referring to no other than the number one fur manufacturer in the world, the Jindo Corporation.

Not only are luxury furs not indigenous to Korea, but the domestic demand is also relatively small. And yet, Jindo was instrumental in developing fur manufacturing techniques and produced a variety of products specifically tailored to the demands of particular markets and was able to succeed on the basis of developing an external market for its merchandise.

Until 1985 Korea registered a current account deficit, and continuing demand for foreign currency resulted in a $46 billion foreign debt. But beginning from 1986 a current account surplus was recorded and in 1988 the surplus reached more than $15 billion. Today, no one in Korea seems to worry about foreign debts.

Korea is the only developing country in the postwar period that has reduced its foreign debts on the basis of its own economic success. But Korea is still not a fully developed country nor a powerful nation. And, the goals of the Korean people have yet to be achieved. In the meantime, we are hopeful that we will become a "developed" country with a per capita GNP of $15,000 annually by the end of this century.

Professors and students,

At the height of the Bolshevik Revolution, the Russian poet Mayakovsky passionately and proudly declared, "Behold and envy; I am a citizen of the Soviet Union."

Seven decades have passed, and today I am a witness to a revolution of a different order, which seeks to renovate the very foundation on which stood a long outmoded ideology and a rigid and long-defunct system. This latest revolution is not only transforming the world through its visionary ideals, but also changing this nation into a free, pluralistic and democratic society.

The experience of the Korean people shows that free competition and creativity are the sources of human progress in a pluralistic society. And, respect for human dignity, liberty and individual drive for the pursuit of happiness are vital motivating forces not only for individual successes but for the progress of a nation as well. These elements are, indeed, the driving force behind social energy, vitality and progress.

Democracy and market economy together have provided us with a framework for economic growth for the past twenty-eight years, and our per capita GNP has increased seventy-fold and exports 1500 times during the period. The quantum jump in economic growth has changed not only the outward appearance of the nation but also our life-style and way of thinking.

I understand that the Soviet Union is facing a variety of difficulties and challenges in the process of carrying out perestroika. To be sure, there are pessimistic views regarding the future of perestroika. However, I do not approve of such a view.

Unlike my own country, the Soviet Union has a vast territory that is 200 times the size of Korea, and it has unfathomable, untapped natural resources. Your country has been, for some time now, one of the two super-powers, and has the scientific and technological know-how advanced enough to reach the moon and the outer space. And, most important, you have a highly talented people that few other countries can match. These are people who pride themselves with brilliant culture and creative mind in all areas of human endeavor, including literature, music, ideas and academic research.

The people of the Soviet Union collectively resisted foreign invasions and preserved not only their own civilization but the world's as well in the First and Second World Wars.

I know you have all the necessary qualities to make perestroika a success. Under the new economic measures adopted last October, the Soviet Union has decided to introduce market economy principles. Should the efforts and patience of the Soviet people be concentrated on the effective development of market economy, the enormous potential of the Soviet economy will be realized.

Seen from the perspective of Korea's own development experience, all of these factors will contribute ultimately to perestroika's success.

As a new friend, Korea is ready to render its support and hope for the success of reforms, which are currently being institutionalized in the Soviet Union.

The great decisions that you have reached in the process of creating a new history will not only propel the Soviet Union along the road of freedom and prosperity but also contribute to world peace and progress.

President Logunov, professors, and students,

Ya pomnew zednoye megnobenye
bele doe menoi ivilasi dui
(I will remember the moment of miracle,
because you have appeared in front of me.)

The people of Korea welcome the newly founded relations with your country in the spirit of Pushkin's "moment of miracle."

This is so because the establishment of official relations between Korea and the Soviet Union symbolizes for our people the end of the Cold War, a period full of pain and tragedy.

And thus, we are hopeful that even though the Korean Peninsula remains divided with remnants of an ongoing confrontation, a new era pronounced by unification and peace will be opened. My visit to Moscow firmly illustrates this very point.

There was an absence of relations between our two countries for the last 86 years, and this was due to an invasion by a colonial power and the confrontations stemming from the Cold War.

After the end of the Second World War, the United States and the Soviet Union divided the Korean Peninsula into two halves and drew a line along the 38th parallel.

But in time, this line evolved into an impenetrable barrier, and in the process solidified the state of division.

To this very day the millions of parents, siblings, and relatives who were separated into the South and the North can neither exchange visits, much less make one single telephone call, nor exchange a single letter or even verify where a relative may reside.

Korea and the Soviet Union used to stand on opposing sides of this wall. A relationship of antagonism and confrontation developed given that the Soviet Union was a country that supported one side, whereas Korea stood at the forefront of the other side.

One result of this confrontational structure was that the giant Soviet Union was perceived as a threat to the security of the relatively small Korea, and our two countries experienced an unfortunate past.

A primary example of such a confrontation was the outbreak of the Korean War during Stalin's period and the downing of a Korean civilian airliner by a Soviet military aircraft. But it is time for Korea and the Soviet Union to clear away the vestiges of the unfortunate past and to turn a new page of history.

Professors and students,

Our bilateral rapprochement can be described in terms of confluence between my "Northern Policy," which seeks to remove Cold War confrontations and to build a world of harmony and cooperation, and President

Gorbachev's perestroika, which has brought on phenomenal changes around the world. The philosophy that we share has provided the basis of our talks.

In the aftermath of the opening of exchanges between the two countries, some 12,000 visits have already been made. You will recall the very warm welcome the people of Korea extended to the Soviet national team when they entered the stadium during the opening ceremony of the Seoul Olympics.

Moreover, critical acclaim was given to the Bolshoi Ballet and the Leningrad Philharmonic Orchestra on the occasion of their performances in Korea as an expression of our newly formed friendship. Any Soviet citizen visiting Korea, including President Logunov, I am sure, will be able to verify the Korean people's warm friendship. I am equally convinced that the same holds true for Koreans who visit your country.

From a personal perspective, this visit has been a meeting with a great people and a grand culture.

As I am speaking to you at this very moment, I am confident in the knowledge that, hand in hand with all of you, we can proceed together to build upon such universally held values as the dignity of man, freedom, peace and prosperity.

The creation of a new era between Korea and the Soviet Union means that the unnatural and abnormal past must be buried and in its place a new history must be built, a history founded on the acceptance of existing realities, a history that is led by reason, a history that restores humanism.

The Korean Peninsula's history of confrontation has long remained as a key source of tension in the Asia-Pacific region.

The effort by Korea and the Soviet Union to break the ice of the Cold War in the Korean Peninsula will not only mean the acceleration of peace and unification for the Korean people but also the cultivation of a new order of cooperation in the Asia-Pacific region.

The Western waterway of the Pacific, which stretches from Korea, Japan, and Northeast Asia to Australia, is emerging as a dynamic region wherein major contributions can be made towards global progress in the upcoming century.

Two out of every three inhabitants of the world live in the Asia-Pacific region, and over 40 percent of global trade and over 50 percent of the world's manufacturing take place in this very region.

For those who are able to see over the horizon, it has been often remarked that the next century will become the era of the Pacific.

After the conclusion of my summit meeting with President Gorbachev today, we pledged to jointly cooperate for prosperity and peace in the Asia-Pacific region, including the Korean Peninsula.

This is a very significant milestone in that it signals the shift to the eastern landmass of Eurasia of a new order and a new peace, which was built in the heartland of Europe upon the foundations of the U.S.-Soviet Malta summit and the concept of a "Common European House."

Peace is not realized on the basis of words or reasoning alone since visible change must be made on the basis of courageous decisions. When seen from this perspective, peace has been achieved in Europe through the implementation of perestroika.

The Korean people watched with excitement when the wall between Eastern and Western Europe was broken and Germany was unified. Korea is the only nation in the world still divided, but the resolution of the Korean problem need not be overly complex.

I believe that when South and North Korea establish a cooperative relationship premised on the recognition of outstanding realities, reconciliation between the two sides can be achieved at a rapid pace.

Koreans in the South and the North can nurture an environment conducive to unification once they perceive each other as partners in a community. For our part, we are committing ourselves to cooperate and to progress jointly as partners and not based on a competitive or confrontational relationship.

In the final analysis, we do not want an isolated North Korea. We hope that while the Soviet Union will further develop its relations with us, it will also maintain its traditional ties of friendship with North Korea.

We also firmly believe that it is time for North Korea to break out from its self-imposed isolation and to build a new cooperative relationship with not only South Korea, but the international community as well.

It is impossible for North Korea to continue to resist the global wave of openness and reform. North Korea's participation in the world community is a necessary condition for its own progress as well.

Just as we extend our support for perestroika, I hope that all of you will render your support for our yearning for peace and unification.

When I spoke before the United Nations General Assembly in 1988, I mentioned that world peace will be definitely achieved when swords are turned into ploughshares on the Korean Peninsula.

President Logunov, professors, and students,

Our two countries possess virtually unlimited potential to foster cooperation for joint progress. Such a prospect attests to the bright future in the relationship between our two countries.

I am hopeful that in the aftermath of my visit to Moscow the foundation will be laid for a strong partnership and that bilateral exchange and cooperation will improve on all fronts including political, economic, cultural, academic, and athletic.

In particular, I am convinced that bilateral economic exchange and cooperation will be enhanced given the two countries' mutually complementary economies.

A sound framework for the future development of economic relations has been set during my visit through the signing of agreements on trade, scientific and technological cooperation and other areas.

At the same time, the Korean economy can provide the Soviet Union with a variety of needed goods and services, and, as I have already alluded to, our own development experience based on the workings of the market economy.

In particular, Korea can provide the Soviet Union with a large number of consumer goods and the facilities that will enable the production of such goods in the Soviet Union.

Moreover, Korean firms can jointly develop with Soviet enterprises the abundant natural resources of the Soviet Union and participate in the construction of roads and harbors and in the expansion of social infrastructure.

At the same time, Korea needs the Soviet Union's advanced scientific technologies and could very well manufacture goods on the basis of such technologies for the world market.

If Korea and the Soviet Union combine their mutual advantages, it will prove to be beneficial to the two sides. I believe that progress can also be achieved in other areas of exchange and cooperation beyond the economic realm. As an example, I sincerely welcome the opportunity for greater exchange and cooperation between the universities of our two countries. Such a development is critical for it will not only strengthen academic cooperation, but also broaden mutual understanding by scholars and students alike, thereby contributing to a brighter tomorrow for all of us.

I am particularly encouraged to learn that the Soviet scholars, including those of you at Moscow University, have been carrying out more extensive research activities on Korea than any other country in the world.

President Logunov, professors, and students,

I am reminded of the dictum that "all the hours of work in the field of literature are but the hours of creation."

You are on the threshold of creating a new history on the basis of universal values and together as a progressing nation, you are building a new world in which mankind can truly prosper in peace.

From this vantage point, Korean-Soviet relations are a very important component of the broader picture. Let us take this opportunity to march together as partners so that we can create a more peaceful and prosperous world as the 21st century beckons us.

I remain convinced that the day will come in the not too distant future when young Koreans can leave Seoul in a high-speed journey across Siberia, join Soviet youths in Moscow, and together travel to Stockholm, Paris, and Istanbul.

Let us proceed, shoulder to shoulder, to accelerate the arrival of that golden day.

Moskba, rei dochi ryunima.
(Moscow, the loving daughter of Russia.)

Balishoe Spaciba.
(Thank you very much.)

5.

Overcoming Difficulties and Marching Forward; Opening Remarks at the New Year's News Conference, Seoul, January 8, 1991

Good morning, ladies and gentlemen,
 I wish a happy New Year to you all.

Overcoming Difficulties and Marching Forward

The year 1990 gave us lots of confidence and hope, although we did not achieve everything we hoped to during the year. Exactly a year ago, prospects were grim and uncertain as we greeted the new year. Such expressions as "total crisis" were used to describe the national scene. Today, however, stability is the predominant trend in every sector of our society, political, economic and social. A framework for political stability emerged when three major political parties merged to form a ruling majority. Subsequently, a national consensus to put an end to the period of political transition has brought about fresh changes in every aspect of our national life. In spite of various adversities and the worsening economic environment, we have achieved a 9 percent growth in our economy and successfully stabilized labor-management relations through the exercise of self-restraint and a spirit of solidarity.

In step with the tidal waves of change that swept across the world and transformed the international order, we have taken positive and vigorous steps to usher in a new era of peace and unification on the Korean Peninsula. The fact that we established diplomatic relations with the Soviet Union and East European countries during the year and that I paid an official visit to Moscow last month illustrate the significant progress we have made, on our own, in leaping forward across the Cold War barrier.

Leadership for Progress and Stability

We are ushering in 1991 amid enormous challenges from within as well as from without. We will, however, accelerate our energetic march toward democracy, prosperity and unification by mobilizing anew the national capabilities that brought about successful national development despite adversities of all kinds. One by one, we will bring the ongoing projects to completion and will ensure that the fruits of our endeavor are equitably distributed among the people.

I have made a number of commitments and pledges, and over the past three years a lot of them have been carried out, including the guarantee of freedom of the press, the removal of the authoritarian style of government, the construction of two million housing units, the development of west-coast areas, the implementation of northern diplomacy and the endeavor to bring about an early national unification.

I believe that it is now time to bring to you the results of and progress reports on what is being done rather than making new pledges and new commitments. The world is changing very rapidly, and we are facing an entirely new situation in terms of new global trends of democratization, liberalization and internationalization. Accordingly, based on fresh and clear assessments of the situation and "new thinking" of our own, the government shall faithfully exercise its leadership role in pursuing our national goals.

For projects that require speedy action, we will take immediate steps. For projects that require time, we will provide the nation with accurate blueprints and detailed plans to carry them out. The administration will lead the nation in a fair, open, just and democratic manner.

This is the fourth year of my administration. This year promises to be a year of great challenge for our democracy, which should take firm root, and for our economy, which should take off to a higher stage of development. This will also be a year of pivotal importance for South-North Korean relations which should move forward toward unification. I am determined to lead the nation to progress and prosperity, under all circumstances, by solidifying the basis of social stability and enforcing law and order.

The 21st century is only nine years away. During the remainder of the 20th century, we will firmly establish the conditions for this country to become an advanced, free and prosperous nation, within the unified bounds of which the entire 70 million Koreans shall enjoy living together.

A Touchstone of Democratic Development

Local elections are to be held this year for the first time in 30 years, and will be the key to a full democracy and an era of local self-government. Fair and clean elections of local council members this spring will prove to be a touchstone of success not only for local autonomy but for democratic development as well.

Should we succeed in maintaining fair and just processes in electing some 5,000 local council members with a maturity befitting our democratic development, the schedule of elections for next year, such as provincial governor elections, general elections and presidential elections, will be more easily and satisfactorily carried out.

If, on the other hand, the elections are mired in disorder and illicit campaigning and add fuel to the parochial dissensions, the future of our country, let alone democratic development, will be decidedly bleak. Furthermore, should the elections become corrupt and the vote-buying practices of the past return, it will threaten the very basis of our economic stability. For this reason, the government will enforce strict supervision to stem illicit money-spending practices, pre-election campaigning and other illegal election-related activities. From this moment forward, the government will regard any activity that breaks the rules and regulations of our democratic elections as anti-democratic crimes and will enforce very strict legal sanctions on all violators regardless of party affiliation and position.

The fundamental purpose of local autonomy is to encourage participation by local leaders and to realize the welfare of the people through local representation. Consequently, in order for local autonomy to succeed, you, the voters, must bring about what amounts to a revolutionary change in our election practices. We must reject gifts and/or money in connection with the elections and maintain watchful eyes to ensure fair and clean elections. We must reject those who seek to promote personal interest in the name of politics, and elect those who will serve faithfully for the development of our local communities.

We are entering the fourth year since we set out to build a new democracy with the June 29 Declaration of Democratic Reforms, and yet our politicians seem to have failed in winning the trust and confidence of much of the nation. Since I am also responsible, let me express my sincere regrets at this disappointing outcome. The impending task for our politicians, it seems to me, is to transform the style of our politics from confrontations that breed instability to compromises and dialogue that produce national harmony and integration. For my part, I will do my utmost to transform the ruling party, based on a thorough self-criticism, so that it will effectively carry out the aspirations of the people and become a party trusted and respected by them as truly democratic.

Social Consensus for Economic Progress and Stability

This is the last year of the sixth Five-year Economic Development Plan, part of a series of plans that began 30 years ago. By the time the seventh

Socio-Economic Development Plan which begins next year is completed, our country will become a highly industrialized country with a per capita GNP of $10,000. At this juncture, the nation is facing the last stage of development for the attainment of the long-awaited advanced nation status. In order for us to attain the advanced economic stage, however, we must achieve a higher level of development by infusing vitality into economic, industrial and technological structures and by introducing fresh approaches to business management and the national work ethic.

This year we are planning to achieve a 7 percent overall growth on the basis of sustained economic and social stability. By the end of this year, we will have moved closer to becoming an advanced economy as we achieve a per capita GNP of $6,200 with a trade volume exceeding $150 billion.

A note of caution is in order, however. Externally, a number of constraining factors tend to thwart our economic growth: namely, the Persian Gulf crisis and unstable oil prices, the worldwide stagflation, and the Uruguay Round and trade frictions. Internally, elements of economic instability persist due to increases in wages and prices, costs of energy, and the tardy recovery of international competitiveness on the part of our industries.

Stability this year in wages and prices and in labor-management relations will be of vital importance for the future of our economic development. Should prices and wages increase at a higher rate, it will stifle the competitiveness of our products, which is showing signs of recovery, and will inflict a crippling blow to our economy. Should this turn out to be the case, not only the 30-year-long national efforts but our aspirations to become an advanced nation will turn into national despair. I would like to urge all of you, businessmen, workers, salaried persons, indeed every citizen, to recognize this unmistakable reality and participate in producing a "societal consensus" for economic stability and development.

At the same time, unless extraordinary circumstances such as unusual oil price hikes in the wake of a deteriorating Persian Gulf crisis so dictate, the government and all the economic entities should exercise tight fiscal self-restraint so that the rate of price increases this year will not exceed a single digit in such areas as consumer products, services, rental housing and real estate. Wage increases for ordinary workers should also be held within the level of price increases. The government will concentrate its policies on the successful implementation of our goals and stabilization of the economy on the basis of a "societal consensus."

Revitalization of Manufacturing Industry

A most pressing task at this point is for our manufacturing industries, particularly export industries, to recover vitality and lead economic growth.

We must do everything humanly possible to revitalize our industries so that factories and manufacturing industries throughout the nation will operate round-the-clock, the diligent hands of our efficient workers will be busy filling orders and our export salespeople will further expand their market shares throughout the world. The results, I believe, will have a significant impact on every sector of our economy.

The government will implement a comprehensive and vigorous plan for industries to recover their international competitiveness at the earliest possible date. The government will also design and pursue effective programs to relieve current pressures on money supplies and manpower shortages. At the same time, the government will help develop readily applicable industrial technology and actively support corporate-level research and development efforts in order to encourage and accelerate technological renovations nationwide.

The rapid recovery of our industrial competitiveness is further hampered by the fact that our harbor and road facilities as well as factory sites have already reached capacity. Therefore, the government will make an extraordinary effort to expand the social infrastructure to help relieve these constraints. The government has already allotted a 2.5-trillion-won budget for this sector, a 35 percent increase over last year. The government also plans to supply an additional one trillion won through such measures as the sale of government bonds and extra tax income. These expenditures will be invested in such projects as the expansion of express and artery highways and of the capacities of Pusan and Inch'ŏn harbors. The government also plans to complete the second Seoul-Inch'ŏn Express Highway and the Seoul-Pusan Express Highway expansion projects by 1993. In order to effectively coordinate these and other similar projects, a social infrastructure planning and investment group is being set up in the Blue House.

The government will continue its ongoing efforts this year to eradicate the sources of illicit real estate investment activities and to discourage the expansion of non-productive service industries. In addition, we will remove unrealistic control measures to allow for more liberal business activities. If we are to modernize farm and fishing villages, increase welfare benefits to the disaffected and the disadvantaged, and improve the quality of life nationally, it is imperative for our manufacturing industries to lead healthy and steady economic growth.

We must also prepare ourselves for the complete liberalization of our economy. Our industries, including the agricultural sector, will have to nurture inner strength and durability in preparation for the forthcoming challenges. The truth of the matter is that even if there were no requirements for liberalization we would not be able to modernize our farming villages by exclusively relying on the strength of traditional methods of farming, consisting of individual manpower and limited operating resources. Consequently, we should take advantage of the Uruguay Round requirements and modernize our farming and fishing villages. The government will actively invest in and coordinate the restructuring of our agricultural sector.

Economic development can hardly be successful with government efforts alone. It requires the determination and participation of every citizen of the country: the workers, farmers and businessmen. I call upon all of you to join the effort.

Four Immediate Tasks to Improve the Quality of Life

Housing, transportation, environment and education are the four areas that demand our immediate attention, and the government will continue to improve the quality and service of these sectors. As for housing, construction began last year for 750,000 new housing units, and this year will see the ground broken for an additional 500,000 units. It means that the construction of the two million new apartment units that I pledged during the election campaigns will be completed by the end of this year. As new housing units are supplied, the housing shortages will be greatly relieved and real estate prices will also be stabilized.

To improve the transportation problem in the Seoul metropolitan area, we will complete a metropolitan express circular route connecting Pangyo and T'oegyewon by 1992. A new electrical rail system connecting Seoul with nearby satellite cities is scheduled for completion by 1993. Seoul City subways will also be extended on a continuing basis. The Pusan subways will be extended and new subways will be built for other major cities.

Our environment is deteriorating as industrialization progresses. During my tenure, I am determined to implement effective long- and intermediate-range environmental protection programs to preserve our natural environment and to provide clean air and clean water which are vital resources for the health of our citizens. The government will shortly issue guidelines for environmental protection to improve the quality of air and water, and to better process industrial waste.

During the three-year period between 1990 and 1992, the government is investing a total of 1.1 trillion won in special accounts to improve the nation's educational environment, and as a result you will notice significant improvements in our schools. We should, however, make adjustments in our attitude—that everybody should go to college or that everyone should graduate from college. College education, of course, is highly desirable, but we should find a better way of educating our children, and the government is currently in the process of restructuring the college entrance examination and high school education systems.

New Life, New Order Campaign for a Healthy Society

Democracy will only prosper in a society where stability, law and order prevail. The nation has paid a dear price and has sacrificed much for this lesson throughout the process of democratization over the past several years.

The New Life, New Order Campaign which was launched in the wake of the October 13 Declaration of War on Crime embodies the consensus of our citizens throughout the country. Everywhere in our society, a fresh movement to uphold the law is spreading, and the campaign is setting new life-styles for our citizens, young and old. The campaign is likely to set the pace for the decade of the 1990s and become a nationwide movement.

The government will continue this year to mobilize all available resources to strictly enforce the law and eradicate from our society crimes, violence and unlawful and disorderly behavior. To reform society, we will address the trends toward delinquent behavior and decadent pleasure-seeking. The government will strictly enforce the law against drunken and dangerous driving and illegal parking, as well as violations of late-night operating hours and the operation of decadent establishments. The government and the civil servants will take the lead in building a safe, healthy and hard-working society.

A safe and orderly society, however, can only be realized when the public voluntarily joins the government efforts. I ask each and every one of you to actively participate in our common efforts to remove the dark clouds hanging over parts of our communities so that our great society will once again be swept clean by a fresh wind.

Road to Peace and Unification

This year, the international situation around the Korean Peninsula is likely to undergo a very rapid transformation, for the waves of reform that changed Europe are moving on toward East Asia. Long before the break-up of the Cold War system, we have taken the initiative and have been pursuing a northern diplomacy. Now, we have to look ahead and wisely respond to the coming challenges from around the Korean Peninsula. The old structure of confrontation that persisted for decades is now collapsing. The task before us then is to be at the forefront of this great change and to remove the threat of renewed hostilities so that our aspirations for peace and unification may soon be realized.

We will further solidify the existing cooperative relations with our traditional friends, above all, the United States, Japan and the European Community countries. On this basis, we will continue to develop substantive cooperative relations with the Soviet Union. Our relations with China will improve further with the concurrent opening this month of offices of trade representatives.

In light of external and internal imperatives, North Korea appears to be approaching a critical stage, and it will soon have to drop its self-imposed isolationist policy. In a not-too-distant future North Korea will have to change, and we may come to a significant turning-point in South-North relations.

Last year, for the first time since the territorial division, we had three rounds of prime ministers' talks and some cultural and sports exchanges. We will continue to sincerely pursue the talks and contacts with North Korea to derive meaningful agreements from them, which will lead to wider exchanges and closer cooperation between the two parts of Korea.

Today, the external constraints on unification are disappearing. Furthermore, the international climate for the unification of the Korean Peninsula is improving. On the basis of an accurate assessment of the situation, we will approach the unification issue realistically without undue haste.

Ladies and gentlemen,

Building a democratic nation . . . Becoming an advanced nation . . . Attaining a unified nation . . . these are no longer idealistic wishes nor do they remain beyond our reach. They are rapidly becoming realities before our eyes.

Today, we are faced with challenges as well as opportunities. Undergoing innumerable trials and tribulations, we have never forgotten the aspiration for national unification. We must now join our strength and wisdom to realize our long-sought dreams. Let us all join and march together. I will stand at the forefront of government and do my utmost. Let us all move vigorously forward.

Ladies and gentlemen, thank you very much.

I will now take your questions.

6.

President Pins His Hopes on Moscow and Peking: Interview, *Far Eastern Economic Review,* May 9, 1991

President Roh Tae Woo has presided over dramatic changes in his country: rapid democratization, continuing economic growth and opening to the communist world. In a wide-ranging interview on 24 April with REVIEW Editor Philip Bowring, Seoul bureau chief Shim Jae Hoon and correspondent Mark Clifford, he discussed these and other issues. Excerpts:

At your recent meeting in Cheju with President Gorbachev, how much did personal rapport contribute to the success of the talks?

Undoubtedly very much. It was our third meeting: the first was in San Francisco in June 1990. President Gorbachev came after a heavy itinerary in Japan, and Cheju Island—away from the capital—provided relaxation, adding to the informal and friendly atmosphere. We had a very intimate conversation on the pains of perestroika, the situation on the Korean Peninsula, peace, the question of our UN admission, and also North Korea's nuclear problem, which your publication helped to draw the world's attention to two years ago by breaking the first story (REVIEW, 2 Feb. '89).

I explained to Gorbachev some of the experiences and achievements gained from our own economic development which must have encouraged him, and offered to help him cope with economic difficulties arising from perestroika. I praised his courage in tackling these problems. Our talks created a good atmosphere and gave rise to hope, making a great deal of contribution to developing our bilateral relations. I have developed a great personal affection for him. It was a valuable opportunity, indeed.

How much influence does Gorbachev have in stopping North Korea's nuclear development?

So far, I am satisfied with the efforts he has made and with his pledge to bring North Korea to accept international obligations. Of course, if North Korea accepted 100% of what the Soviets say, then there should be no problem, but as you know, the North resists all outside pressure so I wouldn't rest assured until we had solid evidence that they are complying with international inspection.

South Korea's admission to the UN will improve your international status, but do you have any assurance that China will not exercise its veto at the Security Council?

We don't have any official signal from high Chinese authorities over this but through informal channels, they have indicated that they will not exercise a veto. Now the two countries have exchanged trade offices, and may soon open up diplomatic relations. In the early 1970s China had bitter experiences of being shut out from the UN for a long time. In view of the universality principle of the UN, China cannot comfortably keep us out; China does not actively oppose our admission, so I am not going to worry too much over this.

In view of North Korea's deepening isolation because of its internal, external and economic problems, do you foresee changes coming before the death of Kim Il Sung?

I can't see any fundamental changes, though I feel that what looks like a prelude to change is already occurring, starting from areas that are relatively easier for them to handle, such as sports. Today a joint South-North table-tennis team starts playing. I don't see any sign of the North Korean system itself fundamentally shaking so long as Kim is alive but the North has responded to talks. We had three rounds of premier-level talks last year and I expect them to resume this year. In the absence of fundamental changes, we have to go on broadening the area of cooperation and exchanges, to keep accumulating small steps so that we can draw them to the outside world, showing them what the world is like, helping to improve their standard of living until they realize the value of economic development and progress.

We don't want abrupt changes creating social and political instability in the North. What we want is a sort of gradual change so that both South and North can develop together in peace and restore our common national identity. This is the road we have chosen to take, and it's the road dictated by our history.

Internally and externally you have presided over many changes while in office. Do you plan to contribute to the cause of unification in any way after you retire?

I have been so busy in the last few years that there has hardly been time to think over what I would do in retirement. But while in office, I hope to put down the roots of democracy and place our northern diplomacy on the right track to reunification. These are historic tasks that have been thrust on me. I just hope to hand over to the next president my personal efforts and experiences from the pursuit of northern diplomacy and reunification.

You have said that the next president should come neither from the army nor from your family circle. What qualities would you like in your successor?

Qualities of leadership should reflect the demands of time, and it should clearly be someone who is capable of mastering the course of our democratization efforts, of satisfying the increasingly diverse aspirations of our people; it should be someone who can stand up to the task of our times. Our country has changed tremendously—it ranks as the 12th-largest trading country and the 15th-largest GNP in the world. Our foreign policy no longer deals with just half of the world, but must be global. The next leader should possess the aptitude and ability to make some tough—and sometimes acutely sensitive—decisions. We have grown through so many tribulations in recent history and I would expect to see people with these qualities stepping forward naturally in the course of time.

Some South Koreans want a strong president, but others want a Japanese form of parliamentary government. Which do you think is better suited for South Korea?

Many Koreans appear to want both. I would wait and see which they like more.

Which would you prefer?

Strong leadership is important for Korea. But personally, I think that leadership strength that rests on the consent of many people, on collective ideas marshalling the support of many people, is preferable to a single leader.

7.

South Korea's President Wants a Polity to Match Its Economy; Interview, *Los Angeles Times*, June 23, 1991

When authoritarian President Chun Doo Hwan anointed Roh Tae Woo as his successor, to run in a rubber stamp election for president of South Korea, in June, 1987, he hardly seemed likely to lead the country into democracy. Both Roh and Chun are ex-generals, and Roh had supported Chun in his 1980 coup. During Chun's repressive presidency, Roh stood by his friend, serving in various Cabinet posts and, for a period, heading the 1988 Seoul Olympic Organizing Committee.

On the day Chun formalized Roh as his choice, South Korean students launched street demonstrations that won the support of the middle class and threatened to deprive Seoul of the international prestige of the 1988 Olympiad. But, on June 29, Roh stunned the nation by pledging to support a direct election of the president and, if elected, to carry out a democratization of South Korea. He threatened to resign as a candidate if Chun refused his recommendations. Chun accepted, calm returned to the streets and, in a December, 1987 election, the people elected Roh by a 37 percent plurality—the opposition ran three candidates against him and so split the field.

Now widespread, if still imperfect, reform has been carried out in South Korea. But public discontent with politics and with his new ruling party continues—as Roh admitted during an extensive conversation on the eve of his trip to the United States on June 29. Labor strife marred the first two years of Roh's administration. Trade deficits have returned, alarming a nation that, since an economic takeoff began in the 1960s, has equated exports with growth.

Continuing is a bitter parochial enmity that psychologically divides the nation east and west—even as the country remains physically separated north and south. Political analysts say regional antipathy between Koreans of the southwest Cholla region—the birthplace of opposition leader Kim Dae Jung—and the southeast Kyongsang region—Roh's native home—supersedes all other issues in Korean politics. As the constitutional limit of one term for Roh approaches—in February, 1993—parochialism again threatens to color a presidential election.

Meanwhile, more than 1.5 million armed forces of the communist North and the capitalist South confront each other along a demilitarized zone 25 miles north of Seoul, with some 43,000 U.S. troops standing guard as a symbol of the U.S. commitment to Seoul's security.

Only in diplomacy has Roh achieved unblemished triumphs—staging of the Olympics, establishment of diplomatic relations with the Soviet Union and East Europe, exchanges of trade offices with consular functions with China, and a now assured entry into the United Nations next fall.

An impeccable dresser, Roh, 58, speaks softly and slowly, by Korean standards, but in a relaxed manner, usually with a smile on his face. He held a felt pen in his right hand while talking but never used it. A pile of notes prepared by his aides sat on a table beside him. Roh never looked at them.

Question: *You cited eight specific reforms in your June 29, 1987, declaration promising to bring democracy to Korea. Which has been implemented most successfully?*

Answer: . . . . One of the most moving experiences for me was to see realized the people's desire to elect the president with their own hands and to see the release of politicians and others who were imprisoned because of their conviction [that the president should be elected directly]. Not only were they given an amnesty. They were permitted to run for political office. [By their release, including freedom for opposition leader Kim Dae Jung], I didn't gain anything as the ruling party's candidate. But my mind was set at ease, and we had a free election. That was one of the best achievements.

Q: *Which least successfully?*

A: . . . . I emphasized that authoritarianism . . . should be removed and that we should renovate both the system and the way of thinking that then prevailed. In my inaugural speech, I asked political leaders and government officials not to turn me into a Don Quixote. I emphasized the need for a completely fresh way of thinking. . . . Although the authority of the president should be preserved, authoritarianism should be eliminated.

Therefore, I told officials of the government and the ruling party to delegate as much authority as possible to provincial and local government authorities. What rightfully belongs to legislatures should be entrusted to legislatures. What rightfully belongs to the judiciary should be returned to the judiciary, so that voluntarism would spring up from all corners of the country. . . .

The area in which the least progress has occurred in catching up with the times is that of the political circles. . . . Our politicians have not matured enough to . . . distill conflicting demands. . . . Rather than grasping and resolving popular demands and frictions, the ruling and the opposition parties have tended to escalate them—making our society suffer even more and pay a greater price. . . .

Q: *In your May statement, you said the people's distrust in politics has reached a dangerous level and the ruling party itself needs to be reborn. Despite your reforms, why does distrust remain?*

A: One of the reasons I just mentioned—the old way of thinking.

As the nation transforms itself into a democracy, the public expects and demands more than ever that politicians and political parties work harder in the best interest of the country, the people and society. Our politicians, however, have given the impression that, on the contrary, they are engrossed in self-serving maneuvers to advance the interests of only their parties, factions or themselves, personally. The process of liquidating such negative political legacies of the old era has progressed more slowly than the people expected.

Furthermore, several politicians have recently been implicated in scandals. Public misgivings about the morality of our political circles, as a result, have intensified.

The other [reason] comes from the merger of three political parties . . . as a result of an agreement between me and the leaders of two opposition parties [into the ruling Democratic Liberal Party] last year. . . . When the parties merged, the entire nation welcomed the move. But later, as conflicts surfaced, the people's disappointment was great. Perhaps, our popularity dropped by as big a margin as it had climbed with the rise of expectations at the time of the merger.

. . . . We must speed up coordination and the process of ironing out the differences of opinions and dissatisfactions to respond to the desires of the people. That is why I said [the party must be reborn].

Q: *Another area where distrust emerges is in the regional antipathies between the people of the Kyongsang region in the southeast and the Cholla region in the southwest. Can something be done to uproot these regional antipathies?*

A: Friction . . . derives in part from our longstanding tradition of valuing blood and community ties. . . . [It] has been growing over the last generation. . . . During the last presidential election [when Kim Dae Jung, a native of Cholla, ran against Roh, a Kyongsang native], those sentiments deepened.

Over the last decades, Korea's economic development focused on the eastern side of the country—in an axis of Seoul, Pusan, and Japan. The southwestern provinces were left out. . . .

Of course, the 1980 Kwangju incident [200 people in the capital of South Cholla Province were killed by government troops sent in to put down demonstrations] added fuel to the fire. In the past several years, the government has been trying to reduce parochialism by taking such measures as enacting a special compensation law for the victims of the Kwangju incident. . . .

With a [new] government program to develop the west coast, the axis of national development will now move to the west side of the country. Within 10 years, the west-coast axis will be strengthened . . . and regional antipathies softened.

Q: On Oct. 31, 1983, you said you had "rearranged the functions" of the Defense Security Command and the Agency for National Security Planning, the former Korean CIA, to ensure neither intervened in politics. Yet, last summer, it was revealed that the Defense Security Command was conducting surveillance of politicians. And no revision of the Agency for National Security Planning Law has been carried out yet. Do you plan further reforms?

A: The National Security Law [banning praise of communist North Korea] has been revised. Still pending in the National Assembly is the revision of the Agency for National Security Planning Law. . . . [It would create] an intelligence committee in the National Assembly . . . to ensure the political neutrality of that agency and strengthen National Assembly oversight of its budget.

The law [establishing] the Defense Security Command does not permit surveillance of citizens. That incident was a case of mismanagement. Subsequently, the government took corrective measures to ensure better management of the command and it is now operating within the law.

Although the revised Agency for National Security Planning Law has not been enacted, management of the agency has been improved. Politicians and the news media point out any mistakes and wrongdoings. Unlike the old days of authoritarian rule, political surveillance of opposition politicians is not possible. Opposition parties and politicians are not restricted in their political activities.

I expect that a revision of the Agency for National Security Planning Law will be enacted in the near future, but there is no restriction on political activities in Korea today.

The mission of the Defense Security Command is to prevent the infiltration of impure elements into the armed forces. To do that, the command must have the means to screen radical students—especially those who believe in the "juche" [self-reliance] thought of [North Korean President] Kim Il Sung and those armed with Marxist-Leninist philosophy.

When those elements enter the armed forces, there is no telling what antistate, anti-military actions they may take. The command needs personal data. But since there has been criticism from political circles, collecting personal data on individuals before they enter military service has been ended. The command now collects personal data only after individuals enter military service.

I hope you will understand Korea's unique situation [of national division and 1.5 million troops of the North and South facing across a demilitarized zone].

Q: *Another big change in politics also appears to have occurred. No one is worrying about armed forces intervention. Will the armed forces refrain from intervening in politics even if an opposition leader should be elected president?*

A: When I made my June 29 declaration and ran for the presidency, many people—especially people in the armed forces—predicted that I would be defeated. But you know the results [a victory by 37% plurality], and the military upheld its integrity and accepted the result. . . . It is no longer possible even to imagine military intervention in politics. In a democratic country, there can be no force that can negate the people's choice expressed through elections.

Q: *When will the ruling party name its candidate for the next presidential election? What role do you intend to play?*

A: I will not be the one to nominate the candidate of the Democratic Liberal Party. . . . He will be chosen through democratic procedures according to the party consultation. . . . It is advisable to nominate a candidate about a year before my term of office ends [February, 1993].

Q: *What is the main topic you expect to discuss with President Bush on your trip to the United States?*

A: . . . . In Europe, the East-West Cold War has ended and a new international order is emerging. I hope that the Cold War in Northeast Asia and the Pacific will soon end. Under these circumstances, the United States is envisioning a "new world order," including new policies for Northeast Asia. We have arrived at a time to think of a "new order" in Asia—for security, cooperation, peace and prosperity. I hope to have a wide-ranging exchange of views with President Bush on these issues, as well as on the future of weapons [in this region]; we should get together and discuss the reduction of nuclear weapons. That, I think, is more logical.

Q: *What is your view about future reductions or removal of U.S. forces stationed in South Korea?*

A: . . . . [Whether] North Korea's recent decision to go along with South Korea in joining the United Nations separately means a change in North Korea's policy toward the South remains to be seen. In these circumstances, I believe that South Korea and the United States must continue to maintain their solid cooperative relationship.

Q: *Do you foresee the establishment of diplomatic relations between North Korea and the United States and between North Korea and Japan in the near future?*

A: . . . . Washington has been following a policy of improving relations with North Korea in return for its signing of a nuclear-safeguard agreement with the International Atomic Energy Agency, meaningful progress in inter-Korean dialogue, and the return of remains of U.S. troops killed in action during the Korean War. North Korea, however, has not altered its militant isolationism and has yet to show signs of positive change in favor of reduced tension and durable peace in the Korean peninsula. . . .

The military threat from the North has not changed in any substantial way. . . . Therefore, I do not foresee any rapid improvement of U.S.-North Korean relations in the near future. Improvement of Japan-North Korea relations, I think, will also depend on how far the North will go in changing its attitude. . . .

Q: *Are you happy that you are going to the United States without a major Korean trade surplus with the United States?*
A: [laughing] Why should it please me to be visiting the United States as the president of a trade-deficit nation? For 10 years, we have had a trade surplus with the United States. . . . It reached a peak of $9.6 billion in 1987, and we have been trying to correct the situation.

. . . . It has continued to shrink—to $2.4 billion in 1990. The latest statistics show that Korea's trade with the United States during the first four months of this year registered a deficit of $1 billion. . . . It is the result of our mutual efforts to balance trade. . . . By the end of the year, trade is expected to attain equilibrium. . . .

There have been many outcries about an economic failure or an economic crisis [in South Korea]. But in the midst of those outcries, we achieved an 8.9% real growth in the first quarter [of 1991]. . . . Foreign observers ask why we Koreans are so pessimistic and critical. The same thing may be applied to politics and the lack of popularity of the government. Even my own popularity has dropped.

Despite the criticism of the government and its low popularity, we won 75% of the seats in the last local elections [in March]. This time, too, we probably will secure more than 50% of the seats in elections for city and provincial legislatures. [Thursday, the ruling party won 65% of provincial and city assembly seats.]

8.

Opening Remarks at the New Year's News Conference, Seoul, January 10, 1992

I wish all of you greater joy and fulfillment in the new year.

For the last four years, I have diligently worked with my fellow citizens to achieve democracy, prosperity and unification in this land. By implementing the steps outlined in the June 29, 1987 Declaration of Democratic Reforms one after another, we have introduced an era of genuine democracy brimming with freedom, individual initiative and vitality.

The Northern Policy that we began pursuing even before the onset of the current changes around the world has opened a new horizon toward unification on the Korean Peninsula, and extended the sphere of activities of our citizens throughout the world.

The year 1991 was perhaps the most rewarding year since our land was divided, as far as our national aspirations for peace and unification are concerned. Only three months after the South and the North entered the United Nations together, the two parts of Korea agreed to end long-standing confrontation and rivalry and to usher in a new era of peace and prosperity. Our endeavors to make the Korean Peninsula nuclear-free on our own initiatives are also making progress as a result of a positive response from the North. Now, unification is no longer a dream, it has become a realistic goal.

Along with these rewarding achievements, we have also had a number of disappointments. For example, although our economy grew at an average annual rate of more than 9 percent for the past four years, we have not yet been able to fully overcome the difficulties stemming from democratization, internationalization and market opening.

The year 1992 is expected to be a year of transition at home and abroad. The revolutionary changes that have been sweeping across the world and brought the downfall of Communism and the disintegration of the Soviet Union are expected to continue this year. The waves of change that have redrawn the world map are now causing fresh movements in Northeast Asia and the Korean Peninsula.

In the post-Cold War world, nations and regions are increasingly involved in fierce competition for prosperity. The European Community is expected to offer a single market for 340 million consumers within this year, leading to a major restructuring of the world economy. North America, our largest export market, is about to enter into a free trade area. The development of Japan, with its leading-edge technologies and huge capital, is being further accelerated. Our neighbors in the developing world are also growing rapidly.

In this manner, the whole world is racing toward the 21st century. This year, the nation must weather these changes around the world and surge ahead toward a glorious future. We must restore our economic vitality this year and leap forward again. We must make the elections this year into a catalyst for bringing our democracy to full maturity. We must properly channel the incipient thaw on the Korean Peninsula into a steady movement toward unification. From such a perspective, I want to enunciate the basic policies of the nation for this year and appeal to my fellow citizens for cooperation and participation.

Restoring Economic Vitality and Promoting Healthier Development

Top priority in national administration will be given to restoring economic vitality and all-out efforts will be made to stabilize prices, while improving the balance of payments position. 1992 is the first year of the seventh Five-Year Economic and Social Development Plan designed to fully transform our economy into an advanced economy. By 1996, the last year of the plan, our per capita income should reach US$11,000, making the land into a developed country where life will be comfortable for all.

However, as we approach the threshold of the developed world, our economy is facing tough internal and external challenges. Even though we achieved 8.6 percent growth in real terms, we have yet to resolve many structural problems. For example, wages have risen faster than productivity. Increases in consumption have outpaced economic growth. Moreover, because growth has come mostly from disproportionate expansion of domestic demand, inflationary pressures have mounted while imports have soared. On top of that, productive activities have been hampered by increasing labor shortages and inadequate public infrastructure. All these factors have combined to blunt our industrial competitiveness and push the trade balance deeply into deficit.

The government intends to lower the economic growth rate this year to around 7 percent with the goal of achieving a healthier economy under conditions of stability. To that end, efforts will be directed, first of all, at stabilizing wages and boosting the supply of industrial manpower. For our economy in 1992, the most crucial factor will be how wages will be settled, because this will have a direct bearing on efforts to restore the competitiveness of Korean industry, to cool the consumption boom, and to keep inflation in check. Wages must be held within the rate of increase in productivity.

The administration will also work harder to curb the construction boom and lower the profitability of services so that more workers can be recruited into the manufacturing industry. Admission quotas, especially for engineering and technical schools at various levels, will be expanded. A system will be instituted to make it easier for businesses themselves to train and educate a greater proportion of the skilled workers they need.

We must curb consumption to help reduce deficits in our balance of payments. Since the national income has doubled over the past four years, leading to a higher standard of living, it has been inevitable for consumption to rise to some extent. However, consumption trends have gone out of normal bounds, and the demand for luxurious goods and services has grown excessively. This was one reason that oil consumption jumped nearly 30 percent last year while we were hardly aware of it. Consequently, crude oil imports exceeded US$10 billion. If we do not save and conserve more, it will be difficult to correct our trade imbalance even if we export more. It is time for all our citizens to return to the virtues of industriousness, frugality and saving.

The administration will continue to implement measures to help sharpen the competitiveness of the manufacturing industry. Businesses must also exert greater efforts to raise productivity and improve product quality. If our businesses do not try harder to produce a range of products that can meet international standards of excellence, they will lose out in today's international marketplace. So, the administration will support technological development and export industries, especially small and medium industries, on a priority basis.

In this connection, 4.2 trillion won is scheduled to be invested this year in the expansion and improvement of roads, ports and other infrastructure under a program initiated last year. As part of this program, ground will be broken this year for a Seoul-Pusan high-speed railway and a new international airport on Yongjongdo Island, both projects designed to satisfy the need of the 21st century.

Our economy is now moving into a stage of full-fledged openness. Our domestic market has been open to foreign investors since the beginning of the new year. When the Uruguay Round of trade negotiations are brought to a successful conclusion, our markets will be fully open to the world.

We must take advantage of market opening as a catalyst for increasing our industrial strength and leaping onto a new level of development, instead of fearing it. In this connection, the government has scheduled a total investment of 2.7 trillion won this year to modernize our agriculture and fishing industry. What is important, however, is the concerted efforts of workers, farmers, fishermen and all other citizens to adapt to the changing circumstances. The administration will do its utmost at the forefront of these endeavors.

Fair Elections for an Advanced Political Climate

This year is important for the future course of the nation. We have ahead of us a great task of electing representatives of the people who will lead our efforts to achieve national prosperity and unification and thus lay a foundation for the establishment of a new government. We cannot, however, let the forthcoming elections disturb the national economy, split national unity and destroy social morale. We must build a consensus on the need to revitalize and further promote national development.

Needless to say it is impossible to choose the right representatives through corrupt elections in which money, false publicity and irresponsible electioneering play a major role. The government, therefore, will strongly crack down on all illegal election campaigns, no matter who's involved, while ensuring a free atmosphere. It goes without saying, however, that it is impossible to ensure fair elections without the active and spontaneous participation of the people. In fact, the political climate is in the hands of the people.

I will now discuss the major political agenda for this year—a topic most of you are deeply interested in. The national convention of the Democratic Liberal Party which is to elect a presidential candidate will be held following general elections for the National Assembly. The presidential candidate of the DLP will be nominated through democratic procedures as provided for by the constitution of the party.

Executive Party Chairman Kim Young-sam will lead the Democratic Liberal Party in the general elections for the 14th National Assembly with the close cooperation of the two co-chairmen. The National Assembly elections will be held sometime in March.

I understand that the idea still persists in some political quarters that the government may opt for a Cabinet system or a dual executive system by revising the Constitution. Such speculation tends to amplify the people's distrust of politics. Therefore, I wish to make it clear once again that I will not seek a Constitutional revision during my term of office. I hope that this issue will no longer be made a subject of non-productive debate.

In addition to the National Assembly and presidential elections there are two more elections scheduled for this year, for the heads of local governments. In this connection, there are some who fear it may not be easy to hold so many elections in a year. Voices are also heard that the mobilization of manpower and funds for the four elections would further depress our economy. Some people also have misgivings that these elections will have an adverse impact on the social stability that we have attained with much difficulty. It is true that the process of opening a new era of democracy cost our economy dearly. It is also true that another blow to the economy would shake it to its very foundation which would in turn endanger the very existence of democracy.

I have sought the counsel of specialists from all walks of life on this issue. All of them said that in view of our current economic reality, it would be practically impossible to stabilize the economy and society if we held four elections this year. They thus urged me to make an important decision in this respect. After a series of consultations and deliberations, I have finally decided that it is best to postpone the elections for the heads of local governments. The timing of the elections will be determined by the 14th National Assembly, of which elections are due in March. I hope the people will understand and support my decision—a decision made for the future of our country and in line with the spirit of my June 29, 1987 Declaration of Democratic Reform.

Creation of a Solid Foundation for Unification

Next, I will translate the Agreement on Reconciliation, Nonaggression and Exchanges and Cooperation between the South and the North into action to open an era of coexistence and prosperity between the South and the North. First, I will see to it that the North will take measures, including international inspection, to free the Korean Peninsula of nuclear arms, and I will also endeavor to replace the armistice agreement with a peace treaty.

Since my July 7, 1988 Special Declaration, commodity trade between the South and the North has amounted to US$240 million, and last year, it rose more than seven times over 1990. Furthermore, trade with the North will rise greatly once an open account is set up, ports are named for direct trade and a common market is established.

Pending agreement between Seoul and P'yŏngyang, South-North joint ventures will be actively sought in specially-designed areas, such as the Demilitarized Zone and the border area with China and the Russian Federation, with a view to jointly advancing into world markets.

Home visit exchanges will be proposed to enable the elderly to visit their relatives in the other part of the Peninsula. Another plan to enable dispersed persons to freely meet with one another at a specially-designated area is also being considered. An increase in the South-North Cooperation Fund is also being considered to further facilitate economic exchanges between the South and the North and to support increased investment in the North.

In addition, relations with our friends such as the United States and Japan will be further cemented. Increased efforts will also be made for a successful conclusion of our Northern Policy.

Stabilization and Improvement of the Living Standard

I shall make continued efforts to further stabilize our society and improve the living standards by improving public security, housing, environment and education. As a result of the October 13, 1990 declaration of war on crime and disorder, crimes decreased while the arrest rate increased. I will do my very best to wipe out crime this year, on the basis confidence gained in our war against crime last year. I will strictly put under control the violent criminals who are prone to take advantage of the upcoming elections.

As for the plan to build two million houses, we have built no less than 2.14 million housing units as of the end of last year, which means that we topped the goal one year in advance. True, there were adverse side effects to building the large number of apartment units and houses over such a short period, but I was pleased to note that housing prices have been declining and that nearly 10 million people now own homes. Under the seventh Five-Year Economic and Social Development Plan (1992–1996), the government also plans to build 500,000 houses a year to help further ease housing problems. For the benefit of low-income citizens and workers, the government will build a total of 200,000 small-size rental units this year; private construction firms will also be encouraged to build small housing units. Efforts will be made to prevent, in advance, speculation in real estate.

Last year, we introduced local autonomy in education, paving the way for the decentralization of education. In order to foster the creative minds necessary for internationalization and the age of information which will characterize the 21st century, the government will continue to promote the reform and modernization of education.

To improve the quality of drinking water, the government will increase investment in water treatment as well as sewer drainage facilities. To improve the environment, the government will boost the supply of liquified natural gas in major cities.

Good Citizenship

Finally, I hope that our people will properly exercise their rights and duties as good citizens this year—a year which will be vital in determining our future. It goes without saying that the most precious asset earned from democratic development is a sense of community. We have been able to overcome the transitional difficulties in an era of democracy in our country, thanks to a public consensus on the need to work toward a better future.

The very fact that labor disputes sharply declined last year from the level of 1987 demonstrates the civic consciousness of the workers. The movement now spreading in the work places across the country to work more and to improve productivity also stems from the spontaneous awareness of the people that we cannot afford to let our country falter at this juncture.

In fact, a mature civic consciousness has been the underlying force for the ongoing New Life-New Order Campaign to drive out excessive consumption, lifestyles and social disorder. I hope and expect that this movement will gather momentum this year. We will be assured of a better future as long as we remain conscious that we are the masters of our country, that we must develop our own community, and that it is for us to choose our own future.

Fellow citizens,

As the one who is ultimately responsible for the affairs of state, I shall do my very best to successfully accomplish my duties this year—a year believed to be most important for determining our destiny. In so doing I hope I will be able to bring my remaining term of office, which is a little more than a year, to a satisfactory conclusion.

I have now outlined the basic direction for the political agenda. I expect that the politicians will assume responsibility for carrying out this agenda, as I plan to turn politics over to the politicians so that I can devote myself to reinvigorating our national economy, while consolidating the foundation for unification.

I will do my best to accomplish what I can. I will never neglect to sow seeds for the future. I hope to go down in history as a president above reproach. I hope to make 1992 a springboard for a great nation. We are at this moment at a juncture that will determine the course of our people and country in the 21st century. Let us all march forward, having made the right choices and with a firm resolution to achieve a bright future.

Thank you.

9.

Reshaping a Nation: Korea's Quiet Revolution; article, *Britannica Book of the Year*, 1992

I was still in high school when North Korea suddenly invaded my homeland in the South in June 1950, touching off a bitter three-year war. My home was in Taegu, in the southwest, the city that for a time became the anchor of the UN defense line against the invaders. I went to war wearing my student's uniform. We fought hard against the Communist aggressors. My original hope was to become a doctor, but due to the war situation, I was enrolled as a cadet in the Korean Military Academy in 1951. There I learned a lot more about Communism, but I also learned a great deal about American democracy. Thanks to Gen. James A. Van Fleet, then commanding the U.S. 8th Army in Korea, our curriculum was modeled on West Point's.

If the war experience taught me the value of liberal democracy, it also made me painfully aware of the tragedy of our divided Korean people. Despite our hardships, the war ended in an armistice without reunifying the country. All of us young people at that time felt the need to end the poverty and misery of our people by rebuilding the economy.

Long inhabited by one people with one language and one culture, Korea has a proud tradition and heritage. This we have preserved despite countless foreign invasions—from the 13th-century Mongols to the 20th-century Japanese. Nevertheless, the country was cruelly divided by cold war politics after World War II. While the South began to pursue the goals of democracy, with a market economy in place, the North established a Stalinist Communist system. This ideological rivalry was at least partly responsible for the Korean War, the wounds of which have not yet healed. More than 10 million Korean people remain displaced or separated from their loved ones because of the military truce line that cuts across the country. The sundered parts of Germany are now united: Eastern Europe and the Soviet Union are free of Communism. But Korea has continued as the worst victim of the cold war.

> **Roh's Reform Platform: The 1987 Declaration**
>
> 1. Revise the Constitution, through consensus between the governing party and the opposition, in order to adopt, among other things, a direct presidential election system favored by the public so that there could be a peaceful change of government in February 1988, when the term of the incumbent President was to end
> 2. Revise without delay the Presidential Election Law to ensure fair management of elections
> 3. Release those imprisoned or detained for political dissent and restore their civil rights
> 4. Institutionalize respect for human dignity and the protection of basic rights
> 5. Promote freedom of the press by abolishing all manner of overt and covert censorship
> 6. Guarantee private initiative and self-regulation and reinstate local autonomy to build a vibrant democratic society
> 7. Create a political climate conducive to dialogue and compromise and guarantee sound political party activities
> 8. Carry out bold ethical reforms to build a clean and honest society

In the South, we have endeavoured to build a new nation from the ruins of war. We have been able to modernize and industrialize a formerly backward agricultural country in a very short period. We now enjoy greater prosperity than at any time in our history. If Germany's postwar resurgence could be called "the miracle on the Rhine," Korea's might justly be called "the miracle on the Han River." The Han River may be far shorter than the Rhine, but the obstacles in the way of the Republic of Korea's modernization and economic success were, if I may say so, far greater.

I am proud that Korea's political development now matches its spectacular economic development—thanks to the recent series of drastic but relatively orderly democratic reforms. Not the least of these was the reinstatement of local autonomy—based on local elections—in 1991 after a 30-year hiatus. These reforms were inspired by my own June 29, 1987, Declaration of Democratic Reforms. With this, I sought to end decades of authoritarian rule and set our country on the road to full democracy. (*See Sidebar.*)

In recent years, Korea's stature in the international community has increased greatly. To a large extent this was due to our success as hosts of the 1988 Seoul Olympic Games and the fruitful pursuit of a "northern democracy." In 1991 we finally overcame P'yŏngyang's resistance to parallel UN membership, resulting in the simultaneous entry of both South and North into the world body. Rapid changes in the world are brightening the prospects for a durable peace on the Korean Peninsula. The end of the cold war and of

Communism in the Soviet Union and other formerly socialist countries increasingly compels North Korea to soften its hard-line isolationist stance, giving us a better opportunity to seek our long-cherished goal of unification.

Setting the Stage for Democratic Reforms. I retired as a four-star general in 1981, after almost 30 years of army service. I began my political career as the minister of state for national security and foreign affairs, a Cabinet post without portfolio. My main task, however, was to win the 1988 Summer Games for Seoul. Our objective in holding the Olympics was to tell the world that the Republic of Korea had come of age. In 1982 I became the first minister of sports in a new ministry created in part to support the staging of the Games. Subsequently, I was chosen president of the Seoul Olympic Organizing Committee. In that capacity, I traveled constantly, talking to a wide variety of people in an effort to ensure the success of the Games.

In 1985 I became a member of the National Assembly, running on the ruling Democratic Justice Party's national ticket. Shortly afterward I was elected chairman of the DJP. Inevitably, I came to be impressed with the important place of the legislature in a democracy. I became convinced that the National Assembly alone—through debate, dialogue, and compromise—could effectively reflect the views of the people. It is true that during those days the Assembly's work was often hampered by lengthy but pointless debate and incessant confrontation and strife between opposing political groups. In addition, we had to cope with complicated parliamentary procedures designed not to strengthen but to weaken the legislature. Without my experience in the National Assembly, I doubt that I could have succeeded later, as the nation's chief executive, in carrying out democratic reforms with patience, in a spirit of give-and-take.

By the mid-eighties popular exasperation over decades of authoritarian rule sparked increasingly massive and wild street demonstrations. Although spearheaded by students, they were supported by an expanding and well-educated middle class that had developed a keen political consciousness. On June 29, 1987, with civil disturbances threatening the Olympics, I acted. As chairman of the governing party and its presidential candidate, I issued the Declaration of Democratic Reforms intended to resolve fundamentally the underlying causes of public discontent. The Declaration may have been a grave risk on my part, but I was determined to end the long-standing unrest and transform the authoritarian government structure we had inherited into a genuine democracy.

To be fair, our past presidents managed to develop the economy rapidly, enhance education, and strengthen national security. Through the economic policy of Park Chung Hee and his successors, the nation rid itself of age-old poverty and hunger while protecting itself from renewed aggression. However, there is no denying that we lagged in building a truly democratic society. We concentrated all our resources and energies on economic development, national security, and little else. As our society grew more affluent and sophisticated, however, I realized that authoritarian methods could no longer be used to deal with the needs, demands, and conflicting interests that had surfaced as a result of our accelerated modernization. The Declaration of Democratic Reforms was almost universally accepted. It quickly ended public unrest, and the subsequent changes opened a new era of political and social advancement.

I was able to win the first direct presidential election in 16 years on December 16, 1987, thanks largely to the popularity of the democratic reforms I was instrumental in initiating. The election was close—and I received a plurality rather than a majority—but the margin was decisive. I was inaugurated on February 25, 1988, in the first peaceful transfer of power since the establishment of the Republic in 1948. This put an end to the divisive controversy over the legitimacy of the government that had plagued the nation for decades.

Reforms in Practice. During my past four years as president, my colleagues and I have worked hard to realize the democratic reforms I promised in the Declaration. In doing so, we have achieved a *quiet revolution*. Freedom of the press has been realized. Korea now can boast 87 daily newspapers and about 5,200 magazines, which circulate freely. The National Security Law has been revised to protect the basic rights of citizens. A Constitutional Court has been established and the Covenant on Civil and Political Rights signed. Trade unions have been allowed to organize and function. Local autonomy has been reinstated to bring democracy back to the grass roots.

Elections were held in March 1991 to establish local councils in small cities, counties, and municipal districts. In June they were held in large cities and provinces. Thus just four years after the Declaration, local autonomy was reinstated. There were many who opposed the elections as premature. I firmly believed, however, that government power had to be decentralized to make democracy work. In the large city and provincial council elections, the ruling Democratic Liberal Party (DLP) won 65% of the seats nationwide and 83% in Seoul—traditionally an opposition stronghold. More than any other evidence, this showed the strength of popular support for continued reform with stability.

In January 1990, after a long period of negotiation, I had succeeded in bringing about the merger of the DJP with two opposition parties, the New Democratic Republican Party and the Reunification Democratic Party, to form the DLP. It was indeed unheard of in Korea for opposition parties to merge voluntarily with the ruling party, so this was a momentous event. The necessity for the merger arose out of the National Assembly elections of April 1988. The ruling party won just 42% of the seats, while the three opposition parties secured 55% between them. This resulted in a deadlocked Assembly.

It was extremely difficult for the minority ruling party to pursue its legislative program. I had to find a way out of this predicament. I believe that the merger of the three parties, controversial though it was, made it possible to achieve the political stability necessary for the nation to forge ahead into the 21st century. We improved an undesirable political climate. We also fostered a new force to spearhead the unification effort in the light of a fast-changing international situation.

During the four-year transition to democracy, however, we experienced many difficulties. A radical leftist image opposed democracy per se in favor of North Korean-style "socialism." Many groups selfishly sought to promote their own interests at the expense of others. Unions often struck illegally or used violence to gain their objectives, resulting in a slowdown in production and the weakening of law and order. I take pride in the fact that the Korean people have overcome these and other serious difficulties with forbearance and with a firm belief in democracy.

The problems stemming from democratic reforms have been largely solved. There are now fewer conflicts of interest and a far more orderly political process. I believe that we must now "internalize" democratic values. To this end, I will endeavor to promote dialogue and negotiation to replace confrontation and struggle. I will also seek to ensure continued fair elections next year and thereafter.

Korea's Economic Growth and Development. Rising from the ruins of war, the Korean economy has achieved rapid growth to emerge as the world's 13th largest trader. Because our land is small and our natural endowments are poor, Korea adopted an outward-looking economic development strategy in the early 1960s. Under that strategy, we were able to build the basis for industrialization and develop heavy and chemical industries. As a result, the Korean economy has grown at an average annual rate of more than 3% in real terms during most of the past three decades. Exports were our top priority. To build up our industry for this purpose, we incurred heavy international debt—a debt that has now been largely paid off. The Korean experience has been cited abroad as a model of economic development.

Unfortunately, rapid economic growth cannot be achieved without some unfavorable side effects. In the late 1980s, as the cold war began to slacken, economic blocs based on regional interests began to emerge throughout the world. I realized that a drastic change in our economic policy was called for if the country was to cope effectively with the new international economic order. Upon assuming the presidency, I set four basic goals:

1. To deal with new economic problems resulting from democratization, especially the implementation of local autonomy.

2. To internationalize the economy in line with Korea's increased international stature.

3. To prepare Korea to join the ranks of the industrialized nations.
4. To prepare the economy for eventual unification.

We decided to modify the government-led growth strategy to emphasize private initiative. Thus the nation could maximize its growth potential through free and fair competition—while promoting the more equitable distribution of wealth. Our government has accordingly introduced and implemented bold policy measures. The medical insurance system was extended to cover the entire population. A national pension system has been introduced and large-scale housing construction begun. Intended to create two million residential units so that middle- and low-income families can own their own homes, the housing program is progressing ahead of schedule.

Sound labor-management relations have been encouraged by ensuring the three basic rights to organize, to bargain collectively, and to strike. We are also implementing an independent labor-dispute arbitration system. This I regard as extremely important. On the way is a program designed to spur rural development for more balanced regional growth. For example, we have announced an ambitious project aimed at realizing the economic potential of the nation's west coast region. This is designed specifically to promote bilateral trade between our Republic and China. In addition, the Korean government has taken measures to halt real estate speculation and resolve imbalance in landholdings. For this purpose, the concept of land as a public good has been introduced and applied on an increasingly extensive scale. We are determined that the land speculation so rife among other countries be checked in Korea. The government also reformed various taxes to ensure fairness in the distribution of income.

The year 1991 marks the end of Korea's sixth Five-year Economic and Social Development Plan. When the plans began in 1961, Korea's per capita gross national product (GNP) was hovering about the $100 mark. In 1987, the year before I was inaugurated, per capita GNP registered $3,100. It is expected to reach $6,300 in 1991, with the economy growing at an annual rate of 9.1% during the first half of 1991 after recording growth of 9% in 1990. The rate of unemployment has been held down to 4%.

Our seventh five-year plan begins in 1992. The economy is projected to grow at a stable annual rate of 7%, boosting per capita GNP to $11,000 in 1996, the concluding year of the plan. In that year, Korea's external trade should become the 10th largest in the world. Under the previous five-year plans, Korea built the foundation of accelerated industrialization in the 1960s, developed heavy and chemical industries in the 1970s, and emphasized economic stabilization in the 1980s. The forthcoming plan aims at leading Korea into the ranks of industrialized economies. When policy goals envisaged under the plan are met, Korea will be able to assume an even greater role in the Asia-Pacific economic region, whose importance in the world economy is increasing greatly. Korea then will further increase economic cooperation with late-coming less developed countries, while sharing with them its development experience.

Internationalization and Liberalization. I have a keen interest in internationalizing and liberalizing the Korean economy. Korea is vigorously implementing market-opening and liberalization measures commensurate with its status as the world's 13th largest trade nation, despite the fact that its balance of payments reverted to deficit after four years of surpluses in the latter half of the 1980s. In keeping with promises made to its major trading partners, Korea has steadily taken steps to open its market in the fields of merchandise trade and services. We are also working to strengthen protection of intellectual property rights. No country can afford to tolerate counterfeit or pirate products. Even the market for some agricultural goods has been opened. Further market-opening steps are being taken involving communications, the financial industry, and the capital market.

By January 1991 Korea's import-liberalization rate (rate of imports without prohibitive tariffs) had reached 97.2%. It will rise to 98.5% in 1994. Korea has so notified the General Agreement on Tariffs and Trade. Because of its big lead in economic development, Japan began its market-opening process 20 years before Korea. Yet Tokyo moved so slowly that it was not until January 1991 that its import-liberalization rate finally reached 98.5%. This illustrates the rapidity of Korea's market-opening pace. We feel that the contrast is revealing.

South-North Relations. Korea was liberated from Japanese colonial rule at the end of World War II, but soon the peninsula was divided into southern and northern segments as a result of cold war conflicts. The ravages of the three-year war triggered by the Communist regime in North Korea not only virtually destroyed the infrastructure of the whole country, it also left deep social and personal scars. During the past half century, Koreans in the South and the North—one ethnic family—have been forced to live in a state of complete separation, characterized by confrontation, distrust, and antagonism.

In the second half of the 1980s, the long ideological confrontation between West and East began to thaw. Driven by economic pressures, the socialist countries, including the Soviet Union and China, started policies of reform, external opening, reconciliation, and international cooperation. As the international mood of détente spread, opening a new era, it was necessary for Koreans to move quickly toward a positive response. We began to view Korea's reunification not merely as a lofty national aspiration but as a realistic task that can and must be achieved within the current century. On July 7, 1988, I made a Special Declaration in the Interest of National Self-Esteem, Unification, and Prosperity. In this statement, I made it clear that we would not regard North Korea as our adversary but rather would seek to develop a partnership in the work for unification.

The Declaration started on the family level. We proposed that the South and North allow exchanges of visits between separated relatives and permit Koreans resident abroad to travel freely to both sides. We also proposed that the South and North help find out the fate of separated relatives, locate their addresses, and allow exchanges of mail and visits. We further proposed to initiate trade, which the South would regard as *internal* trade. We made it known that the South would not oppose nonmilitary merchandise trade between North Korea and South Korea's allies and friends. The statement, finally, called for an end to diplomatic rivalry and confrontation between the two parts of Korea. We urged the North to work together with the South to promote the common interests of all Koreans.

On September 11, 1989, we went further. I proposed a "Korean National Community Unification Formula," detailing a step-by-step approach to unification. This formula was based on the principle that we will seek to achieve national unification: peacefully—without the use of military force: independently—on the basis of self-determination; and democratically—according to the free will of the Korean people. Under this formula, after trust has been established through dialogue and exchanges, a South-North summit would be held and a Korean National Community Charter adopted. In the second phase, a Korean Commonwealth would be set up as an interim stage leading to unification. The Commonwealth would promote the peaceful coexistence and prosperity of the South and North. Finally, a constitution of a unified country would be adopted through democratic procedures, and general elections would be held.

The unified Republic thus established would fully guarantee freedoms, human rights, and the pursuit of happiness to all Koreans. Participation of all Koreans and their freedom of expression, however diverse their views, would be guaranteed. The Republic would promote the welfare of all Koreans and safeguard national security while also contributing to the promotion of world peace.

Further, on July 20, 1990, I suggested that we organize a "grand South-North exchange of people." Again we called upon the North to agree to unrestricted, free travel by all Koreans. The offer reflected a willingness to accommodate the North, whose rulers are still trying to ignore the global tide of change. By setting an example, the South wanted to urge the North to join in efforts to build mutual trust. The proposal would have expanded the scope for exchanges of visits beyond separated families to permit free travel by any Korean, regardless of political ideology.

The only shortcut to peaceful unification for such a divided nation is to increase exchanges on a gradual, sustained basis. Inter-Korean exchanges of people and goods are a sure way to develop a sense of mutual trust. German reunification was made possible through continuous conversations, mutual people exchanges, and collaboration between the former two Germanies. The Korean situation differs substantially from the German case. Animosity, deepened by a three-year internecine war, has existed between South and North Korea for a long time. East and West Germany had built up a degree of mutual trust through 20 years of exchanges of visits and bilateral trade. Between South and North Korea there have not even been exchanges of mail.

In July 1990 the South and North exchanged goods. This was the first direct trade ever in 46 years. In August 1990 our Republic passed a Special Act Governing Inter-Korean Exchanges and Cooperation and set up a South-North Korea Cooperation Fund, intended to support inter-Korean exchanges. The volume of South-North trade, direct and indirect, has increased rapidly. It totaled $94 million during the first seven months of 1991, 12 times the amount registered in the preceding year. The total value of South-North trade, direct and indirect, since 1988 is $142 million. Although we have shipped some rice to North Korea, our exports are largely manufactured goods.

Meanwhile, I have endeavored to create an atmosphere conducive to unification by arranging talks and other events. In September 1990 the prime ministers of the South and North met in Seoul for the first time since the division of the country. On Dec. 13, 1991, at the end of the fifth round of South-North Korean prime ministers' talks in Seoul, an Agreement on Reconciliation, Nonaggression, Exchange and Cooperation between the South and the North was signed. Subsequently, on December 18, I declared that "there do not exist any nuclear weapons whatsoever, anywhere in the Republic of Korea." This stripped the North of any excuse to refuse to sign a nuclear safeguard accord and prompted the North to initial, on December 31 at P'anmunjom, a Joint Declaration for a Non-nuclear Korean Peninsula, thereby paving the way for solid peace on the peninsula.

Efforts have also been made to hold cultural and athletic exchanges to create an environment favorable to rapprochement. In October 1990 a group of South Korean musicians went to P'yŏngyang to take part in a traditional music concert for reunification. This was the first time since the division that a private group had obtained permission to make its own arrangements to visit North Korea. The following December a group of North Korean musicians came to Seoul for year-end "unification" concerts.

In April 1991 the first joint South-North athletic team to participate in international competition went to Japan for the world table tennis championships. This was followed in June by a joint soccer team participating in the world junior soccer championships in Portugal. These events were the first results—after 23 years of off-again, on-again sports talks. Such sports exercises can play a significant role in international relations. I recall that the first post-

1949 U.S. relations with China were preceded by Chinese-American table tennis matches in Beijing (Peking).

I am a firm believer myself in the internationalizing effect of sports competition. In fact, I am something of a sports devotee. When I was younger, I played a lot of rugby. Even now I play a good bit of golf and tennis and occasionally swim and water-ski. My work with the Olympic Committee convinced me that friendly sports competition offers a pathway to cooperation—on this peninsula as everywhere else.

The Seoul Olympic Games. "The grandest festival of mankind, transcending the barriers of ideology and social systems." That is indeed an apt description of the 24th Olympic Games held in Seoul in September 1988. The Seoul Olympics brought East and West together for the first time since the 1976 Olympics in Montreal. The two previous Olympics, in Moscow and Los Angeles, had been crippled by international politics, but the Seoul Games brought together more than 13,000 athletes from 160 countries in all regions of the world. This was the largest and most successful Olympic Games ever. It was also the second such event held in Asia, the first having been the 1964 Olympics in Tokyo. Further, the Seoul Olympics highlighted a new phase in international relations and world history, symbolizing the advent of a new era of East-West dialogue and détente. Fittingly, the theme of the opening ceremony was "Beyond All Barriers."

The Seoul Olympics helped to remove the barriers between the socialist countries in Eastern Europe and our Republic. They opened the way to dialogue that led to successful implementation of our Republic's northern diplomacy. All this paved the way for the simultaneous entry of both South and North Korea into the United Nations—helping create an international environment conducive to Korean unification. The Seoul Olympics will be long remembered.

Not least, the Seoul Olympics provided an opportunity for over three billion television viewers across the world to see the real capabilities of the Republic and the Korean people. Bringing off the Games was a feat hardly expected of a country on a small Northeast Asian peninsula that remains divided—a country that survived the harsh repression of colonial rule only to suffer the ravages of war. The new stadiums and parks, the highways, the high-rise office buildings of Seoul were only the background for this picture of our people at work. The Olympic coverage, I must say, was a welcome antidote to the fragmentary coverage, highlighting Korea's student demonstrations, so often aired by foreign TV stations.

The Seoul Olympics changed the status of our Republic in the world community. There are some who say that "the Seoul shock," this eye-opening rediscovery of the Republic of Korea, helped trigger demands for reform in Eastern Europe. In any case, because I was deeply involved in the Seoul

Olympics from the beginning, this event remains an exceptionally moving experience for me personally.

The "Northern Policy." Dismantling the cold war structure in Northeast Asia was the crucial first step in establishing a durable peace on the Korean Peninsula—and unification after that. From that conviction, I determined that our Republic needed to launch a "Northern Policy." Many years ago, Germany's Chancellor Willy Brandt began the Federal Republic's *Ostpoliitik* (Eastern Policy) of greater association with the socialist countries. Ultimately, Chancellor Helmut Kohl realized its triumphant climax with the reunification of East and West Germany. It was high time we Koreans had a Northern Policy of this sort.

I believed that our Northern Policy would inevitably lead North Korea, the greatest menace to peace in the Northeast Asian region, to reconsider its anachronistic posture. Such a transformation is essential if real peace is to be established in the region. Encouraged by the East-West thaw, our government therefore pursued a three-step approach to dealing with Communist countries. The first step was to promote increased exchanges in the nonpolitical and noneconomic fields—culture and sports. The second was to expand economic exchanges and cooperation. The third and final step is to establish normal diplomatic relations.

Spurred by the Seoul Olympics, our Republic's Northern Policy proved a success. In February 1989 Hungary established diplomatic relations with us. Subsequently, all other Eastern European countries followed suit. The Soviet Union normalized diplomatic relations with us in September 1990. After China exchanged trade offices with our Republic, Seoul-Beijing trade and other forms of bilateral economic cooperation expanded rapidly.

The capstone of the Northern Policy was the rapid improvement of relations between the Soviet Union and our Republic. Soviet President Mikhail Gorbachev met me in San Francisco in June 1990, in the first Korea-Soviet summit. This led to the establishment of full diplomatic relations between the two countries in September of that year. In December I paid an official visit to Moscow, an event hardly imagined by my predecessors. President Gorbachev visited Cheju-do, an island off Korea's south coast, in April 1991 to hold talks with me for the third time. It was the first time in history that any Soviet leader had visited the Korean Peninsula, in either the South or the North. Originally, the ties between Russia and Korea were rather close, but all diplomatic relations were discontinued after the Russo-Japanese War broke out in 1904. After World War II the Soviet Union became an adversary. This hostility lasted throughout the cold war era. Now we have not only political relations but also greatly expanded economic exchanges. Our Republic is providing the Soviet Union with economic assistance amounting to $3 billion.

Similarly, China's relations with our Republic were anything but amicable over the past 40 years. Through past centuries, however, China and Korea traditionally had close political and cultural bonds. China, therefore, is a country from which our Republic should not remain aloof. Moreover, China's interest is directly involved in the security of Northeast Asia, particularly the Korean Peninsula. The establishment of normal diplomatic relations between China and our Republic will be in the interest of both countries. Given China's position with regard to North Korea, however, I decided that it was both realistic and necessary for us first to increase nonpolitical exchanges with China. Consequently, our relations with China have improved significantly. The two countries opened trade offices in each other's capital in 1991. Two-way trade with China reached $3,620,000,000 during the first eight months of 1991, an increase of 60% over a year earlier. The expanding economic relations with China should lead eventually to the establishment of diplomatic relations between us. This will contribute greatly to the security of the Northeast Asian region.

Korean-American Relations. With the reshaping of the international order, the global influence of the United States has become far greater than ever before. American decisions on the role the United States will play on the world scene will determine the emergence of a healthy new order in the 21st century. We are naturally concerned about how American policy will affect Northeast Asia.

Our northern diplomacy, which brought so many dramatic changes in our relationships with the socialist countries, was pursued in the closest cooperation with the United States, traditionally our closest ally. I do not intend to neglect this tradition. We in Korea shall continue to work with the United States to ensure political stability as well as economic prosperity for the region. The United States helped us unstintingly in our growth as a democratic country during very trying times—from the establishment of the Republic following World War II through the Korean War and into the rehabilitation of our country. But as our Republic has grown, our relationship has evolved from one-sided dependency to a more equal partnership.

The United States has been the number one market for Korean products over a period of years. In a very real sense it has served as our engine of growth. Trade between Korea and the United States increased to $36.3 billion in 1990. At the same time, Korea has proved itself a major customer for U.S. exports. We are the third largest importer of U.S. agricultural products, for example. Our people, as they grow into a powerful consumer society, have displayed constant interest in American manufacturers. In any such close relationship there is bound to be some friction. In our case we hope we can resolve any problems between us in the same spirit of dialogue that we have used in the past.

In my four years in office, we have held six summit meetings with U.S.

presidents. Again and again I have stressed how important it is to promote the close ties with our old friend, the United States—even as we cultivate new friends around the world. The ties between Korea and the United States go back more than 100 years, to the 1882 Treaty of Peace, Amity, Commerce, and Navigation. I am sure our friendship will continue to evolve and grow in the 21st century.

Entry into the United Nations. One of the most satisfactory results of our northern diplomacy was North Korea's change in attitude in the matter of entry into the United Nations. North Korea's demand for a single UN membership was seen from the first to be unrealistic and self-serving, given the vast political differences between our democracy and that totalitarian state. Even the Soviet Union and China, North Korea's traditional allies, turned their backs on Kim Il Sung's stand. In May 1991 North Korea reversed its position and accepted our Republic's call for the simultaneous but separate entry of South and North Korea into the world organization.

The Republic of Korea has long enjoyed a close association with the United Nations. The UN supervised our first postwar elections, then intervened to help us fight North Korea's invasion. Indeed, the long-standing Korean armistice has been maintained by the United Nations Command. Since 1949 the Republic has submitted applications for UN membership on eight separate occasions. North Korea made a similar bid four times. All were in vain. Because of opposing views held by some permanent members of the UN Security Council, the result of cold war politics, the Republic has had to be content with observer status in the UN for the past 40-odd years—despite its ample qualifications for full membership. It has taken us almost 43 years to move the short distance from an observer's seat to a member's seat. Surely, there can be no more obvious casualty of the cold war.

Our GNP is the world's 15th highest. We have diplomatic relations with 149 countries and have joined 15 UN specialized agencies. We were host to the Olympics. That our country has been left out of the UN is an obvious contradiction of the principle of universality in Article 4 of the UN Charter. Even before becoming a member of the United Nations, we in South Korea contributed a total of $7 million a year to 31 organizations under the UN umbrella. We have taken part in efforts of the world body to maintain world peace. When Iraq invaded Kuwait in 1990, we contributed $500 million in cash and materials to help the war effort of the UN coalition forces. In addition, we provided a medical unit and furnished transport equipment.

I have spoken twice before the United Nations, the first time in 1988, as the head of state of an observer country, the next in September 1991, as the head of state of a member country, when I presented the following three proposals for the two Korean governments to carry out:

1. The two Koreas should replace the fragile armistice with a permanent peace structure.

2. In order to reduce the threat of war on the Korean Peninsula, the two sides should seek to bring about realistic arms reduction, beginning with measures designed to build mutual confidence.

3. The two Koreas should bring an end to the period of mutual isolation. We must open a new era with free exchange of products, information and people.

True, it is painful for us that the South and the North are seated in different chairs, but I believe that we must tolerate this as an inevitable step toward unification. I expect that as members of the UN the two Koreas will be able to take an active part in the various organizations and activities of that body, and thus together we can contribute to the maintenance of world peace and prosperity.

New International Order and Unification. On the eve of the 21st century, the world is going through great upheavals in all spheres of human activity—ideology, politics, economics, social mores, and culture. The cold war political order was once dominated by the strategic rivalry between the two nuclear superpowers. As a new order emerges, we see the growing influence of economic powers: the European Communities (EC) and Japan, as well as the newly industrializing nations. The Industrial Revolution began in Britain and reached its fullest development in the United States. It has evolved into an information revolution in the late 20th century. The tide of these changes is upon us in Korea. We move with it. We will continue to work out our blueprints for the future, to prepare effectively for the 21st century.

I have established a Presidential Commission on the 21st century, composed of specialists in various fields, charged with developing a vision of Korea in the 21st-century world. I have also encouraged a number of government and private research institutes to study how to strengthen our international economic competitiveness so Korea can join the ranks of the advanced industrialized nations in the coming century.

The goal we must pursue in the 21st century is the realization of a prosperous, unified nation that can provide a satisfactory life for all its citizens and contribute actively to the harmony and prosperity of the international community. To provide a satisfactory life, I believe it is essential to create a clean and comfortable environment, ensure sustained economic growth, and enhance public welfare. At the same time, we must continue to build a democratic society, establish sound values, and provide cultural and artistic opportunities.

In light of current world trends and other domestic and international factors, I think unification will be realized in the not too distant future. In pursuing unification, I will adhere to the three principles of self-determination, peace, and democracy. I believe, furthermore, that we must endeavor to cure the pain of national division and achieve unification with a minimal amount of economic and social disorder. The prosperous unified Korea of the 21st century will be a nation that will make active contributions to international harmony and the prosperity of the world community.

The Korean Peninsula, long a hotbed of international conflict, must be turned into a bastion of peace. I believe that the Korean Peninsula—strategically placed between the Asian continent and the Pacific Ocean and between the advanced and less developed worlds—can play a unique and vital role in forging a new world order. Korea is neither a wealthy nor an advanced country. But we have demonstrated to other newly emerging countries that it is indeed possible to pursue economic and political development simultaneously. In this sense, Korea is a good model for those interested in developing both a market economy and a democratic system of government. Korea must be a bridge between the advanced and emerging countries, while striving to become advanced itself.

Asia will play an ever more important part in the 21st century, which is predicted to be an Asia-Pacific Era. For example, in 1989 America's trade with Asia totaled $314 billion, about 33% larger than that across the Atlantic. Already in 1979 the Pacific Rim countries, as a group, had become a larger trading partner for the United States than Europe. And this trend is expected to continue. Many specialists predict that the weight of the Asia-Pacific region in the world economy will increase because of the high rates of growth in the Association of Southeast Asian Nations member countries and in the newly industrializing countries, including Korea, as well as the abundant material and human resources in the region. If the Asia-Pacific region is to play an important role in the international community, as it should, all the countries in the region will have to exert joint efforts to promote the prosperity of all by integrating or complementing their economic potentials and promoting political and cultural ties. Korea will spare no effort to this end.

Korea's Patient President (By Frank B. Gibney)

The man who presided over Korea's democratic transition is one of those people who seem to appear suddenly on a world stage with a previously unsuspected gift for handling difficult political situations. A graduate of the Korean Military Academy, in the same class as the disgraced former president Chun Doo Hwan, he was first known as Chun's faithful supporter. After retirement from the Army as a four-star general, he entered Chun's Cabinet as minister without portfolio for political affairs, then in 1982 as the Republic's first minister for sports, with the mission of getting the 1988 Olympics for South Korea. His years of international lobbying, first as a member of government and later as the president of the Seoul Olympic Organizing

Committee, proved surprisingly successful. That the Olympics came off in Korea was really his personal triumph.

Even more surprising was Roh's announcement in June 1987, as the ruling party's presidential candidate, calling for drastic political reform.

"The tides of history," Roh told me, "brought me to this position." At the time we met, in September 1991, in the reception chamber of the newly opened presidential office at Chung Wa Dae—the Blue House (literally, "the house with the blue-tiled roof")—he had been three and a half years in office. He speaks quietly, but with assurance and a trace of dry wit showing. His 1987 decision, he was quick to say, "was not something that happened overnight. Of course, my thinking was influenced by outside events. But I had been pondering this kind of thing for a long time. The decision could not have come by accident."

Roh, it is said, is the only patient man in Korean politics. In a country whose explosive politicians have traditionally short fuses, he is a planner who can wait for results to happen. In January 1990 he again surprised the country with the announcement of a merger between his own majority party and two major opposition parties, led by Kim Young Sam and Kim Jong Pil, both of them his election opponents in 1987. The new majority Democratic Liberal Party—all too readily compared with its Liberal-Democratic counterpart in Japan—came into being only after two years of behind-the-scenes negotiations. Neither of the two parties negotiated with knew that the other was involved. In neither was the outlook promising. "When we came to him from time to time and said the outlook was hopeless," one of his political aides recalled, "he would only say, 'Go back and keep at it. Just call them up again.' Once he has set an objective, he never deviates from it."

One objective successfully attained is his "Northern Policy," a three-year effort to build bridges with the Soviet Union, the People's Republic of China, and other Communist (or once-Communist) countries. This diplomacy grew logically out of his experience with the 1988 Olympics, in which Chinese and Soviet athletes—despite North Korea's opposition—were conspicuous by their presence. "Going back over those years," Roh said, "as I went around the world talking to people of different countries, I found that others were as persuaded as I was that harmony is the most important modern political need."

By the close of the eighties, both China and the Soviet Union had already put aside ideology to develop multibillion-dollar trade relations with South Korea, whose manufactures are well suited to their development needs. In June 1990 Roh made history with his summit meeting with Soviet President Mikhail Gorbachev in San Francisco, paving the way for the opening of formal diplomatic relations between their countries. In September 1991 the Republic of Korea was finally admitted to the United Nations, along with Communist North Korea, in the separate two-country formula that the South had long advocated. Double admission was made possible when Beijing refused to veto South Korea's entry, removing the last stumbling block.

In the antechamber outside Roh's reception room hangs a large framed scroll, written in classic Korean Hangul calligraphy, with the headline "Now Let's Open the Way to P'yŏngyang." The statement below it is Roh's. "Once the road to Moscow is wider open," it reads, "the way to Pyongyang will be opened in a matter of time. Now there is nothing which blocks our advance into this wide world." This expresses the hope, as Roh later put it in his September 1991 address to the UN General Assembly, that the "two Koreas . . . [will] open a new era with free exchange of products, information and people."

In December 1991 this new era seemed suddenly nearer, as the prime ministers of South and North Korea signed in Seoul an unprecedented agreement on "reconciliation and nonaggression," including promises for economic cooperation, reopening communications and transportation lines, and free travel between the two Koreas.

There remained two practical obstacles to realizing these promises. The first is the character of Kim Il Sung's regime. There is a world of difference between Roh's emerging democracy and Kim's personalized Communism, where the enforced worship of the "Great Leader" and his son and political heir, Kim Jong Il ("Beloved Leader"), has become a virtual religion.

The other obstacle to early reunification is economic. Its foreign debt payments defaulted, its food supplies dwindling, and its former Communist allies, China and the Soviet Union, now demanding hard currency in their trade, the Democratic People's Republic of Korea is virtually bankrupt. To accommodate its people in any kind of economic union, experts reckon, would cost South Korea a staggering $400 billion—dwarfing the amounts needed to rehabilitate East Germany. So here Roh's gradual approach is necessity.

In working out domestic policies, Roh often has to act more swiftly. When a student activist was killed in a violent demonstration in 1991, he dismissed his interior minister—a reaction inconceivable under his predecessors. Earlier, his move toward democratization in 1987 had brought on some crisis of its own. In the three years following, now that unions were free to organize and strike, the country experienced some 7,000 labor-management disputes, many of them violent. Business and political corruption cases still abound, although now under the public scrutiny of an aroused press. Land prices skyrocketed as they had in Japan; Roh has not yet succeeded in his efforts to make the huge *chaebol* business conglomerates disgorge more of their preempted land for the public's use.

On occasion Roh has himself moved harshly against dissent, recalling less happy times. Nonetheless, he has kept the Army in its barracks. "Civilization" of the government is almost complete. More importantly, this former general has institutionalized a democratic succession process.

"It's true," he told me, "that people think of the military as being very regimented, apart from the mainstream of civilian life. That's not necessarily so in Korea's case. When our Military Academy was founded, our textbooks were translations of the West Point textbooks—at first many of the faculty were American officers. Our cadets were one of the first groups in Korea to study Western institutions this thoroughly. Indeed it was the army which led the modernization of the civilian sector in this country. Outsiders may think of military organizations as intrinsically nondemocratic in nature, but we received many democratic elements as part of our education."

Talking to this thoughtful, quietly determined man, my mind went back 40 years to the time I last interviewed the Republic of Korea's first president, Syngman Rhee, in 1950, and to 1970, when I talked to President Park Chung Hee at an older building in the same Blue House compound. Both Rhee and Park were incorrigible autocrats. The old man, a classic politician in exile, had learned little from his American education, except to use the talk and trappings of democracy, quite cleverly, as a public relations facade. Park Chung Hee, it is true, pulled Korea up by its economic bootstraps. But as a graduate of the Japanese Military Academy in prewar days, Park clearly regarded democracy as a nuisance, to be invoked principally when the early U.S. aid programs seemed threatened.

Roh Tae Woo had gone to a different school, and he has evidently learned far more than some of his classmates from that experience. He had gone out to meet statesmen and business leaders of vastly differing systems and traditions throughout the world. He has learned from that experience also. In the new world of the nineties, both he and his country have a great deal to contribute.

Part II

TOWARD REUNIFICATION OF THE NATION

10.

Riding the Trends of History; Interview, *Newsweek* Magazine, June 18, 1990

Newsweek's Tokyo bureau chief Bradley Martin accompanied President Roh Tae Woo on his flight to meet Mikhail Gorbachev in San Francisco and on to Washington for a session with President George Bush. Martin interviewed Roh in Washington. Excerpts:

Martin: *What are the chances that North Korea's anger over your meeting with Mikhail Gorbachev will drive it to some drastic military response?*

President: I've made it quite clear that we do not want the North Koreans to be further isolated. So I do not expect North Korea to take any drastic military actions. But on the very remote chance that something might happen, we have taken all precautionary measures and we'll try to maintain a watertight security posture. I think the North Koreans will experience some shock, but in the future they will recover their reason. Eventually they will follow the trends of history.

Martin: *South Korean-Soviet détente is likely to fuel demands within the United States to withdraw American troops from the South, on the grounds that the situation is less dangerous than before and the troops therefore are no longer needed. What do you think of that argument?*
President: I can understand that such sentiment will grow in the United States, but the fact is that (South) Korean-Soviet détente does not necessarily mean changes in North Korea. Until North Korea abandons its military scheme for conquest of the whole country, and until North Korea's military superiority is corrected, there will be obvious danger. Under these circumstances a drastic reduction of U.S. troops or a complete withdrawal from Korea would be inadvisable.

Martin: *What happens if those conditions are met and the Americans do go home? Do you worry about some other regional power–the Soviet Union, China or Japan-achieving hegemony in the Far East?*

President: We have to think about that. We have to be careful about that and we have to learn from the lessons of history. Look at the post-World War II period when America withdrew. There was a vacuum and (the Korean War) resulted from that vacuum. Although there will be some détente and some improvement of the security situation, I hope and trust that the United States in the future will maintain its necessary presence.

Martin: *Now that South Korea and the Soviet Union are drawing closer together, there are calls for the United States, in reciprocal fashion, to move closer to North Korea. Do you favor this?*

President: In principle, I have no objection to that, but there are some absolutely essential preconditions. North Korea has maintained a very hostile attitude toward the South. On the Korean Peninsula it has maintained an enormous military, deployed offensively, and has always taken a highly confrontational posture. And internationally the North has been engaging in various terrorist and subversive activities. If North Korea abandons such activities and attitudes, and if there is true openness and reform in North Korea, the relationship of the United States . . . with North Korea can improve.

Martin: *You said in San Francisco that you had asked President Gorbachev to help persuade North Korea to reduce its offensive military posture and begin talks with the South on arms control. Are you specifically asking that the Soviets use their leverage as suppliers of military and economic aid to the North, for example, by withholding or threatening to withhold such aid? Realisticallly, how much can Moscow do?*

President: There wasn't any detailed discussion on this point in my meeting with President Gorbachev. But we know that North Korea depends a lot on Soviet supplies for its military equipment, and in that respect the Soviet Union has substantial leverage on North Korea. On the economic side, I think because of the economic difficulties that the Soviets themselves are undergoing, their influence will be limited.

Martin: *It seems that Gorbachev wanted to downplay your meeting, in publicity terms, in order to avoid overly antagonizing North Korea. Do you think he was right to do that?*

President: Yes, I can understand how Mr. Gorbachev feels about that. He wanted to reduce the shock that North Korea would experience, and at the same time he wanted to achieve what was in his mind.

Martin: *You suggested at your San Francisco press conference that the emergence of a more flexible and realistic group in P'yŏngyang could move North Korea* *toward the great openness you hope for. Does this mean you believe change won't come until President Kim II Sung is out of power?*

President: As you know, Kim II Sung has ruled North Korea single-handedly for the past 42 years. Under those circumstances, there is little chance that the Gorbachevian movement for reform and openness will affect the North Korean attitude in the near future. But in this modern age no country can erect watertight walls against the outside world. Something is bound to seep into even that very tight isolation. We don't know when it will happen. But eventually North Korea will start to crack and will start to open up. We cannot be too optimistic about this, but once Kim II Sung is out of the picture, whoever succeeds him will be quite different.

11.

Special Announcement on Major Inter-Korean Exchange Visits, Seoul, July 20, 1990

My fellow Koreans at home and abroad,

The world today is going through a period of fundamental transformation: The Cold War is receding and a new order of international reconciliation is emerging. At this juncture, and in my efforts to bring about early a peaceful unification of Korea, I would like to announce a major decision aimed at facilitating the exchange of our nationals between the South and the North.

In my special policy declaration of July 7, 1988, I proposed that the South and the North should end confrontational relations and should instead forge a cooperative partnership. On October 18 of that year, I proposed before the United Nations General Assembly that for peace and unification the two Koreas should lift all barriers between them and permit a free flow of people and goods across the dividing line on the Korean Peninsula.

Two years have since elapsed, and the old world order is undergoing a profound transformation. New tidal waves of openness and reconciliation have torn away the Iron Curtain separating the East and the West and are now shaping a new order. Nations have begun to cooperate with each other regardless of ideological and political differences. The tides of reform have brought down the Berlin Wall and are unifying West and East Germany.

The time has come to end Cold War confrontation and the territorial division on the Korean Peninsula. Korea must not remain the world's only land still partitioned by Cold War politics. The reality that Koreans in the South and the North are still unable to visit each other is a state of affairs that should not be allowed to continue, if for reasons of national self-respect of a proud people with a rich cultural heritage.

If we cant to make the 21st century an era of glory for our nation, we must achieve peaceful unification within this century. The South as well as the North should take courageous measures and necessary steps to re-unite our people.

On August 15 this year, we will mark the 45th anniversary of our national liberation. And so, I hereby proclaim the five-day span around this day a period of grand inter-Korean exchange visits. For five continuous days beginning on August 13th, we will keep Panmunjom open and will accept our brethren from the North without restrictions. We will guarantee complete freedom for anyone from the North to visit freely any place in the South and meet anyone whom they choose. We will also provide all possible conveniences to our brethren visiting the South and will, if necesssary, furnish room and board.

We will also permit our citizens to visit North Korea through Panmunjom, without restrictions. We will guarantee our North Korean brethren visiting the South personal safety and a safe return. We expect North Korea to guarantee the same.

I hope that North Korea will open not only the northern portion of Panmunjom, but its entire territory as well and permit people from the South to travel freely throughout the North. I also hope that the North will accept without restrictions their brethren from the South who wish to visit North Korea.

If we succeed in such a free exchange on Liberation Day this year, we should be able to permit mutual visits on and around such national holidays as Ch'usok (The Harvest Moon Festival), Solnal (Lunar New Year's Day), and Hanshik (a day in early April set aside for visits to ancestral graves). We should build upon such exchanges around shared holidays to clear the way for free interchange throughout the year. Mutual visits and exchanges between our compatriots in the South and the North are an indispensable step toward reunification.

On January 1st of this year, President Kim Il-sung of North Korea proposed that South and North Korean societies be completely opened and free travel be allowed between the two parts of Korea. Consequently, I believe that there is no obstacle in realizing an exchange of our compatriots and in fully opening the South and the North on Liberation Day this year. Even if North Korea is not prepared to agree with us this time for some unavoidable reasons, we will go ahead and one-sidedly open our society to our North Korean brethren, who wish to visit the South.

In addition, we will soon permit foreigners to travel freely between South and North Korea through Panmunjom. The government will take all necessary steps and make all necessary preparations to successfully implement the exchange visits.

Fellow Koreans,
It is time that the South and the North exerted genuine efforts to unite the Korean people by transcending ideological and political differences. The 21st

century would truly be a magnificent and great age if only the country were unified and the 70 million Koreans allowed to come together again. With this vision, let us all endeavor to fulfill our national aspirations.

Thank you.

12.

Commemorative Address on the 45th Anniversary of the National Independence Day, Independence Hall, August 15, 1990

My fellow Koreans at home and abroad, distinguished guests, ladies and gentlemen,

Today, we celebrate the 45th anniversary of our national independence. The 20th century, a century that has been checkered by periods of anguish and hope, is coming to a close. We look forward to the 21st century with new hopes and new aspirations.

Today is the first Independence Day of the 1990s, and we greet it with the determination to build within the decade the proud homeland that our patriotic forefathers dreamed of. We are resolved to end within this century the history of trials that the Korean people have had to endure. We must usher in a new century of glory during which our brethren will live in freedom and prosperity in a single homeland, thereby enabling us to contribute to the peace and prosperity of all mankind.

This year also marks the 80th anniversary of that shameful year when we lost our national sovereignty because we were too weak to defend ourselves. Moreover, this year is the 45th anniversary of the painful national division and the 40th anniversary of the outbreak of the Korean War.

Those national tragedies are an indication of the hardships we have had to endure during the first half of the 20th century. And yet, even during the dismal days of foreign occupation, our national ethos lived on. The spirit of our people, presumably tempered by those trials, is stronger today and burns more brightly than ever before.

Braving all manner of oppression and repression, a great number of our forefathers sacrificed their lives in their courageous and relentless struggle at home and abroad for the cause of freedom and national independence. Today, we pay our deepest homage to our patriotic forefathers who devoted their lives in the cause of our nation.

Fellow Koreans,

In the second of half this century, the nation stood up in an amazing outburst of strength, putting an end to the dark history, and produced a number of great accomplishments. The perennial "spring hunger" that used to precede the barley harvest in early spring is now a distant memory. We have transformed an impoverished nation of farmers into a prosperous industrial powerhouse within a single generation.

The volume of our external trade reached some 130 billion dollars a year, which will also serve as a significant contribution to world economic development. The days when most Koreans despaired for the lack of education and were depressed by an overriding sense of defeatism are over. Burning with a zeal for better education and greater achievements, our people today are brimming with a sense of self-confidence and a "can-do" spirit.

No one today will regard Koreans as timid or weak. The nation is emerging as a key actor on the global stage. We hosted a most magnificent festival of global harmoney, even though we live in a divided land which is still threatened by the danger of renewed war. The Seoul Olympics provided a window through which the world saw the dynamic pulse of development in Korea today and marvelled at our achievements and capabilities.

An even greater prize, however, would be the introduction of an era of genuine democracy. Together we are now marching towards an advanced society in which freedom and affluence flourish together.

Fellow citizens,

A broad avenue of freedom has opened for us. We have also paved a road to prosperity. Our people are working to the best of their abilities in their respective fields with high hopes of building an affluent nation in which generation after generation shall live in peace and prosperity.

The paramount national goal then is to unify our divided land before the end of the 20th century. National division has brought suffering and pain seldom found elsewhere in world history.

Today, however, the Cold War, which divided our land and separated our people, is now drawing to an end. The powerful current of freedom, prosperity, and human dignity is knocking down the walls of isolation and repression. This movement toward openness and reform represents an inexorable course of history. The fact that the divided Germanies are about to be fully reunified is testimony to the momentous changes now sweeping the world.

We, too, must open a new era of reconciliation and cooperation between the southern and northern halves of the Korean Peninsula. We must initiate and maintain a process of integrating our divided people into a single national community. Korea must not be allowed to remain the only country on earth still divided by the now defunct Cold War. Although division was inflicted on us by others, we must overcome the division through our own independent national resolve and capabilities. There no longer exist any external constraints to inter-Korean reconciliation and unity. Both the East and the West support our endeavors to transform division and confrontation into a durable peace based on the ideals of co-existence and co-prosperity. The Republic of Korea-Soviet Union summit meeting in June of this year, which represented the consummate progress in our northern policy, is an example of the kinds of change that can be expected of on the Korean Peninsula. We can tell from a falling leaf that autumn has arrived. Likewise, signs are appearing that the Korean situation is headed toward a considerable change. I am confident that the next four to five years will see a decisive movement in the direction of unification.

Fellow Koreans,
For almost 40 years, the armistice line dividing our land and people has made it impossible to exchange even a single letter or telephone call across the line, let alone visits. The many calls for reconciliation and unification would amount to a subterfuge unless actions are in fact taken towards resolving the South-North division. In today's open world, we should be able to go anywhere on this planet.

That parents and children, brothers and sisters should be allowed to get together is a fundamental human right. It should transcend ideological and political considerations, which have so long divided South and North. Members of separated families have been denied this basic human need over the past forty years, and find themselves running out of time as they grow old. There should not be any further delay in fulfilling their fervent wish to see their loved ones once again and revisit their places of birth while they are still able to do so.

In response to the ardent yearning of our people in both the South and the North, I announced on July 20th steps for unrestricted inter-Korean exchange visits, especially the opening of the armistice line during the period around this Liberation Day. I believe such exchanges could also contribute to our goal of national integration. It is truly regrettable that the North Korean authorities chose to persist in their preposterous arguments and conditions to block inter-Korean travel.

Free travel between the South and the North is a necessary step toward unification. Accordingly, we will continue to insist on inter-Korean exchanges of people. We will make all necessary preparations to enable citizens from the two parts of Korea to travel freely during any period agreeable to the North, be it the coming Ch'usok (Harvest Moon Festival), Christmas, or New Year's holidays.

We have opened avenues for exchanges of visits and goods even with countries with different ideologies and political systems and are building closer ties of cooperation with them. Therefore, there cannot possibly be any justification or sufficient reason for refusing to initiate and expand exchanges and cooperation between our own people in the South and the North. Without exchanges, it will not be possible to bridge the gap of mistrust and hostility and build confidence.

Fellow citizens,
Through dialogue with North Korea, we will continue to work with patience and good faith to realize exchanges. It would also be possible to convert the structure of South-North military confrontation into a system of peace through mutual trust and dialogue. We are fully prepared to discuss with the North any and all issues, including political and military questions.

I am convinced that the time has come for the responsible authorities of the South and North to hold talks on an entire range of issues, from the joint renunciation of the use of military force to the signing of a nonagression pact, and from the replacement of the present armistice agreement with a peace agreement to the establishment of permanent representative offices in Seoul and P'yŏngyang. In particular, we are willing to discuss earnestly the issue of arms control in our efforts to eliminate threats of war on the Korean Peninsula, end South-North confrontation, and usher in an era of national reconciliation. I hope that substantive progress will be made in our dialogue at the high-level inter-Korean meeting scheduled for next month. It is also hoped that it will lead to an early South-North summit meeting.

Fellow citizens,
The day of unification that will bring the people in the South and North together under one roof will not come of its own accord. To achieve unification, we must pool all our energies, wisdom, patience, and capabilities. Let us all work with even greater dedication to further augment the prosperity needed to attain unification. Through the united efforts of citizens from all walks of life, we must positively deal with the swift changes now occurring in the world with a view to clearing the way for unification.

A bright future is drawing closer for our 70 million brethren. Our dark past marked by oppression, trials, division, and confrontation is now fading away into history. A recent popular song describes our aspirations as making Korea "a land brimming with freedom, equality, peace, and happiness." I believe it will become a reality within this century as long as we work hard toward that goal.

Let us all rally together to forge an era of unification.
Thank you.

13.

Remarks at the Dinner in Honor of President Richard von Weizsaecker of the Federal Republic of Germany, Seoul, February 25, 1991

Your Excellencies President and Mrs. Richard von Weizsaecker, distinguished guests.

I join the entire Korean people in heartily welcoming Your Excellencies and your delegation to the Republic of Korea. It is a great pleasure to share this evening with you here at Chong Wa Dae.

I wish to take this opportunity to congratulate you once again on your assumption of the first presidency of unified Germany on October 3 last year. You are the first head of a unified German state to visit our country in the more than a century of friendly relations between Korea and Germany.

I remember with gratitude the warm hospitality that Your Excellencies accorded me when I visited your country in November 1989 and also the friendship that the German people showed me at that time. I vividly recall my excitement on setting foot in your great country only 10 days after the Berlin Wall was brought down by the collective aspirations of Germans for freedom amid waves of momentous change sweeping Europe. The great feat of German unification was accomplished last October, less than a year hence.

That event has opened a new chapter in world history in which reason shall prevail. The Korean people have watched this event with envy and have been inspired with new hope. Following the conclusion of World War II, both Korea and Germany suffered the pains of territorial division imposed on them by others and together experienced the traumas of the Cold War.

Germany has been unified peacefully, without going through deadly confrontation and bloody conflict between compatriots in the two parts of its land. It was a triumph of the values of human dignity, freedom, democracy and pluralism. It has brought to reality the ideal that Your Excellency had outlined in a speech in April 1989, when you said:

"It is imperative to replace confrontation with cooperation, to remove separation by frontiers and to thus provide the dignity and rights of man with the respect to which they are entitled."

I pay respects to you for the insight and leadership with which you presented such a vision of German unification and spearheaded the efforts to achieve it.

I believe German unification has laid the cornerstone for the common European house as envisioned in the Paris Charter. Along with democratic reforms now under way in the Soviet Union and Eastern Europe, the German unification is certain to help shape a more peaceful and cooperative world.

Your Excellency,

The prevailing winds of world-wide reconciliation are now blowing eastward. This is illustrated by the fact that the Republic of Korea has established full diplomatic relations with virtually all East European countries including the Soviet Union and is developing new ties of friendship and cooperation with them. Korea and China also have established trade offices in each other's capital.

All the same, however, Korea still remains the only land on earth divided by the Cold War. We are resolved to do everything in our power to end the outmoded Cold War confrontation in our land. It must be a natural course of history that brethren in South and North Korea who have lived as a single nation for more than 1,300 years should seek to form a national community by pursuing a broad avenue of exchanges and cooperation.

We are determined to seek and develop such inter-Korean relations with the goal of attaining a peaceful and democratic unification. Last year, prime ministers of the South and the North held talks for the first time since the land was divided in 1945. In fact, three rounds of the high-level talks were held alternately in Seoul and P'yŏngyang. Cultural and athletic exchanges have also taken place, though on a very limited scale.

And yet, the Demilitarized Zone running across the Korean Peninsula still remains frozen. Relatives separated by the dividing line are still unable to exchange a single letter or a single phone call and have no way of knowing where their loved ones live and whether they are still alive.

We will tirelessly pursue dialogue to achieve inter-Korean reconciliation. The peaceful and democratic unification of Germany inspires us with courage to seek that goal. I am convinced that just as unified Germany is underpinning European peace, so will the unification of the Korean Peninsula bolster peace in the Asia-Pacific region.

Your Excellency,

Even though Germany is geographically separated from us, it is our old friend and a close neighbor, Germany's legal system, institutions, scholarship and arts have had a profound influence on Korea during the early period of our modernization and things German have become an integral part of our way of thinking and way of life. Numerous Koreans enjoy German music and literature and are also fascinated by the Bundesliga soccer games. More than 600,000 Korean high school students are learning German as their second foreign language. On the college level, 10,000 students in 33 universities are majoring in German language and literature. Germany is our third largest trading partner, with two-way trade exceeding $6 billion last year.

I am sure that the "Technogerma" exhibitions being held in Seoul under your patronage will significantly contribute to the furtherance of Korean-German understanding and friendship, as well as to boosting bilateral economic and technological cooperation.

Korea and Germany are pursuing common ideals. Having experienced repressions of freedom and human rights, the Korean people are determined to bring about an era of genuine democracy and uphold the values of freedom.

An Oriental sage said, "Is it not a pleasure to have a friend visit from afar?" Today, I welcome Your Excellency in that spirit. We pledge anew that our two nations are committed to the development of a partnership for peace and prosperity through even stronger ties of friendship and cooperation.

Distinguished guests,

Please join me in toasting the good health and well-being of Their Excellencies President and Mrs. von Weizsaecker, the unlimited development of the Federal Republic of Germany and the everlasting friendship between our two nations.

Thank you.

14.

Interview with CNN Television News, September 22, 1991

MIKE CHINOY: On the Korean Peninsula, the Cold War is not yet over, despite the collapse of communism almost everywhere else. Communist North Korea is believed to be developing a nuclear capability now. 40,000 U.S. troops still guard South Korea.

Following the upheaval in the Soviet Union, will this last East-West flash point now move towards peace? If Germany can be reunified, why not North and South Korea?

From the presidential residence in Seoul, South Korea, this is a special edition of "Newsmaker Sunday." I'm Mike Chinoy, and my guest today for a rare television interview is the president of South Korea, Roh Tae Woo.

For almost half a century, the Korean Peninsula has been on the front line of the Cold War. Even today, South Korea troops, backed by 40,000 U.S. soldiers stand eyeball to eyeball with the massive military machine of communist North Korea.

But in recent years there have been the beginnings of a rapprochement between these two bitter enemies, the austere, communist North, dominated by its Stalinist-style dictator, Kim Il Sung, and the booming, capitalist South. Its democratically elected president Roh Tae Woo has been the primary architect of the thaw.

Since taking office four years ago, Roh has made a deliberate attempt, first to cultivate North Korea's longtime friends, the Soviet Union and China, and then to open direct contacts with North Korea itself. One result, the admission of both Koreas to full United Nations membership this past week. And that's not all.

FORMER U.S. AMBASSADOR TO SOUTH KOREA JAMES LILLEY: They're now talking to each other, and I think there's been considerable progress over the last couple of years. That's fine, but you've got an awful lot of work to do. You've got to reduce mutual suspicion, hostility. There's an awful lot of work to be done.

MR. CHINOY: But, to many South Koreans, the opening to the North and the example of Germany have awakened long dormant dreams of unification, prompting demonstrations, even riots, demands that President Roh move faster to develop relations with P'yŏngyang.

The violence has been a blot on the otherwise impressive record of economic and political development that has marked Roh's tenure, although critics say he hasn't moved swiftly enough to erase the legacy of South Korea's years of military rule.

KIM DAE-JUNG: There's no freedom of organization of trade unions. No freedom of demonstrations or assembly. At the moment there are more than 1,600 political prisoners in prison.

MR. CHINOY: Still, the political landscape over which Roh has presided is vastly different today than when the South Korean president took office in 1987, and he is in no small measure responsible for the change.

MR. CHINOY: *President Roh, thank you for joining us on "Newsmaker Sunday." As one of the frontline countries in the Cold War for many years, what's your assessment of how the collapse of communism in the Soviet Union will affect the situation here in the Korean Peninsula, especially in view of the fact that Mikhail Gorbachev, whose power has now been considerably diminished, has been seen by man as a restraining force on North Korean leader Kim Il Sung.*

PRESIDENT ROH (through interpreter): To tell you the conclusion first, I believe the political development and evolution of the Soviet society will have a very positive impact on the Korean Peninsula itself. The North Korean society right now perhaps will feel a sense of crisis, because the collapse of the communist system in the Soviet Union and elsewhere might have adverse repercussions on North Korea.

But in the long term, and now that the communist background has collapsed behind North Korea, I believe it is inevitable for North Korea to open its doors to the free world.

As we all know, North Korea maintains a very rigid system. But in the near future I am firmly convinced that favorable developments will unfold in the Northeast Asian region.

MR. CHINOY: *Both Koreas have just been admitted to full membership in the United Nations, and you yourself are going to be speaking at the U.N. shortly. What impact do you think this will have on the situation here in Korea, both in the immediate term and especially in terms of the long term prospects for reunification?*

PRESIDENT ROH (through interpreter): The entry of South and North

Korea to the United Nations will have positive impact toward our aspirations for unification, and entry itself is an essential interim step toward achievement of national unity.

The two Koreas have been maintaining a confrontational and rivalrous relationship outside the United Nations framework. But now that we are members of the United Nations which pursues peace and prosperity of all mankind, I believe the Cold War system and confrontation on the Korean Peninsula will proceed to a relationship of cooperation and mutual trust, and that, I believe, would be another step toward realization of Korean unification.

MR. CHINOY: *Your admittance to the U.N. is only the latest in a series of achievements that South Korea has scored on the diplomatic front in recent years as part of a strategy which you designed to improve South Korea's international position, and try and break the stalemate on the Peninsula. That strategy has included major openings, both to the Soviet Union and to China and to the former communist countries of Eastern Europe. Can you give us some idea about the basis of your thinking, and the evolution of that strategy which has had such an important impact on the situation?*

PRESIDENT ROH (through interpreter): The main purpose of our entry into the United Nations was because North and South Korea have been maintaining a relationship that is confrontational and very tense over the past half century, and this, I believe, has been a period of misfortune for the entire Korean people.

Now, Koreans have been living together for a long time, and for the homogeneous Korean nation to pursue unification is only natural and perhaps inevitable.

The Republic of Korea has pursued northern diplomacy, which is to seek friendship and cooperation with North Korea's friends and allies, because we tried to maintain contact and dialogue with North Korea in the past several years without much substantive results.

Consequently, by pursuing a friendly and cooperative relationship with North Korea's friends we wanted North Korea's friends and allies to persuade North Korea and promote cooperative and friendly relationship with the Republic of Korea.

In so doing, we have been successful to establish relationship with these countries, and I believe the 1988 Seoul Olympics has provided a turning point. And today, as we become members of the United Nations, I'm very satisfied with the results of northern diplomacy.

MR. CHINOY: *We have to take a break now, but we'll be back in a moment.*

(Announcements)

MR. CHINOY: *Welcome back to "Newsmaker Sunday." I'm Mike Chinoy in Seoul, South Korea, and with me is Roh Tae Woo, the president of South Korea.*

President Roh, the North Koreans have developed a nuclear reactor which they have so far refused to allow international inspectors to look at. How concerned are you about North Korea's emerging nuclear capability, especially in view of the fact that North Korean leader Kim Il Sung is very elderly, and will no longer be on the scene, and there may well be some instability or dramatic changes in North Korea after he departs the scene?

PRESIDENT ROH (through interpreter): The North Korean attempt to develop nuclear weapons is a source of grave concern for all of us. The previous North Korean behavior pattern indicates that it is nation of military adventurism and it maintains enormous military forces right now on the Korean Peninsula.

Consequently, we cannot be assured of our safety and North Korea might launch any adventurous actions.

The North Korean development of nuclear devices will pose threats, not only to the Republic of Korea, but to China and Japan as well. Therefore, North Korea should immediately and unconditionally sign the nuclear safeguards treaty with the International Atomic Energy Administration, and submit all its nuclear material and nuclear-related facilities for international inspection.

MR. CHINOY: *I've been to North Korea. I was there two years ago, and it struck me as a very brittle kind of place, with a very rigid government and a very sullen population. The man who's ruled North Korea for the past several decades is going to die soon. He's eighty now. Can I ask you in a little bit more detail what you foresee happening in North Korea after Kim Il Sung's death? Do you see positive change or trouble?*

PRESIDENT ROH (through interpreter): I understand there are two schools of thought, and many experts analyze and anticipate the passing of Kim Il Sung and subsequent developments in North Korea. One school anticipates that as soon as Kim Il Sung passes from the scene, North Korea will undergo a rapid transformation and perhaps even rather unfortunate bloody developments in North Korea.

The other school anticipates that because the North Korean system has been maintained so long under rigid control, even after Kim Il Sung passes, the system might be able to maintain for some time.

Now, personally, I believe there are both possibilities. What the Republic of Korea wants for North Korea is a smooth transition to democracy, even if it means time is required, and we do not want any violence and bloodshed on the part of North Korea.

MR. CHINOY: *And you want to pursue this gradual policy of slowly building contact between the South and the North?*

PRESIDENT ROH (through interpreter): Of course, the entire Korean people want to achieve unification in the earliest possible date. However, it is absolutely essential that we achieve unification without incurring any unfortunate turn of events in the process, and we should speed up the process but prudently. And I believe this is the best route to our national unification.

MR. CHINOY: *In view of the dramatic changes that have taken place around the world, and especially in the Soviet Union, what role do you see for the United States now in the Korean Peninsula, and specifically is there still a need for the U.S. to keep 40,000 troops here?*

PRESIDENT ROH (through interpreter): As you know, the Soviet Union, as well as the countries in Central and Eastern Europe have undergone tremendous change in recent years. And in these changes, I believe the United States has played a very important role.

The U.S. posture of sufficient strength and peace through strength has played a very important and critical role. The U.S. contribution toward NATO and other activities in Europe, I believe, has contributed toward the transformation of these societies.

Speaking of Northeast Asia and the Cold War structure, I believe that structure has only begun to change in recent years, and for the Korean Cold War structure to undergo a change, I believe it will take a substantial time. For this reason, the maintenance of U.S. troops on the Korean Peninsula is not only essential, but it is critical for the maintenance of peace and stability on the Korean Peninsula, and the Korean Peninsula, of course, plays a key role for the maintenance of stability of the entire Northeast Asian region.

MR. CHINOY: *We'll be back in a moment to continue our discussion with South Korean President Roh Tae Woo.*

(Announcements.)

MR. CHINOY: *Welcome back to "Newsmaker Sunday." What role do you see China playing now in relation to both South Korea and North Korea? The Chinese have made major strides in improving relations with your country while still maintaining a kind of ideological solidarity with communist North Korea. What do you think the Chinese are likely to do in this next period?*

PRESIDENT ROH (through interpreter): Since you are reporting out of Beijing, Mr. Chinoy, I believe you know the subject rather well. As we know, China is changing right now, and it is only natural that China undergoes certain change.

In the economic and trade sectors, China has shown remarkable changes in recent years. Likewise, slowly but steadily, I believe, Chinese politics will also undergo some change.

China would want no dispute on the Korean Peninsula. Instability on the Korean Peninsula would not be to their advantage either. Therefore, China, I believe, would want reduction of tension on the Korean Peninsula, and the development of a cooperative and friendly relationship between the two Koreas on the Korean Peninsula.

And I hope and expect the Chinese to make contributions toward the promotion of cooperative relations on the Korean Peninsula.

MR. CHINOY: *You've presided over a rather tumultuous transition to a more democratic and open political system here in South Korea. You've made a lot of progress, although your critics domestically say there hasn't been enough and it hasn't come fast enough. How do you see the evolution of democratic institutions here in South Korea, and what impact will the progress that you make toward solidifying those institutions have on the prospects for reunification with North Korea?*

PRESIDENT ROH (through interpreter): Since I enunciated the June 29th declaration of democratic reforms in 1987, Korea has made big strides towards democratization. And I'm very satisfied that I have been able to carry out my pledges to the nation.

As you know, we have today complete freedom of press and of speech. We have independent judiciary and legislature, and labor rights are competely guaranteed.

In the process of democratization in Korea, the Korean people aspire to a lot more in terms of democratic rights and right to pursue happiness. Consequently, I do not believe our pursuit of democracy has been completed so far.

We will continue to endeavor for further progress of a democratic society on the Korean Peninsula.

Now, as you know, the democratic societies have induced the collapse of communism around the world, and the same analogy could be applied on the Korean Peninsula. The freer and the more perfect democracy we accomplish, I believe we will have laid a solid foundation for national unification, and I am firmly convinced of it.

MR. CHINOY: *President Roh, thank you for joining us on "Newsmaker Sunday." From Seoul, South Korea, I'm Mike Chinoy.*

15.

Declaration of Non-nuclear Korean Peninsula Peace Initiatives, Seoul, November 8, 1991

My fellow Koreans,

This morning, I am going to announce an important decision to help build a durable structure of peace on the Korean Peninsula and in Northeast Asia.

In the process of removing the legacies of the Cold War and in efforts to build a world of peace, many courageous and previously unimagined initiatives are being taken around the world today.

Not only have the former adversaries joined hands but they vow friendship and cooperation for a better future for all mankind. What is more, epoch-making measures are being taken to reduce all weapons of mass destruction, which threaten to destroy human civilization in an instant.

Both the United States and the Soviet Union are in the process of reducing and dismantling nuclear weapons on a large scale, and international negotiations are currently under way in Geneva to completely eliminate chemical weapons, which could inflict indiscriminate killing on a massive scale.

Looking at these global waves of reconciliation and cooperation, there are those who mistakenly believe that threats of confrontation have disappeared from our own land also. Unfortunately, however, a situation that is unique in the world and is quite inconsistent with the tides of history persists on the Korean Peninsula.

At a time when reduction and destruction of nuclear weapons are being carried out worldwide, North Korea shows no sign of giving up its efforts to build nuclear weapons, while reneging on its professed duties as a signatory to the Nuclear Non-proliferation Treaty. It has been well documented that North Korea also manufactures, and has a stockpile of, chemical-biological weapons.

As is well known, there has been a tragic fratricidal war in Korea and, subsequently, an intense military confrontation and arms race ensued on the

Korean Peninsula for almost four decades. Under these circumstances, North Korea's development of nuclear weapons has to be a matter of grave concern, and it will escalate the Korean question into an entirely new dimension. Indeed, nuclear weapons in North Korean hands would be so dangerous and destabilizing that they would not only threaten the very survival of our nation, but could in an instant shatter the peace in Northeast Asia and the world.

It is for these reasons that the gravely worried international community joins us in our concerted efforts to deter North Korea from developing nuclear weapons.

In my address to the United Nations General Assembly last September, I made it clear that I was prepared to discuss with North Korea the nuclear issues on the Korean Peninsula as soon as North Korea would sign the nuclear safeguards agreement, renounce the development of nuclear weapons, and agree on inter-Korean military confidence-building measures.

And yet, rather than positively respond to my proposals North Korea continues to evade its international duties on account of groundless charges and excuses.

In an effort to initiate the resolution of nuclear issues on the Korean Peninsula and in my earnest desire to bring about a durable structure of peace on our land, I have come to an important decision and have determined to take steps to carry it out.

Reaffirming our commitment to the cause of peace and in order to eliminate from our land all chemical-biological weapons and to secure a non-nuclear Korean Peninsula, I declare the following to be our policy:

First, the Republic of Korea will use nuclear energy solely for peaceful purposes, and will not manufacture, possess, store, deploy or use nuclear weapons.

Second, the Republic of Korea will continue to submit to comprehensive international inspection all nuclear-related facilities and materials on its territory in compliance with the Nuclear Non-proliferation Treaty and with the nuclear safeguards agreement it has concluded with the International Atomic Energy Agency under the treaty, and will not possess nuclear fuel reprocessing and enrichment facilities.

Third, the Republic of Korea aspires for a world of peace free of nuclear weapons as well as all weapons of indiscriminate killing; and we will actively participate in international efforts toward a total elimination of chemical-biological weapons and observe all international agreements thereon.

We will faithfully carry out this non-nuclear, no chemical-biological weapons policy.

Now, there can be no reason or justification for North Korea to devleop nuclear weapons or evade international inspection of its nuclear facilities.

I strongly call upon North Korean authorities to immediately take steps corresponding to my declaration today.

Just as the Republic of Korea has done, North Korea also should renounce unequivocally the possession of nuclear reprocessing and enrichment facilities.

As soon as North Korea takes these steps, beginning with the signing of the nuclear safeguards agreement, we will initiate bilateral discussions on other military-security issues, including the nuclear issue, and seek to resolve them through South-North high-level talks.

Any and all issues pertaining to the Korean Peninsula should be resolved through direct inter-Korean negotiations in a spirit of self-reliance.

Consequently, I call upon North Korea in the name of seventy million fellow Koreans to immediately abandon the attempt to develop nuclear weapons so that together we may open a new era of peace on the Korean Peninsula, having secured a land free of nuclear weapons.

My fellow Koreans,

Prior to the enunciation of our policy today, the government has very carefully examined its possible impact on the national security. My decision is based on a firm assessment that our national security will continue to remain solid.

It is sincerely hoped that North Korea will accurately evaluate current international realities and decide to join us in our common efforts to eliminate the sources of national tragedy and to achieve national harmony and peaceful unification.

16.

Special Announcement on a Nuclear-free Korean Peninsula, December 18, 1991

My fellow Koreans,

Last week, South and North Korea agreed on a detailed accord in an effort to end the half-century–old Cold War on the Korean Peninsula and to open a new era of peace.

The Accord, which was signed at the conclusion of the Fifth South-North High-level Talks, consists of important measures that are necessary to end national division and rivalry on the basis of mutual trust, to build a structure of peace on our land, and to promote national reconciliation and common prosperity through exchanges and cooperation.

The Republic of Korea fully supports this Accord, for we believe that the development of an inter-Korean relationship based on peaceful coexistence and common prosperity is an essential step towards the goal of national unification.

Together with the parallel entry of South and North Korea into the United Nations in September, the signing of the South-North Korean Accord last week is an epic milepost on our road to the resolution of the Korean Question and the attainment of national unity.

South and North Korea should now march together toward peace and unification.

The tasks and courses of action which lie ahead of the two Koreas are clear.

It is now incumbent on the two Korean governments to implement faithfully the contents of the Accord step by step so that national reconciliation, peace and common prosperity, which are aspirations shared by all Koreans, may soon be realized.

The Republic of Korea pledges to do its utmost in transforming the relationship with the North from one of rivalry to partnership, exchanges and cooperation. In addition, we will seek a speedy resolution of political and military issues between South and North Korea.

The Cold War brought upon our nation untold sorrows and tragedies. The sacrifices and tribulations this nation suffered from division, war and rivalry have been truly enormous and unbearable.

Now, the two Koreas have produced a Charter of peace that will end a dark period in their history and bring forth a new era of reconciliation and cooperation. I firmly believe that this Charter will mark a momentous turning-point on the road to building a new nation in which 70 million Koreans together shall forge a glorious future.

My Fellow Koreans,

Before we proceed with the implementation of the widely supported Inter-Korean Accord, however, there is an important issue that must be resolved at the earliest possible date. It is the nuclear issue on the Korean Peninsula.

On the eighth of November, I enunciated the Non-nuclear Korean Peninsula Peace Initiative, noting that the development of nuclear weapons by North Korea was an extremely dangerous venture which posed serious threats not only to the peace and survival of the Korean people, but also to regional and global stability.

It was for these reasons that I made a public pledge specifically declaring that South Korea would not manufacture, possess, store, deploy or use nuclear weapons, and that we would also renounce the right to build nuclear reprocessing facilities, which could very well have been justified on grounds of economic necessity.

In order to remove any obstacles to nuclear inspections of North Korea, the government, in consultation with the U.S. government, has proposed during the recent High-level Talks to conduct simultaneous nuclear inspections of facilities in the South and North, including the U.S. military bases in South Korea.

To open the military bases of a nuclear superpower to international inspection is a truly exceptional precedent, but we have reached this decision for the sole purpose of a peaceful and smooth resolution of the Korean Peninsula nuclear issue.

It is gratifying to note that last week at the High-level Talks South and North Korea jointly recognized that there should be no nuclear weapons on the Korean Peninsula. On this common ground, I sincerely hope that a definitive agreement on nuclear issues will emerge from the Panmunjom working-level conference later this month.

So that we may come to an early resolution of the nuclear issue, I take this opportunity to make one thing emphatically clear to you, my fellow Koreans, as well as to North Korea and the world at large:

As I speak, there do not exist any nuclear weapons whatsoever, anywhere in the Republic of Korea.

Clearly, then, the non-nuclear policy enunciated in my November 8th

Declaration has now been fulfilled insofar as the Republic of Korea is concerned.

My fellow Koreans,

I want to emphasize the following to the North Korean authorities:

Since the Republic of Korea is now completely nuclear-free and since we have agreed to the simultaneous nuclear inspections proposal, there is no reason or excuse for North Korea to develop nuclear weapons or refuse nuclear inspection.

North Korea must forthwith conclude and ratify a nuclear safeguards agreement with the International Atomic Energy Agency, shut down all nuclear reprocessing and enrichment facilities, and submit unconditionally to international inspection.

It is now North Korea's responsibility to demonstrate to the Korean people and the world that a genuine peace is indeed emerging on the Korean Peninsula, by resolving the nuclear issue on the basis of the letter and spirit of the South-North Accord.

Obviously, we cannot successfully build peace and national reconciliation without first resolving the nuclear question. For this reason, the entire international community is currently searching for ways to deter North Korea's development of nuclear weapons, having recognized it as a significant threat to the peace of this region and as a grave danger that will potentially accelerate the proliferation of nuclear weapons globally.

I believe that the North Korean authorities are well aware of the central issues. Therefore, I hope and expect that the forthcoming Panmunjom conference will yield an agreement which meets the legitimate demands of South Korea and the international community.

North Korea must immediately abandon the development of nuclear weapons. It is an imperative duty that cannot and should not be delayed.

I sincerely hope that an agreement guaranteeing a nuclear-free Korean Peninsula will emerge by the end of this month so that with the New Year South and North Korea together will usher in a new era of reconciliation, cooperation, peace and common prosperity.

Thank you.

17.

Special Statement on the Occasion of Coming into Effect of the Basic Agreement Between South and North Korea, Seoul, February 19, 1992

My fellow Koreans at home and abroad,

Today, the "Agreement on Reconciliation, Nonaggression and Exchanges and Cooperation between the South and the North" and the "Joint Declaration of the Denuclearization of the Korean Peninsula" begin to take effect formally. This means that South and North Korea, which have had to live with incessant confrontation and antagonism for half a century, will now put an end to the unfortunate history of division and proceed together along a path to co-prosperity and unification.

We have exerted every effort to transcend the barriers of ideology and political system so that South and North Korea may enjoy mutual development within one national community. Our efforts have now begun to bear fruit, and it gives us great satisfaction that we have attained such a valuable progress through our own independent efforts.

Now, it is incumbent on both South and North Korea to faithfully carry out the terms of the basic agreement. No pledge will have meaning unless it is faithfully translated into action without fail. In fact, empty pledges often breed distrust and discord. So, the South and the North should promote reconciliation, exchanges and cooperation as well as uphold the terms of nonaggression on the basis of mutual trust. I would like to emphasize once again that this is the only shortcut to the attainment of a structure of peace on the Korean Peninsula and, eventually, national unification.

The government of the Republic of Korea hereby solemnly declares that it will do its utmost to faithfully carry out the terms of both the "basic agreement" and the "joint declaration." I call upon the North Korean leader to issue a corresponding public pledge, declaring that North Korea, too, will faithfully implement and abide by the terms of the basic agreement and the joint declaration.

Once again, I urge North Korea to clear itself of the suspicions and misgivings about its development of nuclear weapons by promptly fulfilling its domestic and international obligations under the pertinent treaties and agreements. Gravely concerned, the entire Korean people are closely watching all related developments on this vital issue, because North Korea's nuclear development will certainly threaten not merely the safety of the Korean people but the stability of the Northeast Asian region as well. North Korea's failure to take the necessary steps would result in deterioration of inter-Korean relations and invite strong criticism from the international community. Consequently, by promptly removing this dangerous stumbling-block, North Korea should make its own contribution toward opening a new era of reconciliation and cooperation under the new inter-Korean agreement.

My fellow Koreans,

This is a day of new hope to all of us, at home and abroad. We all eagerly aspire that our hope will soon become a reality. We should now draw our strengths together to bring about a national unification so that in the 21st century the entire Korean people may step up on the international stage as a unified nation. This is the earnest desire of all our 70 million compatriots living at home and abroad. Indeed, it is an historic task, the completion of which will determine the destiny of our posterity.

It is our generation's duty before history to successfully carry out this national task. We must build a unified country; a country strong enough to determine its own future—a democratic and prosperous country free of military conflict. As we mark a day that has opened a new chapter in our history, we should all renew our resolve to usher in a new era of glory for the Korean people everywhere.

Thank you.

Part III

KOREA'S PLACE IN THE WORLD

18.

Remarks at the Banquet in Honor of President Daniel Toroitich arap Moi of the Republic of Kenya, Seoul, September 17, 1990

Your Excellency President Moi, distinguished guests,

I heartily welcome you and your delegation to the Republic of Korea. I appreciate your making such a long trip to get here.

Today happens to mark the second anniversary of the opening of the Seoul Olympics, a festival of global reconciliation and amity. The Korean people and I are particularly happy to greet you on this significant day because we know that, with profound faith, you have been striving so hard to translate a spirit of love and harmony into action.

I still vividly remember the majestic sight of Kilimanjaro which so deeply impressed me during my visit to Kenya in 1982. The towering volcano soaring out of the vast stretch of grassland with the permanent snow cap glistening in the tropical sun, I thought, symbolized the unflinching spirit of the Kenyans.

Mr. President,

I am happy to note that our two nations have developed close ties of friendship since we established diplomatic relations in 1964. Even though geography separates us by some distance, we have been cooperating with each other as close neighbors. I am confident that your present visit to Seoul will further cement our friendly ties.

Your Excellency,

I wish to pay tribute to you for your outstanding contributions not only to the development of Kenya but also to peace and harmony in Africa by taking the lead in implementing the national philosophy of peace, love and unity expressed by the term "Nyayo." I know that under your leadership, Kenya has steadily developed both politically and economically, thus becoming a model African country with the highest level of industrialization in the continent. We also applaud you for your unlimited endeavor for the security of African nations and for the peaceful resolution of regional disputes.

We know also that as the chairman of the Preferential Trade Area for Eastern and Southern African States, you have been leading the way for regional economic development and integration and have also been playing a pioneering role in international environmental protection. Once more, I salute you for your illustrious achievements and contributions to humanity and hope your efforts will bring forth further successes in the coming days.

Mr. President,

The world now is in the midst of a great upheaval as we approach the 21st century. A new era of reconciliation and cooperation is emerging as Cold War confrontation withers away. Advances in transportation and communication have shrunk the Earth into a global village.

Humanity thus looks forward to the fast-approaching 21st century with new hopes and dreams. And yet, many problems remain to be solved if peace and well-being is to be assured for all. For example, should the Persian Gulf crisis flare up into war, woe will befall not only the belligerents themselves but all other nations as well. Protectionist trade policies and the trend toward economic blocs continue to intensify, while the gaping North-South economic gap remains unmitigated.

The world today offers opportunities as well as challenges. I therefore believe that cooperation among developing countries like Kenya and Korea is more essential than ever before. Our two countries should now become genuine partners in order to realize our common ideals and to march together toward the brighter 21st century.

Your Excellency,

We are hopeful that the tide of détente and cooperation that has brought down the Cold War barriers will reach the Korean Peninsula, too. We believe that the best way for us to contribute to peace and stability is by securing durable peace on this Peninsula and unifying our divided land. We are striving to achieve peaceful unification by removing the bases of confrontation and hostility between South and North Korea and by promoting inter-Korean exchanges and cooperation.

I am grateful to Your Excellency for consistently supporting the cause of the Republic of Korea in the international arena.

Mr. President,

I believe our two nations should now even more actively cooperate, especially in the economic field, for our common prosperity and well-being. Both being developing countries, I believe we can profit much by sharing developmental experiences and expertise.

In particular, both our countries can benefit greatly through the joint development of resources, technology, tourism and other projects.

Let us work closely together in all international endeavors for a more peaceful and prosperous 21st century.

I sincerely hope that Your Excellency and your delegation will have a pleasant and rewarding stay in Korea and hope you will witness first-hand our citizens' unchanging warm feelings of friendship toward the people of Kenya.

Ladies and gentlemen,

Please join me in toasting the good health and well-being of His Excellency President Moi and the eternal friendship between our two peoples.

19.

Congratulatory Remarks on the Awarding of the First Seoul Peace Prize, Seoul, September 25, 1990

Mr. Chairman, Honorable Members of the Seoul Peace Prize Committee, distinguished guests.

Today, we are gathered here for the joyous occasion of awarding the First Seoul Peace Prize which was established to celebrate the lofty ideals of the Seoul Olympic Games and to promote them throughout the world. Korea is still reverberating with the echoes of the 24th Olympic Games held two years ago, during which the global village gathered in Seoul in a spirit of friendship, harmony and peace.

Prior to the Seoul Olympic Games, the Olympic Movement had long been tarnished by the conflicts of the Cold War, racial discrimination and terrorist acts. By staging the Games in a divided country still trying to shake off the vestiges of the Cold War, however, the Olympic Movement was able to rediscover its true dimensions.

In Seoul, the world's young people overcame all the barriers of race, religion, politics and ideology that divide people. Hand in hand, they vowed to live together in harmony and to march toward a more peaceful world.

During the past century which coincides with the history of the modern Olympic Movement, Korea has been a victim of numerous acts of aggression and wars, resulting in national division and confrontation. Those painful experiences have implanted a profound and inherent desire for peace in the hearts of the Korean people. The Seoul Olympic Games were, thus, a wellspring of hope and encouragement for all peoples who suffer from the threat of war, the yoke of rigid ideology, the shackles of poverty and other adversities.

With the dawning of a new century fast approaching, waves of openness and reconciliation are sweeping the whole world. When, at this propitious time, the sacred Olympic flame was lit in Seoul, symbolizing a universal yearning for peace, we came to believe that peace was within our reach, if only we remained as united as on that uplifting occasion. The Seoul Peace Prize embodies this fervent desire.

It gives me great pleasure, on behalf of the citizens of Korea, to congratulate the first recipient of the Seoul Peace Prize, Mr. Juan Antonio Samaranch, President of the International Olympic Committee. The Seoul Olympic Games were a monumental achievement made possible by the concerted and dedicated efforts of both the Korean people and the International Olympic Committee led by President Samaranch. I am well aware of the devoted and unsparing efforts of President Samaranch and the IOC to ensure the success of the Seoul Olympic Games. In order to restore the Olympiad to its original splendor by healing divisions and to make the Seoul Games the fullest embodiment of the Olympic ideals, President Samaranch made almost superhuman efforts and was constantly on the road paying numerous visits to Seoul and other cities. It was thanks to his outstanding leadership and unflinching efforts that the seven years of assiduous preparations by the Korean people for the Games could be rewarded with a sense of fulfillment and glory and the International Olympic Movement could be reborn with greater vitality and magnetism.

All this attests to the great power of the Olympics in bringing the world together in an enthusiastic and friendly spirit and shows us how important and valuable peace really is. The Seoul Peace Prize aims to encourage advances toward a fair, just and more prosperous world where all can live in peace and harmony.

Once again, I would like to extend my warmest congratulations to President Samaranch and also to Mrs. Samaranch who has wholeheartedly supported and helped him in all his endeavors.

May the meaning of today's Prize remain forever in the hearts and minds of all those who love peace.

20.

Remarks at the Banquet in Honor of the President of the Socialist Federal Republic of Yugoslavia and Mrs. Borisav Jovic, Seoul, November 8, 1990

Your Excellencies President and Mrs. Jovic, distinguished guests.

I join the entire people of the Republic of Korea in welcoming you and the Presidential delegation from the Socialist Federal Republic of Yugoslavia. The visit of Your Excellencies to our land less than a year after our two countries established formal relations last December is of major significance because it greatly brightens the prospects for a steady development of our bilateral ties.

Mrs. Roh and I are very delighted to share this evening with Your Excellencies here at Chong Wa Dae. I had the pleasure of visiting your country six years ago to attend the Winter Olympics in Sarajevo. I still vividly remember the beautiful natural sceneries of Yugoslavia and the exquisite harmony between your long history and rich cultural heritage on the one hand and modernity on the other.

I was also deeply impressed by the vision and courage of the leaders and people of Yugoslavia for their successful efforts to overcome numerous adversities and to consolidate diversity and uphold the torch of self-reliance.

Mr. President,

Although our two countries are separated by a great geographical distance, the Korean people have long felt a sense of affinity toward the people of Yugoslavia because we share many similarities in our historical experience. Both our countries have successfully preserved independence and illustrious cultural heritage in spite of numerous trials and tribulations brought on us by great power rivalries.

Stories of gallantry associated with such Yugoslavian national heroes as

Milos Obilic and Karadjordje were sources of inspiration for our own resolve for national independence in the dark days when we were under foreign domination. The Korean people hold your people in deep respect for the determined resistance against foreign aggression. Outstanding Yugoslavian writers and artists such as Ivo Andric and Paja Jobanobic are well known to the Korean people.

Since the end of World War II, Yugoslavia has courageously pursued an independent, self-reliant course, refusing to be involved in the Cold War confrontation. By initiating and leading the Non-aligned Movement, Yugoslavia has greatly contributed to the birth of a new international order today. The world is now in the midst of momentous change. The Cold War system that long dominated the world has now collapsed. The ideological barriers and political blocs that used to divide humanity and the nations of the world are being removed. Human dignity, freedom and democratic pluralism are now being accepted as universal values.

A new wave of détente and cooperation is sweeping the world, and we can therefore have higher hopes for a better tomorrow. We applaud your country for having pursued a pioneering role for the community of nations.

Mr. President,

Korea was divided at the end of World War II as a result of Cold War rivalry. This national division led to a fratricidal war on the Korean Peninsula and tension across the Demilitarized Zone persists even to this day. For forty long years, families dispersed in the North and South have not been able to exchange letters or make telephone calls, let alone exchange visits across the border.

Korea probably is the world's worst victim of the Cold War. This is why we are now making all-out efforts to remove vestiges of the Cold War on the Korean Peninsula, and improve relations between South and North Korea so that the two parts of our land will permit exchange visits and cooperate with each other for the sake of coexistence and coprosperity. When South and North Korea recover our community relations as one nation through such efforts, an avenue to peaceful unification will be opened.

We are cultivating friendly and cooperative relations with all nations of the world. We believe this is the way to promote not only universal prosperity but world peace and global cooperation as well.

We are encouraged by the establishment of diplomatic relations with Yugoslavia and most other countries in Central and Eastern Europe and also with the Soviet Union. We are now rapidly developing cooperative relations with them. We are hopeful that our new European friends will greatly assist us in our efforts to secure peace and stability in Northeast Asia, and to achieve Korean unification.

Having undergone painful experiences of war and confrontation, we sincerely wish that all regional disputes will be settled peacefully. We earnestly hope that the dark clouds over the Persian Gulf crisis will also be dispersed peacefully in keeping with the founding spirit of the United Nations.

Mr. President,
Your visit has now brought our two peoples together as good friends. I am certain that the movement of people and goods, and scientific and technological know-how between our two countries will greatly increase over the bridge of friendship and cooperation we have just built together.

Both our countries are developing nations that are in the throes of democratic reforms. We should actively share developmental experiences and expertise and work together to enhance cooperation among the developing countries throughout the world. Since our two national economies are mutually complementary in many respects, the potential for bilateral trade and economic cooperation is enormous.

I am very pleased that through a summit meeting with Your Excellency today, we have discovered that Yugoslavia and the Republic of Korea share many concurrent views on a broad spectrum of international and bilateral issues. I expect that both our countries will be amply rewarded by the continuing development of our ties.

I understand that Yugoslavia has an old saying: "It is not good to be alone even in Paradise." So, let us now be partners for building a better world.

Ladies and gentlemen,
Please join me in toasting to the good health and well-being of Their Excellencies President and Mrs. Jovic, to the prosperity of Yugoslavia and to the eternal friendship between our two nations.
Thank you.

21.

Remarks at the Dinner for the Diplomatic Corps in Seoul, February 12, 1991

Ambassador Raul Casal, Dean of the Diplomatic Corps, Your Excellencies, ladies and gentlemen.

Two years ago at a dinner for the members of the Diplomatic Corps in Seoul, I believe I said the reason we had to exchange New Year's greetings only in February was mainly because my assistants had scheduled our dinner so late.

I believe I also pointed out that on the golf courses diplomats like yourselves had a habit of waiting for instructions from the home government to go ahead before making the tee shot . . . and that even though I was the president I could not even go out to the field unless and until my staff made a special allowance in my schedule.

This year, my able assistants apparently tried very hard to schedule our dinner earlier than previous years, and ended up scheduling it fully three days before the new year's day, that is, on the lunar calendar.

Well, ladies and gentlemen, I wish each and every one of you a very happy and healthy new year, and hope that all your wishes for the new year will come true. You see, in terms of our lunar calendar, I have just extended new year's greetings to you ahead of time.

For centuries, Koreans followed solar calendars for such calls of nature as sowing seeds, irrigation and other farming chores, but observed lunar calendars for household observances such as Thanksgiving and New Year's.

In fact, the Korean people have been living in a closely-knit community environment for several millennia and the life-style has been preserved almost intact until a few decades ago when my generation of Koreans was still young.

Every year at this time, youngsters and children throughout the country frolicked around in excitement and paid visits to the family and village elders to give thanks for the passing year. On the New Year's morning, children in their colorful dresses would bow to their parents and ancestors and make rounds to bow to and wish the village elders a happy and healthy new year.

On the New Year's Eve, every child in the family had to struggle not to fall asleep early, for they truly believed stories told by their parents that going to bed early on the new year's eve would make them get old overnight and their eyebrows turn grey. The children who had succumbed to sleep early would break into tears in the morning as soon as they looked into the mirror and discovered that their eyebrows had indeed turned grey. You see, the parents and relatives, busy working in the kitchen all night, made sure to play on whichever child fell asleep early and sprinkled rice-cake powder on the eyebrows.

In the past generation or two, some of the old and treasured customs and community traditions seem to be fast disappearing from our society.

A traditional agrarian society, Korea has recently been undergoing a period of rapid modernization, industrialization and urbanization.

One can only describe the transformation of the Korean society as phenomenal, and we are still going through the change.

To our great dismay, however, we are losing in the process many of the admirable customs and attitudes dear to our heart . . . the respect to parents and elders, the traditional manners, the warmth and affinity of community life, the village-wide games and farm dances that used to last for a fortnight from the New Year's Day to the full moon, and the ubiquitous scenes of festivity around the nation.

Perhaps the German philosopher was right when he observed that "human history is built on 'heimatlösichkeit,' or hometown-forgetfulness."

Koreans are a people who would pioneer a new path rather than dwell on past regrets.

Over the years, the Korean people have not only adjusted to changes in spite of tribulations of transition, but succeeded in making progress on the basis of their past experience.

The recent process of transformation in Korea can only be described in terms of unequalled dynamism.

The rapid process of democratization in Korea over the last four years is a case in point. I believe many of you here tonight are firsthand witnesses to the volcanic eruption several years ago of the Korean people's pent-up desire for democracy and against authoritarian rule.

The now famous Declaration of Democratic Reforms on June 29, 1987, marked a watershed and the Republic of Korea has since been moving along a road to genuine democracy. Serving as the president of the Republic over the past three years, I have learned firsthand that the road to democracy is not only long and tortuous but also demands an enormous amount of patience and sacrifice.

Let me give you just one example. The Korean news media today enjoy a complete freedom of the press and they criticize freely. At times, they level harsh attacks on the president, and at other times they indulge in excessive competition and sensationalism, thereby adding fuel to the national dissension. All the same, however, I firmly uphold and subscribe to the higher value that the freedom of the press bestows on our society.

Korea's democracy is on the right track, although it is bumpy at times. Many challenges lie ahead, but I am confident that we can successfully and smoothly carry out the many political agenda in the coming months and years.

Ladies and gentlemen,

The increased size of the Seoul Diplomatic Corps itself reflects some of the big changes that we have gone through recently. The membership has increased by 13 during the past year, reaching a total of 76. In addition, six international organizations are represented here tonight. By the end of 1990 we had established diplomatic relations with all the states in Central and Eastern Europe, including the Soviet Union. Albania now remains the only exception.

It is now clear that the waves of reconciliation and cooperation that transformed the European as well as world order are finally moving toward the Korean Peninsula.

Having undergone a fratricidal war and still suffering from the division of the land, the Korean people place great expectations in the new, friendly and cooperative ties with the countries in Central and Eastern Europe. This is because the more friends we have the sooner can we together remove the Cold War confrontation from the Korean Peninsula and bring forth peace and unification in Korea.

As a matter of fact, high-level inter-Korean talks were held last year for the first time since the country was partitioned in 1945. This took the form of three rounds of prime ministers' meetings held in Seoul and P'yŏngyang alternately. Just this morning, I received a report that the delegates to the South-North Sports Talks have agreed to the formation of single, unified teams for international table-tennis and soccer competitions. It is our honest and sincere hope that more meaningful progress will be made through the on-going high-level dialogue, leading to inter-Korean exchanges and cooperation.

Last year, I visited Japan and the United States in May and June and the Soviet Union in December. I still cannot forget the welcome, the warmth and the hospitality the government and people of these countries have accorded me and my delegation.

Also last year, we had the honor of welcoming as state guests the presidents of Paraguay, Kenya, Yugoslavia and Hungary. The Prime Ministers of Malta, Malaysia and Greece also came to Seoul. A few weeks ago, Prime Minister Kaifu of Japan also visited the Republic.

Through all such occasions, we have even more acutely realized that diplomacy between national leaders can make invaluable contributions to lifting friendly and cooperative bilateral ties onto new and higher planes. Such exchange visits will also contribute to solidifying the foundations for a more cooperative and peaceful world.

I would like to take this opportunity to extend a special welcome to those ambassadors who have recently arrived in Seoul, and are thus the latest additions to our Diplomatic Corps. I would also like to express once again my sincere gratitude to those ambassadors from the countries I visited in the course of the past year, including the United States, Japan, and the Soviet Union. Their meticulous preparations and whole-hearted assistance have made my visits a most successful and rewarding experience.

Ladies and gentlemen,

Although the new waves of reconciliation are sweeping across the world, an important region is currently engulfed in the flames of war. We sincerely hope that the war in the Gulf region will come to an early conclusion, and peace and stability be restored in the region.

Since Germany was unified last year, Korea remains the only country on earth still divided by the Cold War. We will continue to do our utmost to convert this land of confrontation into a land of peace, a land in which the Korean people whether in the South or in the North shall move about freely, and work and live together within the bounds of a unified country.

The Republic of Korea will continue in the new year to cooperate with you and your great countries. We will work with you to build a more open, more cooperative and more peaceful world.

I am delighted to share this evening with you. I wish you all even greater successes in the New Year.

To usher in the year 1991, a year of great hope, may I please propose a toast to our lasting friendship and progress, and to the peace and prosperity of the world.

Thank you.

22.

Address at the Ground-breaking Ceremony for Taejon Expo '93, Taejon, April 12, 1991

Honorable Chairman Jacques Sol-Rolland,
  Distinguished guests, ladies and gentlemen,
  It gives me a great pleasure to join you here at the Toryong plains this afternoon. Two years from today, we will witness a magnificent unfolding of our dreams across this vast expanse, a dream which envisions a more peaceful and prosperous world in the 21st century.
  We are gathered here today to break the ground for the Taejon International Exposition, which promises to visualize ideas and imaginations for our future, embracing knowledge and technology mankind will have been able to marshall for the progress of human civilization.
  This spacious field will eventually house as many as sixty pavilions for overseas participants and twenty pavilions for Korean businesses and organizations.
  It is here that we shall discover in two years fresh ideals and challenges of mankind, and how modern technology proposes to fulfill our dreams and aspirations. Through Taejon Expo '93, we shall be able both to take stock of the present and to experience the world of our future. The Expo '93 is certain to provide as well a meeting ground for the peoples of the world as a festive occasion for reconciliation and harmony among nations and cultures.
  Taejon Expo '93 will be the first international exposition to be hosted by a developing country in the 140-year history of international expositions.
  Only two and a half years ago, in a divided land where the threat of war still persists, we were able to successfully host the much acclaimed Seoul Olympic Games, thereby contributing to the peace of mankind.
  It is of great significance that within five years of the Seoul Olympics we will be hosting an international exposition that is tantamount to the Olympic Games of the combined fields of economics, science and technology.

We are certain that Taejon Expo '93 will serve as a guiding torch illuminating "a new road to development" for both the developed and developing countries of our global village.

I would like to take this opportunity to extend my sincere appreciation to the representatives of the Bureau of International Expositions and the delegates from each country and to all the others who are working so hard to make this project a success.

Ladies and gentlemen,

Mankind looks forward to the 21st century with high hopes and great expectations. For the world will be more peaceful and we can all expect to lead a happier life in the new century. The dark days of the Cold War are behind us and new waves of reconciliation are about us.

The remarkable changes which have taken place have brought with them the realization that a world of harmony in which we can live in friendship and peace is not a mere dream, but is in fact, a realistic possibility.

At the same time, advances in science, technology and industrial development have brought us all together as neighbors in a single global village. The world we saw in science fiction when we were young has become a reality today.

The amazing development in science and technology is certain to bring about a world in which all our lives will be richer, both spiritually and materially. And the foundation of this new world rests firmly upon knowledge and information.

On our road to a brighter future we should of course expect to encounter numerous challenges which are as great as our hopes for the future, but I am confident that we shall overcome them all.

The technological development continues to exacerbate the gap between advanced and developing nations, intensifying the already wide gap between North and South.

It is also true that the rapid process of industrialization carries within it the seeds of destruction, threatening nature and the environment of our one and only planet Earth. Energy and natural resources will be depleted within a few generations if the current rate of consumption should continue.

All of these are formidable challenges, but together through Taejon Expo '93, we shall discover ways of coping with these challenges, and enhance the happiness and prosperity of all mankind.

Fellow citizens,

It must be a unique privilege for all of us to have an opportunity to host an international exposition, and Taejon Expo '93 is worthy of our best efforts.

In 1993 it will be exactly 100 years since Korea first participated in an international exposition in Chicago. The Korean pavilion, a traditional tile-roofed house, had on display such handmade products as ramie, fans, and pottery.

After the Paris Exposition of 1900, however, it took nearly six decades before Korea again took part in an international exposition, because a period of foreign domination and the Korean War, which devastated our land, intervened.

But, like a phoenix rising from the ashes of the war, Korea has re-emerged as an important player on the world stage and has earned the right to host consecutively two high-profile international events, the Seoul Olympic Games and the Taejon International Exposition.

The unprecedented rapid progress we have achieved has made this possible. It has also brought us to the threshold of advanced country status. Taejon Expo will mark a turning point in the nation's science, technology and industry, and will serve as a stepping-stone towards an advanced industrialized society.

Past expositions have showcased the civilization of the day, presenting the most remarkable developments of science and technology of the era. Telephones, nylon, plastics, television, high speed electric railways—all made their debuts at international expositions.

Taejon Expo '93 will help reinforce our conviction that only through strengthened development of science and technology can we surmount the barriers in our path. It will rekindle in our hearts the fires of determination to surge ahead to become an advanced, prosperous and enlightened nation.

The Taejon International Exposition will also give us an opportunity to demonstrate some of the accomplishments we have achieved over the past generation. Perhaps, our determination towards progress will help inspire and encourage the nations that are still struggling to overcome the adversities that we had faced earlier.

My fellow citizens,

At this moment, I cannot help feeling the same excitement and determination I had at the ground-breaking ceremony for the Seoul Olympics. Perhaps you will recall the pessimistic predictions made at the time over the enormity of the task we faced. We know today how wrong those forecasts turned out to be.

Hosting an international exposition is no easier than hosting the Olympic Games. But I am confident that once again the Korean people will rise to the occasion, and will work together to make Taejon Expo '93 a sure success.

The Taejon International Exposition is certain to contribute to Korea's status in the international community, as did the Seoul Olympic Games. It will set us on the road to a broader world and brighter future.

Wherever they have been held, past international expositions have brought tremendous benefits to the host countries and have helped to stimulate development in every sector.

It will certainly require an enormous investment to host an international exposition, but the positive effects of the exposition upon the society and economy of the host country are also enormous.

The fact that this exposition is being held outside of Seoul has many ramifications. Taejon Expo '93 will have a considerable impact upon the development of central Korea, and will help strengthen the pivotal role of the city of Taejon.

Governmental efforts alone can hardly ensure the success of Taejon Expo '93. The active participation and devoted support of the general public are absolutely essential. The Korean participants have a special responsibility to do all within their capabilities to accurately portray the state of our economy and science.

I would like to reaffirm our committment to a successful Taejon Expo '93. Let us all pledge to make this exposition another milestone in our progress so that Taejon Expo '93 will be recorded as another monument of success of the Korean people.

Thank you.

23.

Remarks at the White House Welcoming Ceremony, South Lawn, Washington, D.C., July 2, 1991

President and Mrs. Bush, distinguished leaders of the American government, and citizens of the United States.

I am deeply grateful to you, Mr. President, for your invitation to visit this great country and for the warm and cordial welcome extended to me and my delegation. I am also very pleased to bring warm greetings of friendship from the Korean people to the people of the United States.

The world has changed enormously over the past two years. The Iron Curtain, which used to divide the world into two camps, has collapsed and the Cold War has come to an end. With the sweeping reforms in Eastern and Central Europe as well as in the Soviet Union, freedom, human dignity, democratic pluralism, and the market economy are becoming universal values.

Mankind has been living in constant fear of war due to the East-West confrontation. Today, however, we share the belief that we may now successfully build a more peaceful world.

During the recent Gulf War, all peace-loving nations of the world rallied around the United Nations flag. The coalition victory made it clear once and for all that "aggression will not stand."

I pay my respects to you, Mr. President, for your superb leadership and to the American people for having inspired brighter hopes for a new era.

Having proudly joined the long march toward freedom shoulder-to-shoulder with the American people, the Korean people are very pleased to offer congratulations to America on its success.

Because their land remains divided, and because they acutely remember the tragedies of war, the Korean people are hoping that the currents of peace and reconciliation will soon reach the shores of Northeast Asia and the Korean Peninsula.

Mr. President, since we met in June of last year, significant activities have in fact been taking place in Northeast Asia and the Korean Peninsula. The changing U.S.-Soviet relations, of course, lead the list of events. But, we have also seen exchanges between China and the Soviet Union, and contacts between the Soviet Union and Japan as well as between Japan and North Korea.

At the same time, the Republic of Korea ended decades of enmity and established diplomatic relations with the Soviet Union and the countries of Eastern and Central Europe.

More significantly, North Korea reversed its former position and announced a decision to apply for U.N. membership along with us. These encouraging activities have, of course, been spurred on by close cooperation between your country and mine. We must now focus our attention to removing the legacies of the Cold War from the Korean Peninsula and Northeast Asia so that a durable peace and stability may be secured for the entire Asia-Pacific region.

Our rapid economic development has made Korea a showcase to the former Socialist countries by demonstrating the merits of a capitalist economy, and made us a model to the less developed countries by proving the efficiency of a free-market economy and an open society.

Based on these achievements and having experienced enormous sociopolitical difficulties, Korea has now entered an era of full-fledged democracy.

As the world saw during the 1988 Seoul Olympic Games, Korea's dynamic energies and cooperative spirit encourage a new faith in freedom and hope for prosperity around the world. The Korean people have now become a dependable friend and ally of the American people, and they promise to assume appropriate international responsibilities and make a greater contribution to the international community.

The United States has initiated the current change around the world and is successfully carrying out a leadership role. And, our two countries will march together into the 21st century as partners in trust just as we have come thus far.

Our coming meeting, Mr. President, will be my fourth opportunity to confer with you. Through it, and in my talks with other American leaders, I shall reaffirm my faith in a bright future for our two countries.

I wish you, Mr. President, and Mrs. Bush the best of health, and wish the American people everlasting peace and prosperity.

Thank you.

24.

Remarks at the State Dinner Hosted by the President of the United States of America and Mrs. George Bush, The White House, Washington, D.C., July 2, 1991

Your Excellencies President and Mrs. Bush, distinguished guests, ladies and gentlemen.

I would like to extend my deep appreciation to you, Mr. President, for the kind invitation to visit your great country and for the generous hospitality accorded my delegation. Through our meetings this morning, Mr. President, I can reaffirm that we are indeed living in a great era of change. As you said in your inaugural address, Mr. President, a world refreshed by freedom is indeed being reborn in the past two to three years.

The Fourth of July this year will truly be a unique day in American history. For the first time in 215 years, the American people will be able to celebrate the world-wide realization of the founding ideals of the Declaration of Independence—namely that life, liberty and the pursuit of happiness are inalienable rights bestowed upon all men. On this occasion, the entire Korean people, who have been pursuing these common ideals, join me in extending heartfelt congratulations to the American people.

The Gulf War victory has established that the international community will no longer tolerate wanton aggression and that the rule of law shall prevail in our world. We are at an historical juncture at which a new world order of freedom, justice and peace is being established. I salute you, Mr. President, for your courageous decisions and firm leadership and the American people for their unflagging support for the cause of freedom.

Mr. President,
It would perhaps be impossible today to separate American and Korean

values and ideas in various aspects of Korean life, including the political, economic, educational, scientific, and cultural. In the course of developing such a strong bond between our two countries across the Pacific, many of your people rendered invaluable services and noble sacrifices. The Korean people shall never forget the enormous contributions made on our behalf. Even at this very moment, more than 40,000 American servicemen and women are on the other side of the Pacific on a vigil for peace on the Korean Peninsula.

You deserve to be proud that the Republic of Korea, which received so much encouragement and support from the United States, is now moving ahead toward freedom and prosperity. Despite transitional difficulties, democracy in Korea is on course and is moving inexorably forward. Commensurate with its political-economic development, Korea is determined to assume apppropriate roles and responsibilities in the international community.

I believe that Korea and the United States should closely cooperate, and encourage changes that will remove the tension and instability, and the barrier which divides the Korean Peninsula.

Mr. President,

As valued partners, Korea and the United States together will usher in a free, peaceful and prosperous Pacific Era in the 21st century. Our meeting today heralds this commitment to the Pacific and to the world.

Ladies and gentlemen,

Please join me in a toast to the health of President and Mrs. Bush, to the ever-enduring prosperity of the United States of America, and to the lasting friendship between Korea and the United States.

25.

Korea: Emerging World Power; Interview, *Leaders* Magazine (U.S.A.), July 1991

EDITOR'S NOTE: Roh Tae Woo was born into a farming family in 1932 and grew up in a small village at the foot of Mt. P'algongsan. His early ambition was to be a doctor, but his plans changed when he joined the army at the outbreak of the Korean War in 1950. In 1952 he entered the Korean Military Academy and after a distinguished military career retired in 1981 as a four-star general.

That year he was appointed Minister of State for National Security and Foreign Affairs and in 1982 was appointed the first Minister of Sports. He has also served as Minister of Home Affairs, President of the Seoul Olympic Organizing Committee, president of the Korean Olympic Committee and the Korean Amateur Sports Association and was concurrently a member of the National Assembly and chairman of the ruling Democratic Justice Party.

In June 1987 he was chosen to be the presidential candidate of the DJP. When he was elected in December 1987, the first election of a Korean president by direct popular vote in 16 years, over 90 percent of the population participated. His election marked a peaceful transfer of power after several years of volatile confrontation.

In this interview, President Roh shares his views on the political and economic opportunities created by Korea's reform.

Your third summit meeting with President Gorbachev in April is widely regarded as a turning point both for improved Korean-Soviet relations and for a new Northeast Asian international order. Would you comment on this and put some of the relevant issues in perspective?

It was in June of last year in San Francisco that I had the first summit meeting with President Gorbachev. At the time, it came as fresh and shocking news to those who were used to a Cold War mind-set and the then-rigid situation in the Korean Peninsula and Northeast Asia.

President Gorbachev, himself, as well as the news media around the world, described our first meeting as "a conference that broke the ice between Korea and the Soviet Union." President Gorbachev confided in me that it had required tremendous courage on his part to agree to the San Francisco summit.

For historical reasons, diplomatic relations between our two countries had been suspended for 86 years. The Cold War system that emerged at the end of World War II had brought to Korea territorial division, three years of internecine Korean War and forty years of confrontation and tension.

As the leader of our opponent bloc, the Soviet Union has been directly related to the Cold War realities of the Korean Peninsula, as well as to the painful and distressing experiences of the Korean people throughout the postwar period.

By the end of September 1990, our two countries had established formal diplomatic relations. Then, in December, I paid a state visit to the Soviet Union, and four months later President Gorbachev came to Cheju Island, the first Soviet head of state to set foot on Korean soil.

That these exchange visits have taken place is itself evidence that the long, drawn-out period of Cold War around the Korean Peninsula is at last nearing an end.

President Gorbachev and I were satisfied with the outcome of our talks. The Soviet leader expressed his support for our position that North Korea should submit its nuclear facilities to international inspection and sign the nuclear safeguards agreement required under the IAEA treaty (to which North Korea is a signatory) and for the Republic of Korea's entry into the United Nations.

President Gorbachev expressed his support for our position that, until we achieve unification, South and North Korea should work together to build a mutually beneficial and prosperous relationship through dialogue, exchanges and cooperation.

The current development in Korean-Soviet relations is the result of a confluence between the Soviet foreign policy based on the new thinking and Korea's "Northern Policy," which I initiated in 1988.

In the past two or three years, the Republic of Korea has concluded diplomatic relations with all the former socialist countries in Eastern and Central Europe, except for Albania.

But removal of the confrontational structure in the Korean Peninsula is a prerequisite to an enduring peace and the stability of Northeast Asia, as well as the Asia-Pacific region.

Now, in the wake of improving Korean-Soviet relations, new waves of reconciliation, which have brought a "common house" to Europe, have begun to reach the shores of this region. For example, the Soviet Union has put forward a proposal to host an Asian Foreign Ministers Meeting in 1993 and an initiative for multilateral cooperation under the aegis of Northeast Asia/ Asia-Pacific process.

I would emphasize, though, that before any of these actions are considered it would be necessary to foster a more favorable international atmosphere in this region through confidence-building measures, as well as through the development of closer bilateral relations, including the resolution of the South-North Korean problem.

The Republic of Korea will continue to closely cooperate with the United States, her most important ally, to bring about an Asia-Pacific region in which the regional states join their efforts for the promotion of peace and prosperity.

Your new relationship with the Soviet Union indicates a new stage as Korea emerges as a world power. Given the Soviet Union's current problems, how do you see this future relationship working?

The Soviet reforms appear to be undergoing considerable difficulties at the moment. It must be tantamount to a thoroughgoing revolution to transform a command economy and a 70-year-old Communist system into a market economy and a pluralistic democratic system.

The failure of reform in the Soviet Union would not simply mean ill fortune for the Soviet people. Its repercussions would be felt in all other countries. The world peace structure itself would be affected if the Soviet Union were to revert to conservative extremism or fall prey to colossal chaos.

The Republic of Korea seeks to improve relations with the Soviet Union for the cause of freedom, a market economy and the promotion of regional and world peace. And I believe the development of substantive bilateral relations will produce mutually advantageous and beneficial results.

Further, Soviet cooperation is indispensable if we are to reduce and remove the tension and confrontation in the Korean Peninsula.

For its own benefit, the Soviet Union will continue to improve relations with the countries of the West. It would be indispensable for and conducive to the maintenance of world peace that we extend support and assistance to the success of the Soviet reform effort.

Will the $3 billion Korea has given in economic assistance to the Soviet Union be well used in the face of its current economic and political instability?

The terms we extended to the Soviet Union within the framework of economic cooperation are not those of a grant. They consist of various elements, such as bank loans, delayed-payment commodities and manufacturing plants.

We hope that our commodities will help relieve the acute Soviet consumer goods shortage and that our manufacturing facilities will prove to be of some assistance in Soviet efforts to introduce a market economy.

Much has been said about the unification of Korea. Will it happen during your administration?

Now that the Cold War structure has collapsed around the world and Germany has been unified, I believe the unification of Korea is also possible. I don't believe North Korea can long remain an island in the face of such titanic, historic waves of reform and openness.

Furthermore, in view of the rapid progress being made in Korea's friendly and cooperative relations with socialist countries, it would be impossible for North Korea to insist much longer on a hard-line isolationist policy.

Internally, North Korea is suffering from extreme political and economic difficulties. This means, quite plainly, that change there is inevitable. Should North Korea decide to open its society, I believe a strong national cohesiveness will develop and that unification will come rather quickly. And while it is very difficult to forecast a time frame, it is reasonable to anticipate that a decisive opportunity will present itself by the middle of the nineties.

I believe it is my duty before history to build a foundation for peaceful unification, and I will do my utmost to this end.

You have indicated that, irrespective of North Korea's attitude, the Republic of Korea will seek membership in the United Nations this year. What, in your view, are the advantages and/or disadvantages of joining the U.N.?

The Republic of Korea should become a member in view of the universality principle of the U.N.—and a great majority of nations support Korea's entry.

The United Nations' peace-keeping role is rapidly increasing. Thus, the Republic of Korea should be admitted to the U.N. for the speedier reduction of tension in the Korean Peninsula and for the stepped-up promotion of stability and cooperation in the Asia-Pacific region.

Our desire to join the world body stems from a belief that by formally becoming a member of the U.N. we can better carry out our international responsibilities and work more effectively for the promotion and maintenance of international peace in the Asia-Pacific region and the world.

It had been our position that until we achieve unification both South and North Korea become members of the U.N. In a dramatic policy reversal, however, North Korea recently announced it would apply for U.N. membership this year in tandem with South Korea.

The U.N. membership will certainly encourage North Korea to join the international community as a responsible member. I firmly believe that this will be highly conducive to the maintenance of peace and stability in the Korean Peninsula.

You have been very successful in your "Northern Policy." What is your assessment of the current state of Korea-U.S. relations and your prognosis for them?

I believe Korea-U.S. relations today are better and closer than at any time and under any government of the past.

Four Korea-U.S. summit meetings have taken place since I became president three years ago. Seoul and Washington are in constant contact for purposes of close consultation and cooperation on a wide range of issues. A cordial and friendly atmosphere prevails between our two countries, and we are able to resolve bilateral problems to our mutual satisfaction through negotiations and compromise.

The frictions that existed between Korea and the U.S. during the days of Korea's authoritarian government have been removed since I was put into office through direct popular election.

Korea is today a successful showcase of market economics and democracy, which the U.S. foreign policy has consistently pursued throughout the postwar period. A country devastated by the Korean War forty years ago, Korea has since become a dynamic Newly Industrializing Country as a result of rapid and sustained economic development. In fact, the Republic of Korea today ranks 15th in global G.N.P. output and 12th in volume of trade.

Korea's rapid economic development is looked on as a successful model for development and reform for many newly industrializing countries around the world, including many Eastern and Central European countries, as well as the Soviet Union.

Furthermore, Korea successfully hosted the 1988 Seoul Olympics and is carrying out democratic reforms.

The Republic of Korea, located on the western Pacific, has become a most trustworthy partner of the United States in the Asia-Pacific region, an area of developmental dynamism and home to more than half the world's population.

In a speech before a joint meeting of the U.S. Congress in October 1989, I said, "The Republic of Korea is an ally of the United States and will remain so." Today, I can reiterate that, even as international situations change. Korea-U.S. relations will remain firm and solid into the 21st century.

Scenes of violent Korean student demonstrations, including anti-American slogans and burning of the U.S. flag, are often shown on American TV. What do you think of these phenomena?

I am well aware of some of these phenomena. Among the "democracy fighters" who participated in the anti-authoritarian-government movement was a minority of left-leaning radicals. As democratization proceeded in Korea, and as our society became more open and liberal, their voices appear to have become louder, they are more vociferous.

Given the 40-year-long confrontation with North Korea's hard-line communism and the relentless communist propaganda and agitation, it is perhaps inevitable that some of our young men are confused and misled. But they are a small minority. I would say, in fact, they are only a handful when compared with the overwhelming majority of Korean people who steadfastly support a strong bond with the United States. The followers of violent revolution and class struggle are rapidly losing ground, as are adherents on college campuses throughout Korea, particularly since the democratic reforms in Korea, the onset of perestroika in the Soviet Union and the collapse of communist systems across Eastern Europe.

As opportunities to travel in China, the Soviet Union and Eastern Europe increase, most of the young people are able to see the realities of socialist societies first-hand and quickly cast off their illusions.

To be sure, there often appear criticisms on various aspects of Korea-U.S. relations, but we must not confuse these constructive criticisms with "anti-Americanism." As Korea-U.S. relations improve, mature criticism aimed at perfecting our partnership can be expected, and it is perhaps a sign of the healthy state of our relations.

You said an overwhelming majority of Koreans support strong ties with the United States. Now, what does the United States mean to Korea?

A vast majority of Korean people think of the United States as a friend who rushed to the defense of our freedom when the very survival of this nation hung in the balance at the outbreak of the Korean War. They know that the United States extended support and assistance in the course of Korea's recovery from poverty and the ruins of war to the current stage of economic development and that the American people continue to stand by this nation in its efforts to secure peace and freedom.

In addition, our people are fully aware the United States is our largest export market and that our bilateral trade volume exceeds $36 billion a year. They regard the United States as Korea's closest friend in every sense—political, economic, social and cultural. Above all, they share the ideals and values cherished by the American people.

What does the future hold for military strength in South Korea? Is it necessary? Will South Korea continue to decrease her foreign military presence?

In times of turbulent change, unpredictable challenges often present themselves.

We hope and pray we will never have to face such a situation, but one can hardly rule out the possibility that North Korea, currently under severe internal pressures to change, will seek to relieve the pressure by external venture.

In fact, it is not surprising that the U.S. Defense Department has named the Korean Peninsula the most dangerous area in the world in the aftermath of the Gulf War.

You cannot secure peace by wishing alone. Peace is secured only when there is enough power to deter war. This is the reality in the Korean Peninsula today.

The U.S. forces in Korea are playing a pivotal role in the maintenance of peace and stability in the Korean Peninsula, as well as in Northeast Asia. Depending on the situation and military requirements, I would assume that the size of U.S. troops could be adjusted somewhat, but until the situation in the Korean Peninsula goes through a fundamental change, the role of the U.S. forces in Korea will remain essential and unchanged.

How do you see the future of Korea's trade with other nations?

The volume of world trade is steadily increasing, although problems do persist in international trade. Because the Republic of Korea has achieved economic development through international trade, we shall continue to promote trade with all the countries of the world.

Moreover, we must step up cooperation for the promotion of free trade and guard against protectionist tendencies and the proliferation of exclusive economic blocs. Since the world economy today must resolve not only the North-South problem but also the East-West problem stemming from the reforms of socialist countries, we must bring the Uruguay Round negotiations to fruition in a spirit of cooperation and for the common prosperity.

I believe trade with the United States will increase in a sustained and balanced manner.

Until 1981 Korea's trade with the U.S. showed a chronic deficit. But between 1982 and 1990 we recorded a current account surplus vis-a-vis the U.S. The surplus peaked in 1987, with almost $10 billion in our favor. But the surplus decreased to about $2.4 billion last year, and the trend so far this year indicates that imports from the U.S. will exceed exports. This is a result of market-opening measures and sustained efforts to maintain balanced trade with the U.S.

Because Korea is currently the sixth-largest export market of the U.S. and the second-largest importer of U.S. agricultural products, the improvement of bilateral trade relations would be as important to the U.S. as it is to Korea.

Canada and Mexico are joining the United States to promote North American free trade, and I hope it will develop so as to enhance regional cooperation. Should it, however, degenerate into an exclusive trade bloc, it would work to the detriment of the world economy at large.

Our trade relations with E.E.C. countries are steadily expanding. But our trade deficit vis-a-vis Japan persists, and the chronic deficit has been growing in recent years.

Our trade volumes vis-a-vis China and the Soviet Union are increasing rapidly of late and are expected to grow.

Some U.S. critics point out that the speed of Korea's market opening is below expectations and that some of the commercial practices and con-

sumer austerity campaigns in Korea tend to breach the fairness principle in the eyes of U.S. businesses. How do you respond to this?

I believe that few developing countries are opening their markets as fast as Korea is. We also need to open our markets for our own economic development. We have opened our markets for all items except a few agricultural products. And we are gradually opening service and capital markets.

Just as there are pressure groups in the U.S. calling for import restrictions on specified items, we too have protest by interest groups that perceive damage by specific market opening measures.

Recently, actions by some of these groups, coupled with business and consumer behavior stemming from cultural differences, have caused some worries and misunderstandings in the U.S. But our two governments have been able to remove, and will continue to remove through consultation, the causes of friction that may arise in the course of opening our markets and expanding the volume of bilateral trade.

For those in other nations wanting to invest in Korea, in what areas would they be most successful and in which areas would they be most welcome?

Korea has opened its doors wide to investment from abroad. I have not yet heard of a foreign firm reporting a loss on an investment in Korea.

Investments accompanied by highly advanced technology, I believe, will be both welcome and successful in Korea.

The development of natural resources in the Soviet Union seems to have great potential, and excellent opportunities exist there for Korean and third country firms to form joint ventures and participate in Soviet infrastructure expansion projects.

And I would look to Korean and U.S. firms to jointly participate in the post-war reconstruction projects in the Middle East.

How do you plan to spur investment in technology-intensive industries while balancing the need for foreign technology and maintaining a high level of investment?

The increasing trends in the advanced countries toward protection of technologies and know-how are becoming sources of enormous difficulty for newly developing countries.

Korea has actively and diligently sought to import essential technologies from the advanced countries and in the process has paid a sizable amount of royalties.

We are also actively encouraging research and development in high technology. And many Korean firms are already making heavy investments in R&D.

The Korean government is extending positive support for corporate efforts to improve the R&D environment by assisting in such areas as expansion of research facilities, training of personnel and the timely supply of technical information.

Should government be involved in promoting technological development, in view of the decreasing private financial means in this field?

The development of particular technologies can, of course, be done most efficiently by the particular firm or industry involved. But private sector firms are not expected—nor do they have the capabilites—to develop highly advanced technologies, which require sizable and sustained investment, or technologies for the benefit of the general public.

To accomplish these goals, the Korean government encourages the formation of industry consortia, as in advanced countries, or looks to appropriate government and public research institutes to develop the technologies in demand.

How does Korea's hierarchical tradition harmonize with the modern political-economic system Korea has chosen to follow?

As Korea has industrialized, pluralism and diversity have spread quickly throughout the society. As a result, the much-disdained authoritarian practices in which arbitrary orders are used for uniform compliance downward are no longer complied with nor tolerated by our already diversified and pluralistic society.

Democracy has made remarkable progress in Korea since 1987, and the diffusion of power and local autonomy are now widely practiced in our society. My government specifically supports social diversity and encourages necessary adjustments wherever they are called for.

Authoritarianism is fast disappearing from all aspects of Korean society.

To be sure, the Korean society retains a unique cultural tradition, but this tradition should not necessarily have negative implications for modernization and development.

Looking back on the course of Korea's political-economic development, the traditional culture and modern capitalist system have as much forged harmony to produce unique sinews of national strength as they have clashed head-on.

In addition, the strong leadership of the government has made indispensable contributions in our drive toward rapid economic development, while the charismatic, personalized style of management by the owner-founders of private corporations has served as an essential catalyst to the attainment of Korea's remarkable economic success.

Diligence and the cooperative spirit stemming from a familial community tradition have also been a source of strength.

In the '80s, however, the authoritarian style of government and paternalistic style of corporate management came to meet strong resistance from the public, so even before I became president I called for an era of ordinary people. Since

I came to office I have therefore concentrated on removing the vestiges of authoritarian culture and implementing democratic reforms.

The more Korean society is industrialized, the more the Korean people seem to cherish the traditional culture and the value system ingrained in them through close-knit family life and the communal learning process. So the government will redouble its efforts to preserve and promote Korea's cultural heritage and tradition.

How do you see the world changing in the next ten years? Do you see political stability and harmony? How you see further trade cooperation between certain hemispheres and countries?

The world is still pregnant with many problems and challenges stemming from such issues as race, religion, poverty. . . .

Right now, the world is in the process of casting off the yoke of ideology. No one will now be able to turn back the massive waves of history toward reconciliation and cooperation or to stop the Cold War from its own demise.

The change is now moving toward this area of Asia, toward China and North Korea. As soon as the iron curtains in these countries are lifted, and as they pursue economic development and take advantage of such systems as free trade, market economics and economic cooperation, the trade volume between East and West will certainly see a quantum jump.

The prospects for the North-South problem are not very promising, however. A majority of developing and underdeveloped countries are suffering from chronic poverty and foreign debt. So the gap between the North and the South is expected to further widen, particularly in view of the rapid pace of progress in modern technology.

Thus, if we are to succeed in building a more peaceful and harmonious world, we must step up international cooperation and find effective solutions to the North-South problem.

26.

Remarks During the Reception at the 17th World Jamboree Mondial, Kosung, Korea, August 12, 1991

Thank you, Dr. Moreillon, for your kind words.

There is something that strikes me, here at the Sorak Jamboree campsite. The Scout leaders all look surprisingly young as if they were in their twenties! As you know, people these days would pay a fortune just to look a few years younger, and I think they would gladly hand over a million dollars if you will only let them in on your secrets to staying young. The Scout uniforms no doubt take a few years off your appearance, but I think there is something more to it than that. I believe that the source of your "perennial youth" is that you live surrounded by youngsters with whom you share the dreams, the friendship, adventures and pioneering, the very spirit of Scouting.

Just being with you here at the Sorak Jamboree site, surrounded by the mountains, lakes and open sea in beautiful harmony, even I feel at least ten years younger.

Secretary General Moreillon, World Jamboree Camp Chief Kim Sok Won, distinguished Scouting leaders, ladies and gentlemen,

The young Scouts of today are the leaders of the 21st century. I am very pleased to join all of you here at the 17th World Jamboree Mondial, and welcome you to Korea.

Three years ago, the young men and women of the world came together for the Seoul Olympics. It was a harmonious festival that transcended the barriers of ideology, race, and culture. Following that memorable event, the high walls and barriers that stood between the East and the West began to crumble all around the world.

During those three short years, the world has witnessed revolutionary changes in Berlin, Eastern Europe, and the Soviet Union, as well as in international relations. As a result, mankind has rekindled the hope that they may now live in peace and prosperity, transcending national and ideological barriers.

It is all the more meaningful that the World Jamboree is being held here in Korea, a land that still remains divided despite the arrival of a new era and even as the dark age of division and confrontation is ending.

Almost twenty thousand participants representing some 133 countries have come here, making this by far the largest Jamboree in Scouting history. I am sure this event will mark a memorable turning point of the Scouting movement, not to mention for each individual participant. I am especially happy that for the first time since the end of the Second World War, we have participants from the Soviet Union, and Eastern and Central European countries. It is my sincere hope that through this Jamboree the Scouting movement will be able to realize our motto of "Many Lands, One World."

During the nine days of activities held in these beautiful natural surroundings, the youth of the world will share their dreams, find new friendships, and become one in their hearts within the spirit of Scouting. This is a great opportunity to bridge the differences between the peoples and nations. Though the young Scouts come from lands of different language, religion, and ways of life, I am sure they will discover common youthful ideals and learn the value of cooperation.

I believe the 17th World Jamboree will serve as a beacon of hope for the coming century, just as the Seoul Olympics sowed a seed for worldwide reconciliation.

Ladies and gentlemen,

In 6th and 7th century Korea, the Shilla Dynasty had a system that was perhaps an ancient version of the Boy Scouts. They were called the Hwarang (or the Flowers of Youth Cadets). Under the guidance of a leader, teenagers would join a group organized to learn the duties and responsibilities of an honorable life as leaders. They trained their minds and bodies by such means as exploring mountains and rivers, and singing and dancing. Many eminent leaders were products of this group, and they later became the principal leaders responsible for achieving the first unified kingdom on the Korean Peninsula.

Today's societies are moved not by a few heroes, but by ordinary people with sound bodies and minds, that is, by the democratic citizens. And as democratic citizens of a "global village," we are called upon to contribute as much to our respective nations, as to the world as a whole. The Scouting movement teaches the necessary values for young men and women to be strong mentally as well as physically, and has become one of the major driving forces for instilling hopes in many societies.

As our future leaders now join hands and advance toward "One World," I believe that this Jamboree will become a prominent landmark in our journey towards a brighter 21st century.

During your stay, I hope you will enjoy to the fullest the beauty and hospitality that Korea and the Korean people have to offer.

To all the leaders and able organizers of the 17th World Jamboree, I offer my congratulations and appreciation for the selfless work you have so beautifully put into this event, and I wish you lasting progress of the Scout movement.

Thank you.

27.

Toward a Peaceful World Community; Address to the Forty-Sixth Session of the United Nations General Assembly, United Nations, New York, September 24, 1991

Mr. President, Mr. Secretary-General, distinguished delegates,

Three years ago, I had the pleasure of reporting to you from this very rostrum the refreshing and heart-warming scenes of the Seoul Olympic Games. Those athletes from across the world gave us an inspiring vision of global harmony, transcending the divisions of race, religion, and ideology.

Soon thereafter, revolutionary changes swept across the world. As we look around today and take stock of the changes, we may truly recognize the progress made toward the Olympic ideal of "one peaceful world."

Today, I am proud to stand here once more, this time as president of a member state. To me, this itself represents a significant expression of the new tide of history.

It was forty-three years ago that the Republic of Korea first applied formally to become a member of the United Nations. If you consider the decades of patience we have had to endure, you will perhaps understand the enthusiasm displayed by the Korean people on this occasion.

To those who have supported and encouraged our admission to this august body and to those who have acted and spoken on our behalf during all the years that we had no seat here, I offer the heartfelt gratitude of the Korean people.

Today, the Cold War system, which had prevented our entry to the United Nations, has become a relic of the past.

From the workers of the Solidarity Movement in Gdansk, who raised the banner of reform in Poland to the courageous government in Budapest; from those freedom-inspired crowds who filled Prague's Vaclavske Plaza to those former East Germans who tore down the Berlin Wall—not only did they free themselves, but they opened the road toward a genuine world peace.

In removing the physical walls which denied them liberty, they also brought down the barriers which divided mankind into hostile camps forcing confrontation and rivalry. It was, unquestionably, the Soviet reforms that touched off these great changes. But these changes have also been inspired by the achievements of those nations which attained prosperity on the strength of freedom and individual values. I share a deep sense of satisfaction over this outcome with those who have aspired for a truly harmonious world, and I pay tribute to the courage of those who made into reality what had been considered impossible in the past.

Mr. President,
I offer my congratulations on your election as President of the 46th Session of the General Assembly, and express my confidence that this Session under your leadership will produce fruitful and rewarding achievements.

Mr. President,
I regard it no less significant that along with the Republic of Korea, the Democratic People's Republic of Korea (DPRK) has also become a member of this Organization.

As our North Korean brothers join us in the journey toward peace and unification, I extend hearty congratulations to them on their entry.

The Republic of Korea has long pursued parallel membership of both Koreas in the United Nations in the belief that it is the most realistic approach to the attainment of peace and unification on the Korean Peninsula. A continuation of wasteful confrontation, refusing to recognize each other, will only prolong the painful tragedy of national division.

For this reason, the entry of both South and North Korea into the United Nations marks an important turning-point in inter-Korean relations since the division of our land in 1945.

As responsible members of the international community, the two Koreas are now both bound by the United Nations Charter to carry out the duties incumbent on all members for the maintenance of world peace.

Now that the delegates of South and North Korea have taken their seats together in this hall of peace, we are convinced that a new chapter of reconciliation and cooperation will open on the Korean Peninsula.

The Korean people may live under two separate systems, but we have never forgotten that we are one nation.

Imperfect as it may be, the separate membership of the two Koreas in the United Nations is an important interim step on the road to national unification.

It has taken more than forty years for us to move the short distance from the observer's to a member's seat. It took the two Germanies seventeen years to combine their UN seats. I sincerely hope that it will not take as long for the two Korean seats to become one.

In this hall of peace, the two Koreas will open a new avenue of dialogue and cooperation that will lead to our national unity.

The Cold War system that brought on the tragedy of territorial division in Korea has itself collapsed. Now, we will seek to achieve national unification: peacefully—without the use of military force; independently—on the basis of self-determination; and democratically—according to the free will of the Korean people.

I earnestly hope that all the members of the United Nations will encourage and support Korean efforts to join the human progress toward a more peaceful world by achieving their national unity.

Mr. President and distinguished delegates,

The world is undergoing epochal changes.

Systems that oppressed freedom and human dignity are being dismantled and the tragedies stemming from dogmatic ideologies are coming to an end everywhere.

Around the world nations are seeking to chart their own destinies.

What is truly momentous about this process is that history is being advanced not by the forces of bloody revolution but by the power of reason and free spirit. But, the great change has only just begun.

This epic change brings enormous opportunities and is the source of hope for all mankind. Even so, we must travel a long and tortuous road before we can successfully mold the current process into a new order of world peace.

The recent Soviet political crisis is a clear demonstration of this fact.

The entire world spent those three stressful days in a state of shock and dismay. However, the courageous citizens of Moscow braved the crisis, and placed flowers in the muzzles of tank guns. Indeed, their victory is the victory of all freedom- and peace-loving peoples of the world. Once again, the world has been reminded that indeed "peace is indivisible."

We have to recognize that any attempt at reform, however minor, is bound to require an element of sacrifice and pain. In the cases of the Soviet Union and the Eastern European countries, we know they are currently engaged in through-going reforms of their political, economic and social foundations. In moving away from a system of strict control that pervaded every aspect of their lives for decades, the difficulties and costs of creating new structures must be truly enormous.

We all know that throughout the Cold War period, the nations of the world spent an exorbitant amount of resources on national security and military preparedness. Now, the success of current reforms promises to bring benefits the world over in the form of peace; and we will enjoy this "peace dividend" for a long time to come.

As the benefits of peace are shared, it is only fair that the burdens and sacrifices should also be shared.

Consequently, I call upon all the well-to-do nations to extend active support and assistance to the countries which used to have centrally planned economic systems, in their transition to democracy and free market economies.

Due to the imperatives of the Cold War, the Korean people have had to sustain enormous sacrifices throughout the postwar period. Accordingly, we yearn for a world of peace, perhaps more than any nation on earth.

As a nation that has risen only a generation ago from the ashes of war, and as a recently democratized nation that is growing in prosperity, the Republic of Korea feels a special affinity toward the emerging democracies, and understands from experience the acute imperative that these nations are facing together: to achieve democratic and economic development in tandem.

Korea is neither a wealthy nor an advanced country. But, we are prepared to extend support to the reform efforts not only in Eastern Europe and the Soviet Union but in all parts of the world, and to offer them cooperation to the best of our ability.

Mr. President,

In my speech before the 43rd Session of the General Assembly, I declared that a durable peace would arrive in our world the day we "beat swords into ploughshares" on the Korean Peninsula. I said this because our own land was visited by untold trials and tribulations stemming from the international imperatives of the twentieth century, and because the yoke was still upon us.

However, the external climate surrounding the Korean Peninsula has undergone significant changes over the past years.

Even before the onset of worldwide reform movements, we took the initiative of going beyond the limits of the Cold War. Subsequently, we established diplomatic relations with the Central and Eastern European countries as well as the Soviet Union. We also opened mutual exchanges and cooperative relations with neighboring China.

For the previous half century, Korea's relations with these countries had been officially severed, and in practice were often confrontational. However, with our new friendships and cooperation we sense the onrush of the waves of contemporary history. Indeed, we have discovered the power of reconciliation.

We are firmly convinced that the day of peace and unification is also coming to our land, in spite of territorial division and the ever present military threat.

With the entry of the two Koreas into the United Nations, we have embarked on a new phase of coexistence. Now, it is our task to build on this foundation a positive relationship, which will soon bring peace, stability and national unity.

To this end, I propose that the two Korean governments agree on and specifically carry out the following three measures:

First, the two Koreas should replace the fragile armistice with a permanent peace structure.

Even at this very moment, a total of 1.7 million heavily armed soldiers confront each other on the Korean Peninsula, concentrated along the 250-kilometer-long Demilitarized Zone.

It might come as a surprise to some of you, but we have been living under this unstable condition of neither peace nor war for the last four decades.

In light of these precarious realities, I believe the two Koreas should conclude a peace agreement, thus renouncing the use of force against each other, and proceed to normalize bilateral relations in all areas.

My second proposal is that, in order to reduce the threat of war on the Korean Peninsula, the two sides should seek to bring about realistic arms reductions beginning with measures designed to build mutual confidence.

In order to remove military confrontation on the Korean Peninsula, it is imperative that South and North Korea agree upon a number of military confidence-building measures, including the exchange of military information, the advance notification of field exercises as well as troop movements, and the exchange of permanent observer teams to prevent surprise attacks.

Above all, the development of nuclear weapons on the Korean Peninsula will present a threat not only to the peace of Northeast Asia but also to the peace of the whole world.

Atomic energy must never be used for destructive military purposes, but must only be used for peaceful purposes of promoting the well-being of all mankind. Since the DPRK is a signatory to the Nuclear Non-proliferation Treaty, it should immediately abandon the development of nuclear weapons, and submit, unconditionally, all of its nuclear-related materials and facilities to international inspection.

Once the DPRK abandons its development of nuclear weapons and as confidence-building measures are implemented between South and North Korea, I am prepared to take up discussions with North Korea not only on the reduction of conventional forces but also on the nuclear issues on the Korean Peninsula.

Finally, and on a more humanitarian plane, the two Koreas should bring an end to the period of dissociation, and open a new era of free exchange of products, information and people.

On our Peninsula today, there are over ten million Koreans who live separated from their families and loved ones as a result of the territorial division in 1945 and of the Korean War. They are denied even the most basic humanitarian right of knowing whether or not their parents, brothers and sisters are still alive, let alone exchanging letters or telephone calls. I do not believe we can talk meaningfully about improving inter-Korean relations or mutual confidence-building without first resolving this urgent humanitarian problem.

Just as it is a universal practice among all civilized nations, so must the two Koreas open doors toward each other and guarantee free travel, communication and trade.

We must promote substantive relations by resolving, through dialogue and negotiations, issues of mutual interest including inter-Korean exchanges and cooperation as well as political and military issues.

Next month, for the first time since the two Koreas became members of this Organization, the two government delegations will meet for a fourth round of the South-North High-level Talks. I sincerely hope that the talks will produce an agreement on the basic principles governing inter-Korean relations.

Recently, some limited exchanges between the two Koreas have taken place in such areas as sports, culture, and trade. Small as they are, we value this progress.

For our part, we will do our best to promote a relationship of common prosperity in which the two Koreas offer each other assistance for mutual development.

The Republic of Korea is prepared to actively pursue economic cooperation with the DPRK in all areas, including trade, tourism, joint exploration of underground resources and establishment of joint venture plants.

Please bear in mind that the Korean people have been living as a single national community for over 1,300 years. Therefore, once exchanges and cooperation begin, conditions for a political integration of the two parts of Korea will ripen very quickly, given our historical homogeneity.

I do not believe that the Korean Peninsula should be left as the only land remaining divided by the Cold War. At a time when all the divisive barriers are collapsing, the unification of the Korean Peninsula must be a matter of time and the natural course of history. A unified Korea will be a land of freedom and happiness for all inhabitants, and will become a nation devoted to the promotion of world peace and the well-being of all mankind.

Mr. President,

The Korean people desire to see peace prevail not only on the Korean Peninsula but in all regions of dispute as well.

I am gratified to note that there are real signs of progress in peace-making efforts in many areas of the world, including the Middle East, Cambodia, Angola, Western Sahara, and Central America. I am highly encouraged to see the United Nations play leading roles in these areas, and I wish to pay my respects to the Honorable Secretary-General, Javier Perez de Cuellar, for his devoted efforts.

Along with efforts to prevent regional disputes and to remove their root causes, we should strengthen the enforcement of collective security measures.

The recent war in the Gulf region confirmed that the United Nations is the only independent global body capable of asserting and giving force to the rule of law in today's international community. Our faith that peace and justice will prevail throughout the world under a new international order was bolstered when countries put aside their differences and joined the UN action in a coalition.

Members of this body will of course recall that the Republic of Korea was able to survive and preserve its integrity thanks to the very first collective security action on the part of the United Nations. Now as a member, we will participate more actively in all UN endeavors toward the peaceful settlement of disputes as well as the enforcement of international justice.

Peace can be built only when a common conviction prevails that nations do not threaten each other and that we may in fact live in peace. We shall never win faith in peace so long as we let our safety hinge on the might of formidable weapons that can reduce this world to ashes in an instant.

Confrontations that brought about the "balance of terror" have now disappeared.

We welcome the signing in July of the START treaty between the United States and the Soviet Union. We hope that it will accelerate arms control negotiations around the world.

The Republic of Korea fully supports a complete elimination of all chemical weapons, and will readily join an international convention as soon as it emerges.

In this connection, I believe that the countries of Northeast Asia should now take a fresh look at, and approaches toward, the questions of tension reduction and arms control in this region.

Mr. President,
It is said that peace is more than the absence of war. To ensure real and lasting peace, we must remove the underlying sources of conflict.

Just as the world is passing beyond ideological divisiveness, we must remove all barriers of discrimination: race, color, religion, national origin.

I therefore welcome the positive efforts in South Africa to build a united, democratic and discrimination-free society.

Mr. President,
The Independent Commission on International Development Issues concluded in its final report that where poverty reigns there can be no peace.

Because the Korean people underwent similar experiences, we feel compassion toward the poverty-stricken countries and have a deep understanding of the problems they are presently facing; poverty, hunger, underdevelopment, foreign debts.

Since the Republic of Korea made the transition from an underdeveloped to a newly industrializing country within the span of one generation, we may have become a model for those developing countries, with a message that they, too, can succeed given time and national resolve.

Thirty years ago, my country was a poor agrarian society with a per capita GNP of under $100. Today, Korea has become a country with the 13th largest trade volume and 15th largest GNP in the world. Korea's rapid development is due largely to the advantages of free market economics and the openness of democratic societies.

The vast global market served as the seedbed of development for an industrious people and innovative businesses. The Korean people have continued their efforts for further progress. Many countries around the world as well as the United Nations itself rendered assistance in the process of Korea's development, and became our partners for common prosperity.

Today, the Republic of Korea lies at a midway stage between the advanced and the developing countries. As such, we hope to return the benefits we received from around the world by playing an active role in solving the global North-South problem. In addition to sharing our experience and know-how with the developing countries, we will seek to play the role of a bridge between the advanced and the developing world by promoting global exchanges and cooperation and by facilitating the flow of commodities, capital and information.

The advanced countries should actively extend assistance to the developing countries with a view to mitigating the latter's difficulties.

These measures by themselves cannot fundamentally solve the North-South problem, and so we encourage the advanced countries to move forward with the horizontal specialization of industries among nations by speeding up the process of readjusting their domestic industrial structures. In addition, they should refrain from monopolizing information and technology.

In order to assist the economic growth of the developing countries, global markets should be opened wider and the expansion of trade should be encouraged. Tendencies toward protectionism and mutually exclusive regional economic blocs should be discouraged.

The international community should adopt a more positive posture toward the solution of these critical problems within the framework of the United Nations system. In addition, we should jointly meet such new and serious global challenges as drug trafficking, terrorism and environmental damage.

Mr. President,

A new century is almost upon us. The twentieth century has seen a great number of achievements, certainly much more than was achieved in previous millennia. At the same time, however, this century has also been a period of unspeakable trials and tribulations brought on by wars, confrontations, inequities, and irrationality.

With the twenty-first century near at hand, the human race is embarking on a new era of peace and reason. The irresistible waves of history today are those propelled by freedom, democracy, and respect for human dignity and individual values.

A new era is upon us in which mutual respect prevails among nations and where conflicts are resolved by peaceful means. Revolutionary advancements in science and technology, particularly in the fields of transportation, information and communication, have transformed the world into a global village in which mankind can pursue common prosperity as neighbors.

Ever since the beginning of history, the human race has aspired for a realization of a "peaceful community" on this turbulent planet. That aspiration is no longer a dream but a realistic goal that we can attain. As partners for peace and common prosperity, all the nations on earth should now open their societies and broaden the avenues of exchange and cooperation to build this peaceful community.

As the pivotal organization for world peace, I believe the United Nations is fully capable of fulfilling this historic task by faithfully carrying out the letter and spirit of the charter.

As a full-fledged member of this world body, the Republic of Korea now proudly joins the world of nations in our common task of realizing the long-held dreams of all mankind.

We may ask for your help and understanding with our own problems, but we also care deeply for the welfare of other peoples.

We renew our commitment to the United Nations and will march forward hand in hand with all nations in the cause of this organization.

Henceforth, the Republic of Korea will play a leading role in building a world that will be a blessing to our posterity—a world that will be freer, safer and happier; above all, a world of peace.

Thank you.

28.

Untying the Last Knot of the Cold War; Interview, *Newsweek*, September 30, 1991

Before he left for New York to address the United Nations, President Roh Tae Woo spoke with Newsweek's *C. S. Manegold. Excerpts:*

MANEGOLD: How do you assess the importance of South Korea's entry into the United Nations?
ROH: This is the last knot of the cold war, and we are finally untying it with this entry. Even though the Republic of Korea has had the capability to make a great contribution to the promotion of peace on the international stage, we were unable to do that because we were kept out. Several years ago in Malta, George Bush and Mikhail Gorbachev got together and declared that the cold war was over. But the wind of change apparently was blocked by the Himalayas. It still has not reached us. The cold war persists on the Korean Peninsula to this day.

What specific steps can be taken within the United Nations to diminish the nuclear threat?
We should start off by emphasizing the principle under the United Nations that all signatories to the Nuclear Non-proliferation Treaty are bound by international law. North Korea, being a party to this treaty, should unconditionally sign the nuclear safeguards agreement and open all nuclear-related materials and facilities to international inspection. It should follow the specific steps spelled out by the International Atomic Energy Agency.

Is there some action that South Korea should take to allay the North's concerns?
Once North Korea carries out and fulfills all duties required by these treaties, then the Republic of Korea is prepared to take up discussion for the relaxation of military tensions on the Korean Peninsula.

President Bush advocates a strong U.S. role in the post-Cold-War world. But there is also a growing sentiment in America in favor of a more isolationist approach to foreign affairs. Does that worry you?

The human race has lessons to learn from history, and the United States as well as the world should remember that when the United States pursued a policy of isolationism in the past the result was the eruption of World War II. [During the Cold War] the United States pursued a policy of peace based on strength. This led to the victory of freedom and democracy and the demise of communism. For the United States to return to a position of isolationism would be to forget the lessons of history and invite the possibility of danger. I am against a return to isolationist policies at this juncture and believe that the United States will not return to that policy.

Has the time come for the United States to begin paring down its military forces in the region?

Until the Cold War situation disappears and until there is no external threat, U.S. military forces should be stationed in Korea not only to guarantee peace on the peninsula but to safeguard the entire Northeast Asian region. Assuming the military threat does disappear, the United States will still have to remain involved in political and economic roles because in the 21st century the need for cooperation and economic prosperity will increase.

What do you believe Japan's role should be in the 21st century?

Japan has become an impressive economic power. Japanese people are industrious and very able. But at the same time, Japan's economic achievements have been possible because Japan's friends and allies provided the opportunities and conditions for it. I prefer to have Japan share its economic wealth and technological know-how not only within the region but around the world. Countries in this area of the world remember the unfortunate history of Japan's militarism prior to World War II. So even if Japan may find justification for a role in the U.N. peace-keeping forces, the public consensus in this area is for Japan not to increase its military strength. For Japan to exercise military influence is not desirable.

Part IV

NORTHERN POLICY: OPENING TO SOCIALIST AND EX-SOCIALIST COUNTRIES

29.

Opening Remarks at the News Conference Following the Summit Meeting with President Mikhail Gorbachev of the Soviet Union, San Francisco, June 4, 1990

I have just concluded very productive talks with President Gorbachev of the Union of Soviet Socialist Republics. I found him a man of courage and candor, true to the image of a statesman who has been helping reshape the world. Though this was our first meeting, we exchanged views frankly in an open and amicable atmosphere.

In view of the fact that our two nations have no official diplomatic relations, this meeting was an epochal event. Because the partitioning of our country forty-five years ago and the subsequent Korean War were products of the Cold War, our historic meeting represents an important turning point. After talking with President Gorbachev today, I am convinced that prospects for peace and the eventual unification of the Korean Peninsula are bright. In fact, I am confident that our talks will prove to be a major impetus for the promotion not only of Korean-Soviet relations and the reduction of tension in Korea, but also of peace and security throughout Northeast Asia.

President Gorbachev and I are both encouraged by the fact that the progress toward openness and reform is forging a new world order of harmony and co-operation. We have agreed to make joint efforts to facilitate the development of the new order. We have also agreed that it is time that the waves of openness and detente reached Northeast Asia, especially the Korean Peninsula.

Differences in ideology and political systems should no longer be allowed to obstruct normal relations among nations. All nations should recognize and co-operate with each other to shape a more peaceful and prosperous world. Such a common yearning was well expressed during the Seoul Olympics two years ago, a grand festival of global harmony. It was there that the East and the West first joined hands. As we have seen, this momentum of East-West reconciliation was soon followed by U.S.-Soviet summit meeting at Malta and Washington.

In that context of peaceful cooperation, President Gorbachev and I shared the view that the initial efforts to normalize bilateral relations between the Republic of Korea and the Soviet Union should lead to establishment of full diplomatic relations, and we agreed to expand further economic, scientific, technological, and cultural exchanges and cooperation between our two countries.

As a result of my meeting with President Gorbachev today, our two countries will be able to restore normal bilateral relations after an 86-year interval—transcending the unfortunate events and experiences of that period.

The long separation between our two countries reflects the turbulent history of Northeast Asia. In the 20th century alone, four major wars have been fought in this region, each embroiling the Korean Peninsula in the process. It is such a conflict-ridden historical background that used to hamper the normal conduct of our relations.

In fact, the Korean Peninsula is the only area still remaining under the clouds of Cold War tension. Now that German reunification is a reality, Korea is the only nation on earth that still is divided by Cold War politics.

As a result of today's meeting, the Cold War ice on the Korean Peninsula has begun to crack. It is expected that our meeting will serve as the first major step toward a peaceful and unified Korea.

I have made it clear to President Gorbachev that we do not want North Korea to be isolated. It is my hope that the Soviet Union will continue to maintain interest in and further develop its existing links with North Korea even as the USSR and ROK promote constructive relations. As we work toward our national unification, our immediate goal is to promote peaceful coexistence, common prosperity, and co-operation between the two halves of Korea.

I asked President Gorbachev at our meeting today to support and help our efforts to involve North Korea in meaningful dialogue with us and in increasing exchanges and co-operation. Through this summit meeting, President Gorbachev has demonstrated to the world that the Soviet Union is determined to help end the Cold War on the Korean Peninsula.

The normalization of relations between the Republic of Korea and the Soviet Union should boost bilateral trade and economic cooperation. This should greatly accelerate the development of both our economies, because our countries are close geographically and we share many mutually complementary economic features.

As a result of its northern policy, the Republic of Korea established relations with all Eastern European countries over the past year. We also opened diplomatic relations with Mongolia last year. In addition, 20,000 people

President Roh at a press conference.

President Roh signing the Agreement between the South and the North, February 1992.

President Roh speaking to the 46th General Assembly of the United Nations, September 1991.

President Roh with President George Bush at the Waldorf Astoria Hotel, September 1991.

President Roh with President Carlos Salinas of Mexico, September 1991.

President Roh with Prime Minister Brian Mulroney of Canada, July 1991.

President Roh and President Mikhail Gorbachev signing the Moscow Declaration, December 1990 at the Kremlin.

President Roh with Emperor Akihito of Japan at the state guest house in Tokyo, May 1990.

President Roh with Juan Antonio Samaranch, chairman of the International Olympic Committee in Lausanne, Switzerland.

President Roh with visiting Prime Minister Konstantine Mitsotakis of Greece, November 1990.

President Roh with President Árpád Gönez of Hungary, November 1990.

President Roh with President Richard von Weizsäcker of the Federal Republic of Germany at Chong Wa Dae, February 1991.

President Roh and Prime Minister Poul Schlüter of Denmark at a dinner in honor of the Prime Minister and Mrs. Schlüter, June 1991.

President Roh with Sultan Azlan Shah, King of Malaysia, at Chong Wa Dae, September 1991.

President Roh with President George Bush of the United States at Chong Wa Dae, January 1992.

travelled between South Korea and China last year, while bilateral trade exceeded three billion dollars. We expect our relations with China to develop further.

The Northern Policy of the Republic of Korea will serve to convince socialist countries of the effectiveness and efficiency of democracy and free trade system and help them carry out reforms.

The ultimate objective of our Northern Policy, however, is to bring North Korea to open up its society so that we may secure stability and peace on the Korean Peninsula. The road between Seoul and Pyongyang is presently closed. Accordingly, we have to choose an alternative route to the North Korean capital by way of Moscow and Beijing. This may not be the shortest route, but we certainly hope it will be an effective one.

I believe North Korea is currently plagued by internal and external difficulties. Before long, however, it will have to abandon its isolationist policy in favor of openness and reform. Once change starts there, it will move very rapidly. We absolutely do not wish chaos for the North. Rather, we sincerely hope that change in North Korea will occur in an orderly and peaceful fashion. North Korea is no longer our rival or adversary. We believe it should become our partner for common prosperity.

In this regard, I am grateful to the United States of America for having solidly supported our northern policy and co-operated to make it a success. Tomorrow, I will leave for Washington to see President Bush. We will exchange frank views on my discussions with Mr. Gorbachev.

Two weeks ago, I paid a state visit to Japan. During the visit, I agreed with the Japanese leaders to work together to remove obstacles handed down to us by the unfortunate past and to build a firm partnership for a brighter future for Northeast Asia and the Pacific.

I plan to discuss with President Bush on ways to boost mutual co-operation and to join efforts of like-minded nations to cope with challenges of the changing world. This will be my third meeting with President Bush in about a year, and it reflects the strong ties between the United States and the Republic of Korea.

The Korean question is becoming one of the most urgent problems that must be solved if we are to secure world peace. We are very pleased that progress toward that end has been made in San Francisco, the birthplace of the United Nations. I would like to thank the citizens of this beautiful city for providing me with an excellent venue for this historic meeting.

Thank you.

30.

Remarks at the Banquet in Honor of the President of the Republic of Hungary and Mrs. Árpád Gönez, Seoul, November 15, 1990

Your Excellencies President and Mrs. Gönez, distinguished guests,

I join the entire nation in extending a warm welcome to you and your delegation. Your visit is first ever by the head of state of the Republic of Hungary and we are highly honored and pleased to share this evening with you.

Let me first of all extend congratulations to you for having been elected as President of the Republic of Hungary. For decades you have been at the forefront of the Hungarian struggle for freedom and democracy.

There is an old saying in Korea, "No pleasure is greater than receiving a good friend from afar," and it so aptly expresses the distinct pleasure Mrs. Roh and I have in welcoming you and the members of the Hungarian delegation.

Your presence here tonight makes me recall once again the fond memories I always cherish of my visit to your great country last year.

The beautiful bridges over the Danube, the City of Budapest where historic landmarks compete to exhibit their proud cultural heritage, and above all the Hungarian people and their courageous struggle for freedom are but a few unforgettable impressions that readily come to mind.

The government of the Republic of Hungary, the National Assembly, and indeed the entire nation extended a truly warm and hospitable welcome to our delegation, and I would like to express once again our deep-felt gratitude to you and our Hungarian friends.

Your Excellency,

Since early last year, the world has been going through a series of revolutionary changes. The Berlin Wall was torn down and Germany has finally achieved national unification. The heavy curtain that divided the world into East and West has been lifted for good. No system or ideology can interrupt any longer the free flow and exchange of goods, information and people. A new era is now at hand in which all the nations live in one world, peacefully engaged in their calls of life.

Today, human dignity, democratic pluralism and market economy have become universal values. May I respectfully point out that, in this tremendous change that brought higher hopes for us all, Hungary has played a pioneering role.

Once again, I would like to pay deep respect to the Hungarian people for this great achievement as I have done in my address to the Hungarian National Assembly last year.

The Korean people hold the Hungarian people with special affinity. Like the great nation of Magyars, the Korean people have successfully maintained their freedom, independence and a brilliant culture over a period of several millennia in spite of repeated great power pressures from around the Korean Peninsula.

We Koreans feel particularly close to the Hungarian people, for Hungary was the first among the Central and East European countries to establish democratic relations with us, thereby contributing to a new world order of reconciliation.

Mr. President,

We are quite familiar with the many changes and developments taking place in Hungary over the past year. You have adopted a multi-party system, and through free general elections last spring and local and regional elections this fall you have successfully institutionalized solid foundations for parliamentary democracy.

In the economic sector, you have substantially transformed the system into a competitive market economic system through courageous structural reforms.

Only ten days ago, Hungary took a significant step toward becoming a full-fledged member of the European Community by joining the Council of Europe as a full member. Hungary was of course the first among the Central and East European countries to do so.

Difficulties and discord are endemic on the road of reform toward democracy. But, I am convinced that positive reforms are the indispensable first steps toward building a nation of freedom and prosperity.

Forty years ago, Cold War confrontations erupted into a tragic fratricidal war and reduced the Korean Peninsula into a heap of rubble. The sources of Korea's success in attaining the status of a newly industrializing country and in hosting the highly acclaimed Seoul Olympics have been liberal democracy and a market economic system.

The enormous cultural heritage and intellectual genius and creativity of the diligent Hungarian people, I am quite certain, will provide the solid basis for a remarkable economic takeoff for Hungary.

Mr. President,
That two summit meetings have taken place between our two countries within the space of one year demonstrates that the future of our bilateral relations is brighter than ever. Your state visit has now set a solid landmark for our close partnership.

Our summit meeting this morning has firmly established a framework and we were able to confirm the rapid increases in bilateral cooperation in economic, cultural, scientific and technological sectors.

Our two countries have only begun the development of bilateral cooperation. We will continue to encourage active trade and economic cooperation, strengthen friendship between our two peoples, and share the fruits of cooperation together.

The Korean people are determined to contribute to world peace by accelerating their efforts to bring forth peace and unification on the Korean Peninsula, which remains divided South and North. We are concentrating our efforts to open the road to peaceful unification by seeking dialogue, exchanges and trade as well as co-existence and co-prosperity with North Korea.

Just as Hungary has provided a turning-point in our pursuit of "Northern Diplomacy," we earnestly hope that your understanding and support would be forthcoming in our efforts to bring about reconciliation and unity between South and North Korea.

Your state visit schedule may not be sufficient, but I do wish you will have opportunities to affirm the friendliness and hospitality of the Korean people and take home fond memories of Korea, her culture and people.

Ladies and gentlemen,
May I please propose a toast to the health and well-being of Their Excellencies President and Mrs. Gönez, to eternal prosperity of the Republic of Hungary, and to long-lasting friendship between our two nations.
Thank you.

31.

Responses to Questions Submitted by the Soviet Press, *Tass-Izvestia-Pravda*, December 10, 1990

Question 1) *Mr. President, there is no doubt that in the long distant future historians will mark the current year as the year of major breakthrough in the relations between our two countries. But we are not historians and that is why we would like to ask you about your visit to Moscow: about your expectations, about the main task of your mission, about your personal feelings toward the new partner in political, economic and diplomatic dialogue.*

Answer 1) The Republic of Korea and the Soviet Union have normalized diplomatic relations after decades of interruption. The Korean people welcome this new development in our relations. I am very pleased to convey the warm greetings of the Korean people to the people of the Soviet Union, including your readers.

At the invitation of President Gorbachev, I will shortly be visiting Moscow, and I will be the first head of state of the Republic of Korea to do so. We have normalized relations in September. That the President of the Republic of Korea is visiting Moscow is itself an historic event, particularly when it follows the normalization by only two months.

The Asia-Pacific region, where two thirds of the world population lives, is emerging as a new center to lead the future prosperity of the world. The peace and stability of the Korean Peninsula where tension and sharp confrontations persist, has been at the center of the security issue in this area.

All the nations of this region have been aspiring for the emergence of a new international order in this part of the world just as Europe has succeeded to uniting for a family of peace and cooperation.

The rapid development of Soviet-Korea relations is an encouraging sign to many nations in the area that a new era of reconciliation and cooperation is dawning in the Asia-Pacific region as well.

Through my visit to Moscow, I wish to help lay a firm foundation for the development of Soviet-Korean relations, and to reaffirm the importance and significance of the normalization of our relations at this particular juncture of history in terms of the Korean Peninsula, the Asia-Pacific region and the international situation. However, I do not anticipate to find any fundamental differences in our perceptions since my "Northern Policy" and policies of openness and reform based on President Gorbachev's "new thinking" share many common characteristics.

The question of removing the Cold War structure from the Korean Peninsula is central to the problem of eliminating the danger of war and bringing about a peaceful unification of Korea, and it affects directly the future of the entire Korean people. I plan to review the international situation with President Gorbachev and exchange views on the promotion of peace and cooperation in Northeast Asia.

A framework for the promotion of bilateral exchanges and cooperation will emerge during my visit to Moscow, since a number of agreements that have been under negotiation between our two governments will be signed in Moscow. President Gorbachev and I will explore the direction of cooperation for a sustained development of bilateral relations. I believe the development will proceed in a satisfactory manner since there are many areas that could be developed to our mutual benefit and since both countries have great potentials in their own right.

I hope my visit will help contribute to increasing confidence in the Soviet people toward a brighter future and a new world, as they endeavor to create a new history with their reform policies.

Between our two countries, a new era of neighborly friendship is now open.

The new Soviet Union, where perestroika is being implemented, is not only our new partner for the realization of peace and prosperity but also a partner for the active promotion of stability and cooperation in Northeast Asia.

Question 2) *It's no secret that despite the speed of rapprochement between ROK and USSR the information background, knowledge and general ideas about each other are far from the political changes. The objective information is a key point for mutual trust and understanding. On this ground could we ask you, Mr. President, to point out the main priorities of ROK at present days, what is most important in economics, in politics, in social life? What is most difficult?*

Answer 2) There has been a long interruption in our bilateral relations in the years past. The gigantic wall of Cold War not only interrupted personal and cultural interchanges but it also has cut off and misinterpreted the information on the other side.

Now, the road for mutual exchange is wide open. This year alone recorded a total of one billion dollars in our trade and there have been more than 12,888 visitors between our two countries. There is a saying in Korea, "Seeing in person is better than hearing it a hundred times." By seeing, meeting and talking to each other, we come to realize how unnatural and abnormal the wall in our past has been.

The Soviet athletic delegation to the Seoul Olympics has received an enthusiastic welcome by the Korean people and the performances of the Bolshoi Ballet and the Leningrad Philharmonic Orchestra have seen enormous success in Seoul. Any Soviet person visiting Seoul will be able to find the warmth and friendliness of the Korean people.

As the relations of the two countries develop, the understanding and mutual trust between our two peoples will deepen and exchanges expand. This will in turn provide the basis for a long-term development of friendly and cooperative relations between our two countries.

The Republic of Korea's policy priorities at this time are as follows:

First: To develop and stabilize liberal democracy that came to flourish since my inauguration in every sector of our society.

Second: To build an advanced welfare state by increasing the current GNP per capita of $6,888 and $138 billion trade volume to a level of $18,888 and $288 billion by 1996–97, and to accomplish an equitable distribution of wealth among all sectors of our society.

Third: To remove Cold War confrontations in the Korean Peninsula, to realize reconciliation between the two Koreas and to open the road to peaceful unification.

In order to develop liberal democracy, economic growth and national reconciliation, numerous difficulties and challenges are expected.

Since the partition of our territory at the end of the Second World War, there have been in existence two different political systems in the Korean Peninsula. Because one part tried to deny the existence of the other part under the dictates of the Cold War rationale, the Korean people have suffered a traumatic war and millions of casualties, and we have been living for forty years under constant confrontations, rivalry, and the fear of renewed hostilities. Because of these circumstances, the Korean people have undergone unspeakable pain, sorrow and difficulties.

Consequently, the task of achieving peace and unification on the Korean Peninsula is our most important and urgent priority. The normalization of our relations, which is based on new thinking, and a further development of our relations will greatly contribute to this important objective.

Question 3) *The dialogue between ROK and USSR started from the development of trade and economic relations. Only two years have passed since first direct contacts. But we could see a big program and big results. What do you think about our economic partnership in the future? Is there any connection between your forthcoming visit to Moscow and bilateral economic relations?*

Answer 3) Our two countries are not only close geographically, but our economic structures share complementary characteristics in many respects.

The Korean economy has many elements that are needed by the Soviet Union. We have developmental techniques and experience under the market economy . . . the capabilities to build merchant marines and automobiles, to manufacture and produce electronic appliances and consumer goods . . . the material and technology for construction, communications and other social infrastructure . . . the skilled manpower and managerial abilities . . . These are all items that can provide realistic help in the process of restructuring the Soviet economy.

On your part, the Soviet Union has a large potential market, a wide expanse of territory and abundant natural resources including oil, gas and timber. And, we can benefit from your advanced scientific technologies.

In view of these complementary features of our two economies, the expansion of trade and economic cooperation will benefit us both and contribute to our common prosperity.

The trade volume between our two countries stands at about one billion dollars. Should the Soviet economic development plan proceed at the current rate, the bilateral trade volume is expected to exceed 18 billion dollars by the middle of the nineties, according to economic experts.

With the normalization of our relations and my visit to Moscow, bilateral trade and economic cooperation will greatly be expanded. Many bilateral agreements are currently under negotiation between our two countries, and during my visit to Moscow at least three agreements—namely, the agreements on trade, avoidance of double taxation and science and technology cooperation—are expected to be signed. This is to provide a framework and facilitate the activities of our businessmen, Soviet as well as Korean.

With this basic framework and additional agreements to follow, I believe the bilateral trade will increase at a rapid pace and economic cooperation speed up. During my Moscow visit, more detailed consultations on the direction of our economic cooperation will take place.

A number of important Korean business leaders will accompany the presidential party during my visit to Moscow. These business leaders will discuss with their Soviet counterparts details on our bilateral economic cooperation.

Question 4) *Mr. President, you've said your administration considers the Soviet Union one of the "most important economic partners of the ROK in the Asia-Pacific region." How do you see the prospects of ROK-USSR trade, economic and science-technology cooperation?*

Answer 4) I still believe the Soviet Union is "one of the most important economic partners" in the Asia-Pacific region. Our economic partnership is important in the near term, but it is more important in the long run.

In terms of trade and economic cooperation, we can import such items as natural gas, timber and coal that are found in abundance in geographically-near Soviet Union. Our businesses that have accumulated lots of experience through their ventures abroad, are also interested in jointly developing Soviet resources for purposes of import as well as export to third countries.

They are very competent and maintain high-level international competitiveness in road- and harbor-building, public facilities, housing and construction. I understand that many Korean businesses have conducted extensive surveys and close examinations on these possibilities. We can also supply lots of consumer products, from electronic appliances and other daily commodities to ships and automobiles, that may be in demand in the Soviet economy.

We also have not only the managerial expertise and technical know-how for the upgrading of productivity and quality for export in international markets but also the capabilities to supply facilities and organizations for the production of a wide variety of consumer goods and merchandise. Consequently, the Korean businesses could, through direct investment or joint ventures, build factories in the Soviet Union and provide the products to our markets and export to the world market.

Our businesses are also interested in providing production facilities and manufacturing various merchandise in the process of converting Soviet military industry into civilian purposes.

Our two countries do have different trade and economic structures. For this reason, there exist a number of areas for which we both must exert our efforts to complementary aspects in our economies, adjust to each other.

So long as our two governments and business circles resolve these problems to our satisfaction, trade and economic cooperation between our two countries will bring enormous help to our economies and future prosperity.

The Soviet Union has extremely advanced scientific technologies that even conquered the moon and space. Such Soviet technologies and know-how are in demand for our economic development. We are therefore interested in combining the Soviet know-how and our production experiences to apply in the production of necessary commercial items for sale at home and abroad. Joint venture companies are being set up for this purpose.

The promotion of trade and economic cooperation between our two countries are expected to bring forth valuable rewards to both our nations, and I am convinced of this result, and prospects are very bright.

Question 5) *The winds of peace, which caused the East-West Cold War structure to crumble, have begun to blow in Asia also. The new spirit of international politics starts to affect positively the situation in the region, though the process of confidence building measures seems to be more complicated. What kind of steps, do you think, could be taken to make this trend develop faster?*

Answer 5) Since the Soviet-American summit in Malta, a new international order has been sought and a "new era of democracy, peace, and unity" has arrived in Europe. And yet, the Korean Peninsula remains divided as the last legacy of the Cold War.

The Cold War confrontations in the Korean Peninsula have been the epicenter of tension in the Asia-Pacific region. With the opening of a newly neighborly friendship, our two countries should exert our efforts to reduce tension and institutionalize peace in the Korean Peninsula. Between the two Koreas, we have to build mutual confidence through exchanges and cooperation on the basis of recognition of the other entity.

Once this relationship will have been established, more forward-looking measures can be taken to remove sharp confrontations and rivalry. The problem obviously is in North Korea's decision to maintain an extreme isolationist policy, denying the reality that two political systems have been in existence on the Korean Peninsula for decades.

The development of Soviet-Korean relations, together with the overflowing waves of openness and reform around the world, will stimulate North Korea to revise its posture to a more realistic one. North Korea should open its doors to the world, cooperate with us and become a responsible member of the international community. This will also help their own cause for development.

Once the Cold War structure is removed and a cooperative mood takes hold in the Korean Peninsula, the global wind of cooperation will sweep across Northeast Asia. Our two countries should develop our relations rapidly so we can actively contribute to replacing the confrontational Cold War structure in Northeast Asia with a new structure of reconciliation and cooperation.

In an address before the United Nations General Assembly on October 18, 1989, I proposed a "consultative conference for peace in Northeast Asia" to be attended by interested countries including the Soviet Union, to discuss the introduction of a structure of peace and cooperation in Northeast Asia. The Soviet Union has also enunciated the need for multilateral consultation for the security of the Asia-Pacific region.

The development of close bilateral relations, I believe, could provide a realistic basis for such initiatives, particularly in view of the fact that the relaxation of tension in the Korean Peninsula is the primary issue for peace in Northeast Asia.

Question 6) *What is, Mr. President, your vision of perestroika (reforms) in the Soviet Union and how do you appreciate the influence of perestroika on recent world events and on future situation in the Far East?*

Answer 6) With the 21st century approaching, mankind can at last harbor high hopes that we will all be able to pursue peace and prosperity within one global setting of harmony and cooperation.

Throughout the postwar years, mankind has built high walls that divided them against their nature and persisted in enmity, confrontation and rivalry. The Korean people have experienced excruciating pain, the trauma and tragedy of fratricidal war that the Cold War has inflicted on them. The Korean people were not the only victims of this traumatic experience but the entire humanity whether they are in Europe or on other continents.

Since the inauguration of President Gorbachev, the Cold War structure that dominated the world for half a century has crumbled and the world today is full of new waves of openness and reform emanating from new thinking of your president. To be sure, there still exist elements of uncertainty. But no one can ignore or reverse this predominant historical current of harmony and cooperation that characterizes our world today.

The change led initially by perestroika in the Soviet Union has brought about the Malta U.S.-Soviet summit, progress in arms control talks, the recent success in the Conference on Security and Cooperation in Europe and the European Common House, and a number of other favorable developments around the world. The Berlin Wall was brought down and the barbed wire across the heart of Europe rolled back. Future historians will record this change that has successfully forged one harmonious world out of two divisive ones as the most valuable achievement that mankind has attained in this century.

The normalization of our relations and my visit to Moscow will form part of this great change. This betokens the creation of new history in accordance with human reason, and symbolizes the arrival of a new era in which mankind will respect and put into practice such universal values as freedom, prosperity, peace and human dignity. The ultimate fruits of our efforts will be celebrated by the happiness of all mankind and will be handed down to the 21st century in the form of a more peaceful and prosperous world.

The new waves have not yet fully reached Northeast Asia. With the rapid development of our bilateral relations, however, change has begun to occur. This region alone could not be immune to the global waves that reflect the ultimate human aspirations and the progress of history of our time.

Northeast Asia has seen five major wars in the past century and rivalry still persists in the area. Nevertheless, a new international order of cooperation is emerging amongst the regional nations for a common peace and prosperity.

Question 7) *Do you, Mr. President, consider as a truth such a version that the Soviet Union is a dangerous country producing a military threat to her neighbors in the Far East? Are there prospects that the Japan Sea (East Sea) will become a zone of peace and good-neighbor cooperation of all countries located in its vicinity?*

Answer 7) The path of history our two nations have taken since early this century are very different and contrasting. At the end of the Second World War the world was divided into two blocs by the superpowers and our two nations were set apart into opposing sides. At the conclusion of the war, Korea was liberated from the colonial control, but we were immediately faced with the tragedy of national and territorial division by the dictates of Cold War.

The Cold War has imploded into a hot war in the Korean Peninsula. The land was totally devastated and casualties reached millions. The Korean people carry to this day the scars and national trauma of that war. Standing on the opposite sides of the wall, our two countries remained separated and maintained confrontational relations. The Soviet-Korean relations represented a typical Cold War international order. The Soviet Union was the leader of one camp, and the Republic of Korea was at the forefront of the other camp. In this historical process, the Soviet Union came to be perceived by her neighbors as a source of threat, and unfortunate developments have indeed taken place in the past. The shooting down of a civilian airliner, the Korean Air flight 807, in 1983 by Soviet jet fighters would be the starkest example.

However, new signs of change began to appear once the Soviet Union undertook to pursue perestroika policies. With the pursuit of perestroika by President Gorbachev, the world has begun to transform from the very base.

Although a fundamental change has not yet occurred in the confrontational structure in Northeast Asia, I believe the view that the Soviet Union is threatening to her East Asian neighbors has greatly diminished. We should develop our bilateral relations further and build a structure of peace and cooperation in East Asia so that no country would be perceived as a threat to the other.

As indicated earlier, I have proposed in my United Nations speech a "consultative conference for peace in Northeast Asia." In light of such proposals as President Gorbachev's Krasnoyarsk and recent "all-Asia" security conference initiatives, the Soviet Union has shown a positive attitude toward the building of a security cooperation structure in Asia. The Soviet Union has also announced plans to reduce naval forces in Northeast Asia and remove armed forces deployed in the Far Eastern region.

As neighboring Asian countries, we should endeavor to realize these initiatives by first developing friendly and cooperative bilateral relations with all the interested countries. Then, our East Sea will become not a sea of distrust and rivalry but a sea of neighborly friendship and common prosperity.

Thank you.

32.

Remarks at the Banquet Hosted by President Mikhail Gorbachev, The Kremlin, Moscow, December 14, 1990

Your Excellency President Mikhail Gorbachev, Mrs. Gorbachev, and distinguished guests.

I would like first to express my deep gratitude to you, President Gorbachev, for your invitation to visit this great country, for the warm reception and hospitality you have accorded us since our arrival, and for your encouraging words on the world situation and on the future of Soviet-Korean relations. It is with pleasure that I bring cordial greetings from the people of the Republic of Korea to the people of the Soviet Union.

As the twenty-first century draws nearer, a new era of hope is unfolding before us, and the legacy of the Cold War is disappearing throughout the world. Today mankind is filled with the hope of living together in one global community of peace and prosperity. Your Excellency's courageous leadership and the resolve of the Soviet people to achieve reforms have been a driving force of the phenomenal changes in the world.

I extend my heartfelt congratulations to Your Excellency for the distinction you have earned as the recipient of this year's Nobel Peace Prize. I strongly believe that this event is testimony to the great admiration throughout the world for your unflagging courage, firm convictions, and unequaled leadership to realize the aspirations of mankind.

Your Excellency,

Korea and the Soviet Union are neighbors with a common border. The first recorded encounter between Koreans and Russians traces back to the fourteenth century, though supporting evidence indicates that exchanges between our peoples have occurred since time immemorial. The Kingdom of Chosun and Russia maintained cordial ties for two decades after the establishment of formal relations in 1884.

In current times, Koreans grow up enjoying the great literary works of Pushkin, Tolstoy, Dostoyevsky, and Gorky, as well as the music of Tchaikovsky, Rachmaninoff, and Shostakovich. In 1988, the people of the Republic of Korea enthusiastically welcomed the Soviet athletic delegation to the Seoul Olympics. Every Soviet citizen who visits my country can be assured of the warmth and friendship of the Korean people.

What had interrupted relations between our two peoples for eighty-six years were colonial expansionism and the Cold War.

Your Excellency,

The news of our first meeting in San Francisco sparked pleasant surprise and jubilation. Since then, hopes have filled the hearts of the Korean people that a new era of peace and unification will finally replace the age-old structure of national division, warfare, confrontation, and rivalry.

That our two countries have normalized relations and that we are meeting here in Moscow at this moment attest to the opening of a new chapter in our histories. We are now pronouncing to the world the end of an era that had brought about unspeakable trauma to mankind and the unnatural division of nations and peoples.

This gathering tonight demonstrates that a new era of reconciliation and cooperation is dawning upon the Korean Peninsula and the Asia-Pacific region.

The ending of confrontation on the Korean Peninsula has been at the heart of the aspirations for peace in the Asia-Pacific region. There is a prevailing belief in the world that the wave of peace flowing from the Soviet-U.S. meeting in Malta and the Conference on Security and Cooperation in Europe held in Paris is washing upon the shores of the Asia-Pacific. Our two countries will join efforts for peace and prosperity in Korea and the Asia-Pacific region.

I hope that the fresh wind of perestroika will soon reach the Korean Peninsula, and that our efforts to attain peace and unification will be met with the support of Your Excellency and the people of the Soviet Union.

Your Excellency,

Our two countries must now put behind us the unfortunate past and march together toward a future of friendship and cooperation. I am deeply pleased that my visit is allowing a framework to be established for active cooperation and exchanges between our two countries. As bordering neighbors, we have enormous potential to develop complementary cooperative Soviet-Korean relations. The Soviet Union and Korea should endeavor with confidence and good faith so that economic cooperation will enhance our common prosperity. Cooperation should not be confined to the area of economics, and our efforts should be strengthened to deepen understanding and friendship between the peoples of our two countries.

Your Excellency,
The summit meeting with you today has set a new landmark in Soviet-Korean relations. This visit has brought me in close contact with a great people and a great culture. I am deeply impressed by the bold efforts of Your Excellency and the people of the Soviet Union to build a new nation and to write a new history under the banner of perestroika. Beyond any doubt I believe that your undaunted resolve will lead to the triumph of perestroika. For our part, we the Korean people will continue to support and encourage your reform efforts. As new partners, our two countries should stride forward to build a more peaceful, more prosperous, and more harmonious world.

Ladies and gentlemen,
Please join me now in toasting to the health and well-being of His Excellency President and Mrs. Gorbachev, to the prosperity of the Soviet Union and to the everlasting friendship of the peoples of Soviet Union and Korea.
Balishoe Spaciba!
Thank you very much.

33.

Opening Remarks at the News Conference, Moscow, December 15, 1990

Ladies and gentlemen,

I am very pleased to see you all.

I have just concluded a three-day visit to Moscow and will leave this afternoon.

The visit has been very successful and I am fully satisfied with the results. Although the visit was brief, I believe it was an historic event that has given new hopes and expectations for a new era to the peoples of our two countries.

That the President of the Republic of Korea paid a visit to Moscow symbolizes the encouraging changes around the world today, and I would think it has given new hopes for a more peaceful world to the nations around the world and in the Asia-Pacific region.

Ladies and gentlemen of the news media,

I know all of you closely follow the development of world events. But, I am sure that until quite recently even the members of the news media would not have expected to see the president of the Republic of Korea holding a news conference here in Moscow today.

That the head of state of the Republic of Korea is visiting the Soviet Union for the first time in history and that a ROK-USSR summit meeting has taken place in the Kremlin reflect a most remarkable development.

The Soviet-Korean Joint Declaration that President Gorbachev and I signed yesterday will serve as a charter as our two countries open a new era of friendship and cooperation, and as we cooperate in removing the remnants of the Cold War, in pursuing peace and unification in the Korean Peninsula, and in building a new order of reconciliation and cooperation in the Asia-Pacific region.

It pronounces in effect that Korea and the Soviet Union together have opened a new era of reconciliation and cooperation, bringing to a close the long drawn-out period of Cold War.

Between Seoul and Moscow, there was an interruption of relations for 86 years due to colonial expansionism in the early period and the Cold War in the postwar period. The Cold War has imposed and exacerbated division and enmity between nations and between peoples.

My visit to Moscow opens a new chapter in our history, removing the wall that separated us in the past and ushering in a new era of partnership for the promotion of universal human values such as freedom, prosperity and peace.

Few nations on earth suffered as much pain and hardship under the Cold War as the Korean people. Under the dictates of Cold War, the nation and the territory had to be divided and we had to suffer millions of casualties.

The Korean people have been living for over forty years under the fear and threat of renewed hostilities. Hundreds of thousands of families separated by the Demilitarized Zone have not been able to know the whereabouts of their parents, children and relatives, let alone exchange letters or telephone calls. The tragedy of territorial division persists in Korea to this very moment.

The rapid improvement of our bilateral relations indicates that an important development is taking place in the Cold War setting in the Korean Peninsula. It pronounces to the entire Korean people that the age of confrontation and fear is receding and a new era of peace and unification is approaching.

Yesterday, President Gorbachev and I have had very sincere and useful talks on a broad range of issues. The atmosphere was very cordial and friendly unencumbered by formalities, as this was the second time President Gorbachev and I met since the San Francisco summit last June.

President Gorbachev and I have had serious discussions on such issues as the Korean Peninsula and the removal of Cold War structure around the world. We also recognized that the new era of peace and cooperation, which emerged in the wake of the Malta U.S.-Soviet summit and the recent Conference on Security and Cooperation in Europe in Paris, should also be introduced in the Korean Peninsula and the Asia-Pacific region.

The improvement of our bilateral relations and the Korea-USSR summit meeting in Moscow are not happenstance developments but inevitable consequences of the new historical wave, which none of us can ever reverse.

Our bilateral rapprochement can be described in terms of confluence between my "northern policy" which sought to remove Cold War confrontations and build a world of harmony and cooperation, and President Gorbachev's perestroika which has brought on phenomenal changes around the world. The philosophy that we share has provided the basis of our talks.

Our two countries will join our efforts to bring peace in the Korean Peninsula and to increase cooperation in Northeast Asia, and as we proceed realistic outcome will emerge.

We are living in an interdependent world, and the Korean Peninsula remains as the key issue relating to peace in Northeast Asia and the Asia-Pacific region.

I hope that the Soviet Union will continue to maintain sound relations with North Korea as it improves relations with us, and hope that the Soviet Union will actively contribute to our cause of peace and unification of Korea. For our part, we will continue to develop a brotherly relationship with North Korea, and not as adversaries for rivalry and confrontation but as partners for progress and prosperity.

Members of the news media,

Korea and the Soviet Union are neighbors with common borders. And yet, Korea and the Soviet Union stood on opposing sides during the decades when the world was divided into East and West, and a relationship of distrust and confrontation developed given the dictates of the Cold War period. Due to the nature of the confrontational structure, our two countries experienced an unfortunate past. A primary example of such history was the outbreak of the Korean War during the height of the Cold War and the downing of a Korean civilian airliner by Soviet jet fighters.

But it is time for Korea and the Soviet Union to clear away the vestiges of the unfortunate past and to open a new age of neighborly friendship between the two countries.

Our two countries have boundless potential for mutual cooperation. Since our economic structures share many complementary features, increases in trade and economic cooperation between us will undoubtedly be conducive to our prosperity.

President Gorbachev and I expressed our satisfaction over the rapidly increasing pace of tangible progress in our relationship. The bilateral trade volume which stood at about $100 million four years ago, is expected to reach one billion dollars this year. Travels by the nationals of our two countries, which had been restricted until recently, recorded over 12,000 persons by the end of November. Impressive as the numbers are, we have only begun.

I am very pleased to note that during my visit agreements on trade, avoidance of double taxation and science and technology cooperation were signed between the two governments. Now, a solid framework is in place for further development of exchanges and cooperation between our two countries.

The Korean economy has lots of important ingredients that the Soviet economy has in demand. Our developmental experiences and technical know-how . . . our capabilities to produce and supply consumer goods and electronic appliances, the ship-building and automobile industries, our material and techniques for the improvement and expansion of social infrastructure such as construction and communications, and skilled manpower and management expertise . . . these are some of the areas that we can practically contribute to the Soviet pursuit of economic reforms.

Some of Korea's most prominent business leaders have joined me on this trip.

A large number of Korean firms have conducted extensive surveys and intensive analyses on the prospective areas of economic cooperation, including joint ventures for the production of consumer goods, the expansion of social infrastructure such as harbors and communications, and joint exploration of natural resources.

The Soviet Union has a huge potential market and abundant natural resources on its vast territory. The advanced technologies of the Soviet Union are much in demand in Korea.

President Gorbachev and I were in agreement on the need to actively promote trade and economic relations and expressed a high degree of confidence on this score.

We are prepared to supply consumer products of all variety that may be in demand by the Soviet economy, and to extend long-term credits for the construction, through joint ventures, of factories in the Soviet Union for production of appropriate consumer goods.

Many Korean firms have expressed significant interest in participating actively in the process of converting military industries for civilian purposes, in providing production facilities and in supplying finished products.

Some Korean businesses are actively pursuing the possibility of applying the advanced Soviet technologies to commercial purposes, and providing the products for our domestic markets as well as third country markets.

We are actively pursuing economic cooperation with the Soviet Union, and as various cooperative ventures are visualized the Soviet people will come to understand that Koreans have the capability and willingness to make positive contributions for the success of economic reforms in the Soviet Union.

Many economists estimate that on the basis of current trend it would be possible for our bilateral trade volume to reach the $10 billion level by the mid-1990s. Our cooperative relations will not be confined to trade and economic fields. We will develop a comprehensive relationship that includes exchanges in social, cultural, academic, athletic and other fields of common interest.

Koreans grow up reading the poems and works of great Soviet writers and listening to the music of great Soviet composers. Recent Seoul performances of the Bolshoi Ballet and the Leningrad Philharmonic Orchestra have received enthusiastic acclaim by the Korean audience. The new bridge of neighborly friendship will help enrich mutual understanding and friendship between our two peoples.

I understand there is a saying in Russia, "Nothing is heavy if hearts are together." Well, we have a saying in Korea, "Even a piece of paper is lighter if two hands lift."

Just as our sayings have it, Korea and the Soviet Union will march forward helping each other as new partners for the cause of human prosperity and world peace.

I have extended my encouragement and support to President Gorbachev for the perestroika the Soviet Union is pursuing, because it has already changed much the world and is the source of new hope for all mankind to live in peace in one global community.

The Soviet Union is writing a new page of history based on freedom, democracy and respect for human dignity. It is a task that the Soviet Union has to achieve if further progress and greater prosperity are to be attained.

Korea has become a vibrant and energetic newly industrialized country in 30 years rising from the devastation of war. From this experience, I can assure you that pluralistic society and market economy are two shortcuts to economic development.

I am quite confident that the great Soviet people will overcome the current difficulties and challenges and succeed in perestroika, which in time will bring rich fruits of democracy and prosperity to the Soviet people.

I have had useful discussions with many Soviet leaders.

I have also had a very impressive and meaningful meeting yesterday afternoon with professors and students of Moscow University. In my discussions with them, I was able to understand the intellectual rationale behind Soviet efforts toward perestroika and aspirations for a new era.

I had the opportunity to meet with some of my compatriots living here. In our conversations, it was evident that they are hard-working, loyal citizens of the Soviet Union making significant contributions to the development of this society, although they too had to go through numerous adversities in the years past.

I have invited President Gorbachev to visit Korea at his earliest convenience.

I leave Moscow for Leningrad with the excitement of having opened a new era, and am deeply impressed by the warmth of friendship of our Soviet friends.

In Leningrad, I will have another opportunity to reaffirm my admiration for the great courage of the Soviet people to achieve reforms as well as the greatness of Soviet history and cultural tradition.

I would like to express my sincere appreciation to President Gorbachev and to the people of the Soviet Union for their warm and cordial welcome and gracious hospitality rendered to me and members of my delegation.

May I close by noting that while winter in Moscow is colder than it is in Seoul, my heart is never warmer and brighter.

Balishoe spaciba!

Thank you very much, and I will now take questions.

34.

Remarks at the Luncheon with Business and Academic Leaders, Moscow, December 15, 1990

Distinguished scholars, government and business leaders, ladies and gentlemen,

It is a distinct pleasure for me to have this opportunity to meet and share ideas with the leaders of Soviet society here in Moscow.

As the first president of the Republic of Korea to visit your great country, I had an historic summit meeting with President Gorbachev yesterday, and have just paid him a call at the Kremlin to exchange our parting words.

The Moscow Summit has opened a new chapter of history between the Republic of Korea and the Soviet Union. Now we have opened a new era of neighborly friendship, ending the eighty-six years of interruption in our bilateral relations.

President Gorbachev and I have agreed to join efforts to achieve peace and prosperity in the Asia-Pacific region including the Korean Peninsula. Our two nations will promote economic, scientific and technological cooperation and develop a mutually beneficial relationship for the attainment of co-prosperity.

So that understanding and friendship will deepen, we will accelerate exchanges and cooperation in all areas including cultural, academic, athletic, and media.

Our two peoples share the belief that the development of mutually beneficial relations will not only bring forth abundant rewards for both our countries, but also contribute to the emerging new world order.

Distinguished guests,

The waves of reconciliation and cooperation are moving toward the Asia-Pacific region and the Korean Peninsula. The era of Cold War is receding, and a new era of hope is dawning on this vast region. The rapid progress of Soviet-Korean relations is pronouncing to the world that the age-old framework of confrontation is disintegrating even on the Far Eastern part of the Eurasian continent.

This remarkable development owes much to the wisdom and efforts of the leaders in this room and the courageous resolve and strong leadership of President Gorbachev.

The Soviet-Korean Summit Meeting in San Francisco was a pleasant surprise to many around the world. Long before the meeting, however, you were laying the groundwork for this moment with keen foresight and strong conviction to carry out your vision.

The farmer sowing seeds must work hard to ensure an abundant harvest. We opened Soviet-Korean relations anew and now have the responsibility to strengthen and broaden our ties.

Distinguished guests,

Since our bilateral exchanges began, there have been very encouraging developments. Travels between our two countries this year exceeded 12,000 persons as of the end of November, and our trade volume with the Soviet Union, which has grown rapidly, is expected to reach one billion dollars this year.

We are importing such items as oil, uranium and coal from your country, while exporting manufactured goods. Active consultations are under way for construction of joint-venture factories in the Soviet Union for resource development.

There is enormous potential for cooperation between our two countries, and we have taken only the first steps toward the road to greater progress and prosperity. Because the economic structures of our two countries share many complementary features, there exist unlimited potential rewards through our bilateral cooperation.

We should now promote economic, trade and scientific cooperation actively and in good faith so that we will mutually benefit from the fruits of a new Soviet-Korean era.

I am very pleased to note that a framework for bilateral cooperation has emerged during my visit here as agreements on trade, avoidance of double taxation and economic cooperation have been signed between our two governments.

The Republic of Korea has the capacity to supply various products to the Soviet Union and to provide facilities for the production of consumer goods.

Over the years, Korean construction companies have accumulated extensive experience and technical know-how in transportation, communication, housing, road and seaport projects, which will enable them to help improve and expand the Soviet Union's social infrastructure.

The Soviet Union has bountiful natural resources and advanced scientific knowledge and technology, which the Korean economy needs. Together,

Soviet and Korean enterprises can enter into joint ventures to build factories and collaborate to produce consumer goods, develop resources, and improve elements of social infrastructure. Our two countries could also work together to commercialize various Soviet high-technologies or utilize natural resources to manufacture commodities for export to the world market.

I understand that many Korean firms have actively conducted extensive surveys and intensive research in this area. Our two countries should further combine our respective advantages for a rapid progress of our cooperation.

At the policy level, our two governments should also extend active support to private sector firms so that cooperation between our two countries with divergent systems could proceed rapidly and effectively.

Leaders of Soviet society,

To promote friendship and cooperative relations is to promote proper understanding and mutual trust.

In the past, the channels of communication between us were blocked, and our information and perceptions about each other were either warped or incomplete.

The present state of Soviet-Korean relations owes very much to you. Perceiving reality as it really is, you have pioneered with perestroika and combined "new thinkings" with the ideals that we both cherish.

I convey my deep respect to you for your efforts, and expect your continued contributions for a new order of peace and prosperity on the Korean Peninsula and in the Asia-Pacific region.

In Moscow today, I am witnessing a new revolution that seeks to replace the hardened system of the past with a fresh and innovative system. Just as perestroika is changing the world anew, I am convinced that it will lead this great nation to a bright future of progress and prosperity.

I am confident that perestroika will reap great rewards and that Soviet-Korean relations will develop in a direction conducive to the success of perestroika.

As I prepare to return home by way of Leningrad, I leave Moscow filled with warmth and much hope. I thank you very much and hope to have the pleasure of seeing you in Seoul.

Balishoe Spaciba! (Thank you very much.)

Da, Swidanya! (Good-bye and see you again.)

35.

Remarks at the Luncheon Hosted by Mayor Anatoly Sobchak, Leningrad, December 16, 1990

The Honorable Mayor Anatoly Sobchak, Mrs. Sobchak, and distinguished guests,

I would like first to express my deep appreciation to you, Mayor Sobchak, for your invitation to visit this beautiful city and to meet its leaders, for your warm welcome and hospitality, and for your kind words of friendship. It gives me great pleasure to be here in Leningrad, a city alive and flourishing with its brilliant culture and rich history. To the citizens of Leningrad, I bring warm greetings of friendship from the 50 million Korean people.

That the President of the Republic of Korea is visiting this city for the first time in history is testimony to the receding of the Cold War era and to the advent of a new era of hope. The world is surpassing the dark tunnel of a past era that divided humanity with confrontation and rivalry, and imposed suppression and war. Mankind is now full of hope for living together in one global community under common ideals of peace and prosperity.

Our two countries have passed a long period of separation and are entering a new era of friendship as neighbors with a common border.

Ladies and gentlemen,

The great poet Pushkin praised Leningrad as "the city that opened windows to Europe" and "the city to which boats from around the world gathered" along new waterways. This city, known for its vivacity and free spirit, has been at the forefront of the modernization of Russia. The magnificent palaces, towers, and bridges across the Neva River are emblems of the open and creative minds of the people of Leningrad. Traditional gateway to Mother Russia, Leningrad embraces diverse cultural heritages and successfully enriches them into its own at a higher dimension.

Though we Koreans have had limited contacts with Leningrad, this city is very familiar to the people of my country. Koreans grow up enjoying the poems, prose, and novels by Pushkin, Gogol, and Dostoyevsky, and the images of this great city have been molded strongly in the minds of Koreans by the impressions of the leading characters of *The Bronze Horseman, The Overcoat,* and *Crime and Punishment.* The Kirov Ballet, which performed a superb rendition of *Swan Lake* for us last night, is also held in esteem by the Korean people.

After our two countries established relations in 1884, the envoys of our two countries maintained cordial ties of friendship here in Leningrad. When Korea fell prey to the aggression of colonial powers, our forefathers right here in this city planned the recovery of their fatherland. Koreans are very familiar with the heroic struggle of Leningrad that successfully defended your fatherland and civilizations throughout the world from aggressive powers.

Mayor Sobchak, ladies and gentlemen,

The 1988 Seoul Olympics was a festivity of progress and harmony that brought together young people from around the world—transcending barriers that separate mankind such as ideology, prejudice, race, and religion. Koreans enthusiastically welcomed the Soviet athletic delegation to the festivity two years ago. Last spring, the Leningrad State Philharmonic Orchestra, which came to Seoul as a cultural representative of this city, received much acclaim from Korean audiences for its resplendent talents and for providing a fresh new encounter with your civilization.

Now that we have normalized our relations, our two countries should build a partnership for a more peaceful and prosperous world. President Gorbachev and I have pronounced to the world that we will join efforts to bring peace to the Korean Peninsula and the Asia-Pacific region.

Our two countries will pursue common prosperity by actively promoting trade and economic cooperation, and should encourage active exchanges in other areas of common interest such as the arts, culture, and athletics. As mutual understanding and friendship between our peoples deepen, the neighborly relations between our two countries will strengthen. Now that Leningrad has opened its doors to the world, I look forward to this city's active contribution to the new era of Soviet-Korean relations.

To most Koreans, Leningrad was a distant city. A century ago, it took the first Korean envoys fifty days across two oceans and three continents to arrive at this city. Until recently, even that detour route had been shut for decades. Now a new avenue of exchange and cooperation is open before us in this new era of friendship.

Ladies and gentlemen,

My visit to Leningrad has provided me with opportunity to come in close contact with a great people, who are creating a bold new history. Perestroika stands as a gateway to freedom and prosperity for the Soviet Union as well as to peace and progress for the global community. I am confident that the people of Leningrad, a city that has long stood at the forefront of history, will help lead perestroika to triumph.

Ladies and gentlemen,

Please join me now in toasting to the good health and well-being of The Honorable Mayor Sobchak and Mrs. Sobchak, to the everlasting growth of Soviet-Korean relations, and to the prosperity and happiness of the citizens of Leningrad.

Balishoe Spaciba. (Thank you very much.)

36.

Written Interview with *Far Eastern Affairs* (U.S.S.R.), Vol. I, 1991

Q. 1 *Esteemed Mr. President,*
First of all, let me express my deep gratitude for your readiness to answer the questions which are now of great interest for the Soviet people. We know that the ROK's mass media paid great attention to your meeting with President Mikhail Gorbachev and to the establishment after that of the diplomatic relations between our countries. More than a month has passed since that event and recently we have learned about the appointment of ambassadors to Moscow and Seoul. It is too early to judge about the efficacy of these steps made by both sides, but nevertheless, could you describe the exchange of ambassadors as a new stage in USSR-ROK relations?

A. It gives me great pleasure to convey, through this space, warm greetings of the Korean people to the 300 million people of the Soviet Union. We welcome the restoration, after 86 years, of diplomatic relations between our two countries.

At the invitation of President Gorbachev, I will visit Moscow in the middle of December 1990. The visit will be first ever by the President of the Republic of Korea, and I will have an opportunity to meet Soviet citizens in person.

The very speed of improving ROK-USSR relations, which had been interrupted for decades, is evidence that the cold war barriers that used to stand between our two nations, and between the nations of the world, have begun crumbling down around us, in the Korean Peninsula as well as in the Asia-Pacific Region. The establishment of diplomatic relations between our two countries serves as an unmistakable and encouraging sign that a new era has arrived not only to the 50 million people of the Republic of Korea but also to all the nations in the Asia-Pacific Region, which is home to two thirds of the world population.

That the friendly relations between our two countries were interrupted for nearly a century was due to the expansionist colonialism and the subsequent cold war confrontations. The establishment of bilateral diplomatic relations has in effect turned past events into matters of history. The normalization of our relations is the result of confluence between President Gorbachev's "new thinking" and my "northern policy."

The normalization of our relations will greatly contribute not only to the increased understanding and cooperation between our two nations but also to the relaxation of tension and a durable peace on the Korean Peninsula. It will also serve as a decisive catalyst in forging a new order in Northeast Asia.

The Asia-Pacific Region that stretches from Northeast Asia to Southeast Asia and to Australia and New Zealand, has now emerged as a new center of development that will lead the world to a new era of prosperity. It should be noted, however, that the stability and peace of the Korean Peninsula have always been essential to the security of this region.

In view of the summit meeting between myself and President Gorbachev in San Francisco and the subsequent normalization of our bilateral relations, it seems that the nations of the region are witnessing a process of implementation of the Asia-Pacific peace initiative President Gorbachev adumbrated in his speeches in Vladivostok and Krasnoyarsk.

In a speech before the United Nations General Assembly on October 18, 1988, I proposed a "consultative conference for peace in Northeast Asia" to be attended by the countries having major interest in the Korean Peninsula, including the Soviet Union. I put the proposal forward with a view to replacing the international structure of this region, which saw five major wars in a century, and where cold war confrontations still persist, with a new structure of peace and cooperation. Owing to realistic policies and courageous decisions, Northeast Asia is now entering into a new era of reconciliation and cooperation.

Just as Europe has found a "common house" for peace and cooperation, the nations in this region also aspire for the emergence of a new order in this part of the world. Because the Korean people suffered so much from the territorial division and the Korean War, our aspirations for peace are greater than any other.

As our bilateral relations improve, an increasing number of Soviet and Korean citizens will visit each other's country. And, as exchanges increase, our two nations will rediscover each other and come to greater mutual understanding. More than ever before, we realize the importance of good neighborly and friendly relations and how unnatural and counterproductive the interruption of our relations has been.

Increases in bilateral exchanges and friendly cooperation will certainly contribute to the promotion of prosperity of our two countries.

Because our two countries have between us great potential and a variety of areas of cooperation I believe our bilateral relations will continue to develop to our mutual benefit and satisfaction. And the exchange of ambassadors is but the first step toward that end.

Q. 2 *There were many doubts in our country: Is it possible that after the establishment of diplomatic relations between Moscow and Seoul some kind of weakening of interest on the ROK's part toward the development of full-scale cooperation with the Soviet Union may follow? Are there any reasons, from your point of view, to take such doubts into consideration seriously?*

A. With the normalization of relations and the exchange of ambassadors, the Soviet Union and the Republic of Korea have just opened a new path toward unbounded mutual development. Henceforth, bilateral cooperation will be pursued positively and vigorously in all areas.

Let me point out that only two months have passed since we restored diplomatic relations. Since July when a ROK government delegation visited Moscow for a round of talks, our two governments have been working diligently to build a framework for bilateral economic cooperation. As a result, we are nearing accord on almost all draft agreements. Unlike the case of socialist economies, a country with a market economy like the Republic of Korea has to rely on private businesses to act as the prime movers of economic cooperation with other countries. To encourage private businesses to embark on active economic cooperation, it is necessary to support their activities with positive policies on the part of both governments by providing a framework such as investment guarantees and avoidance of dual taxation.

Many Korean companies have enthusiastically conducted feasibility studies and closely examined a long list of projects, including joint ventures for production of consumer goods, joint development of natural resources and the upgrading of social infrastructure such as telecommunications and harbor facilities. Korean businesses appear to be interested in providing industrial facilities and machine-tool supplies in the process of converting Soviet defense industries into civilian use. Korean companies also seem to be actively looking for opportunities, and joint ventures are being set up, to apply state-of-the-art Soviet science and technology to various commercial products for sale in third countries.

The Republic of Korea is more active than any other in pursuing cooperative relations with the Soviet Union, and as various ROK-USSR cooperative projects take concrete form, I believe the Soviet people will begin to appreciate our willingness and capabilities to actively contribute to the process of perestroika. Recently, Mr. Medvedev of the Soviet Presidential Council paid a visit to Korea. Through in-depth contacts and discussions with a large number of government officials and business leaders he should have personally confirmed our willingness toward Korean-Soviet economic cooperation. His visit also served to strengthen the basis for an effective implementation of bilateral economic cooperation.

I would expect that a framework for the development of bilateral ties and friendly cooperation will emerge during my scheduled visit to the Soviet Union in the middle of December. I hope and expect that during my visit to Moscow, agreements on trade, investment guarantees, scientific and technological cooperation and aviation, all of which are currently under negotiation, will be signed and subsequently bilateral exchanges and cooperation will move forward in earnest.

Q. 3 *Nowadays, the men of business in both countries are linking the progress in bilateral relations mostly with the advance along the road of economic cooperation. The value of mutual trade in 1989 reached 600 million US dollars, and according to the data given by ROK's experts this value will reach 10 billion dollars by the middle of the 1990s. How could you assess these estimates and, if positively, what real efforts must be made by both sides to provide better conditions for further progress in the mutual trade and economic cooperation?*

A. The Republic of Korea and the Soviet Union are geographically close and share many complementary aspects in industrial structures, resources and technology. Accordingly, I believe prospects for bilateral economic cooperation are very bright. The establishment of diplomatic ties and my forthcoming visit to the Soviet Union will undoubtedly stimulate trade, investment and other forms of economic cooperation between our two countries.

There are in the Korean economy today many elements of which the Soviet Union can take advantage. Some of them include our developmental experience and know-how under the market economy; our capacity to build and manufacture automobiles, ships, electronic commodities as well as a whole range of consumer products; our material resources and technology needed to develop social infrastructure such as public works, telecommunications and transportation; and our pool of skilled workers and experienced managers . . . These resources can be put to work to substantively help the restructuring process of the Soviet economy.

On the other hand, the Soviet Union has a vast territory rich in natural resources and a large market with enormous potential. Furthermore, the advanced science and technology of the Soviet Union are what we need in Korea. Expansion of trade and economic cooperation between our two countries will therefore be highly conducive to our pursuit of common prosperity. So long as the Soviet Union continues to pursue market economy as currently planned, the volume of our bilateral trade will exceed one billion dollars this year, and by the mid-1990s will, according to many economists, reach the 10 billion dollar mark.

The Republic of Korea government is taking active steps to assist our businesses so that they can supply various consumer products needed by the Soviet economy and set up joint venture factories in the Soviet Union to produce such goods. The bilateral agreements for investment guarantees and avoidance of double taxation, expected to be signed during my visit to Moscow next month, are intended to provide our private businesses with the basis and assurance to actively engage in economic activities in the Soviet economic environment.

What I would ask of our Soviet friends is that the Soviet businesses should take full advantage of the market economy and the proven qualities of our private businesses. The Republic of Korea was able to rise from the ruins of the Korean War and achieve a rapid economic development primarily on the strength of active private initiatives and creative entrepreneurship.

Because businesses in a market economy are predicated on the rule of competition, they inevitably tend to emphasize profit and efficiency. Since our businesses appear to be keenly interested in and enthusiastic about investment and resource development opportunities in the Soviet economy, I would hope that the Soviet government will take the lead in creating appropriate conditions conducive to their efficient operation.

Q. 4 *In the world mass media we can often find pessimistic opinions about peaceful intentions of the USSR in spite of the positive changes on the many directions of international politics. Taking into consideration our discussions in Seoul, we can draw the conclusion that today the "Soviet threat" myth is not as popular in the ROK as it used to be. In this connection your conceptions of national security may have been revised too. Could you describe at least in general terms, the present-day approach of Seoul officials to the problems of ROK security?*

A. As the 21st century approaches, hopes run high that mankind will finally be able to pursue peace and prosperity in one friendly and understanding global community. Over the past several years, the world has been undergoing extensive qualitative changes, making significant progress in arms control agreements, ushering in sweeping reforms in Europe, and removing the cold war structure. The waves of reconciliation and cooperation toward a more peaceful world have now become an irreversible current of history.

The current change has been spearheaded by President Gorbachev and the Soviet Union through perestroika policies based on new thinking: The decision to award this year's Nobel Peace Prize to President Gorbachev clearly reflects the worldwide recognition of his invaluable contributions to world peace.

Korean aspirations for and positions toward a new world order of reconciliation and cooperation are clearly spelled out in my 1988 address to the United Nations General Assembly. Koreans take great pride in that we have provided a magnificent venue for global harmony during the 1988 Seoul Olympics in which virtually all the nations of the world took part. The Soviet delegation to the Seoul Olympics and many other Soviet citizens that have since visited Korea, have seen firsthand the friendliness of the Korean people and their desire for cooperative relations with the Soviet people.

The Korean War that broke out in June 1950 lasted for three years and inflicted on us millions of casualties and total destruction. For forty years since the war, our people have had to live under continuing military tension and the constant threat of war. It is due to our past experience and persisting realities that Korean officials, indeed the entire nation, place top priority on our national security.

The establishment of our diplomatic relations is expected to help ease tension and promote peace on the Korean Peninsula. This is one of the most important reasons for the support our people rendered to the normalization and development of friendly relations with the Soviet Union.

The rapid development of Seoul-Moscow ties has brought a substantial change in our perception of the Soviet Union. It is sincerely hoped that our bilateral relations and mutual understanding will develop rapidly so that our perception of the Soviet Union as a source of threat will be quickly dispelled. At the same time, it is hoped that the improvement of our relations will propel greater regional peace and cooperation throughout Northeast Asia.

Having suffered unspeakable sorrow and sacrifice from the territorial division, war and cold war confrontations, the people of the Republic of Korea eagerly await the arrival of global waves of reconciliation in the Korean Peninsula. We are currently pursuing, in all sincerity, dialogues and exchanges with North Korea. We are seeking to build mutual trust and a constructive relationship between the two parts of Korea so that North Korea will cease to pose a military threat and threats of war on us, and will instead become our trustworthy partner for peace and prosperity for all.

Q. 5 *The significance of relations between our two countries, as you have just mentioned, goes beyond the limits of bilateral relations and might, as even the existing experience shows, stimulate the establishment of a new international system based on the principles of the new political thinking. So, are there any untapped reserves in cooperation between Seoul and Moscow on the main (in the sense of international security interests) directions of the world politics?*

A. I am confident that the establishment of diplomatic relations between Seoul and Moscow will contribute not only to the development of constructive bilateral ties but also replacing the cold war structure in Northeast Asia with a new order of reconciliation and cooperation. It should be noted that the Korean Peninsula now remains the only unresolved area of the cold war, now that Germany has been unified and a new order of reconciliation and cooperation has been established in Europe. Tension on the Korean Peninsula has been in fact impeding the security and cooperation of the entire Asia-Pacific Region, and a source of confrontation in this part of the world.

Fundamental change has yet to take place in the inter-Korean relations. But we can say that the cold war glacier over the Korean Peninsula has finally begun to break with the establishment of full diplomatic relations between our two countries. In today's world of increasing interdependence, I feel confident that the changes taking place in the Korean Peninsula in the wake of ROK-USSR cooperation will gradually remove the confrontational cold war structure in Northeast Asia. Our two nations, along with the other states of the region, should endeavor together to promote cooperation, peace and stability in Northeast Asia.

Q. 6 *The establishment of ROK-USSR diplomatic relations doesn't change the Soviet side's obligations to the DPRK. The main principles of Soviet foreign policy today rule out any interference of the Soviet side in the internal affairs of the DPRK, as well as of the ROK, and in this connection our role in the process of ensuring security in the Korean Peninsula could be seen by some people as external influence of sorts. What can you say about the possible future role of the Soviet Union in the process of providing international guarantees of peaceful unification of Korea?*

A. Eliminating threats of war and securing peace are tasks that transcend national boundaries and should be a priority agenda not only for the nations involved but also for all the nations of the world. The Conference on European Security and Cooperation, held in Paris in November, has taken a giant step toward creating a European "common house." We should all welcome this achievement as a truly monumental contribution to world peace. Now, the Paris Charter prescribes what the individual signatories should do to advance the cause of peace and cooperation in Europe. No signatory, however, would regard the stipulations of the Paris Charter as interfering in its internal affairs.

Given the historical and geopolitical environment, the maintenance of peace and stability in the Korean Peninsula demands not only our own efforts but contributions of the neighboring friends as well. For this reason, I have proposed in my U.N. speech a six-nation conference on peace in Northeast Asia to be attended by the two Koreas, the Soviet Union, the United States, China and Japan.

The Soviet Union, in my view, is fully capable of taking necessary steps to persuade North Korea to abandon its unrealistic policies and openly and voluntarily join the international community as a responsible member. Moscow should also be able to help create conditions in Northeast Asia that are conducive to inter-Korean rapprochement.

Efforts by neighboring countries will play crucial roles for the Northeast Asian stability as well as for the maintenance of international peace.

Q. 7 *Our academic community, politicians and practical experts are discussing the future of business cooperation within the framework of some kind of Far Eastern structure resembling the common market, including the Soviet Far Eastern region, Mongolia, Northeast China, North and South Korea. What is your opinion of this and other similar ideas and the possibility of the ROK's business circles' participation in the realization of this idea?*

A. There exists a great potential for mutually profitable cooperation among the Northeast Asian nations in view of their complementary economic characteristics in terms of resources and industrial structure. For this reason, the Republic of Korea is actively pursuing economic cooperation with its neighbors. However, it will be necessary first to build up bilateral and multilateral ties of economic cooperation among the nations involved before serious discussions can take place for the creation of such a system. At the present stage, countries in Northeast Asia should first conclude agreements to actively promote trade, investment, resource and technology development and other forms of cooperation. As substantive economic cooperation expands among the regional countries, discussions on the creation of a formal organization for regional cooperation will naturally ensue.

We in Korea are aware of various ideas for regional cooperation in Northeast Asia. But the idea should be preceded by in-depth studies on how to effectively coordinate and promote cooperation among the countries in the area and on the future relationship with existing and emerging movements for economic cooperation in the Asia-Pacific region.

37.

Remarks at the Dinner in Honor of President Gorbachev of the Soviet Union, Cheju-do, Korea, April 19, 1991

Your Excellency, Mrs. Gorbachev, ladies and gentlemen,

President Gorbachev, although you are very busy these days with your many responsibilities both at home and abroad, we are pleased that you could visit us here and, along with the people of Korea, we welcome you, Mrs. Gorbachev and your entire delegation.

In our country, the story goes that housewives who are not very good cooks usually serve their husbands dinner at a very late hour so that their hunger may make the poorly cooked food taste better. Therefore, I hope you will enjoy the humble meal we serve you at this late hour.

This beautiful spot is known as Cheju Island and it is where our newlyweds go for their honeymoons. Tonight, from the bottom of our hearts, we welcome both of you, President and Mrs. Gorbachev, in the same spirit as we welcome newlyweds.

I remember the words you spoke when we first met last June. You said, "the ice between our two countries has melted and relations between us will soon bear fruit."

Your Excellency, I also recall that you said that when this fruit is ripe, we are bound to eat it. At that time, I said to you that we should join our hands in picking that very special fruit.

Last year we had our very first meeting in San Francisco and last December I visited Moscow. This is our third meeting. In the ten months since all this began, we have witnessed great changes that testify to the fact that the world is truly undergoing fundamental and far-reaching changes. On Cheju Island, the flowers are blooming from shore to shore to welcome not only nature's springtime but also the springtime of relations between our two great nations. Indeed the warm spring has arrived and I hope that this warm, mutual feeling and relationship between our two countries will spread across the whole Korean Peninsula and across the continent to open a wave of reconciliation and springtime for all of Asia.

Last December when I visited the Soviet Union, I was able to witness for myself the insight and leadership with which you lead the Soviet people and I also was touched by the enthusiasm with which your people have embraced perestroika. I especially recall the bright eyes of the students at Moscow University whom I met with during my stay. I know that in spite of the numerous difficulties you are facing you are pursuing reform within your own country with courage and strong leadership.

On my part, I am pursuing our Northern Policy with great determination and I am convinced that these two bold initiatives will somehow come together to help build lasting peace and prosperity in this world.

Today we are meeting each other with the hope that our talks here will provide momentum enough to end the Cold War on the Korean Peninsula that has caused distrust, tensions and the threat of war. It is our hope that by joining hands here on Cheju Island we can create a foundation for a lasting peace and reunification on this Peninsula.

Late last year, we signed the Moscow Declaration and, in the wake of it, our mutual ties on economic, political, social and cultural matters are accelerating at a rapid pace with great strength and direction. I am very satisfied with this.

I am also aware that in the Soviet Union you are in a state of transition, that you face various problems and difficulties and that you are making exceptional efforts to overcome all of this for which you have our respect and admiration. I also know that the leaders of the world are sympathetic with your efforts on behalf of world peace and stability. I think all of us must stand on your side to provide you with assistance and encouragement for your efforts.

Let me repeat that, at this very moment, we are witnessing the historic opening of the Pacific Age—a turning point in world history and a chance to achieve many good things for all people.

Your Excellency, I hope your stay here will be a satisfying, productive and significant one. Ladies and gentlemen, for the health of President and Mrs. Gorbachev, for the progress and prosperity of the Soviet Union and to the everlasting friendship between our two countries, I propose a toast. Cheers.

38.

Remarks at the Banquet in Honor of the President of the Mongolian People's Republic and Mrs. Tsevelmaa, Seoul, October 23, 1991

President Punsalmaagiin Ochirbat, Mrs. Tsevelmaa, distinguished guests, ladies and gentlemen,

I have the pleasure of extending to you a warm and cordial welcome on your first ever visit to Korea as the head of the state of the Mongolian People's Republic.

Your visit represents the restoration and renewal, after a hiatus, of traditional friendship our two peoples as close neighbors have maintained throughout our history.

What has prevented us from continuing with our relationship was the Cold War structure in the postwar era.

Today, however, the Republic of Korea and the Mongolian People's Republic have become partners for friendship and cooperation.

Our partnership has transcended the barriers of the Cold War and is at the forefront the human progress toward a harmonious world community. Furthermore, it means that in the Asian continent also a new era has arrived.

As I have the pleasure of welcoming you to Chong Wa Dae this evening, I feel I am among old friends who have been away.

Mr. President,

Perhaps, you are also struck by the fact that it is very difficult among us to distinguish guests from the hosts. Indeed, our two peoples are as close to each other as our features are similar. In our culture, language, ethnicity and custom we share many common traits.

This is probably because our two nations, both belonging to the Altaic cultural sphere, have been engaged in close interchanges from time immemorial, and certainly before the recorded history of mankind. We share innumerable episodes in our history books, as well. For these reasons, the Korean people feel special affinity toward the Mongolian people.

The Korean people are intimately familiar with the history of the Mongolian people: the vast empire you built across the Eurasian continent, Mongolian heroes such as Genghis Khan and Kublai Khan, the magnificent great plains, and the courage and strength of the Mongolian nation.

We also know that the Mongolian people used to call the Korean Peninsula "Solongos," meaning a beautiful country of rainbow. This, then, is evidence that the Mongolian people also have been friendly to the Korean people.

Mr. President,

We know the many changes and improvements that have been made since you came into office last year. Under your eminent leadership, the constitution was revised and dynamic democratic reforms are under way through free elections and multiparty system.

You are building a new nation by introducing free market economy and bold reform measures and by actively pursuing friendly relations with open societies of the world.

I am convinced that these reforms carried out under the banner of *shinechlel* (reform) and *eerchlelt* (openness) will mark an historic beginning of a new Mongolia of freedom and prosperity.

The Republic of Korea pledges to render its support and encouragement to the reform efforts of the Mongolian government and people.

By taking advantage of the merits of a free market economy and democratic system, the Republic of Korea has been able to build a newly industrializing country within the span of one generation, rising from the ashes of war. And, we are prepared to share with you the experience and technology we accumulated in the course of our economic development.

Mr. President,

Your visit today will serve as a shining landmark in the course of developing a closer and more friendly relationship between our two countries.

Since we opened formal relations in March 1990, our bilateral relationship has seen rapid progress in all areas: politics, economy, culture, tourism and others.

By expanding trade and cooperation and through the promotion of friendship and understanding between our peoples, our two countries will become valuable friends to each other.

As soon as a favorable environment for foreign investment emerges, many Korean businesses will decide to participate in various Mongolian projects, including the utilization of abundant livestock resources for woolen products, the foodstuff industry, joint exploration of natural resources, expansion of social infrastructure such as highways, railroad and communications, and construction of residential housing.

The Republic of Korea and the Mongolian People's Republic will also closely cooperate on the international arena, particularly in forging a new international order of cooperation in Northeast Asia.

Improved relations between South and North Korea are a key to the peace of this region. We are seeking to achieve peaceful national unification on the basis of coexistence, co-prosperity, and cooperative exchanges with North Korea. I hope the Mongolian government and people will continue to support our efforts to lie in peace by achieving the long-aspired goal of national unification.

Your visit this time is rather short, but I hope you will find Korea and her people most friendly, warm and hospitable. I also hope your stay in Korea will be most memorable and fruitful.

Ladies and gentlemen,
"I lay out white satin to greet you as we gather around to share the joy." As we share the joy expressed in this Mongolian folk song, I ask you to rise and join me in a toast to the health of Their Excellencies President Ochirbat and Mrs. Tsevelmaa, to the prosperity of the Mongolian People's Republic, and to lasting friendship between our two countries.

Thank you.

Part V

RELATIONS WITH JAPAN: RECONCILIATION WITH A NEIGHBOR

39.

Remarks at the State Dinner Hosted by the Emperor of Japan, Tokyo, May 24, 1990

Your Majesties the Emperor and Empress, esteemed members of the Imperial Family, Prime Minister and Mrs. Kaifu, distinguished guests,

I am very grateful to you for the warm welcome extended to us and for the generous hospitality in our honor. I am also thankful for Your Majesty's warm and friendly remarks about my country and people.

It is a great pleasure for me to visit Japan at a time when Japan has embarked on the new Heisei Era. I consider it of utmost significance that I have this historic opportunity today to acquaint myself with you and extend my personal congratulations to you on becoming the Emperor of Japan. I note with respect that Japan has risen from the ashes of war and rebuilt itself into a prosperous and peace-loving nation, which is the envy of the world. I firmly believe that the Heisei Era will bring peace, prosperity, and fraternity not only to Japan, but also throughout East Asia and the world.

Since time immemorial, Korea and Japan have had close contacts as neighbors. Through interactions across the narrow straits, our two nations have exercised significant mutual influence on each other's cultural development. We have shared many positive things together, but in more modern times, we have also experienced pain. But, compared to the long history of neighborly and amicable relations, the period of darkness was relatively short.

To be sure, it is not possible to erase, nor should we forget, historical facts. But, I do not believe we should remain bound up in the past. Our two nations must now forge a new era of friendship and cooperation based on proper historical perspectives, and put the wrong-doings of the past behind. It is significant that Your Majesty, the symbol of Japanese history and the new Japanese nation, expressed deep regrets about this matter.

If our two nations are to become truly close neighbors in spirit as in geography, we should now strive together to remove the dark shadows of history and overcome residual resentments that have hampered development of bilateral ties. We will then be able to hand down mutually beneficial ties to our posterity.

Your Majesty,
As the 21st century draws near, the world finds itself in the midst of tremendous change. The irrepressible human aspirations for freedom and prosperity have brought down the Cold War structure, and drastically reshaped the geopolitical landscape. Freedom and democracy, the ideals which both Korea and Japan cherish, have begun to reign as universal values.

It has long been said that the 21st century will be the Age of the Asia-Pacific. In today's world, the relationship between Korea and Japan can hardly be a concern of our two countries alone. Our two countries ought to combine our efforts to take a leading role in promoting peace and prosperity throughout the Asia-Pacific region, the new center of world attention, by harmoniously combining the merits of the East and the West. Furthermore, our two nations should endeavor to make greater contributions toward the well-being and prosperity of the world at large. This, I believe, is our duty before history and mankind.

Some 270 years ago, Hoshu Amenomori, who was in charge of Japan's relations with the Choson Kingdom, held "sincerity and good faith" as his motto. His Korean counterpart, Hyon Tog-Yun, had built Songshindang, or the Hall of Sincerity and Good Faith, in Tongnae and received Japanese envoys there. I am confident that our bilateral ties will develop in the future in a spirit of mutual respect, understanding, shared ideals and values.

I believe the future of Korea-Japan relations will be bright so long as we both endeavor to build our ties on sincerity and good faith as well as on a global perspective. An Oriental sage had said, "The relationship between true gentlemen is placid, like calm water." I believe the friendly relations between our two nations should continue likewise.

Distinguished guests,
Please join me in a toast to the good health, longevity and well-being of Their Majesties, and to ever prosperous Japan in the new Heisei Era.
Thank you.

40.

Korea and Japan: New Relations in a Changing World; Address Before the Japanese Diet, Tokyo, May 25, 1990

Honorable President of the House of Representatives, Honorable President of the House of Councillors, Esteemed Members of the Diet,

It is an honour and privilege for me to be the first Korean Head of State ever to speak before the Japanese Diet. I am particularly privileged since this hall is the focal point of the 188-year development of parliamentary democracy in Japan. Today, you proudly represent the 138 million Japanese who have built one of the most prosperous and vibrant democracies in the world.

I have come to this great hall following in the footsteps of our forebears who had struggled and sacrificed themselves through our checkered history for a better Korea-Japan relationship and for a brighter future for East Asia. Upon reflection, I am deeply moved with memories of our past history. At the same time, however, I am gratified to note that history has progressed such that the neighborly and friendly Korea-Japan relations for which our forebears so aspired have been restored on the basis of reciprocity and equality.

I am grateful to the presidents of both Houses of the Diet, the leaders of the various political parties represented here, and all Members of the Diet for affording me this precious opportunity. At the same time, I wish to convey warm and friendly greetings from the people of the Republic of Korea to the people of Japan.

I have come to Japan convinced that now is the time for our two nations to develop a very close partnership on the basis of mutual respect and understanding. In view of the tremendous changes taking place around the world and in the belief that as we approach the twenty-first century we, as next-door neighbors, must forge ahead with a forward-looking relationship, let me take this opportunity to review with candor some of the issues of our common concern.

Korea and Japan each started building a new nation following the end of World War II. Great changes have since occurred in both countries. Both our nations have transformed many things and achieved a great deal.

Rising from the ruins of war, the Japanese people have developed their land into an economic powerhouse that is the envy of the world. Moreover, Japan is now advancing in the forefront of science and technology. The ideas of capitalism and parliamentary democracy which sprouted in Europe some centuries ago are now blooming here in Japan, a faraway land in the East. During the latter half of the nineteenth century, when farsighted Asian leaders urged the blending of Eastern values with Western expertise, Japan began pursuing a dream of overtaking the West. Having realized that dream, Japan has successfully embarked on creative efforts to fuse its national heritage with things Western to create a new culture. I pay respect to the Japanese people and leaders for this great accomplishment.

On the other hand, the joy of the Korean people over liberation from colonial rule forty-five years ago gave way to a sorrow over national partition the next morning. As if this were not misfortune enough, our people were plunged into another national disaster. On the dawn of one Sunday in June 1950, an all-out invasion from North Korea turned the Cold War which was polarizing the postwar world into a hot, savage conflict on the Korean Peninsula. The three-year conflagration of the Korean War not only caused the loss of millions of innocent lives but also deprived us of every possession.

Early in the 1960s, when the Korean people were beginning earnest efforts to develop their newly-rebuilt national economy, we watched the spectacle of the Tokyo Olympics with envy. Japan's achievement inspired us with confidence and courage.

Overcoming their ordeals and despair, the Korean people rose to build a better tomorrow. Development was a formidable challenge, a nearly impossible proposition for the Republic of Korea, which had virtually no natural resources, no capital and no technology. And yet our people did not lose hope or give up. Through hard work and sacrifice over a generation, the Republic has emerged as a newly industrialized country.

The Korean people hosted the Seoul Olympics as a magnificent festival of peace which brought East and West together for the first time in twelve years. In the very trouble spot where young people from twenty countries fought bloody battles just thirty-eight years before, young people from around the world joined hands to surmount all divisive barriers and forge bonds of harmony.

Our achievements, won against all odds, represent a triumph over unkind history. We Koreans are very proud of the fact that Korea's rapid development has set an example for many countries in the Third World and the Eastern bloc, and that a country that has been tormented by a hot war as well as Cold

War confrontation has become able to contribute to the peace and harmony of mankind.

Another rewarding experience for the Korean people is their recent entry into an era of democracy. Throughout nearly forty years of almost ceaseless internal and external turbulence, the Korean people have never given up their burning desire and determined struggle for freedom and democracy.

The new era, which was ushered in by the June 29 Declaration of Democratic Reforms about three years ago, is characterized, among other things, by unrestricted freedom of speech and the press, as well as unlimited political freedom. Korean democratization has meant sweeping changes, not only in the Constitution and political institutions but also in the whole system of values and the civic awareness of the general public. It has thus become impossible to understand the Korea of today by measuring it with an old yardstick.

I must frankly admit to you, esteemed Members of the Diet, that it is truly difficult to practice democracy. In this regard, allow me to cite a portion of a poem by Han Yong-un, the noted poet and independence leader who died in 1944.

> I love you because
> Whereas others love only
> My youthful face and smile,
> You love even my grey hair,
> Even my tears.

Just as the poet loved his homeland when it was darkened by an unfortunate twist of history, I believe we should cultivate democracy with love of even its most messy aspects. Though democracy can hardly be considered a panacea, nothing else enables humans to live like humans, society to be vital and vibrant, creativity to come into full play and progress to occur, as does democracy. In particular, I believe only democracy can bring about a great age in which ordinary people willingly participate with a civic spirit to make their dreams come true.

Though Korean democratization is costing us dearly, it is nonetheless moving along the right direction. There will be no backtracking in this. It is a rewarding and delightful experience not only for myself but for all my fellow Koreans to renew here today our shared faith in freedom and democracy.

Esteemed Members of the Diet,

Since the guns fell silent in World War II, enormous changes have occurred throughout the world, not just in our two countries. With the new century only ten years away, we are now in the midst of great reforms intended to bring the twentieth century to a constructive close.

The Cold War strife and confrontation that have dominated the postwar world are now passing into history, making way for the new tide of détente and co-operation now engulfing the globe. The burning human desire for freedom and democracy has breached the Berlin Wall and removed the Iron Curtain that used to divide the East from the West. Even the Soviet Union is in the throes of reform, and the totalitarian regimes of Eastern Europe have fallen like dominoes.

The European Community has instituted economic integration and is now moving toward a political union. Owing to reforms in Eastern Europe, it is likely that the domain of a united Europe will expand to the Soviet borders. Human dignity, freedom and democracy have thus begun to prevail as universal values.

Esteemed Members of the Diet,

The challenges of the changing world are great, too. Though we are eagerly looking forward to an emerging new world order to replace the Cold War structure, it is still shrouded in the mist of uncertainties. Though the world now yearns for peace and harmony, with reason beginning to prevail over the logic of force, we still have a long way to go before this crystallizes into a new international order. Although arms control is making headway, fears that nuclear weapons may destroy human civilization at any moment have not been eliminated yet.

Uncertainties also plague the future of the world economy. Even the free trade regime that has brought unprecedented prosperity to the post-war world is being challenged. In other words, imbalances in world trade are giving rise to protectionism, leading to ever harsher trade friction. Nor can we rule out the possibility of the rise of regional economic blocs. Although we hope that a united Europe will pursue openness, no one can say with confidence that it will never move in the opposite direction. The moves of Europe and the Soviet Union in the future are certainly of major concern to all of us. I feel acutely the importance of concerted efforts by our two nations to cope with these changes and challenges.

It is noted that Japan has now become the world's largest aid donor. We greatly appreciate Japan's endeavour to meet its share of *noblesse oblige*. Japan's contributions to the community of nations, I believe, will not be limited to the economic field but will include a leading role in realizing universal values throughout the world. The Republic of Korea is also vowing to fulfill its international responsibilities, commensurate with its new status and capabilities.

Esteemed Members of the Diet,

The achievement of peace and unification of the Korean Peninsula is not only the Korean people's own paramount goal but a most important way to contribute to the well-being of this region in particular and the world at large.

Few other countries have been as tormented over the last century by invasions, wars and confrontation as Korea. Therefore the Korean people yearn especially for peace. We believe the way for Korea to respond constructively to the ordeals inflicted on it is by achieving peace in this part of the world. We are resolved to strive to realize the peaceful unification of the Korean Peninsula without fail before the present century is out. The national division imposed on us by the Cold War regime must not be allowed to continue into the next century. We are confident that Korean unification will become a reality, just as the reunification of Germany, which everybody thought would be extremely difficult, is now becoming a reality and just as the Olympic Games, a festival of global harmony, was actually held even in divided Korea which is under a constant threat of renewed war.

Still, in spite of the wave of détente now sweeping the world, the Demilitarized Zone that cuts across the Korean Peninsula is yet to be unfrozen. We are acutely aware of this grim reality, more so than anyone else. However, North Korea is bound to change sooner or later. It will have no choice but to come into the open world. We are determined to do everything in our power to encourage this. North Korea should no longer persist in being our adversary intent only on confrontation, but as a member of the same ethnic family it should become our partner in the quest for common prosperity. We do not at all desire North Korea's isolation. We are seeking the formation of a single national community with the North Koreans, who are one people with us, prior to full unification based on the principles of independence, peace and democracy. In view of the rapid changes now sweeping the world, as well as our people's ardent wish for unification, a change in inter-Korean relations would quickly lead to national integration.

Since last year, the Republic of Korea has established diplomatic relations with one East European country after another and is now actively pursuing improved relations also with the Soviet Union as well as the People's Republic of China. Our northern policy will not only contribute to common prosperity with those countries but will also help create conditions favorable to improving inter-Korean relations and achieving eventual unification. When peace and unification are achieved on the Korean Peninsula, genuine peace will come to East Asia and the world in general, too.

Esteemed Members of the Diet,

Last November, I toured several East and West European countries at a time when the Berlin Wall was crumbling. I was thus able to sense acutely the powerful current of history pushing towards freedom, peace, openness and prosperity. While on the very scene of the momentous changes, I pondered deeply on the future of the Korean Peninsula and East Asia.

In the past hundred years, Northeast Asia, home to both our peoples, experienced five major wars. Since the Korean War, however, a balance of power has preserved a fragile peace in this region. In the light of the current new moves toward East-West détente, a debate is now going on about how to readjust the roles of the superpowers and their policies in this part of the world. Many imponderables still stand in the way of structural changes to ensure lasting peace and cooperation in this region. The time has now come for Korea and Japan to begin earnest joint efforts to promote peace and prosperity in Northeast Asia.

Speaking before the General Assembly of the United Nations in late 1988, I proposed a multilateral Northeast Asian Peace Conference. It will take time for the political conditions to change sufficiently to make such a conference possible. This must include, among others, a change of heart on the part of North Korea. Toward that end, it will be necessary to develop ties of cooperation among more willing nations in more feasible areas to promote the common interests in this part of the world. Increased cooperation among the nations of Northeast Asia will be the prime move for shaping a brighter future for the Asia-Pacific region.

For some time now, it has been predicted that the Asia-Pacific region will emerge as the hub of world civilization in the new century. We now see that prediction coming true. With boundless potential, this region is now bursting with dynamic development. I think it is a mandate of our time to develop an Asia-Pacific community in keeping with the current trends toward regional integration in this increasingly multipolar world.

The well-being of both Japan and Korea in the twenty-first century will also be directly linked with the peace and prosperity of Asia and the Pacific. Our two nations must thus be partners in shaping a Pacific Era. To that end, we should develop an efficient and effective framework for cooperation to benefit all nations on the strength of openness and diversity in this region. Our bilateral relationship is now not simply the concern of our two nations but is also the basis and focal point for Asia-Pacific cooperation.

Esteemed Members of the Diet,

Over the forty-five years since both Korea and Japan began to rebuild themselves into new nations, our bilateral relations have also undergone great changes. Our ties have been growing especially rapidly over the quarter century since our relations were normalized. This is testimony that our bilateral relations are characterized by mutually beneficial interdependence.

This is particularly true in the economic field. Korea and Japan have now become each other's second largest trading partner, next only to the United States of America. Having grown into the tenth largest trading nation in the world, the Republic of Korea now represents a 17 billion dollar annual market for Japanese industry. Considering the fact that Japan's exports to Korea stood at a mere 200 million dollars only twenty-five years ago, it can be clearly seen that Korea's development contributes to Japan's prosperity, too. The presence of a prosperous country as its closest neighbor will be an advantage in the future for Japan, also.

Korea's development will also help to strengthen the economy of East Asia as a whole. I solicit your cooperation in ensuring the continuing expansion and strengthening of trade and economic cooperation between our two nations from such a broad perspective. Attention should be focused, among other things, on the chronic trade imbalance between Korea and Japan. We know your country is making multifaceted efforts to open your market to the United States and Europe and otherwise remedy your trade imbalances with them. I urge you to take similarly determined steps materially to redress trade imbalances with Korea.

Some people point out that Japan is reluctant to transfer its technology to Korea for fear of increased competition. Increases in Korea's exports may indeed pose some competition for Japanese businesses in overseas markets. However, it would be myopic to focus only on such minor possibilities. It must be noted that rises in exports from my country have always led to rises in our imports from Japan at a similar pace. It is my sincere hope that with the realization that Korea's development is in the best interests of Japan also, you will join us in urging and promoting active technological and scientific co-operation between our two countries.

The growth in our bilateral ties has not been limited to the economic field. Nowadays, two million people travel between our two countries each year, with private-level exchanges and co-operation in the political, economic, social, cultural and other fields expanding at an encouraging rate. In particular, exchanges between young Koreans and Japanese are expanding fast and efforts in both countries to study and understand each other are growing more and more enthusiastic. Now our bilateral relations should be taken beyond political and economic cooperation into comprehensive neighborliness and friendship, with all citizens becoming involved in exchanges and mutual help in every possible area.

Esteemed Members of the Diet,

Even though nearly all things have changed and great overall development and progress have occurred, there still remains a psychological barrier that hinders the evolution of genuine friendship between our two peoples. The perceptions and emotions of the Korean and Japanese peoples about past mistakes are yet to be sorted out even now, when, with the passage of forty-five years since the end of World War II, European countries that fought each other in that devastatingly savage conflict are banding together in a single community. In other words, the negative vestiges of the past era continue to hamper the development of our bilateral ties.

For example, I believe you find it difficult to understand the heartache of a Korean child who was whipped by his teacher for using his own name rather than the Japanese name imposed on him, and for using his own native language that he had learned at his mother's bosom. It is not necessary, however, to recount here all the sufferings and trials, the stupendous tragedies, that our people experienced during the past period of darkness. Koreans today merely reflect upon the fact that we were too weak to defend ourselves. We do not dwell on the past and blame, or harbor resentment against, anyone else for what befell us.

What I would like to tell you today is simply this: There must be true understanding between our two peoples on the basis of truth, so that a bright future can be ensured for our bilateral relationship. It should be noted that the French, German and British peoples are now forming one European family; they are able to join together in opening a new chapter of history, having put the past fully behind them on the strength of truth.

Even God cannot change what happened in the past. However, history is a question of how we interpret and understand things past. This means that depending on how we tackle it, we now have an opportunity to discard the shackles of the past and purge the negative residues of what took place in bygone days. All that is required is the courage and effort of all of us.

What I would like to mention to you particularly in this regard is the question of the 700,000 Koreans who for historical reasons have come to live in Japan. Together with the Japanese, they went through the horrors of war, and after the war they participated in the reconstruction and development of their host country. Only when they become able to live in this land as good neighbors of the Japanese and without artificial inconvenience, will both our peoples feel genuine friendship to each other.

Japan has now become a new country, much different from what it used to be. When Japan fully opens up to history and the world, it will be able to present a new image, especially to Asians.

Esteemed Members of the Diet,

If you stand on a beach in Pusan on a clear day, you can see a hazy blue image of Tsushima Islands on the horizon. I think you can see the lights of Pusan from the islands, too. From prehistoric times, our two peoples have travelled across these narrow straits to conduct exchanges as next-door neighbors. In particular, the ancient culture of the Korean Peninsula was transmitted to the Japanese Archipelago and a wave of modernization found its way to the Korean Peninsula from Japan.

Under the isolationist policy of the Tokugawa Shogunate the royal envoy from the Chosun Kingdom was the only foreign envoy allowed to enter Edo. The long route from Izuhara to Edo was punctuated by a series of amicable meetings between the Chosun royal mission and local Japanese officials and scholars. The unhappy phase between our two countries was a short one when compared with our long history of friendly and neighbourly association.

As a Japanese proverb goes, "Water that has flowed by cannot turn the water mill." How true that is. However, new water keeps flowing in to run the mill. An era of genuine neighborliness and friendship between our two nations will also start again in like manner.

The tea ceremony that the Japanese have long cultivated with loving care harmonizes the artistry of ancient Korean potters embodied in the tea cup and the spirit of immaculateness and philosophical values cherished by your people. In this, there is no sense of persecution or superiority on either side. All one appreciates is the beauty and vitality that can only be found in the harmony between nature and man. Such is also the hallmark of a genuine neighborly relationship. Since our two nations share common ideals, we should march hand in hand on the strength of such a relationship toward the world and the future. Let us join forces as neighbors, close both in spirit and geographical location, to shape a more peaceful and prosperous world of freedom and happiness.

Let us work together to forge the twenty-first century into an age in which young Japanese from Tokyo will be travelling to Seoul, via an undersea tunnel beneath the Korean Straits, to join their Korean friends on a journey to Beijing, Moscow, Paris and London on a tour of friendship to link continents and make all humanity one family.

41.

Remarks at the Luncheon Hosted by Japanese Business Leaders, Tokyo, May 25, 1990

Distinguished leaders of the Japanese business community,

Thank you very much for the warm welcome extended to me and my delegation. It is a great pleasure to attend this luncheon today.

Japan has become one of the world's foremost economic powers by reconstructing itself from the ruins of World War II and by making the most of the postwar free economic climate. It is a valuable opportunity for me to meet and speak with you, the principal architects of this Japanese economic miracle.

The spirit of capitalism that sprouted in Europe two centuries ago has found fertile land and blossomed here in Japan. During the latter half of the 19th century, Japan intensively blended Eastern values with Western know-how, thereby starting its rapid modernization. Today, it is still spearheading the work of combining the ideas of the East and the West.

The Japanese people exhibit an innovative entrepreneurship stemming from a rich heritage, which has been nourished by Confucianism and other elements of Oriental culture. I believe the immense success currently enjoyed by Japan is partly the result of these valuable traditions. In addition, there was a balance of well-conceived government policies, competent business management and, of course, the hard work of your industrious and creative people.

Your dynamic growth has inspired your Korean neighbor with courage and confidence. It has also given the people of the Orient something to be proud of on the global scene. In 1964, the Korean people had to watch the Tokyo Olympics with envy, for just over a decade before the Games we had undergone the agonies of war.

But, through hard work and sacrifice over the past quarter century the Republic of Korea has managed to propel itself into the ranks of the industrialized nations. In 1988, in spite of the tensions that exist on the Peninsula, we hosted the Seoul Olympics, a festival in which the East and the West came together in peace and friendship.

Korea has yet to catch up with Japan, but we are nonetheless proud of our rapid development, for which Korea is regarded as a model for many countries in the developing world and in the Socialist bloc.

In the process of development, Korea has learned and received much help from Japan. I would like to take this occasion to express my gratitude to Japan and the Japanese people for the cooperation, especially to the business leaders present here.

Distinguished business leaders,

I know that you have a keen interest in the process and outcome of democratization initiated three years ago in Korea. I am also acutely aware that international concern is growing about the future of our economy, which is now experiencing the growing pains of transition. Korea's current economic health is suffering from such internal difficulties as the vociferous economic and social demands made by various sectors of society, rapid wage increases, declines in business morale and in capital investment, and the appreciation of the won currency. In addition, there are exacerbating external factors such as the deterioration in the international trade environment in the wake of the rising protectionist tendencies abroad.

In order to overcome these difficulties, I believe we need to learn more about how Japan has so successfully overcome its own economic troubles, from postwar labor unrest to the recent sharp appreciation of the yen currency.

However, my administration, myself, and experts familiar with Korea are not pessimistic about the future of the Korean economy. Unreasonable public demands have subsided, while a new, stable democratic order is taking shape. Contrary to perceptions abroad, labor relations have greatly stabilized this year. Wage increase rates, which remained high during the last three years, are now being kept down to single digits.

The Korean economy is anticipated to grow about 7 percent this year, not at all meager by international standards. Korea has a pool of highly educated manpower, and a broad middle class. Together with a new awareness on the part of our workers, these will help us in resolving the economic troubles facing our nation. Three years ago, on June 29, I announced the Declaration of Democratic Reforms and initiated a genuine process of democratization. Although we have made great strides toward reaching our goal, the process has brought on its own obstacles.

But, I assure you, there will be no reversing of Korea's democracy. The government and people of the Republic of Korea are more than capable of overcoming the trials of a political transition. And, the Korean economy will likewise move ahead.

Distinguished business leaders,

Our two nations are neighbors bound together in a close relationship. Our interaction throughout history has significantly influenced the course of each other's cultural identity. Building upon our geographical and historical ties, our two nations are becoming partners in prosperity. Over two million citizens a year now visit each other's land. Korea and Japan are the second largest trading partners for each other, trailing only the United States.

In the economic field, bilateral relations are deepening mutual influences. Korea has now grown into the 10th largest trading nation in the world. As such, South Korea now represents a 17 billion dollar market to Japanese industry—an outlet which will certainly continue to grow in the future. Considering the fact that Japan's exports to the Republic of Korea stood at a mere US$200 million 25 years ago, this is a remarkable expansion. Even though increases in Korea's exports do pose some competition to Japan in overseas markets, they invariably entail an increase in our imports from Japan. Our economies are then symbiotic as our interdependence leads to a greater mutual benefit.

It is in the interest of Japan to have a neighbor who is prosperous, not impoverished. Korea's continued growth will foster not only the prosperity of Japan but also the health of the East Asian economy as a whole. As the international roles of both our economies gain more importance, there is an expanding need for active cooperation between us. Korea and Japan should form a constructive partnership if we are to contribute more effectively to the peace and prosperity of East Asia and, eventually, the world community.

The active involvement of Japanese businessmen, especially the senior business leaders present here, is essential to improving economic cooperation between Korea and Japan. I would especially like to appeal for your greater participation in the following specific fields:

First is in furthering bilateral industrial cooperation. Although concerns about the "boomerang effect" and the "hollowing-out" of domestic industries are now fading away in Japan, the less-than-positive attitude of some segments of the Japanese business community toward technological transfers to Korea needs to be rectified. I believed that Japanese businesses will speed up the transfer technology to Korea if they realize that Korea's economic development benefits Japan as an expanded market for Japanese exports, let alone other benefits.

Today, such leading-edge industries as computers, new materials and mechatronics are advancing at a spectacular pace in Japan. As a result, there have been reports that revealed the increasing shortages of technically skilled manpower, pointing out an urgent need to encourage international distribution of labor. It is in the long-term interest of both our economies for Japanese businesses to help Korean engineers acquire more advanced technologies so that mutually complementary industries can be developed in our two nations.

I suggest the creation of a committee for bilateral technological cooperation in which both the governments and private sectors of our countries would participate in order to expedite the development of such industrial links.

Second is in redressing our trade imbalance. Since the early days of its economic development, Korea has been importing from Japan large amounts of intermediate goods, finished products, technologies, and capital. Of course, we have been doing so out of our own necessity and this has played an important part in the growth of our economy. On the other hand, Korea has consistently registered huge deficits in its trade with Japan.

As a major economic power, Japan, I understand, is making a wide range of efforts to open its markets, especially to the United States and Europe, with the aim of rectifying its large trade surplus. I urge Japan to lower its tariff and non-tariff barriers against major Korean export products as well so that our bilateral trade can continue to grow in a more equitable fashion. Another way to help remedy the imbalance would be to allow Korean businesses to take part in large projects in Japan on a significant level. I am told that the Japanese government is making institutional changes to allow foreign companies to participate in such infrastructure projects as the Kansai International Airport and the Trans-Tokyo Bay Highway. In reality, however, various invisible barriers are still in place to effectively bar foreign participation. A sincere effort should be made to remove such hidden obstacles as well.

When this is done, Korean construction firms are expected to join hands with their Japanese counterparts and carry out such major Japanese projects in a cost-effective manner. Korean construction firms have gained invaluable experiences from their work in the Middle East and elsewhere. In addition, Korean construction workers are perhaps the best-trained and the hardest-working work-force in the world today.

Distinguished business leaders,

As a major economic power, I believe Japan should now fulfill its share of *noblesse oblige* toward the world community. Japan has indeed become the world's largest aid donor. We greatly appreciate Japan's active contributions to remedying imbalances in the global economy and hope that such a role will grow even larger in the future.

In particular, it is my wish that Japan step up its sharing of capital and technology with countries in East Asia and the Pacific Basin to promote regional development. I hope that Japan will also assist in effectively coordinating policies of the industrialized nations to stabilize the world economy and currencies, especially the yen. Korea is also ready and willing to fulfill its international obligations and contribute to the commonwealth of nations commensurate with its new status and capabilities.

Distinguished business leaders,

We must convince ourselves that as close neighbors, Korea and Japan must become genuine partners. If we are to advance our common prosperity, our two nations should join forces in dealing with the epic changes now sweeping across the world, highlighted by the successive collapse of Communist regimes and the progressive integration of Europe into a single entity.

We now see Europe moving to relax their internal borders, despite the hostilities that occurred across Europe during the Second World War. In a world of such changes, regional cooperation in Northeast Asia should be initiated as soon as possible.

We are witnessing the opening of an Asia-Pacific Age. And, to guarantee the prosperity of this region, it would be wise for Korea and Japan to usher in a new phase of relations based on a broad perspective. History cannot be altered. But the past must not be allowed to fetter our present and future progress. It is our responsibility to lift the dark shadow of the past and clean up the vestiges of a tragic period.

In particular, the issue of Koreans who now live in Japan as a consequence of historical circumstances is seen in the eyes of the Korean people as an indicator of Korean-Japanese relations. Only when an environment has been created in which Korean residents in Japan can live in harmony with the Japanese will our people feel a genuine friendship with trust toward the Japanese.

It has been a great pleasure and a memorable occasion to meet the people principally responsible for Japan's great accomplishments. And I once again ask you to play more active roles in improving the Korean-Japanese relations.

Thank you.

42.

Remarks at the State Dinner Hosted by the Prime Minister of Japan and Mrs. Toshiki Kaifu, Tokyo, May 25, 1990

Your Excellencies Prime Minister and Mrs. Kaifu, distinguished guests, ladies and gentlemen,

Thank you very much for this splendid dinner in our honor. I am very grateful for your inspiring words for brighter future relations between the Republic of Korea and Japan.

I have had the great pleasure of talking frankly and candidly with you and meeting many prominent Japanese leaders from both the public and private sectors. All these meetings have been very useful and constructive.

Earlier today, I had the opportunity of being the first Korean head of state to speak before the Japanese Diet. Once again, I would like to express my gratitude to you and your government for helping to make my visit so meaningful and to the people of Japan for the warm welcome.

Your Excellency, distinguished guests,

Rebuilding itself from the ruins of war, Japan has leaped into the very forefront of the rapidly developing world. The ideals of freedom and democracy that evolved in Europe over the centuries have been combined with your cultural heritage to bring about a splendid blossom here in Japan today. Japan's level of prosperity is indeed remarkable, in that it would be difficult for most countries to attain such a level of prosperity. I pay my respects to Japan's leaders and government as well as its industrious and creative people for their great achievement.

I have come to Japan in the belief that our two nations together must usher in a new era of genuine friendship and neighborly good-will as we enter the last decade of the 20th century. From time immemorial, Korea and Japan have had an unbroken chain of interaction, influencing each other's culture as well as progress. Throughout our long history, our two countries have, for the most part, maintained amicable relations. Although there was an unhappy period in modern times, it was relatively brief compared to our long history. To the extent that our past history hampers our efforts towards stronger relations, we should renew our faith and courage to overcome such a hurdle.

Your Excellency,
The world today demands new thinking and actions. Over the past year, the rigid Communist regimes in Eastern Europe have collapsed in rapid succession and a unified Germany is now becoming a reality. Having agreed to economic integration by 1992, the European Community is now moving further ahead toward a political union. As a result of reforms now sweeping Eastern Europe, there is the likelihood that the domain of a united Europe will extend all the way to the Soviet border. As such, the world today is witnessing the old ideological and political barriers dismantled by the insuppressible human desire for freedom and prosperity.

Your Excellency,
We as neighbors are riding together the new waves of reconciliation and cooperation that are currently sweeping the world. Our two nations must become as close in spirit as we are geographically.

I visited Europe last November, at a time when the Berlin Wall was crumbling and the Iron Curtain lifting. I was compelled to reflect deeply on the future of Northeast Asia. One of my conclusions was that in order to usher in a new Asia-Pacific era in the 21st century, our two nations must commit ourselves to a close partnership for the promotion of peace and prosperity in Northeast Asia, a region that had to undergo five major wars over the past century.

Our two countries have before us the momentous tasks of accelerating global progress and promoting the well-being of all humanity. Now that Japan has entered the new Heisei Era, I sincerely hope that this gathering will serve as the symbolic beginning of a new era in Korean-Japanese relations.

Your Excellency,
Transcending the past history, Europe is relaxing its internal borders to become a single community. Our two nations must likewise go beyond the unfortunate historical legacies if we are to achieve a higher level of partnership. Through talks with you, Your Excellency, and recalling your remarks a few minutes ago, I am reassured of our common resolve to open a new era in our relationship.

Since we normalized our relations twenty-five years ago, the relations between our two countries have been rapidly improving. It is very encouraging to note that not only has co-operation between our two governments grown closer, but exchanges and cooperation have been steadily increasing in many areas, including political, economic, social, cultural, artistic realms. Korea and Japan have become each other's second largest trading partner. Furthermore, two million people now travel between our two countries each year. It is particularly encouraging that exchanges between young citizens of our two countries are increasing rapidly with both sides growing more enthusiastic about studying and understanding each other's history and culture.

I wish to take this opportunity to ask everyone here tonight to extend your support for an early resolution of the issue of Korean residents in Japan. They have come to live in Japan as a result of an unfortunate turn of events in our recent history. Only when Korean residents in Japan are able to lead their lives in Japan as bona fide citizens and without undue inconveniences, can we nurture a true heart-to-heart friendship between our two nations.

Your Excellency, Distinguished guests,

May I read two stanzas from the 15th century Korean classical poem entitled *Yongbi och'on ka* (The Song of the Heaven-bound Dragon):

> The tree that strikes deep root
> Is firm amidst the winds.
> Its flowers are good,
> Its fruit abundant.
>
> The stream whose source is deep
> Gushes forth even in a drought.
> It forms a river
> And gains the sea.

Just like the lyrics, we must ensure that the close relationship between our two countries will produce magnificent flowers and abundant fruits as the deep fountain of friendship ceaselessly pours forth.

Ladies and gentlemen,

Please join me in a toast to the boundless development of Japan, to the neighborly and friendly relations between our two countries, and to the good health and well-being of Their Excellencies the Prime Minister and Mrs. Kaifu.

Thank you.

43.

Opening Remarks at the Luncheon for the Japanese News Media, Tokyo, May 26, 1990

Chairman Kenya Mizukami, ladies and gentlemen of the news media,

I am very pleased to meet with you again here in Tokyo. It has been two years and eight months since I last spoke here in front of the members of the international news media, and it is indeed a privilege to do so once again. I would like to thank the Japanese Press Club for this opportunity.

Thirty-two months ago, speaking from this very podium, I outlined my goals and aspirations as the president of Korea's ruling party and as a presidential candidate facing an imminent election. I made a promise at the time that I would return here as the president of the Republic of Korea. I consider myself fortunate in having fulfilled that promise today, and I thank you all for the encouragement and support you have extended to me.

Since I last saw you, Korea's democratic development has been on course, and is moving forward rapidly. Our constitution was revised, and a free and fair presidential election conducted. In addition, freedom of the press is now fully guaranteed, and through the vitality of openness and individual initiatives our society has been restructured.

Admittedly, however, governing a nation that is undergoing democratic transformation is not without its difficulties. And, the tribulations of democratization still linger on. So, I can well appreciate your keen interest in the present and future of the Republic of Korea. Although the price of democratization has been high, the process has nonetheless been moving in the right direction. I assure you that there will be no retrogression.

As enormous social, economic and political changes sweep across the world today, and as the 21st century draws near, I have come to Japan in the belief that our two countries must open a new era of genuinely close, amicable bilateral relationships. In the past few days, I have met with Emperor Akihito who opened the new Heisei Era in Japan and have had two highly encouraging meetings with Prime Minister Kaifu. I have also met with many leaders from the political and business communities. At these meetings, we exchanged views on a wide range of issues, including our bilateral relationship, recent developments in Northeast Asia, and the rapid changes sweeping the world. All of these meetings have been amicable and constructive.

Yesterday, I became the first Korean head of state to address the Japanese Diet. In retrospect, my presence there was symbolic of a new beginning between our two nations, in every respect.

I was deeply moved as I spoke before the distinguished members of the Diet—the representatives of the 130 million Japanese people. My feelings and emotions ran so deep at that moment as, perhaps, never experienced by any other foreign leader standing behind the same podium.

On clear days, if one stands on the beaches of Pusan, the islands of Tsushima are visible over the horizon. The peoples of Korea and Japan have traversed that narrow strait since prehistoric times, exercising a strong influence on each other's cultural development. Perhaps it is God's will that Korea and Japan have been such close neighbors, and will continue to be so in the future.

Although there have been unfortunate periods in our relations, such periods were relatively brief compared to the many centuries of friendly and neighborly interaction between our two countries. We should be humble and sincere before the truths of history. We must, however, not allow the past to impede our progress forward. The residual feelings of antipathy must be wiped away.

Japan and Korea, as they face the advent of a new century, must become the closest of partners in the Asian-Pacific community. I believe the media and other influential opinion leaders of both countries have an invaluable role to play in forging such a partnership.

In the course of my three-day visit, I have observed firsthand the new Japan. I have also experienced the great warmth of friendship on the part of the Japanese people, and have reconfirmed our common enthusiasm in shaping a new era. I shall cherish this precious experience.

Thank you.

44.

Remarks at the Banquet in Honor of the Prime Minister of Japan and Mrs. Toshiki Kaifu, Seoul, January 9, 1991

Your Excellency Prime Minister Toshiki Kaifu, Mrs. Kaifu, and distinguished guests,

It gives me great pleasure to extend a warm welcome to Your Excellency Prime Minister and Mrs. Kaifu and your delegation on the occasion of Your Excellency's official visit to Korea. I am particularly pleased to see you all here at Chong Wa Dae.

I would like to take this opportunity to extend once again my deep appreciation for the warm friendship and hospitality His Majesty the Emperor and Your Excellency as well as the people of Japan have accorded me during my visit to your great country last May.

It has only been eight months since we met last, and yet my pleasure of welcoming Your Excellency again in Seoul is one of meeting an old friend.

A new era of Heisei has arrived in Japan during your tenure as prime minister. The new Japan is rapidly becoming a nation that plays an increasingly important role for the promotion of cooperation in the Asia-Pacific region and a nation that actively seeks to contribute to peace and prosperity of the world. And, as closest neighbors on earth, we are opening a new chapter of neighborly friendship in our long history of interchange. I pay my respects for the superb leadership Your Excellency has demonstrated in pursuing these goals over the last two years.

Your Excellency,

Through my visit to your great country, I have firmly convinced myself of a bright future for the Korea-Japan relations. Your visit to Korea today is certain to add a momentum for our two countries to further strengthen our forward-looking partnership relations.

I believe your favorite motto, "Politics begins with sincerity," also has a powerful bearing on the inter-state relations. Our two countries share a great vision that we as true neighbors shall work together for the attainment of common prosperity on the basis of sincerity and humble introspection regarding the dark histories in our past. Today, as we remove the vestiges of our unfortunate past and the barriers that history has set in our mind, Korea and Japan are moving forward together toward the twenty-first century, a century of common prosperity for all mankind.

The great citizens of our two countries will become more intimate friends as we increase contacts and interchanges based on mutual understanding, respect and open-mindedness. We should actively encourage citizens in all walks of life to participate in cultural, academic, and information exchanges, and facilitate the exchanges between our younger generations, who are the masters of our future.

As a result of brilliant economic achievements of Korea and Japan, East Asia has now emerged as a powerful region of the world, where energy, vitality and development potentials overflow. Promotion of economic and science and technology cooperation between our two countries will not only contribute to our own development but will accelerate the arrival of a more prosperous Asia-Pacific region as well.

Korea-Japan relations will hardly remain within the confines of our two countries.

Your Excellency,

A new century is almost upon us, and the world is undergoing a truly revolutionary change. The Cold War structure that used to breed confrontations around the world has collapsed. The tidal waves of reform have transformed the systems and appearances of the Soviet Union and East European countries. The entire continent of Europe has successfully formed a new structure of security and cooperation under one roof, transcending integration into a community of nations. As revolutionary changes that transformed world order continue, the promotion of friendly cooperation between our two countries becomes all the more important.

We have to join our efforts to promote stability and cooperation in the Asia-Pacific region, while deterring aggressions that endanger world peace and meeting challenges to the free trade system that has brought progress to the world at large.

The reduction of tension and confrontation in the Korean Peninsula has always been at the heart of our task for peace in this region.

That the Republic of Korea is improving relations with the Soviet Union and East European countries through Northern Diplomacy is part of our efforts to bring forth the day of peace and unification in Korea. Now that Germany has been unified, our country is the only place in the world that still remains divided. Although the waves of reconciliation wash the shores of most countries of the world, the Demilitarized Zone in the heart of the Korean Peninsula still remains frozen in the mode of Cold War. It is sincerely hoped that Your Excellency and the people of Japan will join us in hoping that the tides of openness and reform will expedite the arrival of spring in this divided and frozen land.

Your Excellency,
From time immemorial, our two nations have been engaged in mutual exchanges and have shared ideas and culture. And, together we have cultivated an East Asian culture that is the envy of the world.

A new era of neighborly friendship is open between our two countries, and we will join our hands to build a giant bridge of exchange and cooperation across the narrow straits between us.

Together our two countries will raise high a bright torch of hope for the twenty-first century and for a new era of the Pacific.

Ladies and gentlemen,
May I please propose a toast to the health and well-being of Their Excellencies Prime Minister and Mrs. Kaifu, to eternal prosperity of Japan, and to everlasting friendship between our two nations.

Thank you.

45.

Remarks at the State Dinner in Honor of the Prime Minister of Japan and Mrs. Kiichi Miyazawa, Seoul, January 16, 1992

Prime Minister Kiichi Miyazawa, distinguished guests, ladies and gentlemen,

I am very pleased to extend a warm welcome to you, Mr. Prime Minister, and to the members of your delegation. The very fact that Your Excellency has chosen our country as the first to visit following your inauguration as Prime Minister of Japan demonstrates the warm friendship between our two countries.

Your Excellency has long been active as a pre-eminent statesman and renowned leader of the international community. In fact, Japan is about to enter into an even more prosperous era under your excellent leadership. I am sure that the people of the world in general pin much hope on the role Japan will play toward the establishment of a new world order.

I am also convinced that Your Excellency's visit to Korea will further strengthen friendly relations between Korea and Japan and thus consolidate our partnership as we head toward the 21st century.

Your Excellency,

Last year we witnessed a great change in the history of the world: the disintegration of the Soviet Union and the demise of Communism. Democracy and market economics—the common goal of our two countries—have become the common goal of all mankind.

Korea and Japan will closely cooperate to achieve the prosperity and development of the Asia-Pacific region through the promotion of a close future-oriented partnership. Our two countries have already become the first in terms of personnel exchanges and the second in terms of trade with each other in the world. However, the serious imbalance of trade between us remains a grave issue that must be settled for the development of more mature relations. Balanced trade between Korea and Japan is a must not only for the promotion of our sustained prosperity but for the bright future of the Asia-Pacific region as well. Sincere cooperation in industry, science and technology could be a shortcut to balanced trade between our two countries. It also is strictly in line with the current international trend toward interdependence and openness.

We should also further promote exchanges of young people as well as exchanges in culture, scholars and information to further cement ties for the future. We must make sincere efforts to remove all barriers through humble reflection and correct recognition of historical facts. The dark shadows of the past era cannot and should not hinder development of a mature partnership between our two nations in the 21st century. Our peoples who have enjoyed close historical exchanges since antiquity, thanks to close geographic proximity, must now closely cooperate as genuine partners in building a freer and more prosperous East Asia.

Your Excellency,

A stable and peaceful Korean Peninsula is prerequisite to the maintenance of peace and prosperity in the Asia-Pacific region in the 21st century. I have steadfastly pursued a Northern Policy in order to pave the way for peaceful unification of the Korean Peninsula by taking advantage of the new world trend toward reconciliation and cooperation. The Korean Peninsula is in the process of establishing a new order of cooperation and coexistence, ending the half-century-old Cold War era marked by confrontation and hostility.

I would like now to express thanks to the Government of Japan which has been cooperating to achieve a relaxation of tension and progress in the negotiations between the South and the North. There is a saying that "Friendship is like a plant that needs water now and then." I will endeavor to further consolidate our mutual friendship by frankly exchanging views with Prime Minister Miyazawa wherever and whenever possible.

Ladies and gentlemen,

Please rise and join me in a toast to the health and well-being of Prime Minister Miyazawa, to the eternal prosperity of Japan and to lasting friendship between the Republic of Korea and Japan.

Thank you.

46.

Opening Remarks at the Joint News Conference Following Summit Talks with Japanese Prime Minister Kiichi Miyazawa, Seoul, January 17, 1992

I am very pleased to meet you, especially the journalists travelling with Prime Minister Miyazawa.

I have had two rounds of very useful talks, yesterday and today with Prime Minister Miyazawa. We have exchanged wide-ranging views about the global situation in general and affairs in Northeast Asia in particular. We have also discussed concrete measures to further advance friendly relations between Korea and Japan in the future. We have agreed to closely cooperate with each other as genuine good neighbors in the interest of co-prosperity and world peace.

At the outset, I expressed my thanks to Prime Minister Miyazawa for having visited Korea shortly after his appointment as Prime Minister prior to visiting any other country. I also explained our efforts to ease tension and bring about lasting peace on the Korean Peninsula as well as the recent progress in relations between South and North Korea. Prime Minister Miyazawa expressed his full-fledged support for the recent agreements between the South and the North and promised his utmost support to help fully implement the agreements.

Prime Minister Miyazawa and I have agreed to closely cooperate to have North Korea adopt all the necessary measures under the Nuclear Non-Proliferation Treaty and to ensure their implementation as soon as possible. In normalization negotiations with North Korea, Prime Minister Miyazawa also promised to take into consideration whether or not North Korea had fulfilled its obligations to submit its nuclear facilities to international inspection and was observing its agreements with South Korea, and to closely consult with the government of South Korea.

At today's summit conference, we agreed to further promote cooperation to achieve co-prosperity based on a correct understanding of what happened between the two nations in the past and on humble reflection, I have urged the Japanese government to actively probe into the tragic events of the past, including the issue of the Korean "comfort women" and to take appropriate measures if the results so warrant.

Prime Minister Miyazawa explicitly expressed a sincere apology for what Japan did to Koreans in the past and assured me that the true facts will be brought to light and appropriate measures taken.

Noting that the issues of the growing trade deficit with Japan and the transfer of technology have long been pending, I have strongly urged the Japanese government to implement concrete and practical measures to address these questions, rather than procrastinating on their promises. Prime Minister Miyazawa has pledged to positively cooperate insofar as possible to solve these issues.

Prime Minister Miyazawa and I shared the view that the imbalance of trade and lack of industrial, scientific and technological cooperation between the two nations is the most pressing task, that it is necessary to determine the fundamental cause of the problem through frank consultation between the two countries, and that we must find a concrete solution to it. Prime Minister Miyazawa and I have thus agreed that the ROK-Japan Committee for Cooperation in Trade, Industry and Technology should study the problem of the trade imbalance and technological cooperation in detail, prepare concrete plans and submit a report to both governments by June this year.

As for increased access to the Japanese market through lowered tariffs and other measures, Japan has agreed to consider Korea's requests in the course of the Uruguay Round of trade negotiations. It was also agreed that the participation of Korea in Japan's public construction projects will be negotiated between the two governments.

I also have asked the Japanese government to give special consideration to the Korean residents there so that they will be able to contribute, as members of society, to the development of Japan in every and all sectors without discrimination.

In order to enhance mutual understanding between our two peoples we have agreed to actively promote exchanges, including exchanges of young people.

We also shared the opinion that it has become especially necessary for the two countries to further cooperate in the international arena, and have agreed to closely cooperate with each other in the Asia-Pacific Economic Cooperation Forum and the Uruguay Round of trade negotiations. We have committed ourselves to consult with each other whenever necessary for continued development of friendly relations between the two nations.

Ladies and gentlemen, let me ask you now to give Prime Minister Miyazawa an opportunity to speak.

Part VI

KOREA AS LEADER IN THE ASIA-PACIFIC REGION

47.

Address to the 23rd International General Meeting of the Pacific Basin Economic Council (PBEC) (via satellite transmission), May 20, 1990

Mr. Chairman, distinguished delegates, ladies and gentlemen,

It is a great honor and pleasure for me to participate via satellite in the opening session of the 23rd International General Meeting of the Pacific Basin Economic Council (PBEC). I salute the PBEC for its invaluable private sector contributions toward the promotion of cooperation and exchange between the nations of the Asia-Pacific region since its establishment in 1967. Encouraged by the pioneering role of the PBEC over the past 20 years, the region's states have increased their efforts to strengthen Asia-Pacific regional cooperation.

Mr. Chairman,

The winds of momentous change are sweeping across the world. Communism is fast receding in Eastern Europe, as well as in the Soviet Union. The ardent human aspirations for freedom and prosperity have brought down the Berlin Wall, and lifted the Iron Curtain that long separated East from West. Freedom and democracy now prevail as universal values. Furthermore, there has been a near-universal acceptance of the market economy and free enterprise system as the most efficient and effective means of ensuring individual prosperity and happiness.

A new world order of reconciliation and cooperation is emerging.

As the Cold War recedes into history, however, the changing world is still fraught with uncertainties. For example, we do not fully know the ramifications of an integrated European Community (EC) market in 1992. The changes in Eastern Europe raise the possibility that the EC may expand as far as the Soviet border. In addition, demands for political union are also growing within the EC.

I hope that these fundamental changes will ultimately lead to a better future for the world as a whole. At the same time, however, we must guard against the appearance of regional blocs and protectionist tendencies that hamper the growth of the world economy.

This is one of the reasons why I believe your topic, "Pacific Cooperation in the Changing Global Environment of the 1990s," is most timely and appropriate for this General Meeting. We are all deeply concerned about the uncertainties and the impact of the current global changes upon the future of the Pacific region and how we should cope with them.

Mr. Chairman,

With abundant natural and human resources, the Asia-Pacific is brimming with dynamic energy for development. During the postwar period, this region has achieved a higher rate of economic growth than any other area in the world. The predictions of a "Pacific Age" are now becoming a reality.

By combining Western influences with Eastern culture, the Pacific promises to serve as an even greater source of global prosperity in the 21st century. Advances in communications, transportation and other modern technologies have converted the vast Pacific into an ocean of exchanges and cooperation.

But, multilateral cooperation in the Pacific region remains underdeveloped. The failure to institutionalize broad regional arrangements to meet the challenges of the changing world would significantly hamper our progress. But such a structure does not yet exist in this region.

We need to develop a mutually complementary system of cooperation unique to our own region, which will function as an efficient mechanism to harmonize historical, cultural, and economic differences of Pacific nations.

Since regional cooperation will have to be based on principles of the free market and free trade, it is private enterprise that should be the driving force behind growth. Business leaders, such as yourselves, will play pivotal roles in this endeavor. I am confident that the PBEC will meet our expectations for private initiatives. The Asia-Pacific Economic Cooperation (APEC) conference, which met for the first time in Canberra last November, will no doubt serve as a conduit for government-to-government cooperation in our common efforts to encourage and support private sector activities.

Mr. Chairman,

I would like to take this opportunity to discuss principles that I think are essential to a productive Pacific cooperation.

First, the principle of openness. Asia-Pacific regional cooperation should not be inward-looking or exclusionist in perspective; rather, it should be open for all to effectively serve the cause of free trade and free enterprise throughout the world. Such an approach will not only enhance regional economic development, but also forestall other regional attempts to raise protectionist barriers or form trade blocs.

Second, we must uphold the principle of mutual respect in order to foster cooperative interdependence within this region of diversity.

Third, Pacific cooperation should seek to maximize the merits of market economics. We should encourage creative, private initiatives and free economic activities within the goal of promoting mutually beneficial and balanced regional development.

Finally, a more active system of cooperation should be built on the basis of mutual understanding and friendship among the peoples of this region. Intra-regional travel is now growing rapidly due to advances in air transportation, greater economic interaction, and liberalization of foreign travel. Exchanges in the fields of culture, information, and science and technology should also be expanded.

Unfortunately, however, the grievous historical legacies of East Asia have yet to be resolved. The legacies of the turbulent past continue to add fuel to the discord and antipathy between the nations of this region. We must draw lessons from the European example, where nations that had fought against each other in two World Wars are today moving towards economic and political integration. We should take a more progressive and broad-minded approach by leaving the past to history and laying down a more solid foundation for future cooperation. The nations of this region should cooperate together to promote peace and prosperity.

Mr. Chairman, honorable delegates,

I pay my respects to all of you for the tireless efforts to promote Pacific development through more effective regional cooperation. I sincerely hope that this General Meeting will be both productive and successful.

Thank you.

48.

Remarks at the Banquet in Honor of Dato Seri Dr. Mahathir bin Mohamad, Prime Minister of Malaysia, and Datin Seri Dr. Siti Hasmah, Seoul, September 12, 1990

The Right Honorable Prime Minister Mahathir bin Mohamad, Mrs. Mahathir, distinguished guests.

I heartily welcome you, Prime Minister and Mrs. Mahathir, and the Malaysian delegation to the Republic of Korea. I am happy to note that this year marks the 30th anniversary of our official bilateral relations. This makes your visit here all the more significant.

Both my wife and I still vividly remember the hospitality you extended to us during our visit to Malaysia the year before last. We are thus very delighted to share this evening with you here at Chong Wa Dae.

During my visit to your country, I was impressed by the energetic efforts of your people, in conjunction with the dedicated service of the political leaders, to build a free and prosperous nation by realizing the enormous potential of Malaysia. I would particularly like to pay tribute to you, Prime Minister, for further enhancing a fine tradition of parliamentary democracy which has harmonized Malaysia's social and cultural diversity through dialogue and compromise and for injecting fresh air into Malaysian society as a whole through "leadership by example." I understand that under your leadership, Malaysia is successfully diversifying its economy, thereby achieving spectacular growth over the past several years and adding further impetus to regional development as well.

I would like to note also that you, Prime Minister, successfully hosted both the British Commonwealth summit last autumn and the G-15 summit in June this year, thus greatly raising the international stature of Malaysia. Not only the people of Malaysia but all your Asian neighbors should be proud of your outstanding leadership.

The Right Honorable Prime Minister,

I am very pleased that our two nations have steadily developed close ties of friendship and cooperation since we established diplomatic relations in 1960. I am particularly happy to note that our practical bilateral cooperation has taken unprecedentedly big strides forward in all sectors following my visit to your country. Investments in Malaysia by Korean businesses have been rapidly on the increase in recent years, and major Korean corporations are launching their investments in the field of Malaysia's heavy chemical industries. Our bilateral trade rose from US$1.7 billion in 1988 to over US$2 billion last year. As our two economies are complementary in character, I expect that bilateral trade and economic cooperation will continue to expand in the years ahead.

The number of Koreans and Malaysians visiting each other's land has also tremendously risen over the past year or two.

We are well aware, Prime Minister, of your vigorous pursuit of the "Look East" policy and its magnificent accomplishments. I am confident that Malaysia and Korea will develop a model partnership for building a prosperous East Asia by sharing resources, products, technologies and experiences and by further deepening and broadening understanding, friendship and cooperation between our two peoples.

Prime Minister,

The world is now in the midst of the greatest upheaval since World War II at a time when the 21st century is fast approaching. The Cold War that has divided the world for nearly half a century has all but faded away into history, giving rise to a new international order of rapprochement and cooperation. As it enters the last decade before the 21st century, the world is faced with new challenges as well as new opportunities.

In spite of the predominant wave of détente, war clouds are gathering over the Persian Gulf. On the economic front, tendencies toward protectionism and regional blocs are mounting, while the gap is widening between the developed and developing nations. I agree, Prime Minister, with your insightful observation that East-West détente will not by itself resolve North-South problems.

East Asia, which includes both our countries, is a dynamic region that is sustaining the most illustrious growth in the world today. Both being developing countries sharing common ideals and having reached similar stages of development, Malaysia and Korea face many common challenges in this rapidly changing world. Through ever closer cooperation with each other, our two nations should make increasing contributions not only to the development of the Asia-Pacific region but also to the peace and prosperity of the world in general.

The Right Honorable Prime Minister,

I believe that as the chair country of ASEAN, Malaysia has a crucial role to play in regional development. This is of particular importance because the need for closer cooperation between the Republic of Korea and ASEAN is now greater than ever. Korea is keenly interested in developing a framework for regional cooperation through the ministerial conference on Asia-Pacific Economic Cooperation, or APEC. Both being active participants in APEC, our two nations should further strengthen bilateral ties, while also promoting mutual cooperation on the international scene, so that we will be good partners for progress in shaping a flourishing Pacific Age in the 21st century.

I sincerely hope, Prime Minister and Mrs. Mahathir, that during your first visit to Korea in seven years, you will be able to take a firsthand look at our development since then and to reaffirm our citizens' unchanging warm feelings of friendship toward the people of Malaysia.

Ladies and gentlemen,

Please join me in toasting to the good health and well-being of the Right Honorable Prime Minister and Mrs. Mahathir and also to the lasting friendship between our two peoples.

49.

Opening Address at the 47th Session of the Economic and Social Commission for Asia and the Pacific (ESCAP), Seoul, April 1, 1991

Mr. Chairman, Mr. Director General for Development and International Cooperation, Mr. Executive Secretary, distinguished delegates, ladies and gentlemen,

It is a great honor and pleasure for us to host in Seoul this year the 47th Session of the United Nations Economic and Social Commission for Asia and the Pacific (ESCAP), and I join the entire nation in extending to you a warm and cordial welcome.

The ESCAP region has seen tremendous progress and development since the end of World War II. In those early years, there existed in the region only ten sovereign states, and most of the nations in the region had just begun their efforts at nation building.

With the vestiges of the era of colonialism and the global conflagration everywhere, our region was plagued with poverty, ignorance and backwardness.

Forty-four years have since passed, and today the Asia-Pacific region has become a most vibrant and dynamic region with a highest rate of growth in the world.

The number of countries in the region has increased during the period such that the membership of this Commission alone exceeds the number of original founding members of the United Nations.

The Asia-Pacific region accounts for over 40 percent of world's trade volume and more than 50 percent of the global output comes from this vast region.

The transformation that our region has undergone is truly remarkable in all areas, including political, economic, social and cultural.

Exchanges and cooperation between and among the nations of the region have also increased in a rapid and progressive manner . . . this in a region that lacked any cooperative experience between the geographically distant countries.

The nations of this region of diversity have long been alienated from one another, but they are now rapidly forming a strong and friendly partnership for cooperation.

Almost 60 percent of the total population of our global village has joined hands in this region to pursue an Asia-Pacific identity and reaffirm our lasting commitment to world peace and prosperity of mankind.

I join all the nations of the region in our appreciation for the favorable progress of history and in our hopes for a brighter future for the Asia-Pacific in the 21st century.

The Economic and Social Commission for Asia and the Pacific has played vital and invaluable roles in the process of regional development.

As the principal arm of the United Nations in the Asia-Pacific region, the commission has facilitated technology transfers and assisted in the acceleration of numerous economic development programs, and the Republic of Korea was one of the principal beneficiaries. The Commission has laid a firm foundation for such development-oriented functional organizations as the Asian Development Bank, the Asian and Pacific Development Center, and Asian and Pacific Center for Transfer of Technology. This very forum, the ESCAP ministerial conference, designed to promote common prosperity has long been recognized as the most important vehicle of intergovernmental dialogue.

It is my sincere desire that ESCAP will continue to play an important role to strengthen regional cooperation as well as to promote friendly and cooperative relations among members and associate members of the ESCAP region.

Distinguished delegates,

As a new century draws near, the world is going through a systemic change. The Cold War system that had separated the world as well as humanity and caused confrontation and war has now collapsed.

Today, the world is ushering in new tides of reconciliation and cooperation. And, the new waves are certain to bring new and encouraging changes to this vast region of ours.

If, however, we are to attain the world we want, we have yet to surmount numerous challenges. Even at this very hour, disputes stemming from race, religion, ideologies and prejudices rage on in many parts of the world. The Gulf War is a stark reminder that the world we live in is still fraught with uncertainties and instabilities. The gap between the have and have not countries and innumerable endemic issues continue to illustrate the seriousness of the North-South problem.

What has brought unprecedented progress and prosperity to our region in the postwar era was the free trade system.

Trends toward protectionism and regional blocs will only serve to constrict world economy and hamper economic development efforts not only of the developing countries but of the developed countries as well.

If we are to cope with these challenges successfully, our only alternative lies in promoting mutual cooperation and market liberalization.

Distinguished delegates,

The primary challenge before us today is to turn this vast region into a zone of open doors and mutual cooperation by marshalling the unbounded potentials of Asia and the Pacific, the region's enormous dynamism toward progress and our aspirations for peace and prosperity.

The ESCAP region embraces a great diversity of race, religion, history and culture in its vast expanses. It is a large pool of countries with divergent socio-economic systems, developmental stages and industrial structures. As a consequence, cooperation between the regional states may often be hampered by the diversities.

If, however, we remove harmful competitions and resolve conflicting interests with a view to maximizing harmony of interests and common benefits, diversity will, on the contrary, serve to spur the promotion of cooperation among the regional economies.

The Asia-Pacific countries have now set the pace not only in South-South cooperation but also in North-South cooperation, and together we can move forward to promote closer and mutually beneficial cooperative relations.

The industrial restructuring and adjustments that the Commission has been pursuing will undoubtedly facilitate and accelerate technology transfers and horizontal division of labor on the basis of complementary features of the regional economies, and substantially contribute to the progress and prosperity of all parties involved.

Because the Republic of Korea, rising from the ruins of a war, has become a newly industrializing country within one generation, we are perhaps in a unique position, and we are prepared to actively share with everyone our developmental experiences and know-how.

I am confident and full of hopes that the Asia-Pacific countries can and will successfully set an altogether new example of East-West cooperation.

The Republic of Korea has established formal diplomatic relations with the Soviet Union and countries in Central and Eastern Europe. We have also exchanged offices of trade representatives with China. And, we are currently in the process of expanding areas of economic cooperation with these countries.

As a leading developing country, Korea is prepared to actively contribute to the promotion of a harmonious regional cooperation by playing the role of a bridge between the advanced and developing countries and between the market and Socialist economics.

Following on the successful hosting of the 1988 Seoul Olympics, Korea will be hosting the Taejeon EXPO '93, a global fair to be held for the first time in a developing country. Korea's EXPO '93 will provide this nation with an opportunity to demonstrate to the world our commitment and vision toward the 21st century.

The Republic of Korea is acutely aware that the relaxation of tension in the Korean Peninsula and the improved relations between South and North Korea are the keys to the enhancement of cooperation and stability in the Asia-Pacific region.

We are seeking to realize a peaceful national unification by first improving exchanges and cooperation between South and North Korea and by pursuing a relationship in which both will help each other and contribute jointly toward the attainment of common prosperity.

The Republic of Korea continues to seek membership in the United Nations. It is better to carry out our share of international responsibilities and contributions for the Asia-Pacific and the world.

It must be in direct contravention of the principle of universality that the Republic of Korea, a sovereign state with a population of 43 million and world's 12th largest trading country with an annual trade volume of 130 billion US dollars, should remain outside the United Nations.

Entry into the United Nations of both South and North Korea until such time as the peninsula is unified will be conducive to the peace and stability not only of the Korean Peninsula but of the entire region as well.

Mr. Chairman, distinguished delegates, ladies and gentlemen,

The world is currently undergoing a phenomenal change as powerful waves of reconciliation remove the barriers that used to divide mankind and cause confrontations. Mindful of this momentous change, I sincerely hope and ask of you that this Session will set a lasting landmark in the cause of cooperation and open-mindedness in the Asia-Pacific region and for a more peaceful and prosperous 21st century.

I wish you all to enjoy your stay in Seoul, and hope your trip will prove to be a highly successful and rewarding experience.

Ladies and gentlemen,

Now, I declare open the 47th Session of the United Nations Economic and Social Commission for Asia and the Pacific.

Thank you.

50.

Congratulatory Message on the Occasion of the 40th Anniversary of the Colombo Plan, Seoul, May 1, 1991

It gives me a great pleasure to join the people of the Republic of Korea in extending our hearty congratulations to the Colombo Plan International Society on the occasion of the 40th anniversary of the Colombo Plan.

During the last 40 years, the Colombo Plan has made enormous contributions for the promotion of economic and social development of the countries in the Asia-Pacific region. The Republic of Korea, in fact, is one of the major beneficiaries of the support and assistance rendered by the Colombo Plan.

The membership of the Colombo Plan consists of countries with diverse histories, cultures and political and economic systems, but we are in full agreement in our common objective of pursuing a better standard of living for our peoples.

The Colombo Plan has also made a significant contribution to the improvement of the economic and social life of the region by providing a continuing forum for the exchange of information and developmental experiences between and among the member countries. And, those of us in the Asia-Pacific region have come to know each other better through the many ingenuous and highly useful projects of the Colombo Plan.

In recent years, economic cooperation and the exchange of technical know-how, including the exchanges of experts and trainees and the provision of needed material and equipment, are rapidly on the increase among the developing countries in the region. Active promotion of cooperation between and among the developing countries are certain to produce as much benefit to us as cooperation with the advanced industrial countries.

The Republic of Korea is fully prepared to share with the Colombo Plan countries the socio-economic developmental experiences we have accumulated in the process of attaining the current stage of our economic development.

For this purpose, we will more actively seek to promote economic and technical cooperation with the member countries of the Colombo Plan.

It is my sincere wish that the 40th anniversary will mark a turning point for the Colombo Plan toward a yet again dynamic era of regional cooperation and that it will play a central role in ushering in a new era of common prosperity in Asia-Pacific in the twenty-first century.

I would also like to express my sincere appreciation for the devoted efforts of those who have endeavored over the years for the success of the Colombo Plan.

51.

Message to the 24th General Meeting of the Pacific Basin Economic Council (PBEC), May 4, 1991

It gives me great pleasure to extend my hearty congratulations to the Pacific Basin Economic Council as it holds its 24th International General Meeting. I wish to commend the PBEC for its invaluable contributions to the development and prosperity of the Pacific Basin since its founding in 1967.

The vast region surrounding the Pacific Ocean has now emerged as a new growth center of the global economy. This region now accounts for 50 percent of the world's gross national product and 40 percent of world trade. The Pacific is thus turning into a vast sea of international exchanges and cooperation.

The amazing post-war development of nations along the Pacific Basin shows how great has been the contribution of market economies based on freedom and openness to the well-being of man. This example is fueling momentous changes on many continents seeking a more peaceful and prosperous world. The new waves of détente and coooperation that have breached the Cold War barriers in Europe are now rushing toward Asia and the Pacific. I am confident that these historic changes will advance the peace and prosperity of the Pacific Basin by broadening and deepening regional cooperation.

Many experts are predicting that the coming 21st century will be the "Pacific Century." I think this is because with their diverse national, cultural and social characteristics and different stages of economic development, the countries in the Pacific Basin can complement and stimulate each other to the benefit of all, since creativity thrives best when diversity is brought into a harmonious whole.

In this context, I believe it to be of utmost significance that at its annual meeting the PBEC will concentrate on the theme of "The New Pacific Model: Development through Open Economies." I expect that the PBEC will continue to serve as a major catalyst in shaping a bright future for Asia and the Pacific by taking an even more active role in promoting regional trade and economic cooperation and in fostering understanding and friendship among nations on the Pacific Rim. The Republic of Korea also shares the vision of a Pacific Age in the new century and is resolved to take a leading role in advancing regional cooperation.

I wish the PBEC continuing progress and success and look forward to a fruitful outcome of its 24th general meeting.

52.

Room for Joint Ventures with Canada, *The Globe and Mail* (Canada), June 29, 1991

In a recent interview in Seoul's Blue House, South Korean President Roh Tae Woo touched on prospects for reunification with North Korea, recent student demonstrations and the potential for expanded economic ties between Canada and South Korea.

Question: *What sort of time frame do you expect for reunification now that North Korea has decided to apply for a seat in the United Nations and allow inspection of its nuclear facilities?*
Answer: To give you a clearcut answer would be impossible. In 1989, I had occasion to visit Germany and witnessed the collapse of the Berlin Wall. Nobody at the time predicted that German unification would come in one year, including Premier [Helmut] Kohl. But Germany was unified in just one year from that time. The Korean problem will be similar. Although we are not able to predict with any accuracy, in view of the historical precedent, we cannot exclude the possibility of German-style reunification on the Korean Peninsula. We must prepare ourselves for all contingencies.

Question: *How do you explain continuing domestic turmoil in South Korea, particularly the deaths of students last month, some at the hands of the police?*
Answer: The nature of student demonstrations during the days of authoritarian rule and that of student protests these days is fundamentally different. Before the June 29, 1987, declaration of democratic reforms, pro-democracy demonstrations by students received broad public support. However, the recent violent demonstrations staged by radical groups have been given the cold shoulder and severely criticized by a vast majority of the people now that democratization has made much headway.

During the 1980s, a campus rally could easily attract 4,000 to 5,000 activist participants. Recently, however, only 200 to 300 student activists turned out for a campus rally. A large majority of university students do not sympathize with radical causes.

As has happened in many European countries, the United States and Japan, I believe that radicalism in Korea is intensifying its efforts in a desperate reaction to the decline of their ranks and influence. I believe that the radical forces in Korea will continue to wane and lose their ability to galvanize others.

Question: *What are the chief areas for improvement in relations with Canada?*

Answer: I believe there is an enormous developmental potential in Korean-Canadian relations. There is boundless room for mutual complementary and beneficial relations by combining the strengths of Canada—its vast land, rich resources and advanced science and technology—and those of the Republic of Korea, including its abundant human resources.

Korean investment in Canada is expected to increase further in the future. It would be profitable for our two countries to combine our respective strong points to undertake joint ventures in third countries. In this connection, it is our hope that the expected formation of a North American free-trade area will not lead to an exclusionist economic bloc but be open and accessible to all others so that it will contribute materially to Pacific Basin cooperation.

Question: *A number of Pacific Basin countries, including Canada, have made proposals to establish an organization to oversee collective economic and security matters in Asia. What is your view of such proposals?*

Answer: Brisk moves are underway in the Asia-Pacific region these days to promote regional economic co-operation along the lines of the European Conference on Security and Economic Cooperation. I think such moves are driven by the new atmosphere of international rapport and cooperation generated by the end of the Cold War.

It should be noted, however, that major local conflicts still rage in this region and the interests of many Asia-Pacific countries still diverge sharply. The over-all situation in this region is thus still very complex and in flux. Accordingly, conditions for multilateral Asia-Pacific security cooperation are not yet ripe.

—EDITH TERRY

53.

Korea's Emerging Role in a New Pacific Order; Speech Given at the Hoover Institution, Palo Alto, California, June 29, 1991

Doctor Raisian, Secretary Shultz, Governor Wilson, distinguished guests, professors and students, ladies and gentlemen,

It gives me great pleasure to visit the campus of this world-famous Stanford University, the home of many eminent scholars and alma mater of so many prominent leaders. I am particularly privileged to meet with this very distinguished group of scholars, leaders, and friends here at the world-renowned Hoover Institution.

I thank you for your generous hospitality and for the kind invitation to discuss with you some of the vital issues of the day and of our common future.

As I was reflecting on these topics, I was struck by the wisdom, foresight, and vision displayed by this Institution's founder, the late President Herbert Hoover. For it was clear to me that, when he established this great Institution 72 years ago, Mr. Hoover not only foresaw the course of history in this century with remarkable clarity, but he also had a vision of the world to come in the 21st century.

For the themes of "war, revolution and peace" aptly describe the course of history in the 20th century and give insight to that of the 21st.

In the past 100 years, mankind has suffered untold sorrows of war, unspeakable tragedies and tribulations, seemingly endless strife, and revolution. Only now can we look to a new century with realistic hopes for a genuine peace.

As the 21st century approaches, the world finds itself experiencing another revolution. This revolution, however, is not one of rivalry and conflict, but of peace and promise for all mankind.

Even more impressive is that it has taken only two or three years for the world to overcome the preoccupations of the old international order which reigned supreme for the past two generations.

The Soviet Union has chosen to pursue a course of fundamental change.

Seven decades of Communist dictatorship, beginning with the Bolshevik Revolution, have now been replaced by an entirely new form of revolution, perestroika.

Today, human dignity and democratic pluralism are becoming universal values of all mankind.

The attainment of happiness and prosperity is now unimaginable and infeasible without recourse to the market economy system, which draws upon the strengths of openness and freedom.

Aspirations for human liberty and happiness have formed tidal waves of change that are re-writing world history across national boundaries.

No one can reverse or resist these momentous changes.

We were all first-hand witnesses to the moments when those waves of freedom shattered the Berlin Wall and tore down the Iron Curtain that divided the world throughout the postwar period.

Relations between the superpowers continue to evolve from confrontation to cooperation. Their efforts to build a better future continue apace.

U.S.-Soviet arms control negotiations are making progress in reducing the weapons of mass destruction and their delivery systems. The very speed with which these agreements are reached permits us to look forward to a durable structure of peace.

By rallying a coalition of nations, including the Soviet Union, around the U.N. flag, and by successfully repulsing the forces of aggression during the Gulf War, the United States has once again demonstrated its leadership to the world.

One clear message from the Gulf victory is that the nations of the world will no longer tolerate aggression and the use of force, and that henceforth the rule of law shall prevail in the international community.

The great Gulf victory was the result of courageous decisions and timely actions as well as of accumulated efforts and sacrifices of all those nations that cherished peace and maintained faith in the rightfulness of international justice and order. The United States led at the forefront of this venture, shouldering enormous costs and making many sacrifices.

Today, the people of the United States have come to a propitious moment in history when they can see the lofty ideals of their Founding Fathers realized world-wide.

I pay my respects and offer my congratulations to you and the American people for this great achievement.

Today, the era of wars and revolutions is coming to a close.

The world is clearly moving towards a more peaceful community of nations.

The future of our world now depends largely on how we envision and design the new international order, which will ensure freedom and happiness in a world of enduring peace.

Now, Europe is becoming one, whole and free. The Europeans are moving toward a new Europe.

The European Community (EC) is scheduled for full economic integration next year.

With the ongoing reforms in Eastern and Central Europe, the EC is expected to expand eastward as far as the Soviet border, and we may safely assume the emergence of an integrated Europe in the near future.

In addition, the fact that this fine Institution, dedicated to peace and prosperity, was established on the Pacific coast reflects far-sighted vision.

Over the years, many eminent scholars have predicted that the 21st century will be the century of the Pacific.

Indeed, one need not refer to their predictions to say that our future depends heavily on developments in the Pacific region.

In the 16th century, the Portugese navigator Ferdinand Magellan named this great body of water the Pacific Ocean. And, until the dawn of the 20th century, that ocean did indeed remain "pacific."

The United States was the first Western nation to which the "hermit kingdom" of Korea formally opened its doors in 1882. In September of the following year, the Kingdom's first diplomatic mission arrived in San Francisco Bay.

The City of San Francisco and the Chamber of Commerce extended a cordial welcome to this group of diplomats from the Orient, wearing what must have been quite unfamiliar to the Americans: traditional Korean court costumes complete with ceremonial hats and boots. We can assume that the reception was both colorful and peaceful just as the world at large was tranquil and pacific.

The impact of their trip to the United States must have been very shocking to these emissaries; in fact, so shocking and profound that many subsequently devoted their lives as radical reformers or revolutionaries in the cause of modernization of their fatherland.

Upon receiving their credentials in New York, President Chester A. Arthur observed that with the introduction of the steamship, the great ocean between the two countries became a safe public waterway. He then affirmed the friendship between Korea and America.

Today, it took me less than 11 hours to fly over the Pacific, whereas it took our first diplomatic mission 48 days to cross.

With modern transportation, communications, and the arrival of the age of information, the Pacific is now indeed becoming an ocean of exchange and cooperation.

The twelve countries participating in the Asia-Pacific Economic Cooperation (APEC) now produce over 50 percent of total global output. This is more than double the output of all the EC countries combined. Over 40 percent of world trade is now carried out within the Asia-Pacific region.

In the postwar years, the Asia-Pacific region has steadily been growing as a pivotal new force in economic development.

The Asia-Pacific basin is home to more than one-half of the world's population. Vital growth and enterprise are pervasive throughout this vast region, which is endowed with plentiful human and material resources, and with unbounded potential.

Throughout the 1980s, the national economies of this region averaged a five percent growth rate per year. This compares with two percent in the EC countries during the same period, and no other region of the world comes even close.

The region of the Asia-Pacific has continued to develop dynamically on the strength of its diversity and openness. At a time of global transformation, this development continues with ever greater momentum throughout the entire area.

Brisk movements are under way among the region's countries to realign their Cold War relations. Chinese-Soviet relations are changing, as indicated by Chairman Jiang Zemin's recent Moscow visit; the same is true of Soviet-Japanese relations as illustrated by President Gorbachev's trip to Tokyo; and South Korean-Soviet relations are also developing in the wake of South Korea's successful Northern Policy.

Even North Korea is engaged in negotiations with Japan for normalization of relations in an effort to break out of its self-imposed isolation. It has also dropped its stubborn posture and announced its willingness to apply for separate membership to the United Nations along with the Republic of Korea.

In addition to China and the Soviet Union, countries with Socialist economic systems such as Mongolia, Vietnam, and North Korea also have begun actively to seek trade and economic cooperation with highly prosperous Pacific Rim countries.

Furthermore, these countries are eager to join the cooperative systems of our region's market economies.

For example, China and the Soviet Union have already expressed their desire to join APEC.

For realistic reasons of necessity, the countries of the Asia-Pacific basin, for their part, have begun actively to look for ways to form an institutional framework capable of making substantive contributions toward economic and political cooperation within the region.

This trend is quite clear as evidenced by the numerous proposals and initiatives put forward by many leaders of this region.

I believe it is now time to design and frame a structure of cooperation which will ensure a higher dimension of peace, prosperity and happiness to people of this region and all mankind.

Looking ahead to the world in the next century, I would like to propose a broad plan of action based on four fundamental principles to which I am prepared to pledge my own commitment:

First, we must build a solid foundation for international stability across the Asia-Pacific region by removing the last vestiges of the Cold War.

Clearly, mutual cooperation can make little headway without faith in a durable peace.

Therefore, we should welcome to this region the tidal waves of reconciliation, openness and reform that are sweeping across Europe and around the world.

The success or failure of reforms in China and the Soviet Union will most likely be the crucial factor in determining the future peace and stability of this region.

For this reason, all the regional countries, including the United States and Japan, must actively support China and the Soviet Union in their pursuit of development, free market economies, and democratic choices. The efforts of those nations to join international arenas of cooperation must also be facilitated.

At the same time, however, all the countries in the area seem to recognize the need for the United States to continue its leading role if regional stability is to prevail.

History demonstrates that whenever the role of the United States was reduced in this region, the resulting vacuum was quickly filled by the forces of instability with disastrous consequences.

Some nine years ago, Secretary Shultz told a Stanford graduating class to "Learn from your experiences . . ." Our experiences teach us that whenever the United States became isolationist, the Pacific turned into an "Ocean of War."

Tension on the Korean Peninsula has been the central problem hampering the stability of this entire region.

We must, therefore, accelerate the process of removing the legacies of the Cold War from the Korean Peninsula in the interest of promoting cooperation throughout the Asia-Pacific region.

Second, we must work toward a sustained Asia-Pacific prosperity, through openness, free trade and economic cooperation. The free trade system, as we all know, is what has brought to this region unprecedented growth and prosperity.

The share of intra-regional trade in the total trade of the Asia-Pacific nations exceeds 65 percent, indicating a greater interdependency than that which exists in the European Community.

Neither should the United States nor any other single country be expected to provide the entire market. Every country in the region should open its market commensurate with its economic ability and stage of development.

We must all actively coordinate our efforts to resolve trade frictions smoothly in the interest of promoting free trade and common prosperity.

Third, we must direct our efforts toward harmonizing and capitalizing on the diversity of economic structures, developmental stages, cultures and ethnic origins that characterize the various regional states.

In this region of diversity, there are highly advanced countries as well as newly industrializing and developing countries.

By combining the complementary features of our respective economies, we can enjoy the true benefits that come with cooperation. We should encourage interaction between different industries and also intra-industry specialization according to the rule of comparative advantage. In addition, we should share experiences and technology according to levels of development.

If we succeed in combining our efforts to these ends, we shall have practically resolved the global North-South problem in the Asia-Pacific area. I believe that, in this way, we can provide a shining example for all the world.

And, fourth, based on a new Asia-Pacific identity, we must then proceed to develop a formal framework that can help us achieve our objectives. This framework should embrace the entire Asia-Pacific region.

The appearance of sub-regional groups that compartmentalize the region would not, in my view, be desirable because sub-regionalism tends to cause friction and rivalry, and contributes to protectionist tendencies.

In this context, I would look to the Asia-Pacific Economic Cooperation to develop into a respected instrument for the realization of our common prosperity.

The Asia-Pacific community must improve economic efficiency and promote exchange and cooperation in all areas of concern.

The community must also grow in pace with progress elsewhere in the world, and should try to move towards mutual benefit and prosperity, rather than drift away in sub-regional groups with limited goals.

Distinguished guests,

The Republic of Korea is neither a superpower nor an affluent advanced country. Nevertheless, we have been seriously reflecting on what contribution Korea should make and what roles the Korean people should play in the New World Order.

I believe that Korea's unique historical experience and achievements encourage us to play a meaningful role in this promising world of change.

Broadly speaking, the postwar world has been suffering from conflict, rivalry, and tribulation stemming from three major challenges.

The first of these has been the disparity between the haves and have-nots, the so-called North-South problem; the rivalry between different ideologies and systems—the so-called East-West confrontation—the second; and the struggle to build a world which will guarantee human dignity and freedom, the third.

The achievements of the Korean people despite difficulty and adversity can stand, I believe, as a model for others. Our experience may indicate approaches to the solution of larger global problems.

In terms of the global North-South problem, Korea has become a dynamic newly industrializing country, taking off from a lower stage of development and prospering within the span of a single generation. We have demonstrated that hard work and sustained effort can, within a relatively brief period, lift poor and less developed countries to much higher levels of development.

Unlike Germany and Japan, two of the most successful cases of postwar rehabilitation, Korea had little industry prior to World War II and what little we had was reduced to ashes in the course of the Korean War.

Today, however, I stand ready to give you some truly astounding figures: in 1960, South Korea's GNP was 2.1 billion U.S. dollars; her GNP for 1990 stood at about 238 billion dollars. Thirty years ago, Korea's trade volume was 360 million dollars; her trade volume last year registered at 135 billion dollars.

What the world saw during the Seoul Olympics were not long lines of refugees and hungry children—the images of the Korean War—but a proud and revitalized nation full of dynamic energy.

The Korean experience is testimony to the fact that nowhere can today's poverty justify the poverty of tomorrow, nor can poverty ever be justified by a lack of resources.

We have achieved growth in spite of the handicaps of territorial division and a heavy burden of national defense.

The Korean people do not wish to keep this precious experience to themselves, but are anxious to share it broadly with our neighbors and other developing countries for global prosperity.

With a per capita GNP of 5,500 dollars, Korea today may have become a "middle" power.

In terms of the size of GNP, however, Korea is about 15th in the world, whereas the state of California alone ranks 6th.

In ten years, we hope to become an "advanced country" with a per capita GNP of 15,000 dollars.

The Republic of Korea will continue to support liberal market economic principles and to assume greater external responsibilities commensurate with her development.

Thus, Korea will continue to seek new roles as a middle power—between the advanced and developing countries.

In this era of globalization, Korea will seek to play the role of a catalyst in the promotion of economic cooperation and exchanges of technology, capital, market resources, and information.

The Korean people have suffered enormously as a result of the East-West confrontation, yet today we have built a showcase demonstrating the superiority of a free market economy over a central command economy. Today, we feel proud and gratified.

During the Cold War years, Korea had no formal relations with China, the Soviet Union or any of the Communist nations.

However, our Northern Policy, which we began pursuing three years ago, culminated in my summit meeting with Soviet President Gorbachev in San Francisco last year. Within four months, our two countries normalized diplomatic relations. Last December, I paid a visit to Moscow. And last April, President Gorbachev became the first Soviet leader ever to set foot on the Korean Peninsula.

In addition, Korea and China have exchanged permanent trade offices.

The Northern Policy, stemming from our confidence in our political-economic capabilities, has not only opened a new horizon for our foreign relations, but also is contributing to improved inter-Korean relations and to a general reduction of tension in Northeast Asia.

The recent reversal in North Korea's policy and its decision to enter the U.N. reflects the emerging new international order in which South Korea's Northern Policy has played a role.

We expect that the entry of South and North Korea into the U.N. in September will contribute significantly to ending the impasse on the Korean Peninsula.

Through economic cooperation and participation in the European Bank for Reconstruction and Development, the Republic of Korea is supporting and encouraging the reforms in the Soviet Union and the countries of Eastern and Central Europe.

These actions stem from our desire to contribute to a climate more conducive to the peaceful unification of the Korean Peninsula and to a more harmonious world.

Again, as a result of South Korea's Northern Policy, the bridge over the Pacific has widened and the winds of liberal democracy and market economics have begun to sweep across Asia.

Located at a geographical nexus, the Republic of Korea will be pleased to serve as a bridge to introduce and promote international cooperation and reconciliation.

I believe the Republic of Korea has become a model country for having achieved rapid economic growth as well as genuine democracy at the same time.

After national liberation in 1945, the Korean people suffered countless trials and tribulations in their pursuit of freedom and democratic ideals.

Since the June 29, 1987 Declaration of Democratic Reforms, I have pressed on to establish democratic principles in Korea and to implement various democratic reform programs. Today, our country enjoys freedom of the press and speech, a system of free elections, and the separation of governmental powers.

We had to pay a high price and overcome many difficulties in the process of casting off out-dated authoritarianism and ushering in a new era of liberal democracy.

The long pent-up demands of our people and the structural contradictions erupted all at once.

We have also had to face the threat of opportunistic radicals who had sought, and to an extent still seek, to overthrow the democratic system itself by means of violent "class struggle"—a phrase with which I am sure you are all familiar.

Because these anti-democratic elements have been shrewd enough to hide themselves behind "democratic" slogans, the tasks of maintaining law and order have been extremely difficult and complicated.

Fortunately, however, I am able to report to you that liberal democracy has at long last begun to take deep root in Korea on the basis of a solid national consensus.

The institutionalization of our democratic system is proceeding on schedule with the local government elections this year. In the recent City and Provincial Council elections, held just ten days ago, the Korean people delivered a nation-wide landslide victory to the ruling party. Even in Seoul, where voters traditionally voted with the opposition to check the governing party, an overwhelming 80 percent of the seats went to ruling party candidates. The message here is clear: the majority of the Korean people are satisfied with the current progress of democratization and desire stability in the transition to genuine democracy.

Few countries that emerged independent in the postwar period have been as successful in achieving liberal democracy as has the Republic of Korea.

From this point forward, the Korean people will steadfastly march towards democracy.

Our experience is certain to serve as a source of pride to our friends with whom we share common ideals and as a source of courage to those still facing difficulty in achieving democracy.

Ladies and gentlemen,

The people of the Republic of Korea will always remember that Korea owes much to the United States for its unwavering support.

When my country was engulfed in war perpetrated by Communist aggression in 1950, the American people fought alongside us for our survival and freedom.

At this very moment, over 40,000 young American servicemen and women stand on vigil far across the Pacific, along the Demilitarized Zone in the heart of the Korean Peninsula.

American support has been the source of strength for Korea's remarkable progress.

Furthermore, the open American market has been the seedbed of Korean economic growth.

Korea and the United States together have taken a long march towards freedom and prosperity. In economic terms, Korea is the 7th largest trading partner of the U.S.—with imports of 70 billion dollars compared to a meager 300 million dollars 30 years ago.

The bonds between our two countries have been so strengthened and solidified in all areas that we have now become indispensable partners.

The United States of America is truly the country that has carried the heaviest burden and performed the most vital role in safeguarding peace, freedom and prosperity for all mankind throughout the postwar period; indeed, to this very day.

Our two countries have now become the most endeared friends and closest partners.

Korea and the United States will combine efforts toward establishing a New World Order.

It is a partnership that can make a major contribution to a truly peaceful world and in establishing a prosperous Pacific Era.

Many young people from my country have come to this prestigious Stanford campus in a search for truth, knowledge, ideals and dreams amongst professors and other students from across America and the world. In fact, both my children have been privileged to study here. I understand that in one of the cornerstones of the Quadrangle, there is inscribed the motto of Stanford University, "Die Luft der Freiheit Weht" or "The Winds of Freedom Blow."

May those winds of freedom prevail.

Sharing and cherishing common dreams and ideals, together we shall march onward—from the world we save to the world we yearn.

Thank you very much.

54.

Remarks at the Welcoming Ceremony on the Occasion of the State Visit of the Yang Di-Pertuan Agong IX [King] of Malaysia, Seoul, September 13, 1991

Your Majesties Azlan Shah and Tuanku Bainun, distinguished guests, ladies and gentlemen,

I am very pleased to join the nation in welcoming Your Majesties and the members of the Malaysian delegation to the Republic of Korea.

It is a great privilege for me to welcome Your Majesty once again following your last visit to Seoul during the 1988 Olympic Games. I know your state visit marks an important milestone for the promotion of friendship and cooperation between our two countries.

Endowed with beautiful landscapes and abundant natural resources, Malaysia is Korea's very close and valued friend and partner for freedom and prosperity.

Malaysia enjoys the brilliant tradition of the Malaccan Empire and has succeeded in building a dynamic society by harmonizing the diverse indigenous cultures. Today, Malaysia is making remarkable economic progress on the strength of democracy and stability and is a focus of world attention.

Geographically, Malaysia is sitting astride a crossroad between the Indian Ocean and the western Pacific and between the Asian Continent and the Malaysian Archipelago. As such, Malaysia's contribution toward the international community is rapidly on the increase as it plays a pivotal role for the unity of Southeast Asia as well as for Asia-Pacific cooperation.

I would like to take this opportunity to offer my congratulations and pay my respects to Your Majesty for the accomplishments and progress your great country has achieved under your superb leadership.

Your Majesty,

Malaysia and Korea share common ideals, and the two countries have been making rapid progress in promoting friendly and cooperative relations in all areas.

Our bilateral trade has been consistently growing, and the latitude of our trade has been expanding in recent years, including investment, technology exchanges and economic cooperation.

Friendship and understanding between the people also continue to deepen as the number of visitors and exchanges increase between our lands.

We two countries are also closely cooperating on the international stage. Owing to Malaysia's active support, Korea has become a full dialogue partner of the Association of Southeast Asian Nations, and we benefited from your strong voice in our entry into the United Nations.

As leading members of the Asia-Pacific Economic Cooperation, our two countries continue to endeavor for the promotion of peace and prosperity of this region.

We will develop further our already close relationship on the basis of mutually complementary features and abundant potentialities.

Your Majesty,

Our two countries are playing leading roles in building the Asia-Pacific region into a region of the most dynamic progress in the world.

The friendly and neighborly relations between our nations promise a higher future for the Asia-Pacific region, and will contribute toward peace and prosperity of the world.

I still cherish the beautiful memories of my visit to your great country in November 1988, and I would like to once again thank the government and people of Malaysia for their wonderful hospitality.

I would like to take this opportunity to convey the warm greetings of friendship from the Korean people to the people of Malaysia, and I am very happy to welcome Your Majesties.

Thank you.

55.

Remarks at the Banquet in Honor of the Yang Di-Pertuan Agong IX of Malaysia, Seoul, September 13, 1991

Your Majesties Azlan Shah and Tuanku Bainun, distinguished guests, ladies and gentlemen,

I am very pleased to join the nation in cordially welcoming Your Majesties to the Republic of Korea.

Your Majesty's visit provides a propitious occasion to renew the friendly and cooperative relations our two countries have developed over the past thirty-one years. Your visit marks a significant milestone in promoting our friendship at a higher dimension, as our two countries open in partnership a new era of Asia-Pacific cooperation.

Your Majesty has become the focal point of the Malaysian people by achieving a harmonious national consensus on the basis of mutual understanding and respect and by accommodating a diversity of ethnic aspirations. You have also earned the respect and trust of the people by bringing hope to the dark corners of society by leading the campaign to eradicate poverty and illiteracy.

I pay my respects to Your Majesty for the progress Malaysia is making under your leadership. Malaysia's rapid economic development and balanced national growth are the envy of other countries.

During the three years since your last visit to Seoul, the Republic of Korea has also undergone much change. Domestically, rapid democratization has taken place in all sectors of society. In our foreign relations, the successful pursuit of our Northern Diplomacy has brought establishment of diplomatic relations with Central and Eastern European countries as well as the Soviet Union. In addition, we have opened a relationship of mutual cooperation and exchanges with neighboring China.

The joint entry of South and North Korea into the United Nations next week is an indication that we are taking a big step toward peace on the Korean Peninsula. We are moving forward to realize our goals of freedom, prosperity and national unification.

Your Majesty,
As partners in the Asia-Pacific region, Malaysia and Korea have been developing friendship and close cooperation. Mutual understanding is deepening and cooperative relations are strengthened as visits and exchanges rapidly increase between our two nations.

I am very gratified to note that under Malaysia's Look East policy, some 600 young Malaysians have completed their training in Korea and returned home with new-found knowledge and skill.

The trade volume between our two countries reached $2.3 billion last year, and is expected to amount to $3 billion this year. The investments made by Korean businesses in Malaysia are also showing a rapid increase, and are expected to surpass the $500 million mark within two to three years.

In addition, the areas of our bilateral interest have seen an expansion from primary goods and light industries into heavy industries such as steel and chemical products.

Our bilateral cooperation is expected to further expand and develop on the basis of mutually complementary economic structures and great potential, and will bring on fruitful rewards to both our countries.

Your Majesty,
Korea and Malaysia have been maintaining close cooperative ties on the international stage as well. We have been supportive of Malaysia's foreign policies, including South-South cooperation, and your government has equally been supportive of our posture, including our unification and Northern policies.

I am especially grateful for the role Malaysia played as the Chair country of the Association of Southeast Asian Nations in inviting Korea in as a full dialogue partner last July. I also appreciate the support Malaysia has given in the process of our entry into the United Nations.

Korea will continue to strengthen the efforts to develop cooperative relations with ASEAN, and maintain close ties with Malaysia in the United Nations and the international arena.

Your Majesty,
We can both be proud that our two countries have become the exemplary models to other countries for the remarkable growth and development we achieved in the postwar period. In the new century, East Asia, with its long history and brilliant cultural tradition, is expected to rapidly emerge as a new center of global development.

Historic changes are sweeping across the world with the collapse of the Cold War. Our two countries should jointly meet these global challenges and together open a new chapter of peace and prosperity in an era of Asia-Pacific cooperation.

It is my sincere hope that Your Majesties' visit to Korea will be full of pleasant and fond memories of Korea, just as my visit to your great country has been.

Ladies and gentlemen,

Please join me in a toast to the health of Their Majesties Azlan Shah and Tuanku Bainun, to Malaysia's continued prosperity, and to the lasting Korean-Malaysian friendship.

Thank you.

56.

Keynote Address to the Third Asia-Pacific Economic Cooperation (APEC) Meeting, Seoul, November 12, 1991

Distinguished delegates, ladies and gentlemen,

I am very pleased to join the nation in extending a warm welcome to you on the occasion of the opening of the third Ministerial Meeting on Asia-Pacific Economic Cooperation (APEC). It is also a privilege for me to have such a distinguished group of delegates here at Chong Wa Dae (the presidential office building).

Like a warm and cordial town meeting, friends and neighbors have gathered here under one roof. The reason we feel so comfortable is perhaps because we are all like-minded in building a durable framework of cooperation with a view to laying the groundwork for a community of Asia-Pacific cooperation.

The future of Pacific cooperation has become brighter and all the more promising as three new members have decided to participate in APEC beginning with the Seoul meeting, and, ladies and gentlemen, I would like to ask you to join me in extending hearty congratulations and welcome to the People's Republic of China, Chinese Taipei and Hong Kong.

Distinguished delegates,

In the past two years since we inaugurated APEC in Canberra, the course of history itself has changed as the world underwent epic transformations. Strong currents of openness and reform have brought down the Cold War system that used to dominate the postwar world.

The Central and East European countries and the USSR are all in the process of embracing new systems of pluralistic democracy and market economics.

In our vast Asia-Pacific region, too, the dark era of confrontation is fast receding and a fresh movement to realize common prosperity through mutual cooperation is gaining momentum, and our meeting this evening heralds this reality to the world.

The entire world is moving rapidly to forge a new international order, indeed, a new world for our posterity.

Our hearts are full with hopes that the new era will truly give rise to an age of blessing and a world in which human aspirations are fulfilled.

A world in which human reason and the power of freedom shall lead the progress of history, a world in which all mankind shall cooperate for peace and prosperity, is no longer a dream but a reality at hand.

Our dreams and hopes will become reality only when all nations will share the spirit of reciprocal assistance and genuine mutual trust. On this basis, we should quickly remove all divisive barriers and promote openness and cooperation from common progress.

We share the belief that APEC will play a leading role in building a more prosperous and peaceful world by first fulfilling this spirit in the Asia-Pacific region.

Distinguished delegates,

The Asia-Pacific region has seen a most dynamic development in the postwar world, and has now become a focal point of world progress.

The Pacific Ocean is no longer "pacific." Today, it has become an ocean of dynamic exchanges and cooperation.

The volume of trade across the Pacific has been rapidly growing since 1980, and today it is approaching almost twice that of the Atlantic.

The two billion people of the 15 APEC-participating economies are producing one-half of the global output.

Behind the remarkable and unprecedented growth of our region was the driving force supplied by vigorous trade and economic cooperation. And, what has enabled the latter have been the free trade and open-door systems.

During the past 20 years, the total output of our region expanded six-fold, and intra-regional trade twelve-fold.

The ratio of Asia-Pacific intra-regional trade to total trade is 67 percent, and it is approaching a level close to Europe where economic integration has been underway for some time now. It further means that interdependency among the regional economies is rapidly increasing.

Indeed, we are witnessing an enormous eruption of developmental energy in the Asia-Pacific. It emanates from the diversity, openness, and unfathomed potential that are unique to this vast region.

This region, of course, is characterized by diversities, such as different histories, cultures, socio-political and economic structures, and stages of development. At the same time, however, we know that our region evinces a more positive attitude toward harmony than any other region of the world.

Spread over vast continents and oceans, the Asia-Pacific region is abundant with human as well as material resources. What is more, there is a strong desire all across our region to achieve common prosperity by developing and utilizing our resources.

Many economies in our region have gained independence after World War II and rapidly achieved a newly industrializing status from the stage of underdevelopment. It is perhaps a phenomenon unique to this region that these economies are catching up with advanced economies.

As epic changes sweep across the world, the Asia-Pacific region is also ushering in a new momentum for progress. The divisive curtain drawn across the East Asian continent throughout the postwar period is being lifted and the Asia-Pacific region is now building up a new common ground of genuine cooperation.

I am firmly convinced that an efficient fusion of dynamic energies of the Asia-Pacific countries into one cooperative community will generate a driving force powerful enough to lead world history in the new century. I am full of hopes that APEC will serve as a central framework for this task, as it has now become a unique forum for inter-governmental consultation and cooperation in our region.

Distinguished delegates,

Confrontations over ideologies and systems have by and large ended, and a new world order based on economic capabilities is about to emerge.

The world's future and the destiny of mankind will largely depend on whether the new order fosters exclusive and self-centered regional economic blocs or whether it develops in the direction of promoting openness and cooperation among the regional economies.

The reality today appears to be one in which the free trade system is being challenged by increasing trends of regionalism.

European integration is near at hand and a vast Europe, which stretches to the Soviet border, is likely to emerge as one economic community in the near future.

Meeting amidst increasing uncertainties in the world economic environment, the Seoul APEC meeting should seek to produce a meaningful outcome by setting the course and defining the roles both for the future of the world economy and for a sustained common prosperity of participating economies.

APEC should now move onto a higher dimension of cooperation by forging a more effective framework and setting a clear direction of cooperation so that closer intra-regional cooperation may develop.

It was a significant development that we agreed on the work program in our Singapore meeting last year.

APEC has come to a point where we should establish an institutional base through which, internally, we can promote more effective, intra-regional trade and economic cooperation and, externally, common economic interests of the region can be represented.

It is my conviction that the APEC should develop along the following principles and directions:

First, APEC should seek to shape the world economy of the 21st century into an order of economic globalism by first setting an example of open regionalism under the principles of free trade.

APEC should promote free trade within a stable multilateral trading system by strengthening and complementing the system.

To this end, we should exert our utmost efforts for a successful outcome of the Uruguay Round negotiations.

APEC should also promote extra-regional relations on the basis of openness.

In addition to preventing APEC itself from becoming an exclusive regional bloc, we should also develop close cooperative relations with other regions to prevent them from drifting toward inward-looking regionalism.

Second, APEC should play an increasingly active role as a region-wide cooperative body, which includes such sub-regional groups as ASEAN and NAFTA within our region.

In view of the vastness and diversities of the Asia-Pacific, the appearance of sub-regional groups may perhaps be inevitable for purposes of increased economic efficiency. Sub-regional groups, however, must also seek to develop in harmony with the open and cooperative order of the region.

Asia-Pacific cooperation should not, in any case, develop into a competing relationship between East Asia and North America. On the contrary, it should play a central role for the promotion of a harmonious and balanced development of trans-Pacific relations.

Third, APEC should seek to narrow the economic gap between the advanced and the developing economies of the region, to support Socialist economies of the region in their efforts toward openness and reform, and to encourage these economies to join the Asia-Pacific economic mainstream.

To this end, the advanced economies should facilitate market access to the developing economies as well as to those economies that are in the process of transforming into market economies, and should more actively share capital and technologies with them. This is also essential for the stability and peace of the Asia-Pacific region.

And, fourth, APEC should explore, in the long run, the possibilities of moving toward a free trade area encompassing the entire Asia-Pacific.

When free trade should blossom across this region of diversity, we will have made enormous contributions toward the realization of free trade at the global level.

If all of us in this hall reach a consensus on these principles and directions and coordinate our efforts, I am convinced that APEC will develop a most exemplary regional cooperative body for the world.

I hope and expect that the Seoul APEC Ministerial Meeting will set an historic milestone on our road to a brighter future for Asia-Pacific cooperation by clearly defining its directions and approaches.

Distinguished delegates,
Usually, achievements fall far short of dreams. When we achieve something we could not even dream of, we call it a miracle.

As we recall, the Asia of half a century ago was a region characterized by divisive barriers, closed societies, colonial bondages, underdevelopment, and poverty. Today, however, powerful and dynamic energies of development wash the shores of the Western Pacific, and miracle is perhaps a word quite insufficient to describe this phenomenon.

This evening, representatives of two billion people and of the economies that produce one half of the global output gathered here to design a brighter future for Asia-Pacific prosperity, and this is certainly another blessing of history that no one dreamed of.

A new century is only a decade away. As many eminent scholars predicted, the 21st century will be an era of the Pacific. Let there be no doubt that we will be recorded in history as the architects of the new Pacific Era.

Thank you.

57.

I Expect the United States to Remain Involved; Interview, *Newsweek*, November 18, 1991

South Korean President Roh Tae Woo met last week with The Washington Post Company Chairman of the Board Katharine Graham, Newsweek *Editor-in-Chief and President Richard M. Smith and* Newsweek *correspondents to discuss U.S. policy in Asia and other regional issues. Excerpts:*

NEWSWEEK: What was your reaction to the sudden cancellation of President George Bush's trip to the region?
ROH: As far as Northeast Asia's new order is concerned, the role of the United States is very important, and for that reason the visit of President Bush would contribute greatly to our common cause. I hope he will be able to reschedule it in the next few months.

There have been suggestions that Asia needs a regional leader. Could Bush be that leader?
Whenever the United States withdraws from this area and reduces its influence . . . there are disastrous consequences. I would expect the United States to remain very involved in Northeast Asia and Southeast Asia as far as the military is concerned.

South Korea's latest white paper on defense expressed concern about the possibility of Japan's remilitarization. Do you believe that such a change is occurring?
I would simply say that Japan's increase of its military power is basically defensive and hopefully will not pose any regional threats. But defensive and offensive postures are very difficult to distinguish. It's a matter of intent. That's why we will watch [Japan] closely.

What about indications that Japan may send its Self-Defense Forces overseas as part of a United Nations peacekeeping force?

A peacekeeping role is perhaps possible to take into account. The fundamental question is whether Japan's military power would pose a threat to other countries in the region.

Do you believe that Japan is helping or hindering in the drive toward the reunification of the Korean Peninsula?

Some Japanese believe that a reunified Korea would be too strong to handle, so they support the concept of divide and rule. But they are in the minority. As far as I know, [the Japanese government] is supporting bilateral confidence building. I would hasten to add that the reason the Japanese government holds the position it does is . . . because the United States has been supporting our policies, and I'm grateful that Japan is following that.

What is your assessment of the nuclear threat from North Korea?

For North Korea to have nuclear weapons in its possession would be more destabilizing . . . than for the government of Iraq [to have them]. Now there is international pressure on North Korea to submit to international inspections. As that international pressure increases, North Korea can look forward to even steeper isolation.

How soon do you think the North could produce a nuclear weapon?

Accounts reaching Seoul indicate that North Korea may be able to produce a nuclear device in the next two or three years. I believe the most urgent problem not only for us, but for the international community, is the elimination of this threat.

Given that threat, when is reunification possible?

I believe North Korea will have to take the road to openness in the next few years. It is inevitable for North Korea to open its society—not necessarily voluntarily, but because of pressure from outside. For this reason, I think reunification is possible within this century.

Part VII

KOREA AND THE WEST: EUROPE AND THE WESTERN HEMISPHERE

58.

Remarks at the Banquet in Honor of the Prime Minister of the Hellenic Republic and Mrs. Constantine Mitsotakis, Seoul, November 14, 1990

Your Excellency Prime Minister and Mrs. Mitsotakis, distinguished guests.

I join the entire people of the Republic of Korea in extending a hearty welcome to you and your delegation, and it is, indeed, a distinct pleasure for me and my wife to share this evening with you here at Chong Wa Dae.

Your visit today has opened a new era for a further development of our diplomatic relations, which will mark the 30th anniversary next year. Although our two countries are separated by a great geographical distance, Greece has been quite well known to the Korean people over the years. Perhaps, there are few Koreans who are not familiar with the magnificence of the Greek culture.

A significant part of modern civilization and the values we cherish originate from Greece and we are all beneficiaries of the brilliant Greek culture. Greek influence is pervasive in Korea in the teachings of philosophy, arts and sciences, and in imparting knowledge and values such as democracy, equality, human dignity and the love of freedom.

Six years ago, I had the pleasure of visiting your great country in preparation for the 1988 Seoul Olympics. Memories of beautiful scenery and the magnificence of your civilization are still fresh in my mind.

My countrymen shall long remember and never forget the invaluable sacrifices the courageous young men from Greece rendered four decades ago in our common cause to defend freedom in this country.

Let me also take this opportunity to express my heart-felt gratitude to the government and the people of greece for their unsparing support and assistance for the success of the Seoul Olympics, from the lighting of the Olympic flame to the conclusion of the Games.

Mr. Prime Minister,

The Cold War structure that dominated the postwar world has now crumbled and a new world order of reconciliation is emerging. The ideological and political barriers that served to divide mankind have been removed. Today, the waves of openness and reform have formed an enormous historical current that no one can defy.

On our part, we are making every effort to remove the legacies of the Cold War on the Korean Peninsula that a fratricidal war and the East-West confrontation have bequeathed to us. We are seeking with all sincerity to build a mutually trusting and beneficial relationship with North Korea through such means as dialogue, exchanges and inter-Korean cooperation. Our goal is to bring the two parts of Korea together in a national community and peaceful unification.

We hope that North Korea will step forward and join us as a responsible member of the international community. In the wake of the improving international atmosphere and the pursuit of our "Northern Diplomacy," we have been able to establish diplomatic relations with almost all the countries around the world. It is our policy not only to maintain but to strengthen friendly and cooperative relations with all our friends. A diligent pursuit of this policy will not only help realize common prosperity but also contribute to a durable peace in Korea as well as in Northeast Asia.

Mr. Prime Minister,

Rising from the ashes of war, Korea has achieved a rapid economic development over the past two decades. Through democratic reforms, we have also succeeded in building a freer and more dynamic society during the past three years. In the process, however, painful difficulties and high social costs ensued. With courage and determination we are steadily overcoming the obstacles.

Your Excellency's visit today has paved a broad avenue of friendship and cooperation between our two nations that share common ideals. We hope that through this new avenue, mutually beneficial exchanges will continue to expand in all areas, including economic, cultural, scientific and technological cooperation. I believe we can actively share our developmental experience and expertise for economic progress and increased productivity. Korean businesses would also be interested in joint ventures with their Greek counterparts for third country business opportunities within the framework of the European Community.

In times of momentous change, I sincerely hope that our bilateral cooperation will ever be strengthened. Your visit to Korea this time is rather brief, but your visit has set a landmark for the Korean-Greek partnership as we move toward a more prosperous 21st century.

Ladies and gentlemen,

May I please propose a toast to the good health and well being of His Excellency Prime Minister and Mrs. Mitsotakis, to the eternal friendship of our two peoples and to the prosperity of the Hellenic Republic.

Thank you.

59.

Remarks at the Banquet in Honor of the Prime Minister of Denmark and Mrs. Poul Schlüter, Seoul, June 12, 1991

Your Excellencies Prime Minister and Mrs. Poul Schlüter, distinguished guests, ladies and gentlemen,

It gives me great pleasure to join the nation in extending a warm and cordial welcome to Your Excellencies and the distinguished delegation from the beautiful Nordic Kingdom of Denmark. Indeed, Mr. Prime Minister, you are well known to us and the world for your superb leadership demonstrated throughout your current tenure spanning over nine years and because you have made enormous contributions not simply to the progress of Denmark but also to European integration as well as cooperation among nations.

Mr. Prime Minister,

We are located far away from your great country of Denmark. But, your country is as familiar as a neighbor to us because the stories of Hans Christian Andersen and the pioneer spirit of Grundvig and Dalgas are fresh in our minds.

Like Korea, Denmark is a peninsula country surrounded by powerful neighbors. Neither of us is endowed with rich natural resources. And yet, the people of Denmark, known for their unequalled independent and cooperative spirit, have successfully built the best-managed welfare state in the world, which is a model for our nation.

You rushed the hospital ship *Jutlandia* to our assistance when our land was engulfed in a war, perpetrated by the Communists. Subsequently, after the ceasefire was signed, your government and people provided support for the construction of a major medical center in the heart of Seoul to help nurse the wounds of war. The medical center has provided medical service and care to a great number of Korean patients, and continues to do so. The Korean people are ever grateful to the people of Denmark for such help in a time of great national difficulty.

Within the span of one generation, the Republic of Korea, rising from the ashes of war, has become a liberal and dynamic newly industrializing country. I am very pleased to note that you have been able to visit my country three times and witness first-hand the stages of Korea's dynamic progress and development. As you may have noticed, we have continued to move forward during the six years since your last official visit to our country in 1985. During the interim, the Republic of Korea has succeeded in removing authoritarianism from our society and has embarked upon a new era of liberal democracy. In spite of the threats of war and the adversity of territorial division, we have successfully hosted the much-acclaimed Olympic festivities in universal harmony.

The Republic of Korea today has become a nation playing a more active role and making a greater contribution to world peace and prosperity.

Mr. Prime Minister,
We are living in an age of great change. The changes that have taken place in Europe in the past two years have been truly revolutionary. The wall that separated Europe into East and West has been removed, and the many hardline one-party states have set out to transform themselves into pluralistic democracies.

The unification of Germany that came about amid this global change is a source of envy for the Korean people, whose country is now the only divided one in the world. At the same time, however, German unification has given us hope and encouragement.

The tidal waves of openness and reconciliation that have brought all of Europe together under one roof have begun to wash the shores of East Asia. As part of our Northern Policy, we have been improving relations with the Soviet Union and the countries of Eastern and Central Europe. Perhaps, this best represents the changes taking place in this region.

The solution of the Korean problem has long been regarded as the pivotal task for an enduring peace and stability in this region. The Republic of Korea seeks to achieve peaceful unification by first removing rivalry and confrontation between the two parts of Korea and by promoting exchanges and cooperation for mutual benefit and common prosperity.

The admission of South and North Korea into the United Nations this fall will certainly contribute toward easing tension on the Korean Peninsula and toward establishing a lasting peace in Northeast Asia. I should like to take this opportunity to express my deep appreciation to the people of Denmark for their unflagging support and encouragement for our efforts toward this end.

Mr. Prime Minister,
The Iraqi invasion of Kuwait has served as a stark reminder that the

uncertainties and dangers of regional conflict persist even as the world moves forward to a new international order. At the same time, however, the Gulf War has prompted the community of nations to rally around the U.N. flag, and we have demonstrated once again that aggression will not stand in today's international system.

I firmly believe that Korea and Denmark should join hands to develop ever closer and stronger cooperative and friendly relations because the progress of history is on the side of those who cherish the universal values of freedom and democracy and because together we can work to realize the common ideal of world peace.

Mr. Prime Minister,
Over the years, our two countries have been diligently expanding exchanges and cooperation in all areas, but I assure you that your visit today has given a new and powerful momentum to our bilateral relations.

I am also convinced that our close friendship will be long cherished as a solid bridge between Europe and Asia in the new century.

Ladies and gentlemen,
Please join me in a toast to the health and well being of Her Majesty Queen Margrethe II and Their Excellencies Prime Minister and Mrs. Poul Schlüter, to the ever-lasting prosperity of the Kingdom of Denmark, and to lasting friendship between our two nations.
Thank you.

60.

Remarks upon Arrival in Canada, Ottawa, July 3, 1991

Your Excellencies Governor-General and Mrs. Hnatyshyn, the Honorable Prime Minister and Mrs. Mulroney, citizens of Canada, ladies and gentlemen,

I would like to extend to you my deep appreciation for your kind invitation to visit your great country and for the warm and cordial welcome. I am very pleased to come to this beautiful country, where freedom and democracy flourish and wisdom and vitality abound. I am also pleased to bring warm greetings of friendship from the Korean people to the people of Canada. You have indeed turned this vast territory into a land of progress and plenty.

For over a century, Korea and Canada have been friends, and today we have become the closest of partners, together ushering in a new era of common good in the Pacific. The early Canadian missionaries in Korea were pioneers who made enormous contributions to Korea's modernization in such areas as religion, medicine, and education. Furthermore, when the Communists invaded our country, over 26,000 Canadians came to Korea and fought side by side with us, risking their lives for our survival and freedom. The Korean people will always remember with deep gratitude the service and sacrifice of the Canadian people.

I am very encouraged that our bilateral relations have been making rapid progress recently. We have become important commercial partners, and the volume of our bilateral trade is growing consistently. In addition to the increasing cultural and personnel exchanges, expansion is also taking place in cross-border investment as well as in scientific and technological cooperation. The friendly and cooperative relations between our two countries are valuable not only for our mutual development, but also for the promotion of a more peaceful and prosperous world.

Today, liberal democracy has truly become a universal ideal. As the Cold War collapses and the new world order emerges, the international community demands closer cooperation and coordination among nations. The Pacific Ocean, which washes the shores of Korea and Canada, embraces a vast region—full of dynamism and energy for development.

In the 21st century, the Pacific region is expected to play an increasingly important role in ensuring the world peace and prosperity.

Mesdames, Mesdemoiselles et Messieurs,

"C'est l'intention qui fait l'action." Je souhaite que ma venue ici fournisse une occasion de renforcer les relations traditionelles et amicales entre nos deux pays, et de promouvoir la coopération entre les nations de la région du Pacifique.

Our two nations pursue common ideals of freedom, peace and prosperity, and we share a common desire to establish a bright future for the Pacific and the world.

During my stay in Canada, I hope to have a useful and productive exchange of views with Canadian leaders on these and other issues of mutual concern.

Thank you once again for your warm welcome.

61.

Opening Remarks at the Joint News Conference with Prime Minister Brian Mulroney of Canada, Ottawa, July 4, 1991

Today I had a frank and very useful meeting with Prime Minister Mulroney.

We exchanged views on international changes, the situation in Northeast Asia and possible measures to promote cooperation in Asia and the Pacific. We also had serious discussions on measures to further improve relations between our two traditional allies.

I am very satisfied with the results of the meeting with Prime Minister Mulroney.

Cooperation in Asia and the Pacific is important not only for our two countries but the world at large. We agreed upon the importance of the Pacific cooperation and reviewed a number of ideas for its promotion. We noted that together we have to overcome various challenges and conflicting interests in implementing them.

The two of us agreed that our two countries should play leading roles specifically to promote the Pacific cooperation.

The situation around the Korean Peninsula is changing very rapidly as manifested by Korea's improving relations with the Soviet Union and East European countries.

Accordingly, changes began to appear in North Korea as seen in its decision to enter the United Nations together with South Korea and its recent attitude toward the international nuclear inspection issue.

As a result of my meeting with Prime Minister Mulroney this morning, I am convinced that Canada will more actively cooperate with Korea in support of peace and reunification on the Korean Peninsula.

As an important member of G-7 with an increasingly active leadership role in the world community, Canada will develop ever closer ties with Korea at the United Nations as well as in the international community.

I firmly believe that my meeting with the prime minister today and my visit to Canada have given momentum to improved and expanded Korean-Canadian relations.

Korea is prepared to increase its investment in Canada in such areas as steel, automobile and resource development, and bilateral economic cooperation and trade are certain to expand.

As trusting partners, our two countries will further expand contacts and cooperation in all areas, and I am convinced that our meeting today served as an important turning-point for this process.

Thank you.

62.

Remarks at the Banquet Hosted by the Governor-General of Canada and Mrs. Ramon Hnatyshyn, Ottawa, July 4, 1991

Your Excellencies Governor-General and Mrs. Hnatyshyn, the Honorable Prime Minister and Mrs. Mulroney, distinguished guests, ladies and gentlemen,

I am very grateful for your kind invitation to visit this great country of Canada, for the warm welcome and generous hospitality, and for your encouraging words of friendship.

Since you came into office as the 24th governor-general in January of 1990, Canada has made substantial progress toward harmony and prosperity as well as valuable contributions to the international community, and I pay my respects to you for your leadership and achievement. It is a delight for me to have an opportunity to meet you again in this beautiful country, where the grandeur of nature, diversity of culture, democratic values and dynamic potential for prosperity combine themselves enviably. I am also very pleased to bring warm greetings of friendship from the people of the Republic of Korea to the people of Canada.

Your Excellency,

The friendly relations between Korea and Canada began more than a century ago. James Gayle was an early Canadian missionary who came to Korea in 1888. He translated the Bible into Korean, compiled a Korean-English dictionary and established a modern Western-style school in Korea. Indeed, his introduction of Western culture was a fresh wonder to the tradition-bound Korean people. Furthermore, the Korean people remember many Canadians such as Frederick McKenzie and Frank Schofield, who loved Korea as much as any Korean could.

When Korea was invaded by the Communists, 26,000 Canadians rushed to our aid and fought side by side with our people to ensure our very survival and to protect freedom. The Korean people will never forget Canada's noble service and sacrifice.

Rising above the ravages of the war, the Korean people have achieved a remarkably rapid development over the past 30 years. Furthermore, we have entered into an era of genuine democracy based on our economic progress.

During the Seoul Olympic Games, the countries of the East and the West gathered in Seoul, and the world was able to see a new democracy flourishing with the dynamic energies of prosperity. We are proud that our progress, achieved on the strength of democratic pluralism and a market economy, has become a model for other developing countries. And, the Korean people will always be grateful to Canada and other friends and allies for their support and encouragement.

Your Excellency,

In the past two or three years, the world has undergone tremendous changes, transforming the postwar international order. The reforms in Eastern Europe and the Soviet Union clearly confirm that our commonly cherished ideals of human dignity, freedom and democratic pluralism have now become universally acknowledged values.

The Gulf War was a major challenge to the emerging new world order. To repulse the aggressor, the world rallied around the United Nations flag. Both our nations participated in the crusade for peace and freedom.

Now, the new waves of reconciliation have begun to reach the Korean Peninsula. The Republic of Korea has been actively pursuing a forward-looking Northern Policy, and friendly and cooperative relations have been established with the countries in Eastern and Central Europe as well as the Soviet Union. The entry of both Koreas into the United Nations this fall is expected to contribute toward the stability of the Korean Peninsula and the Asia-Pacific region. Amidst these rapid currents of change, Korea and Canada will join hands to build a world far better than the one we inherited—safer, more prosperous, fairer and happier.

Your Excellency,

Endowed with abundant natural resources and unbounded potential, the Pacific Region is brimming with vitality. The awesome innovations and advances in science, technology, transportation and communication, are turning this vast Pacific Ocean into a small lake of instant exchanges. In the coming century, the Pacific region will lead the world's prosperity.

The friendly relations between Korea and Canada are expanding rapidly in all areas. As important trading partners, the volume of trade between our two countries is consistently growing. Canada is the third largest destination for Korea's investment. Korean corporations are increasing investment in Canada in such areas as the automobile and steel industries as well as in natural resource development. Personnel exchanges between us are on the rise; and the 60,000 Korean residents in Canada act as a bridge for the promotion of friendly and cooperative relations between our two countries. Therefore, I am convinced that our two countries will increasingly value and respect each other as trusting partners in a New Pacific Era. My belief has been further reinforced through my conversations with you as well as with leaders of various sectors of Canadian life.

Your Excellency,
We have a saying in Korea, "Friendship grows bigger the more you share." I understand you have a saying here, "Good friendship is a second relative." I know the friendship between our two countries will be as beautiful and lasting as the water flowing along the Rideau River.

Ladies and gentlemen,
Please join me in a toast to Her Majesty the Queen, to the health and well-being of Their Excellencies the Governor-General and Mrs. Hnatyshyn, and the Prime Minister and Mrs. Mulroney, and to Canada's everlasting prosperity.
Thank you.

63.

Remarks at the Welcoming Ceremony on a State Visit to Mexico, Mexico City, September 25, 1991

President and Mrs. Carlos Salinas de Gortari, distinguished officials and citizens of Mexico,

It is truly a pleasure for me to visit the great country of Mexico, a land with a brilliant heritage of the Aztec and the Maya civilizations. I thank you, Mr. President, and the people of Mexico, for inviting me and my delegation to your beautiful country and for the warm hospitality you have extended toward us.

I consider it an honor that I am the first Korean head of state to make an official state visit to Latin America. I believe this visit will not only be a turning point in the development of bilateral relations between our two countries, but will also make a significant contribution to the relations between Korea and other Latin American states.

Korea and Mexico share the common ideals of freedom, peace and prosperity, and since the establishment of diplomatic relations in 1962, our two countries have maintained and developed close ties in many areas including politics, economics, and culture. The Korean people are especially grateful for the deep understanding and support that the Mexican government and people have shown us in the international arena.

The "Ibero America" summit talks that were held last July in Guadalajara highlighted the emergence of Mexico, under the government of President Salinas, as a key nation in this region. Mexico is playing a unique and important role in the development of the American continents. It is also stepping into a new era of greater prosperity thanks to the stimulation of regional free trade.

With its immense potential and dynamic growth, the Asia-Pacific region is emerging as a new center for global development. On the foundation of rapid growth, Korea is striving to increase its role and contribution to the commonwealth of this region.

The advancement of friendly and cooperative ties between Korea and Mexico will not only stimulate the prosperity of our two nations, but will also serve as the driving force behind the opening of a new century of "Pacific Prosperity."

During this visit, I am hoping to exchange candid views with President Salinas, who has displayed exceptional leadership in fostering solidarity among the people and in the development of Mexico. It is also my wish that through this visit there will be a significant improvement in the bilateral relations between Korea and Mexico as well as for the peace and prosperity of the Pacific and the world.

To our "amigos," the Mexican people, I bring a message of friendship from the Korean people, and thank you once again for your warm welcome.

64.

Remarks at the Dinner Held by President Carlos Salinas de Gortari of Mexico, Mexico City, September 25, 1991

President and Mrs. Carlos Salinas de Gortari, honored guests:

I would first like to thank you, Mr. President, for this invitation to Mexico, a land where the heritage of the Aztec and Maya civilizations, and the revolutionary spirit lives on. And I thank you also for the warm hospitality you have extended toward us.

I am sure everyone in my delegation, including myself, will have fond memories of this banquet you have held in our honor as a token of the friendship between our two countries.

I consider it a great privilege that you have awarded me the highest medallion of Mexico, and I am honored to accept it as a symbol of the close relations between the Republic of Korea and Mexico.

Mr. President,

In 1984, I visited Mexico to attend the General Assembly of the Association of National Olympic Committees as the chairman of the Organizing Committee for the Seoul Olympics. I was deeply impressed by the unique culture of Mexico that is a fine amalgamation of indigenous, European, and modern cultures. This reflects the creativity and wisdom of the Mexican people, and is testimony to their independent cultural heritage. It is indeed a pleasure for me to return after seven years to once again meet close friends and the great citizens of this beautiful land. But this time, I have the honor of visiting as the Korean head of state, the first to visit Mexico.

Today's Mexico is experiencing dynamic growth on a sturdy foundation of security and harmony thanks to the exceptional leadership of President Salinas. The national development plan implemented by the president is producing concrete results in Mexico's political, economical, and social development.

From the results of the general elections that were held last month, it is easy to see that you have overwhelming support from the Mexican people for your policies of nation-wide modernization and reform efforts. I agree wholeheartedly with the citizens of Mexico and offer you my respectful congratulations.

It is evident from the Ibero America summit talks and the Guadalajara Declaration last month, that you are leading the way in efforts for solidarity among Latin American nations and for their development. Mexico is becoming an increasingly important nation on the world scene.

Mr. President.

The Pacific region, in which Korea and Mexico are cohabitants, is brimming with the forces of development thanks to the region's plentiful natural and human resources. It possesses immense potential. The production in the Pacific region already accounts for over half of the total production in the world. Korea, situated in East Asia, on the Western rim of the Pacific, has undergone one of the most dynamic growths of any country in the postwar era.

Scholars have predicted that the hub of world civilization will shift over to the Pacific. We are living in a time when this prediction is becoming a reality. Pacific Rim countries, including Korea and Mexico, should improve mutual understanding through active interaction, and should stimulate trade and economic cooperation by cultivating mutually complementary economic structures.

Korea will do its utmost in building the framework for a more effective means of cooperation in the Asia-Pacific region. I welcome Mexico's efforts, such as the establishment of the Pacific Committee in 1988, to strengthen exchanges and cooperation between nations of this region. Korea and Mexico will be marching into the 21st century hand in hand, as valuable partners.

Mr. President.

Next year will mark the 30th anniversary of the establishment of diplomatic relations between Korea and Mexico. During that time, our two countries have developed close ties in many areas. The rate of increase in bilateral trade, for instance, has been dramatic, averaging 40 percent annually in the last five years. Mexico is, without dispute, our most important economic partner in Latin America.

Optimistic signs abound, such as the opening of a Common Economic Committee in April of this year, and the rapid increase in the investment by Korean businesses in Mexico.

By promoting free trade in North America, including Mexico, the region of economic cooperation is growing ever larger, and I hope this will also contribute to the strengthened relations between our two countries.

Mr. President.
As the 20th century draws to a close, we are witnessing revolutionary changes sweeping across the globe. Cold War structures that divided mankind for over 40 years during the postwar period have now all but disappeared. Communism has lost ground almost everywhere in the world, even in its principal nation, the Soviet Union.

Thanks to these momentous changes, Germany has achieved unification. And there is now a strong movement for peace and unification on the Korean Peninsula—the only country in the world still to be divided by the effects of the Cold War. The simultaneous membership of South and North Korea into the UN last week will no doubt provide stimulus for further unification efforts.

We are doing our utmost to bring about a peaceful and independent unification. The first step is mutual recognition, then the building of trust through dialogue and exchanges. I thank the government and people of Mexico for the support you have given us in the international arena, and hope that you will continue your support as Korea works toward unification.

Mr. President,
In Mexico's Museum of Human History, it is noted that the natives who created the magnificent ancient civilizations here on this continent were settlers that had crossed the Bering Straits tens of thousands of years ago from East Asia.

The history of Mexico's independence movement during the 19th century, and the revolution in the year 1910 gave impetus to Korea's own national movement. The art of Diego Rivera and the poetry of Octavio Paz are familiar to Koreans as well. And the song "Besame Mucho" is a favorite among Koreans, including myself.

The 1968 Mexico Olympic Games were a great source of inspiration to Korea and many developing nations of the world. In 1988, we were ourselves hosts in the Seoul Olympic Games, a marvelous festival of world harmony.

As these examples show, our two countries have much in common, with a shared historical and cultural background, along with common ideals of democracy, peace and prosperity.

I recall a phrase that describes Mexico as "a country as beautiful as the soap bubbles blown by children, a place where spirits lead people into the world of the future." Mexico is indeed a land of such beauty, and I believe the friendship between Korea and Mexico will be as everlasting as the blue "Los Piños" pine tree.

Ladies and gentlemen,

I would like to propose a toast to the health of President and Mrs. Carlos Salinas de Gortari, the endless prosperity of Mexico, and the everlasting friendship between our two countries.

Muchas gracias.

65.

Opening Remarks at the Joint News Conference with President George Bush of the United States, Seoul, January 6, 1992

I want to congratulate you on the good job you are doing. I am especially delighted to meet again with the journalists traveling with President Bush.

Today, I have had very useful talks with President Bush for an hour and a half. We have exchanged views on a wide range of issues, including the ongoing changes in the world and the shifting situation in the Asia-Pacific region.

President Bush and I have discussed the roles of the Republic of Korea and the United States in promoting durable peace and security on the Korean Peninsula, as well as ways to advance our bilateral cooperation. We have also exchanged frank and candid views on such questions as how to strengthen the free international trade system and how to expand economic and trade ties between the Republic of Korea and the United States.

At the outset, I expressed my deep appreciation for the outstanding leadership of President Bush in dismantling the Cold War structure and in freeing all mankind from nuclear terror. I emphasized that the roles of our two countries in promoting lasting peace and prosperity in the Asia-Pacific region and the cooperation between us are growing even more important. In the quest for those common goals, all nations in this region, including the Republic of Korea, ought to fulfill their responsibilities commensurate with their capabilities.

President Bush made clear that, as a Pacific power, the United States will continue to play a constructive role in advancing peace and common prosperity in this region.

I explained to him the initiatives and endeavors that we have put forth to ease tension and secure peace on the Korean Peninsula and the subsequent progress in relations between South and North Korea. President Bush reaffirmed the principle that the problems of the Korean Peninsula should be settled directly by the South and the North. He fully supported the accords that have recently been reached between the two parts of Korea.

President Bush and I jointly reaffirmed our shared position that North Korea must sign and ratify a nuclear safeguards agreement without delay and that the recently initialed Joint Declaration for a Non-nuclear Korean Peninsula must be put into force at the earliest possible date. We also discussed ways in which the United States' contacts with North Korea might be gradually expanded, provided that close consultation is maintained between our two countries and progress both on the North Korean nuclear issue and in intra-Korean relations is made.

President Bush once again stressed that the United States' security commitment to the Republic of Korea remains unchanged and will continue to be honored. We agreed that our two nations should further strengthen bilateral ties in the diplomatic, security, economic, scientific, technological and all other fields and further develop an enduring partnership so that both will prosper together through the 21st century.

Having reaffirmed the principle that common prosperity must be sought through free trade, we pledged that our two nations would closely cooperate to that end. I emphasized that my government is taking positive approaches to all areas with the aim of helping to bring the Uruguay Round of trade negotiations to a successful conclusion. As for negotiations in the agricultural sector, I explained that because of our peculiar situation, it will be exceedingly difficult to fully open our market in the immediate future and asked for America's understanding and cooperation in resolving the issue.

I also stressed the fact that our trade balance vis-a-vis the United States registered a deficit last year, and explained our current economic realities. I emphasized that a healthier development of the Korean economy will benefit the United States also. President Bush and I agreed to have the governments of both countries mutually support and promote Korean business activities in the United States and U.S. business activities in Korea. To that end, we agreed to institute Korea-U.S. Subcabinet Economic Consultations to develop ways to promote economic partnership between our two countries. We agreed on the need to further expand bilateral cooperation in the fields of science and technology also. Thus, a new Science and Technology Agreement and a Patents Secrecy Agreement were signed between our two countries this morning.

Ladies and gentlemen, let me ask you now to give President Bush, our guest of honor, an opportunity to speak.

66.

Remarks at the State Dinner in Honor of the President of the United States of America and Mrs. George Bush, Seoul, January 6, 1992

President and Mrs. Bush, distinguished guests, ladies and gentlemen,

I am very pleased to welcome President and Mrs. Bush and the members of the Presidential party. I am truly privileged to have such a distinguished group of American leaders here at Chong Wa Dae this evening.

We have just begun the new year with a resolution that lasting groundwork will be laid this year so that the 21st century will see an era of durable peace and prosperity, and we are highly honored and inspired by the fact that Korea's best friend, President Bush, came to our country at this particular juncture.

Mr. President,

Your strong leadership is always a source of inspiration and courage for nations around the world, just as it is for the American people.

You led a coalition of nations last year and successfully carried out a brilliant campaign to repel a wanton challenge against international peace and justice. You have also laid an important cornerstone for regional peace by bringing Arab and Israeli representatives together at the historic Middle East Peace Conference.

I pay my respects to you, Mr. President, for your dedicated efforts to build a new structure for international peace and stability.

Mr. President,

Freedom and democracy have finally triumphed over the ideological confrontation of the Cold War era.

The calls for freedom and democracy that swept across the world are rapidly turning into voices of hope everywhere for peace and prosperity.

Now, these calls and voices have finally reached the Korean Peninsula, too.

The Korean people are hopeful that on the basis of the recently signed South-North Accord we will be able to remove the barriers of rivalry and distrust between the two Koreas and attain a peaceful national unity through the promotion of exchanges and cooperation.

To ensure the stability of the Asia-Pacific region, reduction of tension and a structure for peace on the Korean Peninsula are essential.

As you pointed out, Mr. President, North Korea's development of nuclear weapons is a grave threat not only to the Korean Peninsula but also to the peace of the Asia-Pacific region.

We must therefore exert our utmost efforts to eliminate this threat.

In my efforts to discourage North Korea from developing nuclear weapons and to build a structure for peace on the Korean Peninsula, I have enunciated a Non-nuclear Korea Peace Initiative and declared that the Republic of Korea is completely nuclear-free. These measures of course have been taken in line with your courageous decision to make the world safer from the nuclear threat.

As a result of these efforts, significant progress was made late last year between the two Koreas in the form of an agreement on a Joint Declaration for a Nuclear-free Korean Peninsula.

In cooperation with the United States, we plan to continue to exert every effort to make North Korea submit to a comprehensive nuclear inspection by the International Atomic Energy Agency, and renounce development of nuclear weapons in accordance with the Joint Declaration for a Nuclear-free Korean Peninsula agreed on by the two Koreas.

Mr. President,

The Republic of Korea, despite many economic difficulties, will continue to uphold the principles of free trade and market economics.

Free trade and openness are important to our economic development as much as they are to the U.S. economy. We sincerely hope that the Uruguay Round negotiations will produce a satisfactory consensus. The Republic of Korea will continue active cooperation with the United States and other countries for a successful conclusion of the negotiations.

Today, the Asia-Pacific region, a region of dynamic growth and development, is about to enter into an era of increased cooperation for peace and common prosperity.

The peace and prosperity of countries in the Asia-Pacific region are highly interdependent, and continued economic growth of the United States is bound to have a significant impact on regional stability.

In this context, your Asian tour at this time is very timely and is certain to provide important momentum toward the promotion of economic cooperation among the Pacific-rim countries.

Mr. President,

Having struggled together through turbulent years of trials, tribulations and confrontation, the Republic of Korea and the United States have become the closest of friends and allies.

The Republic of Korea was able to cope with the many adversities of war, poverty and confrontation, and today has become the 12th largest trading nation in the world, largely owing to the support and assistance of the United States.

Every year, a great number of our businessmen, intellectuals, students, and visitors travel between our two countries, and we have developed a relationship that has become an inseparable part of our daily lives, in many realms: political, economic, cultural and scientific.

The Republic of Korea has now become a most trustworthy ally and friend of the United States and is a fully committed U.S. partner for a more prosperous world in the 21st century. The Korean people are truly proud of this.

Our two countries are partners for freedom and democracy, and we are partners for a new world order. We have today become partners for free trade and market economics that will bring common prosperity to all mankind.

The friendship and cooperation between our two countries are durable and our partnership will last beyond the day of Korean unification to a future when all mankind shall forever live in peace and prosperity.

Ladies and gentlemen,

Please rise and join me in a toast to the health and well-being of President and Mrs. Bush, to the prosperity of the United States, and to lasting partnership between the Republic of Korea and the United States.

Thank you.

APPENDICES

1.

Grand National Harmony and Progress Towards a Great Nation; Special Declaration on June 29, 1987

My dear fellow citizens,

I have now come to a firm conviction about the future of our nation. I have anguished long and hard over the genuine mission of politicians at this historic time when deep-seated conflicts and antagonisms have so accumulated among our citizens that they have erupted into a national crisis. I have also solicited the wisdom of people from various walks of life—academicians, journalists, businessmen, religious leaders, workers, and young people, including students, and have thus ascertained the will of the people.

Today, I stand before history and the nation with an extraordinary determination to help build a great homeland in which there is love and harmony among all segments and strata of the population, in which all are proud of being citizens and in which the government can acquire wisdom, courage and genuine strength from the people.

I will hereby forthrightly present my ideas. I intend to recommend them to President Chun Doo Hwan and am resolved to translate them into concrete action with the enthusiastic support of my party colleagues and the general public.

First, the Constitution should be expeditiously amended, through agreement between the government party and the opposition, to adopt a direct presidential election system, and presidential elections should be held under a new Constitution to realize a peaceful change of government in February 1988. This does not mean a change in my belief that a parliamentary cabinet system, under which the majority of the cabinet members are National Assemblymen directly elected by the people and under which the principles of democratic and responsible politics can be most faithfully realized through free and open dialogue and compromise, is the form of government best suited to enabling democracy to take hold in our country. However, if the majority of the people do not want it, even the best-conceived system will alienate the public, and the government which is born under it will not be able to dream and suffer together with the people.

Accordingly, I have come to the conclusion that a presidential election system must be adopted at this juncture in order to overcome social confusion and achieve national reconciliation. The people are the masters of the country and the people's will must come before everything else.

Second, in addition to switching to a direct presidential election system through constitutional revision, I think that to carry out elections democratically, it is necessary to also revise the Presidential Election Law so that freedom of candidacy and fair competition are guaranteed and so that the genuine verdict of the people can be given. A revised election law should also ensure maximum fairness and justness in election management, from the campaigns to the casting, opening, and counting of ballots.

Even under a direct election system, there should not be groundless character smearing and demagoguery to incite hostility, confusion, disorder and regional antagonisms, thereby undermining national stability and impeding genuine democratic development. There must be a solid framework to ensure that elections are bona fide competitions in policies and ideas.

Third, antagonisms and confrontations must be resolutely eradicated not only from our political community but also from all other sectors to achieve grand national reconciliation and unity. In this connection, I believe that Mr. Kim Dae-jung also should be amnestied and his civil rights restored, no matter what he has done in the past. At the same time, all those who are being detained in connection with the political situation should also be set free, except for those who have committed treason by repudiating the basic free and democratic order on which our survival and posterity hinges and a small number of people who have shaken the national foundation by committing homicide, bodily injury, arson and vandalism. I ardently hope that all those people will thus be able to return to society as democratic citizens.

There can be no present without a past. However, I believe it is important at this point in our history to create an occasion for all to rejoice heartily. In such an event, the next presidential elections will be elevated into a national festival, and the new government thus elected with solid and broad public support will be able to work even more effectively to build a great nation.

Fourth, human dignity must be respected even more greatly and the basic rights of citizens should be promoted and protected to the maximum. I hope that the forthcoming constitutional amendments will include all the strengthened basic rights clauses being proposed by the Democratic Justice Party, including a drastic extension of habeas corpus.

The government should take utmost care not to let human rights abuses occur. The Democratic Justice Party should make greater efforts to effectively promote human rights. For example, it should hold periodic meetings with the lawyers associations and other human rights groups to promptly learn of and redress human rights violations.

Fifth, to promote the freedom of the press, the relevant systems and practices must be drastically improved. The Basic Press Law, which may have been well meant but has nonetheless been criticized by most journalists, should promptly be either extensively revised or abolished and replaced by a different law. Newspapers should again be permitted to station their correspondents in the provinces, the press card system should be abolished and newspapers should be allowed to increase the number of their pages as they see fit. These and other necessary steps must be taken to guarantee the freedom of the press to the maximum.

The government cannot control the press nor should it attempt to do so. No restrictions should be imposed on the press except when national security is at risk. It must be remembered that the press can be tried only by an independent judiciary or by individual citizens.

Sixth, freedom and self-regulation must be guaranteed to the maximum in all other sectors also, because private initiative is the driving force behind diverse and balanced social development which in turn fuels national progress. In spite of the forthcoming processes of amending the Constitution, local councils should be elected and organized without any hitch according to schedule. The establishment of municipal and provincial councils should also be studied in concrete terms and carried out soon thereafter.

Colleges and universities—the institutions of higher learning—must be made self-governing and educational autonomy in general must be expeditiously put into practice. To that end, the personnel and budgetary policies and general administration of universities and colleges should be free of outside intervention. Enrollment and graduation systems should also be improved to allow them greater autonomy. Scholarship systems should be improved with sufficient budgetary provisions made so that good students need not be frustrated by financial difficulties.

Seventh, a political climate conducive to dialogue and compromise must be created expeditiously, with healthy activities of political parties guaranteed. A political party should be a democratic organization that presents responsible demands and policies to mold and crystalize the political opinion of the people. The state should exert its utmost effort to protect and nurture political parties, so long as they engage in sound activities and do not contravene such objectives. Within such a framework, political parties should abide by the laws of the nation and exercise their political capabilities to resolve social conflicts and contradictions through dialogue and compromise in an amicable and harmonious manner to forge and maintain national coherence. As long as there exists an opposition party which is intent on pressing its unilateral demands by all means, even through violence, the governing party cannot always make concession after concession.

Eighth, bold social reforms must be carried out to build a clean and honest society. In order that all citizens can lead a secure and happy life, crime against life and property, such as hooliganism, robbery and theft, must be stamped out, and deep-seated irrationalities and improprieties that still linger in our society must be eradicated. Groundless rumors, along with regional antagonism and black-and-white attitudes, should be banished forever to build a society in which mutual trust and love prevail. In that way, we must ensure that all citizens can live an active life in a stable social environment, free of anxiety and with pride and confidence. I believe that these are the immediate tasks which must be accomplished if we are to resolve the current difficult situation and project the nation forward.

My fellow countrymen,
On the strength of your expectations that there will be continued development rather than disruptions, I dare to make this proposal today in humble veneration of history and the people. These ideas stem from my genuine patriotism, and I am confident that they will blossom with support from all the people, not only President Chun and members of the Democratic Justice Party.

When these basic ideas have been accepted, additional details can be worked out. If they fail to be accepted, however, I want to make it very clear that I will resign from all public duties including the presidential candidacy and the chairmanship of the Democratic Justice Party.

My fellow countrymen,
The shining achievements of the government of the Fifth Republic should at no time be underestimated. We have begun to root democracy deep into the soil of our nation's constitutional history by implementing a single term presidency. We have realized a trade surplus by stabilizing prices and improving our international competitiveness. We have drastically bolstered national security and obtained the right to host the Olympic Games.

Under no circumstances must we neglect to safeguard and promote the liberal democratic system. The task of peacefully changing administrations is the immediate task at hand. Furthermore, now that the Olympics are approaching, all of us are responsible for avoiding the national disgrace of dividing ourselves and thus causing the world to ridicule us.

With the sacred right to vote at hand, let us all work together to create a society where young people develop their capabilities to realize their ideas, where workers and farmers can work free of anxiety, where businessmen exert even greater creative efforts and where politicians exercise the art of debate and compromise to work out the nation's future. I pledge my utmost efforts to help create a dynamic, developing and genuinely democratic society where law and order prevail.

This country belongs to us. It is our historic duty to both exert our efforts and exercise restraint and wisdom to more successfully develop the country which was founded and nurtured with the blood of our forefathers and the lives of the patriots, and to proudly hand it over to the next generation. I sincerely hope that national wisdom will be pooled to demonstrate to the world that the Korean people will not go backward but will go forward to make a contribution to world history.

My fellow countrymen, my party colleagues and opposition politicians,

I earnestly pray that my genuinely well-meant proposal will be accepted and will solve our current problems, that it will be a breakthrough in the effort to create a great nation where all our people can live stable and happy lives.

Thank you.

2.

We Can Do It; Inaugural Address, February 25, 1988

My sixty million compatriots; President Yun Po Sun and President Choi Kyu Ha, both of whom have been so instrumental in developing constitutional government; President Chun Doo Hwan, who has set a historic precedent of a peaceful change of administration; congratulatory envoys; distinguished guests,

Today, we gather in front of this sacred hall of the people to proclaim a new beginning, an era of hope which will see Korea, once a peripheral country in East Asia, take a central position in the international community.

As I assume the presidency forty years after a democratic government was first established in this country, there is a strong wind of change blowing over the land. Nevertheless, I think we should pause to remember our ancestors, who struggled constantly to shape the nation. With an indomitable spirit of independence, they created our illustrious culture and maintained our national integrity uninterrupted, overcoming numerous foreign invasions and other ordeals. We should emulate their great spirit.

I think we should also pay tribute to those persons whose hands show the marks of hard work in the face of adversity. We grew up in a world of poverty and war, and our hands were empty. However, with our empty hands, we toiled with enthusiasm and single-minded determination to improve our lot. As a result, this country has emerged as a dynamic, newly industrializing nation. It has grown into a full-fledged democracy with the start of a tradition of peaceful changes of government.

We have thus proved to be a truly great people. Korea's extraordinary inherent capabilities are an inexhaustible source of encouragement for all of us who are endeavoring to propel the country into the ranks of the advanced democratic countries before the twentieth century is over. As I take on the challenge of leading the nation toward that goal, I am profoundly grateful to all those whose hard work has made Korea what it is today.

My fellow citizens,

The Korean people have faced numerous challenges and have triumphed over all of them with courage and tenacity. Now we have a new challenge—to create a vibrant era of national self-esteem. I hereby solemnly declare before the nation that just such an era has opened.

My fellow citizens,

We can do it, and we must.

We must successfully meet that challenge by reforming ourselves. A bird must itself break out of its egg before it can learn to fly. Now is the time for us, too, to break out of our shell of old habits and, with the creative enthusiasm that characterized the pioneers who made something out of nothing, create a unified, powerful and self-respecting nation by enabling all citizens to enjoy democratic rights and privileges, as well as prosperity. It is certainly a time for change, renovation and quantum leaps—a time for dynamic progress.

Accordingly, the time has come to put an end to excessive internal squabbling. The past can undoubtedly be put to good use as a mirror by which to examine ourselves, but it should not be a shackle to hamper indefinitely our progress toward a bright future. The great democratic choice made by the people last December eliminated the sources of strife that had built up over the past forty years. Let us here and now bury regional antagonism, partisan and factional egoism and personal resentment. If all of us yield a little in the spirit of reconciliation and forgive each other and bury the residue of hatred, our children will be able to enjoy the abundant fruit of democracy and welfare.

Fellow citizens,

From this moment on we will sail full steam ahead toward a land of hope brimming with freedom and happiness. We have a new chart of democracy and a new compass of national reconciliation that you, my fellow countrymen, examined and agreed to use when you elected me president.

With the launching of the new Republic, we will sail steadfastly toward democracy. This is not at all because democracy is the fashionable word today, but because democracy represents just values that give dignity and worth to our lives. Only a democratic society will guarantee freedom, dignity and full participation.

The day when freedom and human rights could be slighted in the name of economic growth and national security has ended. The day when repressive force and torture in secret chambers were tolerated is over. At the same time, the day when confusion was irresponsibly created on the pretext of freedom and participation must also come to an end. We will have an era of mature democracy, when human rights are inviolable and freedom with responsibility prevails, so that both economic development and national security are assured.

We are determined to create a society in which honest and hardworking people have nothing to fear and can live dignified and productive lives. We will also create a democratic body politic in which all citizens can creatively participate in national development as the true masters of the nation.

With the new Constitution incorporating the will of the people now going into effect, I declare that the new administration will be a government of the people. It will open an era of democracy in which each citizen can reach his full potential. It will help make every segment of our diversified pluralistic society free and dynamic and able to exert its inherent rights to the greatest possible extent.

The people want an honest and ethical government. I intend to give them one. All leaders, including myself, will be honest and truthful. Promises to the people will be kept without fail.

The cheers of support I heard in the recent campaign have given me strength and the criticisms have been good medicine. I will listen to the views of those who did not vote for me and will reflect them in government policies without fail. I will not disregard their criticisms. In this spirit, I earnestly appeal to the opposition parties and others who opposed me. With a shared concern for the affairs of state, let us start a dialogue; and with a spirit of cooperation, let us work together to make democracy work, to unify the nation and to bring prosperity to everyone.

Fellow citizens,

Our goal is national reconciliation. The history of development since the 1970s teaches the grim lesson that no matter how high or sustained economic growth may be, it alone cannot ensure that we will attain our ideal of a harmonious, balanced and happy society. Of course, high growth has raised our living standard and transformed the agriculture-dominated traditional Korean society into a pluralistic, industrial one.

At the same time, this has created obstacles all along our path. Growing disparities between social strata and geographical regions have bred strife and schism, seriously undermining national cohesion. Unless this problem is effectively addressed, our endeavors to build a democracy ensuring the welfare of all may be frustrated. Accordingly, we all desire reconciliation warm enough to melt the ice of conflict and divisiveness.

The time has come for the government and all segments of society to strive in concert to achieve a just and fair distribution of income, so that every citizen can share the fruits of growth. I will ensure that no one will be disadvantaged or, on the other hand, receive unjustifiable favors because of birth, sex or political persuasion.

Individuals who have not received a fair share because of the emphasis on the development of the nation as a whole will no longer be sacrificed. Efforts will be made to see that the sick are treated and the poor and weak are given aid and support. The creative initiative of businessmen and the principle of free enterprise will be further encouraged, while the rights and interests of farmers, fishermen, workers and small- and medium-sized merchants and industrialists will be promoted to the maximum extent.

Everything possible will be done to provide the young, who still shoulder the future of the nation, with the best possible education. Meticulous efforts will be made to foster the ideals and dreams of young people and to shape a progressive society that constantly reforms and renews itself. Since the new era that we are going to create will, before long, have to be turned over to the care of the next generation, their dreams and passions will be an invaluable stimulus for progress. We will energetically promote academic studies, culture, and the arts, so that there will be a cultural renaissance to match our economic miracle. Thus all citizens will have access to rich cultural experiences.

All citizens will be encouraged to make life better by trying to understand and help their neighbors. My administration will resolutely reject any form of privilege, irregularity and corruption that obstructs social justice and deepens conflict. I intend to stamp out violence, property speculation and inflation. The era of the great common man will feature a society in which unjust accumulation or concentration of wealth is done away with, and in which everyone profits by honest work and can thus plan for the future with hope. We must now open a great era for the common man through democratic reforms and national reconciliation.

However, national reconciliation cannot be achieved by government policies alone; it must grow in the heart of every citizen. Accordingly, I ask my fellow citizens not to leave the task of national reconciliation in the hands of the government alone. Let us all reflect on the issue ourselves and approach it from a realization that it must be first planted in the heart of each of us. Those who are strong must help the weak. Those who have plenty should show self-restraint and magnanimity toward those who have less.

Fellow citizens,

The Seoul Olympics, which will be a grand event for all Koreans and a festival of peace for all the five billion people on earth, are fast approaching. On this occasion, when Korea will burst on the world scene, there should be no family squabbles. Let us make joint, concerted efforts to make the Seoul Olympics long remembered by the inhabitants of the global community as the most successful.

Let me emphasize, moreover, that the greatest historic significance of the Seoul Olympics is that it will bring the day of unification closer. The sonorous chorus of reconciliation which will emanate from Seoul when East and West meet together for the first time in twelve years will be a signal to the entire world that an era of unification is finally opening on the Korean Peninsula.

In response to that great chorus, the Republic of Korea will intensify its diplomatic efforts to promote international peace and co-operation with all nations in the world. While further consolidating ties with Japan, the United States and other Western countries, we will further cultivate friendships with the Third World. We will broaden the channel of international co-operation with the continental countries with which we have hitherto had no exchanges, with the aim of pursuing a vigorous northern diplomacy. Improved relations with countries with ideologies and social systems different from ours will contribute to stability, peace and common prosperity in East Asia. Such a northward-looking diplomacy should also lead to the gateway of unification. Here I appeal to my fellow countrymen who yearn for an early end to the territorial division. Unification is a goal which we cannot forget, even in our sleep. We cannot be optimistic about attaining it but we need not be pessimistic, either. We should simply do our best to reach it. Coincidentally, our national self-esteem has grown much stronger. It is going to be the major driving force behind our endeavors to achieve unification as well as eminence in the world. We must thus nurture our democratic capability on the strength of national self-esteem, so that we can go through the gateway of unification while strengthening national security.

We must keep in mind the object lesson that opportunity comes first not to those who wait for it but to those who are well prepared to seize it. If only I can perceive a path to peace and reunification on the Korean Peninsula, I am prepared to go anywhere on earth for a sincere dialogue with anyone.

I propose to North Korea that they discard the wild dream of compelling the free citizens of this land, who have internalized democratic values, to accept their doctrinaire ideology that has been rejected even by other communist countries; and that they acknowledge that dialogue, not violence, is the most direct route to ending the division and bringing about unification.

I reaffirm that the door to dialogue will always be open. In keeping with our new national self-esteem, let us have dialogue. Let us coexist peacefully and on that basis cooperate so that spring can come to the Demilitarized Zone. In that way, let us begin to pave the way for unification together.

I would like to say this to other nations interested in Korean unification. Fundamentally, South and North Korea—the parties immediately involved—will work to resolve the Korean question peacefully through democratic means. However, we will welcome to Seoul without fear or favor any messenger of peace and unification from any place on earth.

Fellow citizens,

The twentieth century began for us with suffering and frustration, but as it comes to an end we have the wherewithal to overcome anything. The vision of a unified Korea looming just beyond the horizon of the twentieth century is beckoning us. When our soaring capabilities and self-esteem are fused into a burst of incandescent energy, Korea will certainly emerge as a brilliant young giant in the world and will be a leader in the Asia-Pacific Age. But let us not forget how many patriotic ancestors and compatriots have had to sacrifice themselves and toil so that we could have this excellent opportunity.

The era of the common man has arrived. From now on, everyone, not just a single person, will have a say in what is good for the country. This will be an era during which cooperation among many people with old-fashioned common sense will be more important than the outstanding talents of a few. It will also be an era in which national development will directly translate into freedom, affluence and well-being for all individual citizens.

Fellow citizens,

Today, I stand on this grand platform at the behest of all of you, my fellow countrymen. As it was raised by you, it does not separate me from you. Bearing that fact in mind, I vow today to be a president who shares your heartbeat and thoughts.

I do not want to be a president who bullies his fellow countrymen. But I will not be one who is bullied by mobs, either. The kind of president that I truly want to be is one who rubs shoulders with his fellow citizens and shares their dreams and pains.

We are now lined up on the starting line of democracy. Having built this glorious platform together, let us all take energetic forward strides together with courage, drive and confidence in the future.

Let us march toward "a land of hope, brimming with liberty, equality, peace and happiness"—to quote the words of a much-loved song.

My fellow citizens,
Let us march together.

3.

A Single National Community; Special Declaration in the Interest of National Self-Respect, Unification and Prosperity, July 7, 1988

My sixty million compatriots,

Today, I am going to enunciate the policy of the Sixth Republic to achieve the peaceful unification of our homeland, a long-standing goal dear to the hearts of the entire Korean people.

We have been suffering the pain of territorial division for almost half a century. This national division has inflicted numerous ordeals and hardships upon the Korean people, thus hindering national development. Dismantling the barrier separating the South and the North and building a road to a unified and prosperous homeland is a duty that history has imposed on every Korean alive today.

The South and the North, divided by different ideologies and political systems, have gone through a fratricidal war. The divided halves of the single Korean nation have distrusted, denounced and antagonized each other since the day of territorial partition, and this painful state has yet to be remedied. Though the division was not brought about by our own volition, it is our responsibility to achieve national unification through our independent capabilities.

We must all work together to open a bright era of South-North reconciliation and cooperation. The time has come for all of us to endeavor in concert to promote the well-being and prosperity of the Korean people as a whole.

Today, the world is entering an age of reconciliation and cooperation transcending ideologies and political systems. A brave new tide of openness and exchange is engulfing peoples of different historical and cultural backgrounds. I believe we have now come to a historic moment when we should be able to find a breakthrough toward lasting peace and unification on the

Korean Peninsula which is still threatened with the danger of war amidst persisting tension and confrontation.

My fellow compatriots,

The fundamental reason why the tragic division has still to be overcome is that both the South and the North have been regarding each other as an adversary, rather than realizing that both halves of Korea belong to the same national community, so that inter-Korean enmity has continued to intensify. Having lived in a single ethnic community, the Korean people have shaped an illustrious history and cultural traditions, triumphing over almost ceaseless trials and challenges with pooled national strength and wisdom.

Accordingly, developing relations between the South and the North as members of a single national community to achieve common prosperity is a shortcut to realizing a prosperous and unified homeland. This is also the path to national self-esteem and integration.

Now the South and the North must tear down the barrier that divides them and implement exchanges in all fields. Positive step after positive step must be taken to restore mutual trust and strengthen our bonds as members of one nation.

With the realization that we both belong to a single community, we must also put a stop to confrontation on the international scene. I hope that North Korea will contribute to the community of nations as a responsible member and that this will accelerate the opening and development of North Korean society. South and North Korea should recognize each other's place in the international community and cooperate with each other in the best interests of the entire Korean people.

My sixty million fellow compatriots,

Today, I promise to make efforts to open a new era of national self-esteem, unification and prosperity by building a social, cultural, economic and political community in which all members of Korean society can participate on the principles of independence, peace, democracy and welfare. To that end, I declare to the nation and to the world that the following policies will be pursued:

- We will actively promote exchanges of visits between the people of South and North Korea, including politicians, businessmen, journalists, religious leaders, cultural leaders, artists, academics, sportsmen and students, and will make necessary arrangements to ensure that Koreans residing overseas can freely visit both parts of Korea.
- Even before the successful conclusion of the North-South Red Cross talks, we will promote and actively support, from a humanitarian viewpoint, all measures which can assist separated families in their efforts to find out

whether their family members in the other part of the Peninsula are still alive and to trace their whereabouts, and will also promote exchanges of correspondence and visits between them.
- We will open doors for trade between South and North Korea, which will be regarded as internal trade within the national community.
- We hope to achieve a balanced development of the national economy with a view to enhancing the quality of life for all Korean people—in both the South and the North—and will not oppose nations friendly with us trading with North Korea, provided that this trade does not involve military goods.
- We hope to bring to an end counter-productive diplomacy characterized by competition and confrontation between the South and the North, and to cooperate in ensuring that North Korea makes a positive contribution to the international community. We also hope that representatives of South and North Korea will contact each other freely in international forums and will co-operate to pursue the common interests of the whole Korean nation.
- To create an atmosphere conducive to durable peace on the Korean Peninsula, we are willing to cooperate with North Korea in its efforts to improve relations with countries friendly to us, including the United States and Japan; and in tandem with this, we will continue to seek improved relations with the Soviet Union, China and other socialist countries.

I trust that North Korea will respond positively to the measures outlined above. If the North shows a positive attitude, I should like to make it clear that even more progressive measures will be taken one after another.

I hope that this declaration today will serve to open a new chapter in the development of inter-Korean relations and will lead to unification. I believe that if the entire 60 million Korean people pool their wisdom and strength, the South and the North will be integrated into a single social, cultural and economic community before this century is out. On that basis, I am confident that we will accomplish the great task of uniting in a single national entity in the not so very distant future.

4.

Feelings of Great National Pride; Remarks on the Eve of the Seoul Olympic Games, September 14, 1988

My fellow citizens at home and abroad,

The Seoul Olympics, for which we have been preparing so wholeheartedly over the past seven years, are now set to begin in three days' time.

People from all over the world are gathering in Seoul. Inhabitants of the global village are coming together in spite of differences of race, language, culture, religion, ideology and political persuasion. They are rising above any and all barriers that have separated them and are resolved to make the Seoul Olympics a festival of friendship and harmony.

Now that all preparations for the Seoul Games, due to become the largest Olympics ever, have been concluded, we are counting down to the lighting of the sacred Olympic flame.

This evening, I wish to share, not only with my fellow citizens but with all people on earth, the joy of holding here in Seoul an Olympiad that will genuinely be a grand festival of global harmony as it was originally conceived to be; the Seoul Olympics are bringing the East and the West together for the first time in twelve years. I appeal for even more enthusiastic involvement until the Seoul Olympic flame is extinguished so that the Seoul Games will be the most magnificent Olympiad ever.

I am confident that the Seoul Olympics will be the most successful in athletic terms also, with young men and women from 160 nations putting forth their best efforts and setting numerous world and Olympic records.

The Seoul Olympics are striving to attain the lofty dreams of the Olympic movement to forge common ideals for all mankind by bringing the East and West—and Korea and the world—together not only in sports but also in culture, the arts and learning.

I believe every one of us is filled with overwhelming excitement and soaring hope because of the fact that this festival of world peace is taking place on the Korean Peninsula, which only a generation ago was a bloody battlefield on which young people from around the world fought over ideological differences and which is still haunted by dangers of violence. To plant the seed of lasting peace in this land, the Seoul Olympic flame will burn brightly, symbolizing a resounding message of peace and harmony among all mankind. The sacred flame will also light the path to reconciliation and unification for our people who have been pained by territorial division, a subsequent fratricidal war and all the grim consequences.

My fellow citizens at home and abroad,
The Olympics first filled us with deep emotions in 1936 when Sohn Ki-jong won the laurel crown in the marathon in Berlin, although he had to run with the flag of another nation on his chest. People of that older generation were thus inspired with a sense of national self-confidence that we could also do as well as others. At the same time, they cried out from the pain and anger of the loss of national sovereignty.

Only half a century later, we have grown into an independent nation capable of hosting the largest Olympics ever. This has been the result of decades of hard work and dedication of the people who have made today's national development possible. At this moment, I want to share with my fellow countrymen a feeling of pride over the continuously expanding abilities of the nation. I am confident that the strength of the people will ensure a safe and flawless Olympic Games.

My fellow countrymen at home and abroad,
Throughout history, no festival has attracted more world attention than the Olympics. At this moment, the eyes and ears of the five billion people on earth are turned to us and our country. Perhaps there has been no previous occasion in which we have been so united, with one mind and heart, amidst rising hope and joy.

Our Olympic officials and athletes have been working and training hard day and night over the past seven years. Tens of thousands of people from Korea and abroad are now serving as volunteer workers without any remuneration. Both the governing party and the political opposition, and all other segments of society, have gladly joined hands in the interest of the national task of hosting the Games. All our citizens are spontaneously participating in and supporting the Olympics as their own important business; all are co-operating for the success of the Games in spite of any inconvenience attendant on them. This evening, I wish to express my deep gratitude to my fellow citizens for everything they have done and are doing for the success of the Seoul Olympics.

Having personally experienced numerous domestic and international trials from the time of bidding for the 24th Olympic Games until the present, and having been constantly concerned for the success of the Games, I am now deeply moved to observe the proud present state of affairs. Together with my fellow countrymen, I feel confident of the nation's bright future.

Out of the rubble of war, our people have worked an economic miracle that has astonished the world. They have overcome a national crisis by creating a democratic political miracle. Now our people are about to achieve a cultural miracle on the Han River by staging a more magnificent Olympic Games than any previous ones, most of which were hosted by industrially advanced nations. With the Seoul Olympics, we will arrive at the threshold of the developed world, the entry to which has been our long-standing national goal. The Seoul Games will also provide a powerful impetus to improving our relations with all the nations of the world, and especially with North Korea, thereby opening the door to unification.

Let all of us living today do our utmost to make the Seoul Olympics an illustrious and proud event to be remembered throughout our lives. Let us thus join hands with all people on earth to create a world filled with hope, peace and prosperity.

5.

Dialogue for Peace; Address at the Forty-Third Session of the General Assembly of the United Nations, October 18, 1988

Mr. President, Mr. Secretary-General, distinguished delegates,

Forty-three years ago, as World War II came to an end, the world began taking steps toward the creation of the United Nations with great hope for lasting peace. The new body was to be entrusted with charting a new international order of peace and stability.

In my country, the end of World War II gave rise to overwhelming jubilation and hope as the Korean people were liberated from the yoke of colonial rule and recovered the land which had been theirs for thousands of years. The joy of liberation, however, soon turned to despair over the tragic division of our homeland. As a matter of convenience in the process of disarming the defeated colonial forces, a line of artificial division was drawn through the midsection of the Korean Peninsula along the 38th parallel. The decision to divide our land, dictating the fate of the nation in the decades to come, was made against the will of the Korean people. Overnight, this cruel division turned brother against brother and plunged the Korean Peninsula into a violent storm of the Cold War.

On a peaceful Sunday morning in June 1950, war broke out on the Korean Peninsula, and soon the whole nation was in flames. Over the next three years, tens of thousands of young people from twenty countries entered the war and eventually over three million lives fell victim to the clash of ideologies. The war also reduced nearly everything on the Peninsula to ashes.

Experiencing the battle as a volunteer soldier still wearing my high school uniform, I saw the young and innocent die in the flames of war and came to long for peace and reconciliation. I also came to believe that we must make all possible efforts to end the division and confrontation which were causing such great suffering in our nation.

Dialogue for Peace 311

The conflict ceased in 1953 with the signing of an armistice, but this did not bring about genuine peace. A state of tension and confrontation between the two parts of Korea has persisted ever since. Even though many seasons have come and gone, and the world has changed dramatically over the decades, this hostile confrontation along the Korean Armistice Line has remained frozen in time and continues to be a source of danger which could trigger hostilities involving the whole world.

Beyond these political and strategic implications, the human costs of this standoff have been enormous. Ever since the war, millions of family members—fathers and mothers, husbands and wives, brothers and sisters—have been separated by the North-South divide, unable to exchange even letters or phone calls. The emotional strains caused by this situation run deep in both the North and the South of Korea.

Is there no way out of this impasse?

I stand here today to answer this question with a message of hope. We must henceforth do everything possible to hasten the coming of the springtime of peace and reconciliation on the Korean Peninsula. In this connection, I wish to welcome, on behalf of the government and people of the Republic of Korea, the timely decision of the General Assembly to adopt the agenda item entitled "Promotion of peace, reconciliation and dialogue on the Korean Peninsula."

I should also like to congratulate you, Mr. President, on your election as President of the General Assembly. I hope that this session of the General Assembly will produce fruitful results.

Mr. President,

In the world today, we can see movements toward openness and reconciliation. The Cold War conflicts which dominated the international scene since the end of the Second World War have begun to surrender to the power of human reason and common decency. Mankind's expectations are changing from confrontation to coexistence, from antagonism to reconciliation. I join all of you in welcoming these trends.

I would also like to express my gratitude and respect to His Excellency the Secretary-General, Mr. Javier Perez de Cuellar, for his insight and leadership, which have helped achieve a cease-fire in the eight-year-old Gulf War. Thanks to the secretary-general's role, all of us have greater confidence and expectations regarding this bulwark of peace. The Nobel Peace Prize just awarded to the United Nations Peace-Keeping Forces is a testimony to this.

In Afghanistan, Cambodia, Namibia and the Western Sahara, steps are being taken toward peaceful resolution of outstanding conflicts. Furthermore, it is highly encouraging that through their summit meetings, President Reagan and General Secretary Gorbachev have been able to reduce the number of deadly weapons capable of annihilating mankind.

Mr. President,

I have come here in the spirit of "harmony and progress", the theme of the Seoul Olympiad which ended exactly two weeks ago. The XXIV Olympic Games were a great festival of cooperation and understanding, in which young people from 160 countries gathered together despite differences of ideology, race and religion. Furthermore, the East and the West met in sporting arenas for the first time in twelve years at the Seoul Olympiad.

As one of the most successful Olympics ever, the Seoul Games instilled in all of us the hope that at last peace and reconciliation are beginning to spread throughout the world. Still, it is ironic that this wonderful festival of peace should be held in a land where the danger of conflict still looms large. But this also gives us great hope for the future. In fact, the historical drama I am referring to must be seen as a part of the larger global development that is being engendered by man's aspirations for peace and common prosperity. I would like to take this opportunity to express gratitude to the peoples of all the countries whose participation and support helped make the Seoul Olympiad a successful and safe festival for all mankind.

Only a generation ago, the Korean nation lay in ruins, shackled by great suffering, hunger and poverty. We have overcome these adversities and made great progress through diligent work mixed with blood and tears. We are proud of our achievements, which we believe have contributed to tapping wellsprings of harmony among diverse peoples. It is also our sincere wish that these achievements offer hope and courage to all people in developing nations who are struggling in similar circumstances.

Only three decades ago, we were a poor, agrarian society dependent on other nations' help for survival. We were able to transform ourselves into a newly industrializing nation only through our people's great desire to achieve, together with a passion for learning. We also took advantage of an open and competitive political and economic system which allows individuals to achieve their highest potential. Mankind's inviolate rights and inborn creativity are essential elements for making social progress. International trade also has played an important role in our rapid economic growth. As the twelfth largest trading nation in the world, we are keenly aware of the fact that the growth of world trade has helped promote the rise in income and employment of trading partners. In this, the Republic of Korea has been especially fortunate. So, although the world brought national division and other trials to Korea, it also made it possible for us to grow and make substantial progress.

There are undoubtedly many problems facing mankind today, but it can be discerned, nevertheless, that progress is being made toward reconciliation, peace and prosperity. In order for man's hope to survive and progress to be realized, we must spare no effort to promote openness and mutual exchanges, cooperation and reconciliation. There is no alternative. Isolation and confrontation will bring only calamity and suffering to every corner of this global village.

As far as the Korean people are concerned, we believe we have been able to progress through international cooperation and openness toward others. That is why we are looking to the future with optimism and confidence that we will eventually achieve democracy, prosperity and national reunification for all Koreans on the Peninsula.

There is vitality in every corner of the Republic of Korea today as well as in every individual, thanks to the freedoms protected by our social system. I am sure that this new vitality will accelerate our progress and bring nearer the springtime of peace and reconciliation on the Korean Peninsula.

Mr. President,

Today our world stands at an important turning point that marks off one era from another. It has been said that the only thing that does not change is the inevitability of change itself. The world of confrontation and conflict is giving way to a world of détente, a trend which is taking place right here at the United Nations. Serious efforts are also commencing to bring peace and a relaxation of tension to the Korean Peninsula, one of the last arenas of the Cold War.

The distrust left behind by the Korean War gave rise to the confrontation between North and South Korea. During the 35 years since the Armistice Agreement, enormous military forces have continued to confront each other across the Armistice Line. In order to put an end to this hostile standoff, there is no alternative but to build mutual trust by engaging in exchange and cooperation and destroying the wall that separates us. To achieve this, we need a fresh approach. And that is precisely what I unveiled on July 7 this year.

I have declared that North and South Korea should immediately end all forms of hostile, confrontational relations. For instance, we should immediately cease publicly attacking each other. I have made clear that we are determined to pursue a partnership with North Korea. Our cultural and historical unity demands that we devote ourselves to the pursuit of common prosperity and mutual well-being for all Koreans.

In the same declaration, I proposed that we allow not only the reunion of millions of separated family members, but also free exchanges among political, economic and religious leaders as well as ordinary citizens. I have taken concrete steps to pave the way for free trade between the northern and southern sides of Korea. We must transform the North-South Korean relationship so that we can reconnect every roadway, whether major highway or little path, liking the two sides which remains disconnected now. Then we shall be able to develop our common land, combining our human, technological and financial resources.

If there are difficulties for North Koreans in opening their doors just now,

I believe that we could work together toward this end by building a "city of peace" in the Demilitarized Zone. Within such a city, family members who have remained separated for more than three decades could freely reunite. Broad trade and other kinds of exchanges could also be facilitated by establishing in the new "city of peace" such venues as a home for national culture, a center for scholarly exchanges, and a trade center.

Similarly, I stated in the same July 7 Declaration that we are determined to end confrontation with North Korea in our external relations. It is our sincere hope that North Korea may participate fully in the international community. Doing so can only benefit the North Korean people, not harm them. Within the world community, the North and the South must recognize each other and cooperate to promote the common interest of the entire nation.

It is our wish that our allies and friends will contribute to the progress and opening of North Korea by engaging P'yŏngyang in expanding relations. It is also our belief that those socialist countries with close ties to North Korea should continue to maintain positive relations and cooperate with North Korea even as they improve their relations with us.

The pursuit of mutual respect and prosperity through increasing cooperation, however, is not our ultimate goal. It is a necessary process which we must go through in order to build the relationship of trust essential for the nation's reunification. When such a relationship is firmly established, we can look forward to realizing peaceful unification.

Mr. President,

On the anniversary of our national liberation last August, I proposed to North Korean President Kim Il-sung that we hold direct talks. Since the Peninsula became divided, both sides have put forward many different proposals concerning peace and reunification. But what is necessary now is that the leaders of both sides who hold the ultimate responsibilities in their areas meet together without setting any preconditions. We must initiate discussions with a new spirit of openness and explore together possible avenues of compromise acceptable to both sides. We must find common ground on which to build institutions for peace and create a single national community. Hence I have taken particular notice of the fact that President Kim Il-sung has reacted to my proposal for a North-South Korean summit meeting. I hope I can visit P'yŏngyang as soon as possible. When the summit meeting does take place, I would like to propose that we agree to a declaration of non-aggression or non-use of force in order to better construct a framework for mutual trust and security. In order to end the military confrontation which has now lasted for more than three decades and to build a new relationship dedicated to shared peace and prosperity, we need to create a new basic framework for progress. Creating such a framework, of course, can be accomplished only at the level of direct contact between the leaders of the North and the South. In this connection, I want to make it absolutely clear—even before a non-aggression declaration is made with the northern side—that the Republic of Korea will never use force first against the North.

We cannot expect lasting peace on the Korean Peninsula without ending the current military confrontation. I propose that at our summit meeting we discuss sincerely and resolve all the problems raised by either or both sides with regard to disarmament, arms control and other military matters. We must also explore institutional structures for peaceful relations, mutual contacts and cooperative ventures, and, of course, ways of bringing about reunification. We can at the same meeting also search for concrete ways to transform the Armistice Agreement into a permanent peace arrangement.

Mr. President,
Clearly the problems between North and South Korea must be dealt with and resolved by the independent efforts of the Korean people themselves. But due to Korea's geopolitical situation, the problem of lasting peace on the Korean Peninsula cannot be considered in total isolation from its relations with the surrounding nations. If peace is to prevail on the Korean Peninsula, not only must the northern and the southern Korean sides reach rapprochement, but each of them must build and maintain more rational and normal relations with all the nations that have interests in peace on the Korean Peninsula. The Republic of Korea will continue to maintain and expand close cooperation with her traditional allies and friends, including the United States. In particular, we will continue our consultations and common efforts for the maintenance of peace and stability on the Peninsula.

In tandem with such efforts, we are also taking positive steps to improve our relations with various countries, including the People's Republic of China, the Union of Soviet Socialist Republics, and many East European nations with which we have in the past had only remote relationships because of our ideological differences. By conducting normal relations with each other under the principles of equality and mutual respect, all the nations of the world will contribute to mutual prosperity. This also serves the cause of world peace, since through dialogue and mutual understanding, nations can work to eliminate sources of conflict while cementing friendship and partnership. It is from this perspective that I welcome as an encouraging development the fact that socialist countries such as China and the Soviet Union are showing a forward-looking attitude in recent months concerning mutual exchanges and cooperation with the Republic of Korea in a number of fields.

I find it significant that China, a nation which has traditionally been a good neighbor of Korea, is moving to overcome the wall of separation that has lasted for nearly half a century and is expanding its mutual exchanges and cooperation with the Republic of Korea. I have also taken careful notice of the positive signals being made by General Secretary Gorbachev of the Soviet Union.

At the same time, we will continue to deepen our cooperative relationships with developing countries and, in fact, intend to strengthen our political, economic and cultural ties with many nations of the Third World and the Non-Aligned Movement. It is our intense desire to do all that we can to share our developmental experience and technical resources with developing nations. To be able to contribute to the development of the Third World would give immense satisfaction to the Korean people, who are themselves living in a developing country.

Mr. President,

The Asia-Pacific region is marching toward a new era of prosperity. This is taking place through the strengthening of international cooperation as well as through the strong will of the peoples of the region to achieve progress based on their infinite potential and dynamism. Within the Pacific Rim, Northeast Asia is the cradle of age-old Oriental civilizations. Yet this region has challenged world peace as it endured a century of conflicts—the Sino-Japanese War, the Russo-Japanese War, the Pacific War and the Korean War.

It is my belief that without peace in Northeast Asia there cannot be peace in the world, and without cooperation among the nations of the area an era of Pacific prosperity cannot commence. Therefore I take this opportunity to propose a consultative conference for peace between the United States of America, the Union of Soviet Socialist Republics, the People's Republic of China and Japan, as well as North and South Korea, in order to lay a solid foundation for lasting peace and prosperity in Northeast Asia. Such a conference could deal with a broad range of issues concerning peace, stability, progress and prosperity within the region.

To be sure, it may not be easy to gather these states together at the same table because of the outstanding differences in ideology, social systems and policies among them. But I am sure we can overcome such difficulties if we all acknowledge the fact that we are inseparable partners in the pursuit of peace and prosperity. The realization of this proposal would certainly create an international environment more conducive to peace in Korea and reunification of the Peninsula.

Mr. President,

Looking ahead to the twenty-first century, I sense that a new chapter of human history is unfolding. Indeed, changes are taking place in this global village, and mankind is increasingly guided by tenets of reason and wisdom rather than ideological obsessions. Nonetheless, there is no guarantee that mankind will not someday be plunged into the whirlwind of global conflict. If we are to avoid this tragedy, openness, peace and cooperation are the only options left to us. I look forward to this new chapter of history, wherein peaceful efforts toward cooperation and progress will be the norm rather than the exception.

Likewise, the time will certainly come on the Korean Peninsula when the brotherhood of all Koreans, North and South, will triumph over our differences, leaving the Korean nation free of tension, conflict and the threat of war. I believe that the present ordeal will finally come to an end and the blessing of peace and reunification will be bestowed upon the Korean people— a people who have never attempted an invasion of a foreign country throughout their five millennia of history. On the day when swords are beaten into ploughshares on the Korean Peninsula, the opportunity for lasting world peace will be strengthened.

Believing that this day will come, I will continue my efforts, together with my 60 million compatriots, in seeking lasting harmony in our nation. This is the solemn responsibility for my generation and the dream and passion of the younger generation in Korea. Through concerted efforts, we are determined to overcome whatever difficulties we may encounter. As the most successful Olympics ever held has just been concluded in a land once dominated by conflict and poverty, so too the day will come when the wall of separation on the Korean Peninsula will fall and harmony will prevail.

Mr. President, Mr. Secretary-General, distinguished delegates,

In conclusion, I earnestly appeal to you all to support and encourage the aspirations of all the Korean people who, as expressed by the theme song of the Seoul Olympics, so strongly desire to go "hand in hand over the walls" and realize the goals of peace and unification.

May I also assure that that the Korean people will demonstrate that they are worthy of your support as we build a unified, peaceable nation on our Peninsula.

6.

Partners for Progress: ROK-U.S. Relations in a Changing World; Address before a Joint Meeting of the United States Congress, October 18, 1989

Mr. Speaker, Mr. President, distinguished Senators and Representatives,

I would like to express my gratitude to you for awarding me the rare privilege of speaking before a joint meeting of the United States Congress—the august representative body of one of the world's oldest and most powerful democracies. As the democratically elected leader of one of the world's newest democracies, I feel honored and proud to be standing here today.

I am honored, not only because it is within these halls that democracy has flourished, but also because the work of this great institution has brought freedom to many people of the world and has nurtured the best in human achievement.

I stand here proudly because I have a story to tell, the story of a people who, while enduring great hardship, have cultivated a free and vigorous democracy within a single generation.

Syngman Rhee, the first president of the Republic of Korea, came to this rostrum in 1954 in order to express the heartfelt gratitude of his countrymen for the courage and sacrifice that the people of the United States had rendered in protecting and preserving freedom and democracy in Korea.

At that time, the sounds of gunfire still echoed in the memories of President Rhee's countrymen in a legacy of the terrible Korean War. Thirty-five years have passed since then and much has changed.

From the depths of despair during the war, a spring of hope and confidence welled up in Korea. What was once a trickle soon grew into a rising tide of political and economic strength that continues to carry my people forward. And so, instead of long lines of hopeless children or hungry refugees, what the world saw at the 1988 Olympic Games was a prospering, confident people striding proudly toward the future.

Much has changed, indeed, Mr. Speaker, but the lofty ideals which bind Korea and the United States have endured, tested through sweat and, at times, blood. When Korea's very survival was in danger, the United States rushed to defend the security and liberty of our people.

While my country strove endlessly to build a thriving democratic nation from the poverty and ruin of war, the United States stood beside us, shoulder to shoulder. For that, the Korean people's gratitude has never wavered.

For my part, I feel a particularly deep affinity for the United States. When my country was in flames, I volunteered, still wearing a student uniform, to fight for our liberty. At that time many American soldiers fought alongside me and my colleagues. Many gave their lives so that Korea might be free. Later I fought in Vietnam together with young American soldiers. I know that there are many of my fellow soldiers among the members of the House and Senate present here today.

I thank those legislators and the thousands of other, brave Americans who fought for our freedom. Our people will long remember your sacrifice.

If you ask a Korean what America means to his country, his answer will be simple and clear: we are allies. And if you ask your constituents what Korea means to America, I am sure the answer will be the same. For us, the word "ally" resonates with deep feelings of friendship, trust and enduring commitment.

Korea and the United States developed this alliance not only out of common national interests, but also because we share the common ideals of freedom and human dignity. Your Declaration of Independence proclaims that "life, liberty and the pursuit of happiness are inalienable rights." That spirit mirrors our traditional belief that "Man is as sacred as heaven."

Mr. Speaker, Mr. President,

The world is now undergoing momentous changes, which are reshaping the international order of the past four decades. Across the walls and fences of the Cold War, a movement has begun which seeks to transform societies that restrict human liberty into societies that promote it; to change systems that suppress aspiration into systems that nurture it. These warmer winds are inducing obstinate and obsolete societies to shed their outmoded ideologies and to join the community of free nations.

The climate of openness and reconciliation throughout the world inspires hope in us all, and notwithstanding the pains of division and the dangers of conflict, the Republic of Korea is committed to sharing the burden of building peace and prosperity throughout the world.

Korea has transformed itself. Our nation has emerged from the authoritarianism of the past and is now propelled by the momentum of liberty, openness and democracy. This new atmosphere not only led to the success of the Seoul Olympics but has also provided the catalyst for change unique among nations, whether developed or developing. The people of the Republic of Korea have made extraordinary strides toward democracy and we are ready to face new challenges along the way.

You may recall the scenes in my country only two years ago, when the streets of our cities were crammed with protesters, chanting and clamoring for democracy. The force of those demands prompted me, as a Presidential candidate, to prove my faith in the essential principle of democracy—that power emanates solely from the people. Shortly thereafter, I issued a statement which became known as the June 29 Declaration of Democratic Reforms, embracing the aspirations of the Korean people.

The process of instituting democratic change began with that declaration. For the first time in Korean history the Constitution was revised with the concurrence of both the government and opposition. In a free and competitive election process, I was entrusted with the presidency, and the perennial controversy over the legitimacy of the government came to an end. Then in the general election of April 1988, the opposing parties, for the first time in Korean history, won a combined majority of seats in the National Assembly. This enhanced the framework for representative democracy by providing a rigorous system of checks and balances.

Significantly, the elections reinforced our commitment to democratic principles as my administration accepted the reality of a legislature controlled by the opposition. To you, of course, this is not a new experience. To us it is indeed a political novelty.

Our liberalization has gone well beyond politics. The media now enjoys uncensored freedom to criticize every aspect of society, including the presidency. No one who encroaches on civil rights in Korea can escape the sanctions of public opinion or the rule of law. The changes in Korea are so diverse, rapid and far-reaching that they can truly be called revolutionary.

It has become clear to me that founding democratic institutions and making them work is no less difficult a task than promoting economic development. The pace of reform has stirred mounting expectations and competing demands in every corner of society. Rapid changes have shaken the fabric of existing political, social and labor relations and placed the burden of reshaping them on my government. At times, social stability has been threatened, and we have had to take measures to protect it.

Regrettably, certain radicals have resorted to force and committed unlawful acts to pursue their aims under the guise of democratic reform. Elements seeking to overthrow the basic principles of democracy through class struggle can be found among them. Here also are the tiny band of extremists who parade anti-American slogans and perpetrate attacks on U.S. facilities.

It is my belief that our political development will follow the example of the Western democracies and that the extreme elements in Korea will diminish in influence as the benefits of democracy and prosperity are enjoyed more and more. As one who pioneered reform in Korea, I will confront squarely every challenge to our young democracy, whether from within or from without. My pledge to carry out democratic reform was a solemn promise before the people of Korea, and I have proudly honored that pledge. Democracy in Korea has already become an unstoppable force which no one can divert.

Out of the ashes and ruin of the war, Mr. President, Korea has emerged like a phoenix to become what is now termed a "newly industrialized country." The diligence and creativity of our people have made this transformation possible, harnessing the twin energies of a market economy and free trade. While the United States helped Korea revitalize its war-torn economy with direct aid, access to the U.S. domestic market for Korean goods has been no less important to Korea's economic development.

The United States is Korea's largest and most important trading partner. In turn, Korea is now the seventh largest market for U.S. goods and the second largest market for your agricultural products. Although the potential for trade friction naturally increases with the expansion of trade volume, I am certain that all of these issues will be resolved to our mutual satisfaction through close and cooperative consultation. I find our success in settling trade disputes thus far encouraging.

My government firmly believes that free enterprise will best serve our economy and that of the world as a whole. Thus, Korea is moving vigorously toward a more open, liberalized and self-regulating economy. It would be hard to find a country, developed or developing, which has moved so far so swiftly in opening markets, liberalizing capital flow and reducing tariffs.

I fully understand that the interests of constituents oblige you, their representatives, to seek ways of strengthening industrial competitiveness, protecting workers and saving jobs. These are the same demands my people make of their government. Consider, for instance, our agricultural sector. Nearly 20 percent of all Koreans work on small, traditional family farms. Thus, our efforts to expand agricultural imports have important political and social consequences for nearly one-fifth of our population. Only with the passage of time can Korea ultimately adjust and achieve openness in the agricultural market without causing political and social trauma.

We are undergoing an inevitably painful transformation in adapting ourselves to the principles of free trade, but we are making astonishing progress. Within only four or five years from now, we may expect the Korean economy to have achieved the same degree of openness as is found in the OECD countries.

Even as a wave of reconciliation brings about changes all over the world, the tide, distinguished members of Congress, has not yet reached all shores.

The confrontation on the Korean Peninsula has resisted all efforts for its resolution. Korea has lived under great tension each day of the 36 years since the ceasefire. The Demilitarized Zone, or DMZ, lies only 26 miles north of

Seoul, our capital, with a population of 10 million. Along the 155 mile-long DMZ more than one-and-a-half million troops face each other, making it the most densely militarized area in the world. Imagine, if you will, hostile and combat-ready forces positioned as close to this Capitol as Dulles Airport!

Since the ceasefire of 1953, stability on the Peninsula has been maintained not because P'yŏngyang's attitudes or intentions have changed, but because strong Korean and U.S. military cooperation has deterred further aggression. Any hint of weakening in the U.S. defense commitment or a precipitate lessening of the U.S. military presence might cause North Korea to misjudge the U.S. commitment to peace in the region. The results would be tragic.

Thus far, security cooperation between our two countries remains strong and effective. Let us not disturb it until necessity dictates change. For this reason, I welcome and applaud the pledge of President Bush and the American government that U.S. ground troops will remain as long as the Korean people want and need them. And on this point, I must tell you that the voice of the Korean people is clear: a very recent poll has shown that 94 percent strongly support the presence of U.S. troops. Moreover, where this issue is concerned, the usually vocal opposition parties stand together with us as one.

Koreans have shouldered a greater burden of their own defense than any other American ally. They spend 5 percent of GNP, more than 30 percent of their government budget, on defense. As our economy grows, so Korea will assume a larger role and take more responsibility in our common defense. And needless to say, a strong Korea-U.S. security relationship is an essential element in the process of inducing North Korea to accept positive change.

In today's climate of openness, Mr. Speaker, it is inconceivable that North Korea can cling forever to its extreme, self-imposed isolation. Meanwhile, we are exerting every possible effort to move our divided land toward reconciliation and to convince North Korea that nothing will be achieved by force.

In July of last year, I announced a policy to reduce the long-standing hostility which divides our Peninsula. The aim of this policy is to create a partnership between the South and North, in which each contributes to the other's development.

Last month, I went further, proposing concrete steps to achieve reunification by joining the two parts into a "Korean National Community". At the heart of the proposal is the formation of a Korean Commonwealth as an interim measure. Eventually, we shall reunify Korea as one nation under the principles of independence, peace and democracy.

I have been urging that a summit meeting take place between Seoul and P'yŏngyang. At this summit all issues, including disarmament and an agreement on non-aggression between South and North Korea, could be discussed freely and without preconditions.

On this very day last year, I made a proposal at the United Nations General Assembly that a "Conference for Peace in Northeast Asia" be convened. The time has now come for the countries in the area to discuss seriously the question of how to lay a solid foundation for lasting peace and prosperity in Northeast Asia.

Through our active open-door policy, we have built a road for exchanges and trade with socialist countries with whom Korea has had no previous formal contact. We hope that our improved relations with socialist countries will deter North Korean aggression, ease tensions on the Korean Peninsula and contribute to bringing North Korea out into the open world.

Ladies and gentlemen,

The forces of freedom and liberty are eroding the foundations of closed societies, and the efficiency of the market economy and the benefits of an open society have become undeniable. These universal ideals, symbolized by the United States, have now begun to undermine the fortresses of repression.

There is no longer a need for hesitation; we know which social system best realizes human aspiration. In all parts of the world, the prosperity of a free society based on the common ideal of liberty has sparked a revolution in thought and action.

My friends,

The nations of the Pacific Basin have made an open society and market economy the engines that drive the fastest growing region in the world. The Pacific will become even more important to the U.S., and Korea will begin to contribute more to the prosperity and peace of the region and become an increasingly important American ally.

I am confident that Korea and the United States of America will be "partners for progress" allied to open a new era—an era in which nations around the world will enjoy the freedom and prosperity we both so deeply cherish. Let us renew this relationship to foster prosperity and contribute to world progress.

Mr. Speaker, Mr. President, distinguished Senators and Representatives,

Although I am about to leave this rostrum, the message I came to deliver is not complete. That is because I look forward to the day when some future Korean president may be invited to address this distinguished assembly and describes the vision I spoke of today as an achievement fulfilled, not as tomorrow's hope. When that president speaks before you as I have today and reflects on those triumphs, all of us will be able to take great pride. For we will have risen to the challenges of our day and passed on to our children a world far better than the one we inherited: safer, more prosperous, fairer and happier.

God bless America and I thank you all.

7.

Partners for a New Era of Harmony; Address to the Hungarian National Assembly, November 23, 1989

Mr. President, distinguished members of the Assembly, ladies and gentlemen.

It is a great honor and privilege for me to speak before you in this magnificent hall, so rich in its history and tradition. Let me extend my deep appreciation of your invitation to address this distinguished group of parliamentarians.

I am extremely happy to be the first Korean president to visit your beautiful land since the establishment of diplomatic relations between our two countries. I believe it is particularly significant that we meet today at a time when a new chapter is being opened in the history of the Republic of Hungary and on the very spot where a new trend was set for political changes worldwide.

On October 23 I was one of the millions across the world who witnessed with admiration and respect the declaration of the birth of the Republic of Hungary from the balcony of this honored house. All 42 million people of the Republic of Korea applaud your launching of a new republic and wish you every blessing for the future of your country.

As the Korean head of state, I am very pleased to bring a message from our people to the people of the Republic of Hungary, a message of warm greetings, deep affinity and everlasting friendship. Our two countries and peoples have now joined together to open a new era of partnership.

The heroic decision of the Republic of Hungary made in the spirit of self-determination and national accord to open and restructure their society has played a pivotal role in building a bridge of friendship and cooperation between a nation in East Asia and a nation in the heart of Europe.

The establishment of diplomatic relations between Korea and Hungary has beamed a message of hope and harmony not only to our own peoples but to other peoples around the world, for the occasion has highlighted for the entire world the courageous and momentous decision of the Hungarian people to accept the challenge of building their nation anew. At the same time, our mutual decision has served as a harbinger of hope, ushering in a new era of harmony and declaring the inevitable disappearance into history of the bipolar international system that developed in the postwar era.

Our diplomatic relations may be new, but our two nations have long shared mutual respect and goodwill through the invisible bond of centuries-old history and culture. Just as Hungary is a nation with a long history and culture, so too is Korea. Even our languages stem from the same source, the Ural language family. We can surmise that the Magyars and the Koreans must have had some ties or cultural bonds in the prehistoric period.

Historically, our two nations underwent similar experiences. If the Hungarian people have displayed throughout their history unequalled patriotism and love of freedom, the Korean people have also repelled aggression by their stronger neighbors many times and have succeeded in preserving their independence and national integrity. Just as Hungary's modern history has seen many trials and tribulations, Korea has also had to withstand the trials and tribulations of the rivalries between the great powers.

In the nineteenth century, the Hungarian people under the leadership of Kossuth Lajos waged a heroic struggle for independence. In the twentieth century the Korean people also fought for their independence against foreign domination.

During this period of national struggle, the late Maestro Ahn Iktae, the composer of our national anthem, studied under the renowned Hungarian composer, Zoltan Kodaly and, of course, Bela Bartok and Franz von Liszt are both familiar names even to high school students in Korea, for the Korean people have long admired the musical and artistic genius of the Hungarian people.

Geography separates us, but we share much in common and we each feel affinity for the other. The separation of the two nations for so long by the artificial gulf of ideology was indeed a most unnatural misfortune. Having overcome all these barriers, we find today common ideals and common national tasks that we must achieve together.

Our two nations have paid dearly under the imperatives of the postwar system. The common ideal of our two peoples, therefore, should be the attainment of a peaceful world on the basis of universal equality, reciprocity and cooperation.

The Korean people are watching with great anticipation the recent upsurge of more free and open political and economic policies around the world. For the Koreans have suffered, more than any other people in the world, unspeakable pain, sorrow and sacrifice due mainly to confrontations between opposing ideologies and systems in the Cold War period.

For us, the end of World War II meant liberation from the colonial yoke and a joyful return to us of the nation that we had defended for thousands of years. Our rejoicing over our national liberation at the end of World War II was replaced overnight by a tragic territorial and national division. The Cold War system suddenly descended upon us and separated into two parts a nation that had lived for centuries as one state and one community. Furthermore, on one morning in 1950 the Cold War confrontation turned the Korean Peninsula into an inferno. The war ravaged the country for three long years, and millions of innocent people were injured or lost their lives.

Distinguished members of the Assembly,

I am still deeply indebted to the Hungarian people for your active participation in the Seoul Olympics last year, in which nearly all the nations of East and West joined in a truly universal Olympiad for the first time in twelve years. Our people enthusiastically applauded your young athletes, who left a lasting impression in Korea, and Miss Kristina Argessy's presence in the center court symbolized the courage and elegance of your great nation.

We still vividly remember, as I am sure you do, the emotions and the excitement of the Seoul Olympics. It was truly a festive assembly for the harmony of mankind. The athletes of the world crossed all barriers and overcame all differences: race, religion, ideology, poverty and wealth. The entire Korean people pulled together for the Olympics so that the seeds of peace and reconciliation could take root on a permanent basis, for the Korean Peninsula is a land where tension and confrontation could lead to hostilities at any moment. I believe all nations of the world drew closer in friendship and harmony through the Seoul Olympics, and the Korean people are proud to have served the cause of world harmony.

Distinguished members of the Assembly,

The Republics of Hungary and Korea will join hands in opening the world to reform and accelerating our march toward prosperity and development. Your open door policy, structural reforms and liberalization measures bear many similarities with the policies of my own country. And, in the process, we have learned that progress can be attained only through competition within a pluralistic social structure. Human dignity, freedom and individual motivation for improvement not only provide guarantees for individual creativity and happiness but also generate new energies for national development. An open society and a market economy that offers equal opportunity for all has brought us prosperity by leading us to compete efficiently in the world community. This is the direction Korea has followed, and the success of this approach has made Korea what it is today.

Methods may differ, but as long as we strive for our common ideals, I am confident that the wise choice of the Hungarian people will be vindicated. I am also convinced that the changes in the Republic of Hungary will make an enormous contribution not only to the development of Hungary itself but to the attainment of a better world.

Distinguished members of the Assembly,

The time has come for all the nations of the world to harness their energies and strive together to enhance our common prosperity, happiness and wellbeing through increased mutual trust and respect. We are living in a world which is rapidly growing smaller, thanks to the advances of technology, commercial interchange and political sanity. We must move on from a period in which wasteful competition and destructive confrontation prevailed to a period in which all nations together contribute to peace and harmony through cooperation and goodwill.

On the basis of this belief, the new Republic of Korea government has been pursuing a diplomatic policy aimed at opening relations with socialist countries. The establishment of formal relations between the Republic of Korea and Hungary has served to solidify our belief in this policy, and only a few weeks ago we established diplomatic relations with Poland.

We will continue actively to pursue exchanges, cooperation and improved relations with China, the Soviet Union and the Central and Eastern European countries.

Distinguished members of the Assembly,

Just as the Republic of Hungary removed the barriers separating the East from the West, we in Korea are also trying our utmost to bring down the barriers that divide the Korean Peninsula into North and South.

Even at this moment, the 65 million Koreans suffer the pain of national division. We have millions of brothers and sisters, parents and relatives who have been separated by the Demilitarized Zone that runs across the Korean Peninsula. For almost a half century, they have not even known the whereabouts of the beloved members of their families. They are not even allowed to send postcards or make telephone calls, let alone freely exchange visits.

On July 7 last year, I made public a major policy decision to end the confrontation between South and North Korea, and to develop a new relationship as partners. Since South and North Korea will not be able to attain national unification within the foreseeable future, we must first recognize each other and then search for ways to coexist and achieve common prosperity. Through dialogue and exchanges, the two Koreas, I believe, should build the basis for mutual trust.

Toward this end I have recently put forward the "Korean National Community Unification Formula." Under this proposal, the South and the North will first form a commonwealth as an intermediate step toward unification. Within the commonwealth, we would seek to build community relations sector by sector. This would in time create favorable conditions for political integration. We would then become one country in accordance with the principles of independence, peace and democracy.

I have been urging the North Korean leader to join me in a North-South summit meeting. At this summit we could freely discuss and resolve, without any preconditions, any and all issues, including arms control and mutual non-aggression.

In our efforts to reduce tension on the Korean Peninsula and to open a path of reconciliation, I ask the support of the Republic of Hungary. We hope that the nations with which we are establishing new diplomatic relations will maintain their good relations with North Korea just as they develop good relations with us. I do not want our new friendship to cause any cooling of Hungary's relations with the North.

We do not want to isolate North Korea. We desire to see North Korea join the world community and cooperate with all nations, joining us in paving the way toward reconciliation and unification of the Korean people.

Distinguished members of the Assembly,

Just as Hungary is undergoing a major change, we in Korea have also been going through a democratic transition which one might call a quiet revolution. Since its foundation in 1948, the Republic of Korea has maintained a parliamentary democracy based upon the principles of pluralism and a multi-party system. But the 40-year history of constitutional democracy was too short to overcome the age-old authoritarian tradition. A strong government was required in the process of nation-building, and this established a pattern of unidirectional leadership, while suppressing the people's needs and demands.

Two years ago, tens of thousands of Korean people poured out into the streets demanding democracy, and the situation reached crisis proportions. As the leader of the ruling party, I decided to accommodate the fervent wishes of the nation, and enunciated what has since been known as the June 29 Declaration of Democratic Reforms. I did this solely in the belief that power in a democracy emanates from the people.

From that point onward, the shackles of authoritarianism began to give way to a democratic transition on the basis of free, open, and self-regulating processes. Subsequently, a new Constitution drafted jointly by the government and opposition parties and approved in a national referendum was adopted. The new Constitution provided for the direct popular election of the President. Shortly thereafter, we had a closely contested Presidential election. In the general elections a few months later the opposition parties together won a majority of seats in the National Assembly for the first time in our history. As a result, parliamentary democracy in Korea is currently going through a new experiment in checks and balances.

As is natural in a democracy, the news media freely criticize government policies and the president, and disclose to the nation any and all social injustices that come under their scrutiny. In short, the new wave of reform has presented us with an enormous challenge.

In its wake, rapid democratization provoked a sudden eruption of the many demands of the people that had been pent up for so long. As conflicts and contradictions concealed by the imperatives of rapid economic growth abruptly surfaced, the system was unable to accommodate them all at once and suffered the strains of transition.

To make the situation worse, there appeared all too soon those who attempted to make quick profits by short-circuiting the legal system and democratic processes. It has taken an extraordinary effort to maintain law and order and social stability.

I can tell you from personal experience that the task of institutionalizing democracy and making it work smoothly is perhaps more difficult than the attainment of economic development. As one who has been at the forefront of reform in Korea, I have tirelessly endeavored to withstand and overcome the many challenges that have arisen, without compromising the principles of democracy.

The many transitional phenomena are being overcome in Korea as we unite our efforts for this purpose. Challenges and instabilities, I believe, are inevitable once the path is taken toward political and social reform. Sometimes, they entail threats to the system itself. In order to master the situation, we all need unflinching courage, perseverance and strong willpower.

The current reform process in Hungary, I fear, may witness similar difficulties to those we have had in Korea. But I have no doubt that the Hungarian people will ultimately prevail over all difficulties and succeed in their national reform programs before the watchful eyes of the world.

Mr. President, Distinguished members of the Assembly,

The Republics of Hungary and Korea are each striving to build a prosperous nation and are making progress toward it. Having previously undergone a period of colonial occupation and then war, Korea was a poor country on the verge of starvation. Natural resources were very limited and we were an agricultural nation with 60 percent of our population living in a traditional style on small farms.

In the early 1960s, when we began our economic development programs in earnest, our per capita GNP was under US$100 and our exports amounted to no more than a few tens of millions of dollars. We had to depend on aid and assistance from abroad, not only for food but for our government budget as well. For the 27 years since 1962, when Korea launched its first Five-Year Economic Development Plan, we have recorded an average economic growth of 8.7 percent per year.

Today, Korea has been transformed into a newly industrializing country that exports to world markets items ranging from fiber-optics and computers to automobiles and ships. With an annual export volume in excess of US$60 billion and an annual trade volume of over US$120 billion, the Republic of Korea has now become one of the ten largest trading countries in the world.

One of our most important assets has been the human resources we have been able to marshal. The diligence, creativity and collective strength of the workers were behind Korea's economic success. In addition, the civilian-led businesses operating in a free enterprise and market economy faithfully followed the active and efficient lead of the economic development plans of the government, and the result was dynamic economic growth.

From the very outset the government adopted outward-oriented economic development policies. In the initial stages, investment was concentrated in the industries given priority for development, such as basic plants, export-oriented factories, and others that manufactured items with relatively great import-substitution values.

At first we had to rely on foreign capital and technological know-how, and import or secure loans for production facilities from abroad. The government placed the highest priority on exports, and our "can do" spirit led us to the open world market. Step by step, but steadily, the national economy became stronger, and the nation began to grow quickly.

By 1985 Korea had accumulated a total debt of over US$46 billion. Since 1986, however, our current account has recorded a surplus for the first time in our history, as a result of increased exports and rapid economic growth. Today, Korea is about to become a creditor nation. Consequently, we can no longer justify import restrictions for reasons of balance of payments. Therefore we are now moving fast in the direction of an open, free and self-regulating market system.

With a per capita GNP of less than US$5,000, Korea is still a developing country. But with our unprecedented speed of economic growth, I believe we have given hope and courage to other developing economies of the world.

The Hungary I see today is open and progressive and has a pool of well-educated manpower. Hungary is also endowed with abundant agricultural products and vast arable plains. For these reasons, I firmly believe that Hungary has the human assets, the culture and the natural potential to generate prosperity.

The unprecedented development of the Republic of Korea is often called "the miracle on the Han River." I believe that the Hungarian people will achieve "the miracle on the Danube." As Hungary's new partner, the Republic of Korea will make its utmost effort to contribute to Hungary's development.

Distinguished members of the Assembly,
Since the establishment of diplomatic ties last spring the relationship

between our two countries has progressed by leaps and bounds. Agreements have already been concluded on trade, investment guarantees, the prevention of double taxation, cooperation in science and technology, and cultural exchanges. Yesterday I witnessed the signing of an aviation agreement which allows the airlines of our two countries to fly to Seoul and Budapest. I am confident that much will flow freely over this bridge of friendship in the years to come, be it ideas and ideals, commerce and culture, or just simple human stories that enrich our lives.

I, for one, am committed to developing our bilateral relationship into an exemplar of friendship and cooperation in the world. I will do my utmost to ensure that our two nations share development techniques and know-how and promote economic cooperation. To the extent that it is helpful for Hungary, we will encourage Korean businessmen to construct plants here through direct investment or joint ventures with appropriate Hungarian counterparts. The Korean businesses that come to Hungary would be able to manufacture goods that are not only needed in Hungary but also marketable elsewhere in Europe. In finance and service industries, too, there are many opportunities to promote our common interests.

Some time ago, in Seoul, I watched a superb performance by the Hungarian National Ballet. It was one of our many recent exchanges in culture, arts, and sports. Plans are being made for inter-university cooperation between the two countries to increase understanding of each other's language and culture.

From now on, more and more Koreans will visit this beautiful country of yours. May I extend an invitation to all Hungarians to visit the Republic of Korea and enjoy our hospitality? Though our partnership has just begun, we have already established firm ground for friendship and cooperation well into the twenty-first century.

Mr. President, distinguished members of the Assembly,

The Hungarian leaders and people have been at the forefront of reforms to change the face of Europe. A new chapter of history is being opened, in which the world order is restructured on a basis of human rationality and not by wars as in the past. By the combined efforts of its leaders and ordinary citizens, the Republic of Hungary has achieved through peaceful means a new birth of liberty, democracy, and humanism.

The Republic of Hungary was the first nation to breach the wall of Cold War division. Now the Berlin Wall is tumbling down in response to your example. We hope that this strong wave of aspirations will overcome all barriers and open the door to a "world of harmony."

At this very moment, you and I are witnessing the realization of our common ideal. At this very hour, we are announcing to the world the passage of an era of confrontation and the arrival of a new era of friendship, harmony and progress. Let us resolve to make the new relationship between the

Republic of Korea and the Republic of Hungary a symbol of a harmonious world.

Mr. President,

The Asia-Pacific region has enormous potential and resources. With its vibrant energy for development, the region is emerging as a new pace-setter of economic progress. Currently, the Pacific Basin countries together produce more than 50 percent of total world output. Due to its strategic position in the Pacific, the Republic of Korea is playing a pivotal role in the peace and prosperity of this vast region.

The Republic of Hungary is a leader in this age of change and hope. Our two countries have today opened a new chapter in our history. As new partners, let us resolve to make a maximum contribution not only to the prosperity of our two nations but also to the peace of the world.

The Korean people and the people of the Republic of Hungary are now firmly committed in our joint efforts to create a new era of greater harmony, greater justice and greater prosperity.

God bless the Republic of Hungary, and I thank you all.

8.

Declaration on General Principles of Relations Between the Republic of Korea and the Union of Soviet Socialist Republics, Moscow, December 14, 1990

President Roh Tae Woo of the Republic of Korea and President Mikhail S. Gorbachev of the Union of Soviet Socialist Republics, having met in Moscow on December 14, 1990 and having discussed the state and the prospects of the bilateral relations as well as a wide range of relevant international issues, expressing a mutual interest in the development of comprehensive cooperation between the two countries; aware of the importance of peace on the Korean Peninsula for that of Northeast Asia and the world at large; recognizing the aspiration of the Korean nation for unification and welcoming the expansion of South-North contacts, including the recent negotiations between the Prime Ministers of the Republic of Korea and of the Democratic People's Republic of Korea; being firmly committed to the building of a new, more equitable, humane, peaceful and democratic world order; declare that the Republic of Korea and the Soviet Union shall be guided in their relations by the following principles:

- Respect for each other's sovereign equality, territorial integrity and political independence, noninterference in the internal affairs of the two states, and recognition that all nations are free to choose their own way of political and socioeconomic development;
- Compliance with the standards of international law, respect for the purposes and principles of the United Nations, set forth in the UN Charter;
- Inadmissibility of the threat or use of force, of providing one's own security at the expense of other states, and of settling international controversies and regional conflicts by any means other than reaching political agreements on the basis of reasonable consent by all the parties concerned;

- Development of a broad mutually beneficial cooperation among states and nations, leading to their rapprochement and to a deeper mutual understanding;
- Joining the international community's efforts to deal, on a priority basis, with the global issues of reducing the arms race, nuclear or conventional; preventing the environmental disaster facing mankind; overcoming poverty, famine and illiteracy; narrowing the dramatic gap between the development levels of various nations;
- Establishment of a secure and equitable world which would ensure progress for mankind and a decent life for all nations in the coming millennium.

Proceeding from the above-mentioned principles and opening a new page in history of their relations, the Republic of Korea and the Union of Soviet Socialist Republics are determined to build these relations in the spirit of good neighborhood trust and cooperation in the interests of peoples of both countries. To these ends, the two states will conclude a variety of agreements with a view to establishing and improving links and contacts between the two countries in the political, economic, trade, cultural, scientific, humanitarian and other areas. The Republic of Korea and the USSR will ensure priority of universally recognized international legal standards in their domestic and foreign policies and will implement in good faith their treaty obligations.

The presidents support the willingness of businessmen from both countries to deepen an effective and mutually beneficial cooperation in economy, trade, industry and transport, to exchange advanced technology and scientific achievements and to develop joint entrepreneurship and new forms of cooperation, and welcome the development of and investments into mutually beneficial projects. An exchange of ideas, information, spiritual and cultural values, an expansion of human contacts in the field of culture, art, science, education, sports, media and tourism, and a reciprocal travel by citizens of their countries will be encouraged. The sides will coordinate their efforts to control international terrorism, organized crime and illicit trafficking in drugs, and to protect the environment and to that end will cooperate in international and regional organizations.

The Republic of Korea and the Union of Soviet Socialists Republics are committed to the ideas of establishing in Asia and the Pacific region equal, mutually beneficial relations based on the balance of interests and self-determination, and of making Asia and the Pacific a region of peace and constructive cooperation through a process of unilateral and multilateral consultations.

The presidents reaffirm their conviction that the development of Korean-Soviet relations contributes to the strengthening of peace and security in Asia and the Pacific, is in line with the changes underway in the region, deepens the processes leading to the removal of confrontational mentality and to the elimination of "the Cold War" in Asia, contributes to regional cooperation and facilitates the relaxation of tension and the establishment of the climate of trust for the eventual reunification on the Korean Peninsula.

The Soviet Union stands for the continuation of a productive inter-Korean dialogue for the removal of the political and military confrontation between the two Korean sides, for a just and equitable settlement of the Korean problem by peaceful, democratic means in accordance with the will of the entire Korean people.

The Republic of Korea, welcoming the global turn from the era of confrontation to reconciliation and cooperation on the basis of universal values, freedom, democracy and justice, emphasizes a success of the Soviet reform policy as a major factor of future international relations, improvement of the situation in Northeast Asia and progress in relations between the two countries.

The presidents proceed from the general understanding that the development of links and contacts between the Republic of Korea and the USSR must not in any way affect their relations with third countries or undermine obligations they assume under multilateral or bilateral treaties and agreements.

The Republic of Korea and the Union of Soviet Socialist Republics have agreed to pursue a political dialogue at the highest level, and to hold regular meetings and consultations at various other levels on matters of deepening the bilateral relations and on relevant international issues.

ROH TAE WOO   M. GORBACHEV

Moscow,
December 14, 1990

9.

Agreement on Reconciliation, Nonaggression and Exchanges and Cooperation Between the South and the North, Panmunjom, Korea, December 13, 1991

WHEREAS in keeping with the yearning of the entire people for the peaceful unification of the divided land, the South and the North reaffirm the unification principles enunciated in the July 4 (1972) South-North Joint Communiqué;

WHEREAS both parties are determined to resolve political and military confrontation and achieve national reconciliation;

WHEREAS both desire to promote multi-faceted exchanges and cooperation to advance common national interests and prosperity;

WHEREAS both recognize that their relations constitute a special provisional relationship geared to unification; and

WHEREAS both pledge to exert joint efforts to achieve peaceful unification,

THEREFORE, the parties hereto agree as follows:

South-North Reconciliation

Article 1: The South and the North shall respect each other's political and social system.

Article 2: Both parties shall not interfere in each other's internal affairs.

Article 3: Both parties shall not slander and vilify each other.

Article 4: Both parties shall not attempt in any manner to sabotage and subvert the other.

Article 5: Both parties shall endeavor together to transform the present armistice regime into a firm state of peace between the South and the North and shall abide by the present Military Armistice Agreement (of July 27, 1953) until such time as such a state of peace has taken hold.

Article 6: Both parties shall cease confrontation on the international stage and shall cooperate and endeavor together to promote national interests and esteem.

Article 7: To ensure close consultations and liaison between both parties, a South-North liaison office shall be established at P'anmunjŏm within three (3) months of the effective date of this Agreement.

Article 8: A South-North Subcommittee shall be established within the framework of the Inter-Korean High-Level Talks within one month of the effective date of this Agreement with a view to discussing concrete measures to ensure the implementation and observance of the accords on South-North reconciliation.

South-North Nonaggression

Article 9: Both parties shall not use armed force against each other and shall not make armed aggression against each other.

Article 10: Differences of opinion and disputes arising between the two parties shall be peacefully resolved through dialogue and negotiations.

Article 11: The South-North demarcation line and areas for nonaggression shall be identical with the Military Demarcation Line specified in the Military Armistice Agreement of July 27, 1953 and the areas that have been under the jurisdiction of each party respectively thereunder until the present.

Article 12: To abide by and guarantee nonaggression, the two parties shall create a South-North Joint Military Committee within three (3) months of the effective date of this Agreement. The said Committee shall discuss and carry out steps to build military confidence and realize arms reductions, including the mutual notification and control of major movements of military units and major military exercises, the peaceful utilization of the Demilitarized Zone, exchanges of military personnel and information, phased reductions in armaments including the elimination of weapons of mass destruction and surprise attack capabilities, and verifications thereof.

Article 13: A telephone hotline shall be installed between the military authorities of both sides to prevent accidental armed clashes and avoid their escalation.

Article 14: A South-North Military Subcommittee shall be established within the framework of the Inter-Korean High-Level talks within one (1) month of the effective date of this Agreement in order to discuss concrete measures to ensure the implementation and observance of the accords on nonaggression and to resolve military confrontation.

South-North Exchanges and Cooperation

Article 15: To promote an integrated and balanced development of the national economy and the welfare of the entire people, both parties shall conduct economic exchanges and cooperation, including the joint development of resources, trade in goods as a kind of domestic commerce and joint investment in industrial projects.

Article 16: Both parties shall carry out exchanges and cooperation in diverse fields, including science, technology, education, literature, the arts, health, sports, the environment and publishing and journalism, including newspapers, radio, television and publications in general.

Article 17: Both parties shall guarantee residents of their respective areas free inter-Korean travel and contacts.

Article 18: Both parties shall permit free correspondence, reunions and visits between family members and other relatives dispersed south and north, shall promote the reconstitution of divided families on their own and shall take measures to resolve other humanitarian issues.

Article 19: Both sides shall reconnect railroads and roads that have been cut off and shall open South-North land, sea and air transport routes.

Article 20: Both parties shall establish and link facilities needed for South-North postal and telecommunications services and shall guarantee the confidentiality of inter-Korean mail and telecommunications.

Article 21: Both parties shall cooperate on the international stage in the economic, cultural and various other fields and carry out joint business undertakings abroad.

Article 22: To implement accords on exchanges and cooperation in the economic, cultural and various other fields, both parties shall establish joint committees for specific sectors, including a South-North Economic Exchanges and Cooperation Committee, within three (3) months of the effective date of this Agreement.

Article 23: A South-North Exchanges and Cooperation Subcommittee shall be established within the framework of the Inter-Korean High-Level Talks within one (1) month of the effective date of this Agreement with a view to discussing concrete measures to ensure the implementation and observance of the accords on South-North exchanges and cooperation.

Amendments and Effectuation

Article 24: This Agreement may be amended or supplemented by concurrence between both parties.

Article 25: This Agreement shall enter into force as of the day both parties exchange instruments of ratification following the completion of their respective procedures for bringing it into effect.

DATE: December 13, 1991

Chung Won-shik Prime Minister Republic of Korea	Yon Hyong-muk Premier Administration Council Democratic People's Republic of Korea

Index

Afghanistan 311
Agency for National Security Planning 47
Agreement on Reconciliation, Nonagression, and Exchanges and Cooperation 54, 65, 102
Ahn Iktae 325
Albania 128
Andersen, Hans Christian 270
Andric, Ivo 113
Angola 145
arap Moi, Daniel Toroitich 107, 109
Argessy, Kristina 326
Armistice Line 310, 311, 313
Arthur, Chester A. 245
Asia-Pacific Economic Cooperation Forum (APEC) 224, 228, 232, 245, 248, 254, 258–262
Association of Southeast Asian Nations (ASEAN) 71, 231, 232, 254, 261

Bainun, Tuanku 253, 255, 257
Bartok, Bela 325
Beijing 66, 67, 73, 94, 155, 207
Beijing Asian Games 11
Belinsky, Vissarion 22
Berlin 308
Berlin Wall 14, 19, 141, 157, 165, 202, 203, 227, 241, 244, 331
bin Mohamad, Mahathir 230, 232
bin Mohamad, Mrs. 230, 232
Bolshevik Revolution 24, 26
Bowring, Philip 41
Brandt, Willy 67
Budapest 156, 331
Bulgaria 19

Bush, George, President of U.S. 48, 77, 123–126, 149, 155, 286–288, 290, 322
Bush, Mrs. 123–126, 288, 290

Cambodia 145, 311
Canada 133, 241, 242, 273–279
Canberra 228, 258
Casal, Anibal Raul 14, 115
Central America 145
Cheju Island 41, 128, 189, 190
Chekhov, Anton 22
Chicago 120
China 10, 11, 19, 17, 39, 42, 45, 54, 62, 63, 65, 67–69, 72, 78, 88, 90, 92–94, 124, 132, 133, 136, 143, 155, 187, 203, 235, 246, 247, 250, 255, 258, 315, 327
Chinese Taipei 258
Chinoy, Mike 90–95
Choi Kyu Ha 298
Cholla Region 45, 46
Chun Doo Hwan 44, 71, 293, 296, 298
Chung Won-shik 339
Clifford, Mark 41
Cold War 3, 10, 14, 15, 21, 22, 28, 33, 39, 48, 51, 57, 80, 84, 85, 87, 88, 90–92, 96, 99, 100, 108, 113, 117, 120, 124, 127, 128, 130, 136, 140, 142, 143, 145, 150, 153, 154, 157, 160, 161, 163–168, 170–172, 175, 178, 185, 191, 198, 200–203, 219, 220, 222, 227, 231, 234, 239, 246, 247, 250, 257, 258, 268, 273, 284, 286, 288, 310, 311, 313, 319, 325, 326, 331, 335
Colombo Plan 237, 238
Covenant on Civil and Political Rights 60
Czechoslovakia 19

Index

Dalgas 270
Danube River 156, 330
de Cuellar, Javier Perez 145, 311
Declaration of War on Crime 39
Defense Security Command 47
Demilitarized Zone 11, 15, 19, 88, 113, 144, 171, 203, 220, 251, 302, 314, 321, 322, 327
Democratic Liberal Party 46, 48, 53, 60, 72
Democratic Justice Party 59, 60, 127, 294, 296
Democratic Republican Party 60
Denmark 270–272
Dostoyevsky, Fyodor 168, 179

Economic and Social Commission for Asia and the Pacific (ESCAP) 233–236
Edo 206
Europe 16, 48, 159, 182, 185, 205, 212, 229, 239, 242, 245, 259, 271, 324
Europe, Central 14, 94, 113, 117, 123, 124, 131, 138, 143, 157, 235, 245, 250, 255, 258, 271, 278, 327
Europe, Eastern 10, 14, 18, 30, 33, 45, 57, 66, 88, 92, 94, 113, 117, 123, 124, 131, 132, 137, 138, 142, 143, 154, 157, 202, 203, 214, 219, 227, 235, 245, 250, 258, 271, 278, 327
Europe, Western 14, 30, 203
European Community 39, 51, 70, 133, 157, 202, 227, 245, 247, 268

Far East 187
Five Year Economic and Social Development Plan 35, 36, 51, 55, 62, 329

Gayle, James 277
Geneva 96
Genghis Khan 192
Germany 30, 57, 58, 64, 65, 84, 87, 88–89, 90, 118, 130, 186, 203, 214, 219, 241, 271
Germany, East 19, 65, 67, 73, 80, 141
Germany, West 19, 65, 67, 80, 154
Gogol, Nikolay 179
Goncharov, Ivan 22, 23
Gönez, Árpád 156, 158
Gönez, Mrs. Árpád 156, 158
Gorbachev, Mikhail 21, 29, 41, 67, 72, 77, 78, 91, 127, 128, 149, 153, 154, 159, 160, 165–167, 169, 170, 172, 173, 175, 176, 179, 181, 182, 189, 190, 246, 250, 311, 316, 333, 335
Gorbachev, Mrs. 167, 169, 189, 190
Gorky, Arshile 168
Graham, Katharine 263

Greece 117, 267–269
Grundvig, Nikolai 270
Guadalajara 280, 283

Han River 58, 309, 330
Han Yong-un 201
Hand In Hand (Olympic song) 14, 317
Hasmah, Siti 230
Herzen, Aleksandr 22
Hnatyshyn, Mrs. Ramon 273, 277, 279
Hnatyshyn, Ramon 273, 277, 279
Hong Kong 258
Hoover, Herbert 243
Hoover Institution 243
Hoshu Amenomori 198
Hungary 10, 19, 67, 117, 156–158, 324–332
Hyon Tog-yun 198
Hyundai Corporation 26

Inch'on 37
International Atomic Energy Agency 49, 93, 97, 61, 149, 289
Iraq 69, 264, 271
Istanbul 31
Izuhara 206

Japan 10, 17, 39, 41, 46, 48, 49, 51, 63, 65, 72, 73, 78, 93, 117, 118, 124, 133, 150, 187, 197–224, 242, 263, 264, 302
Jiang Zemin 246
Jindo Corporation 26
Jobanobic, Paja 113
Joint Declaration for a Non-Nuclear Korean Peninsula 65, 287, 289
Jovic, Borisav 112, 114
Jovic, Mrs. Borisav 112, 114
June 29, 1987 Declaration of Democratic Reforms 4, 23, 35, 48, 50, 54, 57, 59, 60, 95, 116, 201, 209, 250, 320, 328
Jutlandia (ship) 270

Kaifu, Toshiki 117, 197, 213, 215, 217, 218, 220
Kaifu, Mrs. Toshiki 197, 213, 215, 218, 220
Kandinsky, Wassily 22
Karadjordje, (Dorde Petrovik) 113
Kenya 107–109, 117
Kenya Mizukami 216
Kiichi Miyazawa 221–224
Kim Dae Jung 45, 46, 294
Kim Il Sung 42, 47, 69, 73, 79, 81, 90, 91, 93, 314
Kim Jong Il 73
Kim Jong Pil 72
Kim Sok Won 137

Index

Kim Young-Sam 72
Kodaly, Zoltan 325
Kohl, Helmut 67, 241
Korea, Democratic Peoples' Republic of (North Korea) 10–12, 15, 18, 19, 30, 40–42, 48–50, 54, 57, 63–67, 69, 72, 77–81, 65, 86, 90–94, 96–103, 113, 124, 128–130, 136, 141, 144, 145, 149, 154, 155, 158, 164, 172, 186, 187, 200, 223, 246, 250, 255, 264, 268, 271, 275, 286, 287, 302, 304–306, 311, 313–315, 322, 323, 327, 328, 336–339
Korean Military Academy 57, 71, 74, 127
Korean War 15, 23, 24, 49, 57, 68, 83, 121, 127, 131, 132, 144, 153, 182, 185, 186, 203, 249, 313, 316, 318
Kosung 137
Kublai Khan 192
Kumkang, Mt. 11
Kuwait 69, 271
Kwangju 46, 47
Kyeldish 22
Kyongsang Region 45, 46

Lajos, Kossuth 325
Leningrad 174, 177–180
Lilley, James 90
von Liszt, Franz 325
Logunov, Anatoly 21, 28–31
London 207

Magellan, Ferdinand 245
Malaysia 117, 230–232, 253–257
Malta 117
Malta Summit (U.S. and Soviet Union) 154, 163, 165, 168, 171
Manchuria 19
Manegold, C. C. 149
Margrethe II, Queen of Denmark, 272
Martin, Bradley 77
Mayakovsky, Vladimir 26
McKenzie, Frederick 277
Medvedev, Mr. 183
Mexico 133, 280–285
Mexico City 282
Middle East 145, 211
Military Armistice Agreement 337
Mitsotakis, Constantine 267, 269
Mitsotakis, Mrs. Constantine 267, 269
Mongolia 154, 187, 192, 193, 246
Mongolian People's Republic 191, 193
Montreal 66
Moreillon, Secretary General 137
Moscow 19, 28, 30, 33, 142, 155, 159, 161, 162, 165, 168, 170, 171, 174, 175, 177, 181, 183, 184, 186, 190, 207, 246, 250, 333
Mulroney, Brian 273, 275, 277, 279
Mulroney, Mrs. Brian 273, 277, 279

NAFTA 261
Namibia 311
National Community Unification Formula 10
National Security Law 47, 60
NATO 94
Neutral Nations Supervisory Commission 11
Neva River 178
New Life, New Order Campaign, 39, 56
Nobel Peace Prize 167, 185, 311
Non-Nuclear Korean Peace Initiative 289
Northeast Asian Peace Conference 204
Northern Policy 10, 28, 54, 67, 72, 85, 128, 130, 155, 160, 171, 181, 190, 222, 246, 250, 271, 278
Northern Diplomacy 68, 158, 219, 255, 268
Nuclear Non-Proliferation Treaty 96, 97, 100, 144, 149, 223

Obilic, Nilos 113
Ochirbat, Punsalmaagiin 191, 193

P'algongsan, Mt. 127
Pacific Basin Economic Council (PBEC) 227, 228, 239
Pacific War 316
Paekdu, Mt. 12
Panmunjom 65, 81, 101, 336, 337
Paraguay 117
Paris 31, 121, 187, 207
Park Chung Hee 59, 74
Paz, Octavio 284
Peoples' Republic of China, see China
Perestroika 41, 132, 164, 165, 169, 171, 174, 177, 180, 190, 244
Persian Gulf Crisis 36, 108, 114, 123, 125, 132, 145, 231, 234, 244, 272, 278
Poland 10, 19, 140
Portugal 65
Prague 140
Pusan 37, 46, 52, 206, 217
Pushkin, Aleksandr 28, 168, 178
Putjatin, Admiral 22
P'yŏngyang 54, 58, 65, 73, 78, 86, 88, 91, 117, 155, 314, 322

Rachmaninoff, Sergey 168
Raisian, Dr. 243
Rangyo 38
Reagan, Ronald 311

Index

Reunification Democratic Party 60
Rhine River 58
Rideau River 279
Rivera, Diego 284
Roh, Mrs. 112, 156
Romosonov, Mikhail 22
Russian Federation 54
Russo-Japanese War 67, 316

Sakhalin 19
Salinas de Gortari, Carlos 280–282, 285
Salinas de Gortari, Mrs. Carlos 280, 282, 285
Samaranch, Juan Antonio 111
Samaranch, Mrs. Juan Antonio 111
Samil Movement 17–20
San Francisco (site of Soviet-Korean summit) 41, 67, 72, 77, 127, 128, 155, 168, 171, 176, 181, 189, 245, 250
Sarajevo 112
Schlüter, Mrs. Poul 270, 272
Schlüter, Poul 270, 272
Schofield, Frank 277
Seoul 31, 37, 38, 45, 46, 52, 54, 59, 65–67, 88, 89, 95, 110, 111, 115, 117, 119, 131, 155, 171, 173, 174, 181, 183, 185, 186, 207, 218, 236, 241, 255, 260, 264, 270, 307, 322, 331
Seoul Olympic Games 4, 10, 18, 23, 29, 45, 58, 59, 66, 71, 72, 84, 92, 107, 110, 111, 119, 121, 124, 131, 137, 138, 140, 153, 157, 161, 168, 179, 185, 200, 203, 209, 249, 253, 267, 271, 278, 283, 284, 296, 301, 307–309, 311, 317–319, 326
Seoul Peace Prize 110, 111
Shah, Azlan 253, 255, 257
Shanghai 117
Shim Jae Hoon 41
Shostakovich, Dmitry 168
Shultz, Secretary 243, 247
Siberia 31
Singapore 260
Sino-Japanese War 316
Sobchak, Anatoly 178, 180
Sobchak, Mrs. Anatoly 178, 180
Sohn Ki-jong 308
Sol-Rolland, Jacques 119
South-North Korea Cooperation Fund 65
South-North Summit 11, 19, 64
Soviet Union 10, 14, 18, 24, 26–31, 33, 39, 45, 50, 57, 58, 63, 67, 69, 73, 77, 78, 85, 88, 90, 91, 96, 113, 117, 118, 123, 124, 127–129, 131–134, 137, 138, 141–143, 146, 153, 154, 159–190, 202, 214, 219, 221, 227, 235, 244, 246, 247, 255, 258, 260, 271, 278, 284, 315, 327, 333–335

Stalin, Joseph 28
START Treaty 146, 224
Stockholm 31
Syngman Rhee 74, 318

T'oegyewon 38
Taegu 57
Taejon International Exposition 119–122, 236
Tchaikovsky, Pyotr 168
Team Spirit 1990 11
Tokyo 63, 66, 200, 207, 208, 211, 246
Tolstoy, Leo 168
Tongnae 198
Toryong Plains 119
Tropin, Vice-President of Moscow University, 21
Tsevelmaa, Mrs. 191, 193
Tsevelmaa, President 191
Tsushima Islands 206, 217
Turgenev 22

United Nations 10, 30, 41, 42, 48, 50, 57, 58, 66, 69, 72, 73, 80, 91, 92, 97, 99, 114, 123, 124, 128, 130, 140, 141, 143, 146, 148–150, 155, 164, 181, 185, 187, 204, 244, 234, 236, 244, 250, 255, 256, 263, 271, 272, 275, 278, 284, 311, 313, 322, 333
United States 10, 11, 16, 17, 28, 39, 48, 49, 68, 69, 71, 77, 78, 94, 96, 100, 117, 118, 123, 124, 126, 130–134, 146, 150, 155, 187, 204, 205, 210, 242, 244, 247, 252, 263, 264, 286–290, 302, 315, 318–323
Uruguay Round 36, 37, 52, 33, 261, 287, 289

Van Fleet, James A. 57
Vernadsky 22
Vietnam 246, 319

von Weizsäecker, Richard 87, 89
Western Sahara 145, 311
Wilson, Governor 243
World War I 27
World War II 57, 67, 68, 78, 87, 113, 128, 138, 150, 165, 200, 201, 205, 208, 231, 233, 249, 260, 310, 311, 325, 326
World Jamboree Mondial 137–139

Yang Di Pertuan Agong IX 253, 255
Yon Hyong-muk 339
Yongjondo Island 52
Yugoslavia 10, 19, 112–114, 117
Yun Po Sun 298